ECONOMICS II

Microeconomics for Sustainable Growth

By Dr. Edward Schellhammer

2nd Edition 2014, revised.
© Copyright. Dr. Edward Schellhammer. All rights reserved.

ISBN-13: 978-1478244578
ISBN-10: 1478244577

www.EdwardSchellhammer.com

Table of Contents

In Somnis Veritas for Economics II

Dreams tell the truth. Dreams stay above theories, ideologies and dogmas. During the last 33 years I had over 12,000 dreams about the state of humanity and the planet. I had estimated 3000 dreams about humans' evolution and all processes of the Archetypes of the Soul. Examples:

A big assembly. I am talking. I reproach the people about how they did not take serious what I said, not even the problems of the environment with the consequences we have to expect. And I say: "Your children will have to live like in the Middle Ages, cholera included."

Scenes about a war in preparation like in the Middle Ages. Unbelievably perverse. They throw poor people into boiling water. They are the capitalists on highest level with their greed for gain.

An endless long earthquake, esthetically devilishly beautiful. It's night. Fire and disruption are everywhere on the ground. Nobody wants to see this danger. The scenery extends to half of Europe. I can feel the ground trembling. I call the people: "... !" But nobody listens to me.

I tell people: "I told you 20 years ago that the chemical composition (the chemical interactions) of all components ..... (in the body) ..... ."

The dominator of the world is doing his work, everyday!

The rivers in the North are all about to overflow, frighteningly deep and strong whirlpools, very dangerous speed. Nobody wants to see it.

They have placed a packet of dynamite in the town. One targeted shot and half of the earth explodes.

Many people are trying to cross a river. Most of them are drowning. This is because of the inability of the politicians to lead people.

I'm able to draw the sword of the king of the Grail from the rock and then I'm given an orb.

I see the Kings of the Grail sitting at the round table. They're discussing gravely the lack of love, the disregard for psychical life, the lack of truth and the denial of the Spirit in the soul.

An expedition around the world which boils down to: The complete love is the most valuable thing that there is, and nobody has it anymore. I realize this, while I'm walking four white, long-haired, graceful, endearing, healthy, positive and extraordinarily beautiful dogs.

Within me is the temple of the Holy Grail. Actually I know everything; I can reveal and help other people to experience this.

I receive 'cosmic scissors' and with it I cannot only cut and separate, but also join together and create wholeness. It is an enormous, very unfamiliar and alien gadget. I protest, because I think that this does not fit into my hand. But it does, it fits perfectly.

On the branch of a tree there sits an eagle with its wings spread, as if he wanted to show me the pattern of his wings. I take a closer look and discover: This is an image of the king-archetype on the one hand and of the reality of the living king of the Grail on the other hand.

A king has got two pharaoh birds, very colorful and marvelously beautiful. It is said that these are magic birds. We come to the city of Jerusalem. I'm very glad we've finally reached the goal together with the kingly birds.

The truth and the Archetypes of the Soul are the primordial foundation and aim of science, human life, and society. 'Economics' doesn't have both of it! The entire social sciences do not have it. That's the scandalous drama of science. The absence of the truth and of the Archetypes of the Soul produces enormous destructive energy and developments in sciences and societies. It shows clearly that sciences do not take care of the archetypal, psychical and spiritual evolution of mankind nor do they have any respect for the creation. Such science is a sham. Such sciences dehumanize mind and soul, and eliminate the dignity of humans. Such sciences are infected with the most toxic virus ever existed: the dynamic code for regicide and deicide. In the end, it will irreversibly and unstoppably lead to the doom. It can happen within decades if drastic measures are not soon taken globally.

Dr. Edward Schellhammer

Introduction

Economics, Humanity and the World

With an unimaginable brutality and unscrupulousness countless universities and schools of economics and business abuse the most valuable words such as love, happiness, fulfillment, truth, humanism, integrity, ethics, justice, harmony, independent thinking, creativity, intuition, dreaming, etc., and convert such words into a bunch of hot air and hype, of lies and deceit, in order to seduce and lure with images of an unattainable splendid professional future, with wealth and economic success, always worshipping the aim of 'maximizing profit' – the golden calf.

The American dream with its hands full of blood, a heart full of guilt, and hidden suffering from murdering and evil doing, calls for a renaissance (in Europe): "Economics must come back to the art of dreaming". But this kind of dreaming is nothing other than a very dangerous sick psychosis calling for "Be a King! And the Kingdom will come!" [1] The most perverse joke celebrates its victory! And the supreme academic speaker in ecstasy has lost reality with the orgasmic explosion declaring: "Resources are not limited!" The psychotic religious lunacy has broken through. The root lies in the Archaic Age. Archaic and magic understanding of human life and God is abused for economic and (indirectly) for political power. Relate all this to another question is: Who wrote Verse 28 in Genesis I?

About the unlimited resources: Several scientists and economic institutions have calculated: if humanity would want to live on the level of the living standards in the West, then in 20-30 years we would need 2, 3, or even 5 planets. The WWF warns (translated for us): "If humanity continues, we will need by the year 2030 two planets to cover our needs of food, water and energy: Until the year 2050 it would be nearly three planets." [2]

Now, this mortal virus has infected countless students of economics and has made them addicted with an effect similar to that of heroin. The perfect making of a fool has herewith hit the students in their heart. The academic authority (or economics) has erased the dignity of the students and of all humans on earth in general. It's like multiple child abuse from the father or the high priest.

---

[1]   http://www.eselondon.ac.uk/news-and-events/president-elio-d-anna-address-to-the-graduating-class-of-2012.html
[2] http://www.n-tv.de/wissen/Mensch-pluendert-Erde-masslos-aus-article6259136.html

One must be extremely ignorant, false and incredibly evil if he preaches the inner royal Kingship without the inner Spirit and without the holistic psychological-spiritual evolution. Do you know which religion teaches this 'inner royal Kingdom'? "Believe it and it becomes true!" is the classical religious trap with no evolutionary progress, no inner Spirit, no vivid Archetypes of the Soul, and with no way out – transferred from generation to generation since Abraham and Moses. The Western (capitalistic) economics has now also become a religion.

If an address to students or to student candidates starts with the conversion of the truth into lies and glorifying these lies as the truth, and with that producing a fire of ecstasy, then everything that follows is a scam! More evil doing for an academic institution is not possible. This is then compounded and spread globally by the academic 'accreditation' system - a miserable 'good-for-nothing' and valueless sham! But it is correct: Whatever we see and touch, is a projection (the materialization) of the inner being of humans. What do we see and can touch around the world? Everywhere we see is the result of indescribable (supported by academic teachings) that has all but erased the soul of human beings. Even the science of psychology and education has become a sham – slave to economic principles - as they all ignore the fact that 'psyche' actually means more than just behavior and brain activities; it means: 'soul'.

Many scientists, experts, and institutions state:

"In a few decades the world will collapse."
"A world population of 9-10 billion is not sustainable."
"An apocalyptic catharsis is inevitable."
"Already today too many people live on earth."
"We strive for utopia and all we have created is dystopia".

The total collapse is guaranteed. The state of the world has got a lot to do with the current understanding and practice of both micro and macroeconomics:

Unemployment, economic inferno, public debt, poverty, misery, riots, wars, contamination, pollution, climate change, inhumane mega-cities, slums, collateral damages of car traffic, industrial accidents, increase of sea level, drought, floods, tornados and hurricanes, nuclear waste, waste, sewage, dirty water, industrial food and meat, famine, destroyed fish resources, exploitation, damaged eco-systems, illnesses, mental disease, behavior disorders, epidemic plagues, melting of glaciers, elimination of species, destruction of the environment, crimes, mafia, corruption, lack of health care, analphabetism, lack of drinking water, decrease of agricultural land and forests, chemicals and pharmaceuticals and heavy metals in the food chain and already in the body of human beings, lies, cheat, distortion, brainwashing, manipulations, and billions of humans radiating toxic mental energy with their mad mind…

→ It is a repugnant hypocrisy of economists to ignore these effects of economics!

Humanity slithers into the Abysm: Nearly 7 billion people are imprisoned in a dark labyrinth of lies and deceit. Madness, falseness, and manipulations govern over nearly everything and everyone in the world. Most of humanity is dehumanized, degenerated, and brain addled: programmed to be soulless robots! There is absolutely no sustainability for 8, 9, and 10 billion world citizens, not in 40 years, not in 60 years, and not in 100 years. The young generation today and those humans who will be born in the 21st century will experience dystopia.

This is all human made, with very special (human made) contribution by (academics), economists, economic theory and economics policy:

- The unlimited capitalism has enslaved humanity, shaped consumers and decayed human's soul. This is what I interpret given that capitalistic ideology is the core mechanism of Western economics.
- Psychotic greed and complete arrogance of capitalists exploits all resources and every vivid thing. Even some TV channels *(better to replace with media?)* report extensively about it!
- 95% of humanity will be enslaved from suffering, lack of money and from debt. Look around the planet at the United States and in the European Union!
- All ecosystems are irreversibly poisoned and damaged from toxins and climate change. Thousands of pioneering scientists have examined this matter and describe the upcoming nightmares for all.
- Fish resources and healthy agricultural land will become extremely scarce. It's already common knowledge and there is no doubt about it, just mass denial and the optimism that science will somehow solve all problems.
- Endlessly more extinction of species, more deforestation, and more wonderful islands will disappear. Already 30% have disappeared. There are many published statistics; something must be true.
- Glaciers worldwide are incessantly melting and with that water resources are rapidly decreasing. Go for a walk to the high mountains around the globe and you see it for yourself.

- Expect more floods, drought, fires, hurricanes, weather changes, riots, social unrest, and civil wars. Read the newspaper (and all critical media) and you can follow these tragedies.
- Immense amounts of CO_2 and methane gas are being released constantly into the air. All reports say that this is an increasing problem with nightmare perspectives for humanity.
- The chain reaction of nature is all embracing: also the air will be thin in 40-50 years. That's a logical matter based on facts. People soon will have to pay to breathe fresh air.
- The increase of sea level will hit half of humanity and change the life of all humans within decades. There are maps about these disastrous changes, which can be found on the Internet.
- Billions will migrate in search of and fight for a new home, for land, work, food, and drinking water. Migration is already a very big problem for many countries.
- The toxic cocktail of global contamination will create plagues and kill billions of people in the near future. That's a realistic scenario with politicians factoring it into their plans.
- Fine dust everywhere also produces more and more painful illnesses, cancer and even mental dysfunction. Nobody likes to talk about it; it would immediately destroy the car-industry.
- Medicine and drugs and chemicals are already in all food chains and water supplies. Many scientific institutions and NGOs have proven it; some have even started questioning the toxic cocktail effects.
- Sewage from 2.6 billion people, waste from 7 billion, and nuclear waste from around the globe is poisoning humanity. This dance around the "golden calf" of growth is the code for collective suicide.
- The Western media, including Google, Facebook and other social networks are in the hands of an evil cabal. Experts have proven it time and again and shown that it's only the world of economic elites that gets the benefit of their actions.
- Western media operate with brainwashing, deceit, fabrications, distortion, poisoning and dehumanizing human's minds in the interest of profit. This is the everyday experience for billions.
- Accreditation bodies suffer from "compulsive disorder" and operate with totalitarian control in capitalistic interests. Read their instruction manuals and you will feel and see it!
- Accredited public and academic education destroy inner potentials, genuineness, and pioneering solutions. Just experience, think and analyze it critically, and then you too will know it.
- Increasing unemployment, poverty, misery, and natural catastrophes will affect billions of people. Over 1,000 scientists say that. There are numerous authoritative books and reports on the subject.

- Religions have failed terribly in their mission for love, peace, the truth, fulfillment, and real human values. It's even worse than that; it's an outrageous disaster and the litany of facts detailed in this book and Economics I prove it.
- Christianity, with its 'Holy Bible' is an archaic, fabricated, and distorted disaster to subordinate human's soul. This has been proven time and again and the knowledge is free of cost and can be easily found on the Internet or any reputable public library.
- Christianity killed a billion people during its history in the name of J.C.: Christian teachings are a scam. This is historically evident! Who paid the agents of colonialism, imperialism, and slavery – Glory, God and Gold was their mission.
- An absolute madness, someone in Western golden palaces is trying to dominate the entire humanity with an iron grip. Where are these people and their golden palaces? Is it just a phantom from a daydream? Or is there evidence to support it?
- These psychopathic and psychotic predators, programmed with an archaic mental structure, are allotted positions of power allover the world and are usually of Western origin.
- Can this all be just a failure of leadership or an intended and orchestrated plan from mad elites with a long lunatic history!
- It is as if a supernatural evil force is controlling these speculators, rating agencies, central banks, Stock Markets, IMF, World Bank. Is their power really global or do they only have power over the Western world?
- Most leaders in international corporations and in capitalistic governments appear to be just paid puppets. Who pays them so generously that they have lost their soul? Who gets the resulting benefit of their mad actions?
- Are there puppet masters pulling the strings behind the scene for more than 2,000 years and responsible for a litany of atrocities? Are these strange entities real or only a hypothesis to be proven?
- These monsters destroy governments, countries, people, economies, cultures, infrastructures, and the planet. Could the hundreds of thousands of conspiracy theorists be right after all?
- Wars over and over again, since Roman times have been started by these profit hungry monsters; also the upcoming WWIII. Who is triggering them? Who has financed all these wars? Who always benefits from these wars?
- The root of all this evil lays, in the Judeo/Christian scriptures of Genesis: "You are the chosen people; dominate the world and every vivid thing!" Is it all people who are "chosen" or just the "believers"? Who must be dominated, the unbelievers, those with a different color skin? Why must they be dominated, to what end? Do you agree with this? You did not write it, I did not write this, but it is our problem!

Now that you have in your mind the state of humanity, you can compare it with: "Money is a state of being. Money manifests in time what you have conquered through inner responsibility and creative victory. In the same way, any fault in your being makes you weaker and poorer. Any crack in your dream shatters the foundations of your financial power. Money like love is an inner matter. Love means absence of death (a-mors) and in absence of inner death you are an unlimited, omnipotent being." [3] Let us analyze this statement from this academic institution and compare it to reality:

- Money is a being: A stone is a being, the ocean is a being, animals and humans are beings.
- The money and the victory: Corruption, betting, speculating, exploiting, cheating, enslaving, etc.
- Fault in your being: Being or living? Sounds like a genetic defect and a wrong mental coding.
- Fault makes weaker/poorer: All humans have faults or make mistakes. Learning makes strong.
- Money as an inner matter: Greed, falseness, unconscious complexes, deficit compensations, etc.
- Money is like love: A material tool for living becomes a spiritual value, even an archetypal value.
- Inner death: A problem of a spiritual or psychopathological state that produces megalomaniacs.
- Presence of (inner) love: Unlimited, omnipotent being; means: you are a perverse, psychotic psychopath with the mad characteristics according to scientific definition! Herewith revealed!

The outrageous lie of economics is, for example: "Our standard of living depends on our ability to produce goods and services." [4] Such an exorbitant arrogant claim ignores the prices billions of (suffering) people have to pay for it today and in the future.

Now, that hopefully you understand we can begin our analysis of microeconomics with an exploration of the humans, because humans made and make economics and the economy in theory and in practice; and it's for humans, for human's life, and for the evolution of mankind as a whole that economics must serve.

The strategies and ways of thinking of our analysis are evolutionary:

---

[3] http://www.eselondon.ac.uk/bachelor-s-degree/bachelor-degree-in-business-administration/course-modules.html
[4] Mankiw (et al.), p. 393

14

- Identifying the connotations (fields of meaning) of the words and terms
- Multiplying the parameters by hundreds of millions and even by 5 billion
- Extrapolating the growth of figures by 30, 50, 100, and even 200 years
- Expanding the fields and areas of activities to the global dimension
- Identifying the psychological and spiritual meaning of the statements
- Finding out what is hidden, not mentioned, but is an intrinsic reality
- Focusing on the dynamic of construction of the laws and principles
- Giving a view to the multi-dimensional interrelations in the real world
- Putting consumer behavior in the context of mind and soul and real life
- Putting business behavior in the context of mind and soul and real life
- Interpreting the human factors behind principles, theories, laws, and formulas
- Putting the realities of principles, theories, and laws into the real life of society
- Understanding the production entities as a systemic part of society
- Identifying the cash flow that results from laws, theories, and practices
- Comparing small firms with medium sized firms and the big corporations
- Finding an understanding with visualization, intuition and creative thinking
- In general finding an approach to the systemic effects of multiple variables

1. The Economic Agents

1.1. Economics Must Include Humans

The Species called 'Human'

The 'homo economicus' is only one aspect from which to view humans; there are many more:

We all have images about human beings in our mind, partly as simple patterns of images, partly as prejudices, partly as well-founded theory. The whole history of philosophy and education is also a history of changing images about human beings. Let's touch on some sketches:

- A human is from his nature good and bad
- A human is the wolf of the man
- A human is God's image
- A human is the species which has a will
- A human is the undiscovered animal
- A human is a sick animal
- A human is the first to be freed from nature
- A human is a defective creature
- A human is a social creature
- A human is the animal which can create wars
- A human is a biological creature
- A human is what education and environment has made him
- A human is a thinking creature
- A human is the highest creation of God
- A human is lazy, incalculable, lying, and egotistic
- A human is a spiritual creature
- A human is a driven creature
- A human is a creature who can create culture
- A human is the 'homo faber', talented for technique
- A human is the 'homo sapiens', endowed with reason
- A human is the 'homo ludens', a 'player'
- A human is able to think

- A human is able to love
- A human is needy and capable of being educated
- A human is a creature which can sin
- A human is pure race, or is impure race
- A human is a learning organism

We can also see humans from the perspective of the result of education and acculturation:

Educational career / level	Physical health sustainability
Life long further education	Mental health sustainability
Vocational education	In touch with nature
Learning, studying attitudes	Focus on sustainable decisions
Attitude for working daily	Understanding the world
Attitude for life long working	Understanding politics
Moral character, integrity	Understanding society
Knowledge about inner life	Critical view about religions
Skills for mastering life	Critical view about ideologies
Communication skills	Critical about media content
Reading to understand	Care for environment/nature
Ability to love and care	Skills to manage people
Reliable and trustworthy	Skills to manage peace
Living human values	Clear, complex perception
Living inner potentials	Precise, analytical thinking
Knowing the spiritual source	Using spiritual intelligence
Holistic personal growth	Picture: past-present-future
Authentic being and living	No compensatory behavior
Systematic self-knowledge	Pioneering, vanguard spirit
Achieved inner fulfillment	Sexual satisfaction
Humble, decent, responsible	To stand for the truth
Interpreting one's dreams	Exploring the unconscious
Skills for family life	Conscious way of living
Sustainable personal lifestyle	Fulfilled personal catharsis
Care for baby/child/teenager	Ready for global renewal
Inner archetypal experiences	Free from brainwashing
Generally critical, vigilant	Inner male-female balance

→ The diversity of educating, forming, molding, and shaping humans is always present in the manifold economic context!
→ The complexity and variety of 'formed' humans influence on other humans, society, and consumer behavior in the 'free market'.

About the species, called 'humans':

Most people live predominantly without a reflective consciousness about their human images. They don't ask about the psychical reality. As a substitute they have prejudices, ideologies and dogmatic doctrines. Each of us has his own philosophy, his own 'theory' about human being, about life and God or the "golden calf" of economics. A transcendental reality exists for some people; for others not. The doctrines and theories about human beings are always developed from the personal psychical-spiritual state.

In every day life we are used to giving animal names to simplify human matters. Those selling products see others as buyers. Those looking after governmental business understand human beings as a mass, to be guided with instruments of power. Those who possess nothing perceive others as the propertied classes. Those who go to the church, interpret others as godless people. He, who studies philosophy in his room, develops his ideas about human beings according to tradition (and based on what he has in his mind). The doctor sees the patient and the injured as his focus. A psychotherapist analyses psychical diseases. Each psychologist looks around and works according to his studied (copied) theories. Do any of these consider the 'soul', the inner life of humans?

One is analyzing (consumer) behavior; others are looking for the depth of the soul. Priests gain a perspective from their dogmas. A teacher experiences his students as learning people (without soul). Whites differentiate from blacks (without soul). The fundamentalist is limited in his perception from 'holy' texts (without soul). Everywhere people see others as alien (without soul), that is to say, those who don't fit in with their own 'theories' and 'right' ideas or dogmas.

All around the earth many people exist, have always existed, who want to explore and get to the bottom of human nature and existence (including soul). We have a need to understand ourselves and our life (with soul). We search after sense and values (to find in the soul). We live between procreation and death (ignoring the soul). The question of a valuable image of human beings is a very serious matter for our style of life and for our (self-) education, especially if we include soul.

Each of us has his own images about human beings depending on his position, his state and his life history. Most people don't want to change or to widen their images. They don't see that their images encompass less than one percent of the human reality (including soul). After all they claim everybody should coincide with their images. If they don't do so, they are seen as hostile.

We could conclude: if you include the soul, then you are hostile to most of the rest of humanity.

Many people teach numerous images about human beings and a lot of ideas of how life has to be lived (without soul or with a distorted soul). And economics also has its own understanding of what is a human, especially as a consumer or producer for the 'free market' – and here there is absolutely no soul.

→ Also the doctrines, principles, laws, and theories of economics are based on the psychical-spiritual state of the professors, authors and other experts.
→ The psychological and spiritual understanding of mankind in economics is archaic, primitive, extremely reduced to human biomass, and absolutely inefficient.

We have developed during 30 years the most advanced concept of human's mind and soul based on thousands of books, manifold explorations, and meticulous analysis especially also of the unconscious mind and the collective unconscious. Our additional experiences with more than 250,000 dreams from clients and an estimated 15,000 personal dreams have generated and led to the vivid processes of the Archetypes of the Soul, including the supreme Archetypes of the Soul. [5]

Based on these experiences we conclude:

→ There can never be a solution through economics without the vivid Archetypes of the Soul.
→ There can never be a solution through politics without the vivid Archetypes of the Soul.
→ There can never be a solution through religions without the vivid Archetypes of the Soul.
→ There can never be a solution through education without the vivid Archetypes of the Soul.
→ There can never be a solution through humanity without the vivid Archetypes of the Soul.
→ Solutions that exclude the mind and soul of humans dehumanize humans and end in deicide.
→ Solutions that exclude the Archetypes of the Soul are technological and therefore will fail.
→ All sustainable solutions require the inner archetypal processes of leaders

---

[5] http://www.rcigi.com

and experts.

We clarify these conclusions in this Trilogy: 'Economics I, II, and III'.

1.2. The Mind of Consumers and Economics

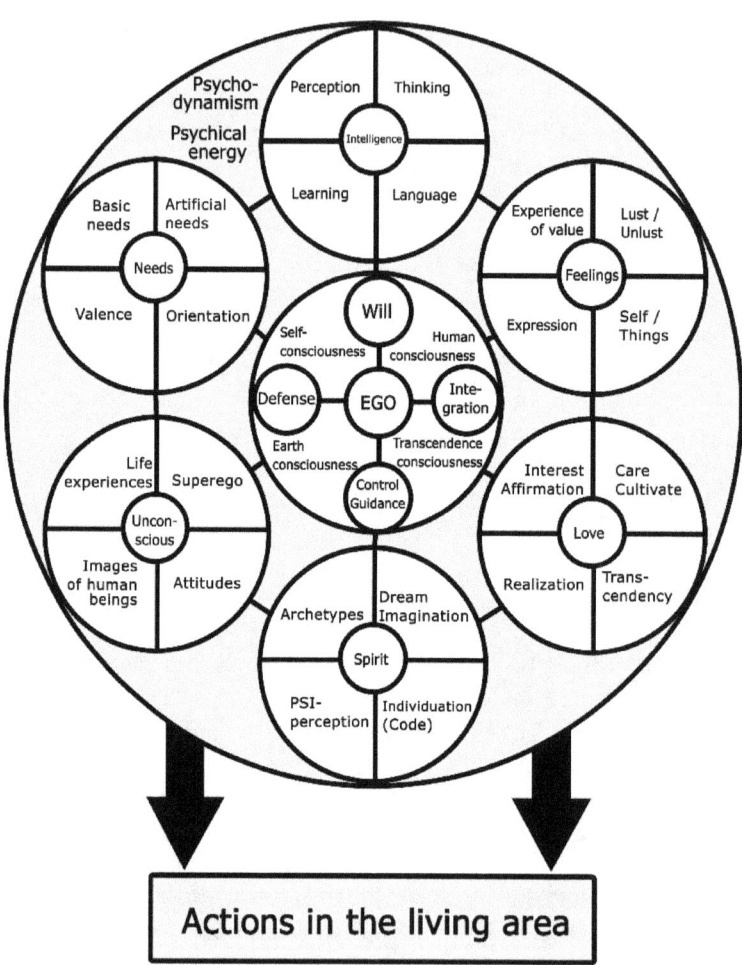

Humans of minor and major qualities:

Our explorations here are not in favor of a race theory. The term 'quality' as used here is not a moral or racial category. We do not develop a value doctrine of humans. Humans with minor qualities are not 'worth' less in a philosophical-anthropological sense than humans with major qualities. We do not use the term 'quality' for any physical state (physical constitution, disability, illness) of humans. 'Quality' does not refer to wealth, reputation, social class, religion, ideology, power or money in general. 'Quality' is a functional determination.

→ *We use the term 'Quality' limitedly for the empirical psychical-spiritual functions and these functions are of highest importance for economics.*

The psychical and spiritual functions and its use or way of operating are:

- The 'I', called also 'ego'; understood as control-instance with a will and a self-identity
- The defense mechanism: rejection and projection, suppression or integration
- Perception (with all senses) and its way of identifying elements of realities
- The consciousness: the present and active content in the conscious mind (inner 'screen')
- Ability to identify meaning in the conscious real world and in the mental/inner world
- The unconscious mind ('coding'): the biography (with complexes) since prenatal time
- The unconscious mind: Super-ego with attitudes, norms, values, rules, morals, ethics
- Love for partner, children, people, life, nature, animals, earth, creation, transcendence
- The psychical needs: e.g. security, protection, support, love, care, learning, growing, working
- Dreams and imagination, intuition, emotional intelligence, spiritual intelligence
- Thinking, questioning, analyzing, interpreting, concluding, judging, learning, and communicating
- Feelings and emotions: the entire positive and negative quality-scale
- Psychical gender dispositions (inner polarity) with male and female sexuality
- Talents, potentials, interests, and creativity as a psychical disposition (to be

developed)

- Dealing with knowledge, life, politics, economics, religion, spirituality, human values

→ What is a human being without these psychical functions? He is nothing but a pure human biomass.

→ Economics understand humans as a human biomass with only physical needs and wants.

It's obvious that a human being would be unable to live without formed psychical functions. Unformed functions would mean a pure instinctive way of living. This would also mean: Level 'quality 0' of psychical functions. On the other end would be the top quality; let's say, level 'quality 100'; so, we can determine on a scale of 0-100 points expressing the sum of the levels of qualities of all psychical functions. Quality also means: efficiency in real life.

Some psychical functions (such as thinking and learning) have instrumental purposes. Others (such as love and morals) influence more directly the existential and factual (spiritual) quality of human life. All these functions are formed by, family, institutions (religious and political), social environment, education, media, and personal performances (learning, working). The entire biography of a person determines these general forming processes. In this context a person is not responsible for his/her state as long as they can't freely operate within these areas of influences and whilst these areas remain mendacious and manipulative.

Fact is: a weak ego and will, with strong and rigid uncontrolled defense mechanisms (including projections), inappropriate norms, attitudes, values (etc.), a very low level of thinking and judging, a complete lack of dealing with dream messages or imagination and intuition, uncontrolled and extreme emotions, an over-loaded personal unconscious (biography), and a strong lack of abilities to deal with their own and other gender, with life and issues, political and religious matters, etc., means: a very low level of constructive and evolutionary qualities of the essential psychical functions.

As a consequence, these functions as a whole are not able to constructively and evolutionary deal with all or most life issues, including consumer behavior and management of economic matters. The simple conclusion is: human beings need a complex education (forming) of all these psychical functions to enable them to constructively and evolutionarily deal with all their life issues.

→ A very low level of qualities of these psychical functions produces enormous damages in the life of a person, in their family life, in their social and political life, in their economic life, in the world of nature and animals, and in earth matters.

Certain combinations of low level of quality of some psychical functions produce psychical disturbances such as neurosis, narcissism, dogmatic and fundamentalist thinking, psychopathic character, depression, anxiety, phobia, rigidity, hallucinations, obsessions, paranoia, psychotic reactions, illimitableness, arrogant and ignorant attitudes, magic thinking and living, and other disturbances. Above that, certain combinations of low level of quality of some specific psychical functions produce psychosomatic reactions and critical behavior such as addictions and compulsion, exaggerated greed, envy, hate, dogmatic and fundamentalist behavior, megalomania, perverse and amoral (criminal) behavior.

We also have to distinguish between low level of forming, with wrong forming, imbalanced forming, and lack of forming. Low level of forming, wrong forming, imbalanced forming, and lack of forming can be understood as a grade of quality of 'efficiency for managing life'. The critical result can be individual, social, and collective on the one hand and local, national, and global on the other depending on the interdependences and culmination of singular effects. Therefore, an individual critical result has no global importance, not even national importance.

But if hundreds of millions of humans have a low level of forming, wrong forming, imbalanced forming, and lack of forming, then it becomes of national importance. With billions of people having a low level of forming, wrong forming, imbalanced forming, and lack of forming, then it becomes of global importance.

→ This collective lack of efficiency for constructive and evolutionary living destroys humanity and the earth.

From another point of view a single individual or a small group of people with low level of forming, wrong forming, imbalanced forming, and lack of forming become of high regional, national or global importance, if this person or group gets economic or political power (instruments) in their hands. The consequences can be and are fatal:

→ A folk, a nation or even the entire humanity can end in a mass disaster.

Let's take four examples to show another aspect of low level of forming, wrong forming, imbalanced forming, and lack of forming that affects human's life, including economics in theory and practice, in the real world.

Example 1: Neurosis

Today the general understanding is: Suppression of sexual and genuine psychical needs and / or a deficit of an authentic satisfaction of psychical and spiritual needs.

Psychical needs can be: security, protection, care, love, support, attention, estimation, respect, (natural) interests and curiosity, development of one's potentials and talents, freedom of speech (and thinking), autonomy (relative to the age), creativity, learning, discovering, etc. Spiritual needs refer to meaning of life and to holistic and archetypal growing (of the soul).

Repressing the genuine (natural) needs produces a drive, which piles up; its psychical energy must be discharged by means of a compensating (replaced) satisfaction. This development causes inappropriate adaptations to the environment. The person lives in a life of lies, self-punishment (for having this need or for ignoring and suppressing inner needs), and this is lying or playing false games. He keeps out of his self-being, blocks against his authentic inner forces and reduces his existence and his genuine being to the remaining external and accepted possibilities.

The suppressed themes (drives, needs, complexes, unsolved conflicts, denied potentials, etc.) convert into a powerful projection. Money and properties, power and lust for objects, often destruction and sadism, replace the genuine self-realization. The character of such a person becomes rigid, inflexible, insensible, insensitive or hypersensitive. In the end all that remains is guilt; and the neurotic person has to deny, even magically, this guilt.

→ Neurosis is what we have in heaps all around us, in individual and social life, in economics, commercial enterprises, politics, public education, and religion.

Example 2: Narcissistic disorder

Narcissism is a type of neurosis; characteristics are: A self-image that is in the tendency grandiose, infantile, archaic and overvalued. Performances serve as a compensation for a weak ego. The world of the objects (material possessions) serves for the increase of the ego; this can be e.g. car, money, furniture, clothes, properties, and jewels.

The identification with a leader figure and the 'best of the world' in politics, economy, sport, show business, etc., serves for the increase of the ego.

Narcissistic persons admire and idealize highest performances, the 'Number 1', the best, the most powerful men, the most beautiful women, and the richest in the world, etc. A strong identification with a football club or other clubs with special highest performance demands, with esoteric or religious communities also serve the increase of the ego. In economics they speak about 'maximizing profit' the ultimate in narcissistic fulfillment.

The identification with objects, persons or institutions has in most cases a background tone of sexualizing an object or person – as if it would have to do with sex or being enamored. Narcissism also reflects a deficit of ability to accept anxiety, an insufficient drive control, inaccessibility as a mask, a deficient relation to the reality (perception and dealing with), a lack of outpace, partial excess, over idealizing father and mother and often teachers or priests, politicians and economists.

→ Narcissism is what we also have heaps of in individual and social life, in economics, commercial enterprises, politics, public education, and religion.

Example 3: Psychopathy

The essential characteristics of psychopathy are:

- Extreme ego-centricity
- Failure to learn from experience
- Unscrupulousness
- Ignorance towards truth
- Amorality
- Incapacity to feel guilt
- Brutal mind
- Unlimited arrogance
- Perverse lust-experiences
- Soulless being and acting
- Antisocial behavior
- Inability to love
- Absence of spiritual intelligence
- Inability to establish meaningful personal relationships
- Complete absence of empathy and devoid of any guilt

→ Psychopathy is what we have with about 10-15% of the general population, and with some 80% in the management of economics, commercial enterprises, politics, public education, and religion.

Example 4: Psychosis

- Delusions
- Loss of contact with reality
- Deteriorated social functioning

→ Psychosis is what we have on a lower level with up to 50% in individual and social life, and with up to 90% in the management of economics, commercial enterprises, politics, public education, and religion.
→ Psychosis is generated mainly through radical ideologies and dogmatic-fundamentalist religions.

Causes of neurosis, narcissistic, psychopathic, and psychotic disorder are:

- A deficit of love, warmth, goodness and human attention during childhood.
- A strong determination through others with rigid roles during the educational phase.
- Repressing genital lust through educational norms and control.
- Experiences of loneliness, abandonment, separation and exclusion.
- Deficient positive esteem as a person during childhood and youth.
- A strong tendency to hold low one's own values, forced through education.
- Repression of feelings, problems with trust and dedication.
- A very strong super-ego, coercing to suppress and with that to life lies.
- Emotions of powerlessness and ego-weakness (etc.) caused by education.
- All kind of traumas and shocking experiences, abuse, punishments, arrogance, etc.

We identify with these examples: Natural psychical functions converted into ineffective functions, destructive functions, and compensatory functions. The person's natural development and growing process from his inner source of life and genuine being is disrupted, distorted, and blocked.

On an individual basis this has little importance for a person or even a nation. But the sum total of all psychical functions of 7 billion people the whole of humanity on this earth who are predominantly distorted, disrupted and blocked in their inner source of life and genuine being, is a very big problem. Additionally, just visualize this picture: we will have an estimated 8 billion people by 2025, 9 billion people by 2040, and then 10 billion people by 2050! These figures could be reached either a bit earlier or a bit later.

There isn't one statistic showing how many people in the world of politics, commercial enterprises, public education, economy and organized religion have neurosis, a narcissistic or psychopathic or psychotic disorder; but based on current and historical actions it must be well over 65%. The main causes are the low level of forming, wrong forming, imbalanced forming, and lack of forming of human psychical functions which leads into inefficient ways of living and doing business, into psychical disorder and especially into heavy social and environmental damages exemplified in mass neurosis, narcissism, psychopathy, and psychosis.

The predominant characteristics of the collective psychical forces are an immense lack of love, respect of the inner life (mind, soul) of humans and in human values, of rootedness in the inner Spirit; and everywhere in all of life fields dominates a major absence of this all-sided balance, especially in the economic world.

→ It does make sense and it is even crucial to discuss human nature before we enter in the world of microeconomics.
→ If the science of economics and the economic worlds are made by deformed, distorted, self-alienated, greedy, possessive, neurotic, narcissistic, mad, false, perverted, psychotic, psychopathic, dehumanized, degenerated, brainwashed, manipulated, and mentally enslaved people, then the science of economics (with its principles, laws, and theories) and the economic reality they create can't be better off and must therefore mirror their distorted values.

1.3. The Meaning of Life and Economics

Philosophical and Psychological Anthropology

Philosophical Anthropology gives us orientations for life:

☐ Forming all psychical functions is a natural need of every human being.
☐ The forming of a function must be in an adequate relation to the other functions.
☐ The most valuable aim of life is an all-sided balanced state of all functions.
☐ Suppressing and neglecting singular mental functions always has a destructive effect.
☐ The spiritual intelligence is informative, corrective, educative, supportive,

and normative.

- ☐ The most essential meaning of life is forming the psychical-spiritual organism.
- ☐ Love is as essential as rational intelligence for living and realizing the meaning of life.
- ☐ Ideals, values, and norms must be in an appropriate network with mental functions.
- ☐ Everything excessive and over-dominant by ignoring other functions is destructive.
- ☐ The unconscious world is more powerful than the conscious mind and ego.
- ☐ An unelaborated unconscious means disequilibrium and is always destructive.
- ☐ An unelaborated collective unconscious produces wars and world destruction.
- ☐ Real life today demands extensive forming and shaping processes of all psychical functions.
- ☐ A claim to power by ignoring the aim of an all-sided balanced being is destructive.
- ☐ Ignoring authentic and genuine growth and living ends in illness and destructivity.
- ☐ The qualities and values of all mental functions must be higher than external values.
- ☐ There is no peace, no happiness, and no fulfillment without these shaping processes.
- ☐ The state of humanity is an expression of the results of collective wrong formation.
- ☐ Giving priority to mindless fun, assets, reputation, prestige, and power destroys humanity.
- ☐ Economics as a science and as practiced the real world is an expression of the 'quality' of humans.

→ Philosophical Anthropology confronts us with the fact that all humans and all human life are much more than just a human biomass.
→ Economics cannot separate humans' economic 'needs and wants' from the intrinsic philosophical-anthropological dimensions of human's existence (being).

Philosophical Anthropology initiates decisions about the psychological and spiritual 'needs':

- To live a holistic positive life philosophy with real hope
- To understand our feelings and to be able to manage them
- To live love, our genuine psychical needs, with truthfulness
- To see through, to think profoundly and also in creative ways
- To understand ourselves, our inner life, and our behavior
- To acquire knowledge and skills to efficiently master life
- To become an authentic, fully self-realized and strong person
- To have real, efficient, constructive ideals, values, norms, and rules
- To live a new, authentic life style with an excellent self-management
- To prepare ourselves for a happy relationship and family life
- To live our desire for sex and tenderness with a lot of love
- To live free from biographical burdens and unconscious complexes
- To be able to solve difficulties, crises, problems, and conflicts
- To live the deepest eternal (archetypal) meaning of marriage
- To succeed with our children by making them authentic and strong
- To live and grow with a genuine meaning of life, rooted inside
- To understand our dreams – the messages from the inner Spirit
- To correctly meditate and practice mental training for wellness
- To live all Archetypes of the Soul for our complete fulfillment
- To care for health, for the environment, for humanity and the planet
- To strive for peace, global balance of power, fair distribution of resources
- For all politicians, CEOs, and leaders to be rooted in the inner Spirit
- For the media to inform us about what is really important on this earth
- For freedom of speech and thought and transparency in political life
- For a new education that respects and promotes inner life and the truth

→ Psychological and spiritual 'needs' are intrinsic and indispensable needs.
→ Psychological and spiritual 'needs' are internally tied to the real needs and wants.
→ Economics cannot separate human's inner needs from economic theories.

A decision is on the table:

Do we collectively want to live genuine human values? Or do we decide to eliminate genuine human values? Do we accept the destruction of genuine (inner) human values or do we want that also economics (as a science and a real world network) protects and promotes human values with their actions and aims? Do we want to live with a soul or with a dehumanized mind (brain) and a lost dignity?

Human values are:

Firmness	Energy, vitality
Integrity	Patience
Self-consciousness	Readiness to help
Self-confidence	Willingness to compromise
Strong will	Relatedness and empathy
Health	Able to deal with tension
Self-identity	Happiness about life
Holistic self-experience	Satisfied sexuality
Performance ability	Stimulating hobbies
Personal 'Style'	Talents
Flexibility	Freedom
Open to learning	Taking responsibility
Free of fear/anxiety	Capacity to suffer
Acceptance of life	Moral Character
Self-management	Fulfillment of life meaning
Being adaptable	Life planning
Self-contentedness	Ideal of life
Endurance	Control of situation
Vegetative stability	Body relation
Self-motivation	Judgment
Ready for performance	Pleasure and joy
Maturity relative to the age	Ability for healthy roles
Determination	Self-esteem
Competences (skills)	Hope
Emotional stability	Faith

→ Psychological and spiritual human values are intrinsic and indispensable needs to be fulfilled.
→ Economics as a science cannot therefore separate economic 'needs and wants' from human values.

Consumers and workers, and most humans do not want this hell on earth:

Consumers and workers don't want superficiality, lies, life lies, cheating, falseness, bigotry, rigidity, narcissism, stubbornness, big mouths, arrogance, ignorance, unreasonableness, sadism, disrespect, stone-cold coolness and unscrupulousness.

Consumers and workers don't want people that poison humanity with their immorality, blown up ego, megalomania, perversion, dogmatism and fundamentalism, superstition, lunacy, madness, extreme greed, evil purposes, and religious psychosis.

Consumers and workers don't want to be deceived, lured, brainwashed and manipulated, oppressed and led into sick meanders, exploited as a human and financially abused like slaves, and treated as vacuous soulless humans to make a few selected individuals into super-billionaires.

Consumers and workers don't want pollution, contamination, climate change, environmental destruction, exploitation of resources, financial speculations, global poverty and misery, injustice, nuclear waste, armament, wars, fascism, and the new Nazi-like laws and practices in the United States and the European Union.

Consumers and workers don't want façades or masks that hide or distort realities; we don't want to be the puppets of politicians and the economy or the industry, and we don't want to be detracted from the truth and misled with false promises.

→ Is there any human that really desires this hell on earth? So, why do they and why does economics still continue to worship the "golden calf" leading to this hell?

Critical thinking and constant questioning can lead us to build the essence of a new economic science:

Does public education teach children to question parents, authorities, society, government, the military, or religion? Do academic programs question psychology, education, business and economics? Is there any Christian school that questions all the dogmas and protagonists in the Holy Bible? Is there an economic science that truly questions itself? The answer is a big No!

Public schools and academic (university) education memorize and in that sense reproduce information, knowledge, culture, attitudes, belief, principles, goals, and the corresponding expected behavior. Memorizing only reproduces existing knowledge, behavior, and performances it does not lead to understanding or the exploration of alternatives.

Public schools and academic (university) education practice mechanical transfer of knowledge (information) and with that they only create human robots. Such learning cannot produce critical thinking based attitudes. It's all a way of memorization that does not produce any evolutionary effect on the learner's attitudes, aims, and behavior. Learning by memorizing is simply filling a brain with ideological and dogmatic scrap.

Granted that, any alternative way to learning such as 'learning by thinking' or 'creative learning', also requires first memorizing the basic elements (knowledge, facts) of a topic.

But, critical thinking requires understanding and includes meaning, often of a holistic approach. The past, the present, and the future of a topic are part of this holistic approach. Critical thinking also includes creative and intuitive approaches that sometimes are a cul-de-sac and not always comprehensible; but often an open way of exploring realities, knowledge, and theories. A critical consciousness is a fundamental part of critical thinking. Indoctrination is the opposite of critical learning.

Understanding has to do with approaching human factors, activities or performances, purposes and aims, mind and soul. The learner connects with human realities, relates to the world with humans and the humans with ideals, goals, and purposes. Such an approach goes in line with intuition, reflections and contemplations, with digging into the connotations of words and into the fields of meaning. Words and meaning are related to human life.

Critical thinking and creative learning, pioneering explorations and intuition or visualization operate in the direction of the truth. Critical thinking does not simply accept and copy what's on the table (in the study books), written on the package, or thought of by teachers, professors and experts.

Every consumer or buyer, including students, must know the very old and extremely successful effect of packaging: operate with words of truth and quality, full of positive emotions guaranteeing perfect happiness or satisfaction, whilst hiding within the content of toxic sewage, rubbish and scrap for the primary objective, of 'maximizing profit', or 'power', or 'control', or 'imperiousness'.

→ There is no human evolution without critical, creative and intuitive thinking together with understanding of the meaning (for humans) and its consequences.
→ Economics is fundamentally and intrinsically related to humans' inner life (mind and soul) and with the external real individual and social life in it's wholeness with the entire humanity.

1.4. Humans in Mutual Trade Offs

Economics and Psychology: 80% of the world of business has to do with psychology!

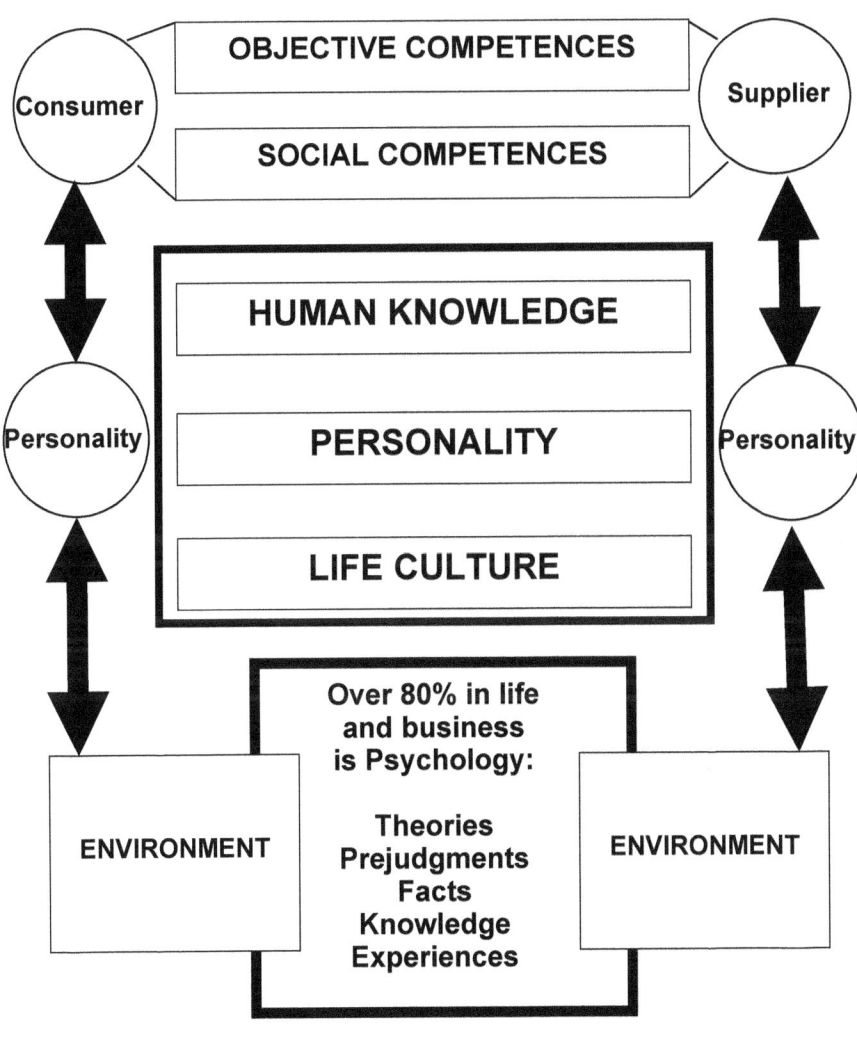

The Consumers and Producers: a Humane World

In many businesses, the labor group for production and services forms a big part of the budget. In this context we have on the one hand, producers who examine carefully and place great store on the raw material they get, whilst on the other hand they should also give equally high attention to the labor that finally assembles and physically produces/provides products and services. Ultimately these finished products/services are purchased and used by consumers.

Collectively consumers and producers are not simply a human biomass, or human robots with certain professional knowledge and skills, for use in the production processes or obediently hand over their money and just consume. Producers and consumers act in the context of the market (demand and supply) whether it is the supply of a skill as a producer or the demand for a particular product or service as a consumer, whilst they are all constructing their lives within a greater society for themselves with and for their partner, their children or even their (old) parents. Therefore, in all economic contexts' we need to understand humans in their vast complexities as psychical, spiritual and biological beings.

Are you a healthy consumer or producer?

- ☑ Mostly I am aware what sensual feelings I have.
- ☑ I can stand up for my opinions and interests.
- ☑ I can speak about anger, rage and my temper.
- ☑ I can accept strong and also unsettled feelings.
- ☑ I like new and uncommon ideas.
- ☑ I can 'do nothing' without losing the floor under my feet.
- ☑ Sometimes I like being alone and I can occupy myself.
- ☑ I can spoil myself now and then.
- ☑ I don't feel forced to always solve every problem immediately.
- ☑ I can live well if things don't go well.
- ☑ I occasionally walk (instead of taking the lift or using the car).
- ☑ I often like going out into the fresh air.
- ☑ I regularly let fresh air into my home.
- ☑ I consciously avoid noise and bad air, if possible.
- ☑ I don't always need background music.
- ☑ I switch off the television if the program bores me.
- ☑ I ensure that I have a regular life pattern.
- ☑ I am moderate in my consumption of cigarettes, alcohol, coffee, sweets and eating in general.
- ☑ I enjoy eating with time and calmness.

☑ I often enjoy my work.

☑ I can manage time pressure without 'swerving'.

☑ I see sense in my work as well as in my leisure.

☑ I am content with my life situation, I feel good and comfortable.

☑ I like the environment around my living space.

☑ I handle electricity, petrol, gas, detergents, medicines, etc. with discretion.

☑ I experience and treat waste ecologically.

☑ When driving I respect others, and I drive sensibly.

☑ I take interest in the biographies of others in my leisure environment.

☑ I often visit cultural, social and political events.

☑ If necessary I forcefully put my interests on the table.

☑ My life makes sense and has psychical and spiritual value.

☑ The basic values of human beings are very important to me.

☑ I can accept inner suffering in life.

☑ I don't think that I missed important things/events in my life.

☑ Today I can accept difficult life phases from my past.

☑ I am confident about how I create and master my life.

☑ I respect the natural environment and the other species that share it.

→ Here we are at the point: Nobody likes this kind of self-knowledge. Why?

→ Self-knowledge is for most people an extremely embarrassing challenge.

Health is defined according to the World Health Organization (WHO): "... as a complete bodily, psychical and social well-being and not only as the absence of illness and disease." [6]

Another definition about 'health' is given by the same source: "Health is a culture of all life means; health is assimilation of body and environment through social actions; health is a path which is formed by going along it."

Factors of health are also methodical principles as 'aspiration for appropriateness', 'respond to feelings', 'nearness to life', and much more.

Self-responsibility and self-determination are valued as an important part of a healthy personality development.

Health is understood as a part of the individual life course development, as a process, which is only possible, if an individual flexibly manages at the time the best reachable state of coordination of inner and external requirements, ensuring a satisfactory continuity of the self-experience (self-identity). Health

---

[6] Schellhammer, Individuation I. 2011

is related to the high capacity of adaptability of human beings to physical, psychical and social burdens and the whole way of living. [7]

→ Capitalistic economics (theories, laws, principles, practices) avoid methodical principles such as 'aspiration for appropriateness', 'respond to feelings', and 'nearness to life'.

Factors that form psychical health are: [8]

- Productivity, creativity, being active, working interest
- The objective-rational contact with reality
- Adaptability
- Internal balance, ego-integration
- Ability to satisfy needs
- Genital sexuality
- Being free from (or limited) use of defense mechanism
- Tolerance of frustration, control of impulses, strengthened against stress
- Power of resistance against psychical illness
- Being free from symptoms
- Realistic definition of aims
- Balance between dependency and independency
- Balance between stability and flexibility
- Basic confidence
- Ego-identity
- Realization of individual potentials
- Autonomy and resistance against enculturation
- Self-responsibility
- Autonomous morality
- Self-understanding
- Realistic self-image
- Self-acceptance, self-esteem, and self-confidence
- Naturalness, spontaneity, sociability, genuineness, being free from facades
- Openness to experiences and feelings
- Experiences of transcendence, 'positive feelings'
- Mind-expanding
- Acceptance of one's own body
- Aiming for the 'good', the truth, the beauty
- Humor
- Democratic character-structure

---

[7] Schellhammer, Management of Knowledge. 2011
[8] Schellhammer, Concept of Individuation. 2013 (in German: 2011)

- Need for privacy
- Orientation in meaning and values
- Ability to a constructive mastering of suffering
- Will-power

This list makes it obvious that health means much more than the 'absence of illnesses'. Health isn't something someone has or not, that we can lose and gain back. Health also isn't something, that is added to the human life and that can make life inside more beautiful and more fulfilled. Health is much more than 'satisfaction' or 'well-being' or 'good life standard'.

→ Health is a way of living, the realization of a genuine life, and a sustainable way of mastering life.

→ How does this understanding of 'health' match with the concept of economics and the greater economy in the Western world today?

1.5. The Archaic Consumer and Producer

The Archaic Consumer and Producer

The archaic consumer and producer are characterized by the negation of the psychical life, by neglecting the psychical organism as well as suppressing love and spiritual intelligence (soul). At the same time this kind of human being is more or less completely tied to the personal and collective unconscious psychical life.

The consequences are disruption (inner conflicts) and decomposition, lack of inner freedom, and infantile dependencies. Such an unformed and wrongly formed psychical life (mind, soul) is expressed in greed, envy, hate, destruction, exploitation, violence, unscrupulousness, ignorance, arrogance, belief and dogmas as well as in ideologies, despotism and egocentrism.

The essential characteristics of archaic consumers and producers:

- Ignoring the psyche as the genuine life; therefore no holistic development
- Rejecting the spiritual intelligence and the performance potential of the power of love
- Pushed from suppressed burdens and the tendency of projecting strongly
- Not living with dreams, imagination, contemplation, and introspection

- Only partially conscious forming of the psychical forces – if at all
- Defense from and suppression of all uncomfortable, weak and different realities
- To a large extent an unconscious way of living without being aware of the psychical life
- Personal and life culture are rooted in ideologies, dogmas and fundamentalism
- Extensively being fixated by material goods, events (fun), and external securities
- Undifferentiated unilateral experiencing of love, lust and sensuality
- Performances with increased gain to the extreme have highest value

→ If a society is created by these archaic consumers and producers, then one can see the result in the environment. And we see the disasters! Economics excludes these disasters (externalities).

The essential characteristics of the evolutionary consumers and producers:

- Accepting the psychical life and a conscious forming of all psychical forces
- Liberation from inner burdens of the biography and becoming free from projecting dynamics
- Elaborated images in the unconscious constructively and progressively promoting life
- Continuous inner orientation through dream interpretation, imagination and contemplation
- Integration and elaboration of all the uncomfortable, weak and different 'things' in life
- Creating relationships, politics and economy (etc.) from the understanding of Individuation
- Dealing with nature, the world of animals, and the environment with Spirit and love
- Differentiated development and use of the power of love and spiritual intelligence
- High flexibility and inner freedom towards material goods and external values
- Psychical-spiritual performances, characterized by love and Spirit have highest values

→ If a society is created by these evolutionary consumers and producers, then one can see the result in the environment. Unfortunately, there is not much evidence to see on this earth!

The real picture of consumers and producers, now:

- Most people know themselves on a level of 3-5 %; the rest they avoid to see/face.
- Most people don't think about tomorrow and the inner network of their living.
- Most people believe that they are totally right with the way they think and judge.
- Most people have no idea about their unconscious inner world – their true being.
- Most people believe it is enough what they learnt; but that is only blind obstinacy.
- Most people cannot distinguish between infatuated and inflated appearance and realities.
- Most people want to be cheated spiritually, religiously, ideologically, and economically.
- Most people don't want to learn for love, Spirit, joy, happiness, peace and balance.
- Most people don't have the necessary knowledge and skills for their own self-fulfillment.

→ Mankind wants evolution and is always in an evolutionary process.
→ But the evolution is currently on a regressive spiral back to the Middle Ages.
→ The collective psychical-spiritual state of mankind now requires a breakthrough for the psychical-spiritual evolution.

The Archetypes of the Soul

Archetypal principles of the soul for human's evolution are of highest importance also for economics:

1) Accepting and turning to the whole inner life

- Not accepting leads to tension, lies, distortion, aggression, etc.
- Not accepting consumes a lot of psychical energy for suppressing
- Not accepting leads to wrong decisions, wrong solutions
- Accepting produces inner peace and genuine self-confidence
- Accepting is an expression of love (self-love) and care
- Accepting gives strength for realistic dealing with humans

2) Discovering and forming all inner forces

- Not discovering leads to 'shadows' following oneself permanently

- Not discovering leads to ignoring these realities by other people
- Not discovering means completely devaluing human's inner life
- Discovering is an expression of love, of accepting one's being
- Discovering leads to realistic knowledge and correct interpretation
- Discovering is the first step that leads to a balanced soul-management

3) Developing the true Self by conscious forming

- Not developing means remaining on an archaic state of being with regressions
- Not developing leads to inner chaos, imbalance, psychopathological growth
- Not developing leads to ignoring or neglecting one's inner potentials
- Developing is an expression of evolution and a dynamic of human's behavior
- Developing is an expression of love and care, of responsibility in oneself
- Developing is the calling from life and psyche to become genuine and strong

4) Integrating the inner Spirit as guidance (Dreams)

- Not working with the inner Spirit enormously reduces the understanding of humans
- Not working with the inner Spirit hinders access to the unconscious world
- Not working with the inner Spirit obstructs the path towards holistic growth
- Working with the inner Spirit facilitates all-sided balanced development
- Working with the inner Spirit activates genuine spiritual power for solutions
- Working with the inner Spirit anchors human life in the Archetypes of the Soul

5) Proceedings of dying and becoming new

- One cannot become new as long as everything (psychical subsystems) remains unchanged
- One cannot become new without re-forming or changing inefficient psychical functions
- One cannot become new without identifying and elaborating the unconscious coding
- Becoming new gives enormous relief, strength, with power of self-control, and inner peace
- Becoming new produces a breakthrough in forming and living one's inner potentials
- Becoming new means also becoming genuine, truthful, just, authentic, and constructive

6) Unification with the inner opposite gender pole

- Not forming this unification leads to the endless stupid war between man and woman
- Not forming this unification makes a man either rigid or stubborn, or a blind tyrant
- Not forming this unification makes a woman an emotional chaos or a hysterical witch
- Forming this unification leads to a creative, constructive and complementary relationship
- Forming this unification makes a man become a real man and a woman a real woman
- Forming this unification is a psychical-spiritual process creating totality and completeness

7) Integration of the spiritual principles

- Ignoring the spiritual principles always creates imbalance, wars, exploitation, and destruction
- Ignoring the spiritual principles makes man into a rational animal with highly criminal energy
- Ignoring the spiritual principles leads to lies, deceit, falseness, distortion, crimes, and wars
- Integrating the spiritual principles creates harmony, balance, justice, peace, and strong love
- Integrating the spiritual principles allows solving the problems of humanity and the planet
- Integrating the spiritual principles leads to fulfillment and with that towards God and Paradise

8) Balance between external and internal life

- People live the way they are formed in their soul, mind, and inner life
- The state of humanity and the planet shows how people are now rotten to the core
- Not forming inner life (psyche) leads to an imbalance of the world as a whole
- Living within the Archetypes of the Soul leads to a world according these Archetypes
- Optimal inner balance and developed psychical functions make external life efficient
- The newly formed inner qualities of people will be transformed in the external life

9) Fulfillment of the completeness and wholeness

- No fulfillment of the completeness and wholeness of people leads to wars and doom
- No fulfillment of the completeness and wholeness must be compensated with dogmas
- No fulfillment of the completeness and wholeness must be compensated with dictatorship
- Fulfillment of the completeness and wholeness is the highest meaning of human's life
- Fulfillment of the completeness and wholeness creates the vivid paradise on earth
- Fulfillment of the completeness and wholeness leads to be in God and in Paradise

Conclusions: Those experts of economics and agents of the economic world that reject these archetypal principles have in their mind the evil coding that leads to the elimination of humanity and the destruction of the planet, and in the end to deicide.

→ Economics must become evolutionary – worldwide – because of its importance in determining human life and the evolution of mankind!

1.6. Satisfaction, Well-being and Happiness

Economics teaches us about wellbeing, satisfaction and happiness:

"Welfare economics (is) the study of how allocation of resources affects economic wellbeing." [9]
"Wellbeing (is the) happiness or satisfaction with life as reported by individuals." [10]

"Subjective wellbeing refers to the way in which people evaluate their own happiness. This includes how they feel about work, leisure, and their response in the events which occur in their life. Objective well-being refers to measures of the quality of life and uses indicators developed by researchers such as educational attainment, measures of the standard of living, life expectancy and

---

[9] Mankiw (et al.), p. 137
[10] Mankiw (et al.), p. 138

so on." [11]

Consumer surplus measures wellbeing: "...is the amount a buyer is willing to pay for a good minus the amount a buyer actually pays for it." ... The author concludes: Consumer surplus measures economic wellbeing. "...a lower price makes buyers of a good better off." ... A corresponding thesis is: The rise of well-being is the response to a lower price. Consumer surplus measures the 'benefit' "...as the buyers themselves perceive it." [12]

This is the fooling formula:

Economic wellbeing = subjective and objective wellbeing = well allocated resources
Economic wellbeing = satisfaction (of needs and wants) = happiness about work, leisure, and life
Explorations of meaning and the related human's realities:

Economics often uses the words 'satisfaction', 'wellbeing', happiness, and rather rarely 'fulfillment' and 'joy'. Let's have a closer look at these words.

Satisfaction: expresses the achieved contentment of a need, desire, want or appetite. It is a state of being satisfied.

Wellbeing: means welfare; in other words a contented state of being satisfied. The focus refers also to health and prosperity.

Happiness: expresses an emotional state of pleasure or spontaneous inclination; sometimes simply 'I am fortunate'.

Joy: marks the emotion of happiness. It includes obviously a specific satisfaction, but is more than that. It's an intense expression of a positive feeling.

Fulfillment: can express 'satisfaction'; something is consummated. The feeling goes deeper than a simple satisfaction when it refers to an inner state as a result of something: completed, brought to an end. It means a feeling of having achieved the satisfaction of a desire, a performance, or an aim.

We can approach this meaning with some examples:

---

[11] Mankiw (et al.), p. 139
[12] Mankiw (et al), p. 140-143

Example 1: John finally cleaned up his apartment. He says: "I am satisfied now that I have done it." John would not say "I am happy", not 'I am fulfilled', not 'I am pleased', but maybe also 'I am content now'.

Example 2: Mary prepared the dinner and after dinner the entire family was satisfied. 'Happiness' is not appropriate here; 'fulfilled' is not appropriate here; 'I am pleased' is also not the right way to express that all the members have now a full stomach. 'Joy' does also not really fit to the situation here.

Example 3: A couple, both in love with each other, is walking on the beach and enjoys the sunset. They would not say 'I am satisfied', nor would they say 'I am fulfilled'. But they would say 'I am happy and joyful'.

Example 4: Carl has worked hard to realize a project during a period of some months or a year. The moment the work is done, he can say 'I am satisfied with my work'. Or he can say eventually 'I feel fulfillment when I work because I can use all my talent'.

Example 5: Peter has worked hard during years and he feels that he has lived his potentials to the fullest. He will say: 'I am fulfilled with what I have achieved. Or: 'Giving everything in a performance creates fulfillment.'

Example 6: Eve truly loves her man and he loves Eve; they have had sex and she is happy. She would rather not simply say to her man 'I am satisfied now' because love touched her deeply.

Example 7: Toni went shopping, comes back home with all the goods. He would not say 'I am fulfilled now'. Maybe he would say: 'I am content that I have bought the right goods.' Would he say 'I am satisfied', or 'I am glad', or 'I am pleased'? Rather not.

Example 8: Robert bought a new car, drives around and then he says: 'I am happy'. It's obvious that this happiness expresses a rather superficial joy that does not touch inner human values.

Example 9: After one year of searching, Julia finally found a job. She would say: 'I am happy that I finally have a job now'. She would not say 'I am fulfilled'. 'I am satisfied now' is also not appropriate. But she would express joy.

Example 10: Rolf is 16 years old and goes to high school. During summer he works in a restaurant washing the dishes. At the end of the summer he gets the money to buy his dream bicycle. He is very happy now; but not because of the bicycle, much more because he can now go to school with the bicycle and doesn't have to walk 45 minutes. He is also proud, not because he is the owner of a bicycle, but much more because he worked for it.

→ These examples show us that the use of the abovementioned words (happiness, fulfillment, joy, satisfaction, wellbeing) is not appropriate for all possible contexts of economic or consumer issues.
→ 'Fulfilled' has a spiritual connotation and is in general not appropriate for economic realities. Happiness expresses also something with deeper inner (emotional or spiritual) roots.

In economic contexts 'satisfaction' says clearly: the need or want is satisfied. 'Wellbeing' refers to a more general emotional or physical state of satisfaction of needs and wants: 'I feel well with myself, with what I have, with my health, and my way of living, with my life as it is'.

The use of the word 'satisfaction' gets here another meaning than in the context of just having had dinner. If somebody finally got a long term employment contract with an acceptable wage, this person can say 'I am happy', but this happiness refers to a human value: having work and being able to make life with the wage. Such use of a word refers to much more than the economic issue.

→ 'Satisfaction' and 'wellbeing' are related to a need and to a more complex state of a current pattern (or mainstream) of life.

To use the words 'happiness', 'joy' or 'fulfillment' in the economic world is a cheat, a deceit, and a camouflage. It reveals how superficial economics perceives the human being and human life, and how superficial people are when using these words in an economic context. This distortion of important words also reveals strong manipulation and brainwashing of people for profit interests. It's soulless.

In a few words: Money doesn't make us happy; and being penniless doesn't allow us to be happy. One can't buy true love; but true love and not having money for making a life, does destroy true love.

→ Economic conditions of humans are the frame and foundation to achieve and get happiness, fulfillment, and joy (of life) – or in case of lack of money not to experience any of these inner (emotional) states that express genuine human values.

The collective use of the word 'satisfaction', 'wellbeing', and 'happy':

We should also consider the consumer's side: How do people use these words? Without putting the lipstick on the pig:

- Some people are happy if they succeed to get up in the morning.
- Some people feel well if they succeed to arrive punctually at school.
- Some individuals are satisfied with a bottle of beer; others with a bottle of wine.
- Some individuals feel fulfilled if their bank account is increasing daily.
- A bath or a long midday rest gives a feeling of wellbeing.
- Business people are satisfied it they can exploit other people.
- Many people feel well if they can hang around and be 'good for nothing'.
- Spending hours in the bar blabbering rubbish gives satisfaction to some people.
- Most people enjoy watching television every day for at least 4 hours.
- Eating the altar bread and drinking the transformed wine produces a sensation of joy.
- Special people are happy to have 50 pairs of shoes at home.
- Shopping can satisfy an addiction whatever people buy.
- Identification with a brand provides often a feeling of fulfillment.
- If one's football team wins, then some people are very happy.
- Getting praise, special attention, or confirmation makes people happy.
- Stimulating the narcissistic ego of people makes these people satisfied.
- If one can afford a better car than the neighbor, then this provides satisfaction.
- Winning with stubbornness creates a feeling of (perverse) satisfaction.
- Humiliating other people provides (perverse) satisfaction to a lot of people.
- Bob, already 180 kg, is not satisfied until he has eaten 8 huge pizzas.
- 50-65% of people however don't feel well as they suffer from constipation.
- 80% of people are neurotic and therefore they distort the word 'happiness'.
- Being convinced that one has the 'right religion' produces a sensation of fulfillment.
- Cantankerousness produces a feeling of triumph and satisfaction.
- Fill peoples' mouth and they are sedated, means: satisfied, quiet, and well adapted.
- Two billion people would be satisfied and happy with one good meal per day.
- A seller can make a consumer 'happy' with a respectful word and a kind smile.
- Unemployed people are happy when they get a job; for those who have a job, it's 'normal'.
- Tell somebody "You look good", and then this person already is a bit happy or delighted.

- Joe says to Max "Morning, how are you?" and the neighbor answers: "Thanks, I am fine".
- Millions of times people lie during their life saying "Thanks, I am fine; and you?"
- Max could also answer: "Are you stupid, do you really think I would tell you how I feel?"
- Imagine: Somebody asks you "Are you happy"? You answer: "No, not at all! Life is shit!"
- "Thanks, I am fine" is the fundamental conditioning of accepting the worst scam in economics.
- Tolerance of the intolerable is what economics depends on and therefore manipulates our tolerance level.
- Always striving for maximum profit produces an unlimited hubris of perverse satisfaction.

There are billions of little balloons of happiness, wellbeing and satisfaction in the market. Most of them have a lifetime of seconds, minutes, sometimes just a few hours. With such balloons the majority of people tolerates and covers or compensates for the fact that they are chronically or permanently unhappy, feel sad, are frustrated, have deep sorrow, feel lonely, are depressed, feel inner emptiness, don't have any joy of life, and are zero fulfilled in their inner being and with their capacities to make a meaningful life.

→ Economics is well advised to use such words in the right context or to clearly explain what they mean with such words in that context.

The crucifix (a symbol of suffering and rejection of the truth) of economics:

Essential in the economic models are: profit, maximizing profit, and lowest possible costs. Everything that could question this concept is considered as an irrelevant 'externality'. Logically human factors and nature form part of externalities and therefore the economic model is static and 'absolute', and disrespects the fact that the world and people are permanently changing and evolving.

The economic model can't be changed. It is ideological (infallible like all dogma) and therefore it leads to damages for most humans and in the end for the entire society and for humanity as a whole. The people are not better off with such an economic system that creates externalities that generate and increase poverty, take away the wealth from people (money, houses, work, achieved social status), damage environment and natural resources, and abuse workers (especially in developing countries).

➔ Capitalistic economics creates constant imbalance and is a complete failure!

Employment under the conditions of creating externalities does not lead to prosperity. A closer look at Western societies shows that the majority of people in employment are not 'better off'. The words 'satisfaction', 'wellbeing', 'happiness', 'fulfillment' and 'joy' in economic concepts must therefore be questioned in the context of the hidden economic aims, ideals, and the creation of externalities.

Free market economics creates conditions in which producers are principally 'better off'. In the end, they get all the money. The result of lowering the wages has led most people to become 'worse off'. The capitalistic economic concepts enslave people through economic practices (principles, mechanisms, power abuse, quality decrease, cost cutting, and debt). No economic theory has included the complexity of these realities. In any financial transaction between consumers and producers that are profit-oriented, the seller wins and the consumer loses because the 'highest possible profit' leads to a price that does not express the production costs or a calculated profit for future production improvements or to bridge a business decrease-gap.

Certainly, a consumer gives money away and gets for example a very cheap chicken of a very low quality. The consumer eats the chicken. Multiplied by hundreds of millions we detect the real result: the chicken is gone and nothing is left than a short satisfaction and some elements of chemicals used to produce the cheap chicken now in the body of the consumer; but the producer gets high profit (as we multiply by hundreds of millions of chickens sold per year) meanwhile the local family chicken businesses that rears quality chickens naturally for the same price as the cheap chicken (e.g. in Ghana) are destroyed. Where have the 'satisfaction' and 'wellbeing' gone now?

The chicken corporations and their calculations: "The average cost to process a chicken on a farm was $1.17. Off-farm processing costs ranged from $1 to $4 per bird. If the unusually high $4 charge is excluded, the average cost to process a bird off-farm was $1.41. Because of differences in income and other costs, producers processing on-farm were not necessarily more profitable than those doing so off-farm." [13] And another source says: "…the cheapest chicken at 1.50€ costs 0.075€ to produce!" [14] There are chickens at a market price of 2.30€ (dollars) and there are other chickens at a market price of 6.80€

---

[13] http://www.cias.wisc.edu/crops-and-livestock/large-scale-pastured-poultry-farming-in-the-us/

[14] http://www.fao.org/docrep/008/y5169e/y5169e09.htm

(dollars); same weight. If people only knew what they got for 2.30 € (dollars) considering the production cost of for example 22 cents [15] or from our other source: 0.075€ [16] ... Statistics: More than 50 billion chickens are raised annually as a source of food, for both their meat and their eggs. [17]

It is practically impossible to convince the believers of a religion with a hundred and more arguments and facts that their beliefs are outrageously wrong. It's the same problem with economists and followers of capitalistic economics (an ideology) that it's also outrageously wrong. We have identified and elaborated this scam in the 'Principles of Economics' (Economics I) and we will uncover more about this scam in the following chapters.

→ The capitalistic master minders protect their outrageous scam with nuclear power, fear, fascist politics, concentrated economic power, and with hysteric defense mechanisms distorting and twisting every truth into a lie, and a lie into a truth.

In 'Economics I' I have shown that this leads to deicide, that the ultimate intended aim of capitalistic economics is inevitably deicide – firmly rooted in the abuse and perversion of the Judeo/Christian mission in Genesis I, Verse 28 now embedded in the psyche of all Western thinking and actions.

1.7. The Planet sets Limits

Destruction of Humanity and the Planet through Economics

In 'Economics I' I have already explored the limits of the planet, especially considering the manifoldness of frightening global problems with the increasing world population. I will draw here some new perspectives to show where the limits with a 'marginal benefit' for all consumers and producers could be:

Be aware of the collective network with its consequences for the planet:

- You think love isn't important. Others also. Everyone thinks the same. What then?
- Professors don't want wisdom; students don't want wisdom. The

[15] http://animalscience.ucdavis.edu/avian/pfs20.htm
[16] http://www.fao.org/docrep/008/y5169e/y5169e09.htm
[17] http://en.wikipedia.org/wiki/Poultry_farming

consequences?

- Some think self-knowledge is nonsense; others too; finally everyone thinks that. And now?
- Some say, only money is important; others also agree. Finally everyone says that. What then?
- One says: you have to be faster than others; everybody says that. What does that turn into?
- First, one wins with lies, cheating, and deceit; then several; then many; then all. What remains?
- Many people go as far as to say 'feelings are not important'. What comes after that?
- Weak and ill people are ostracized. Imagine: from the age 58-85 you are weak and ill. Painful?
- Men haven't got any psychical-spiritual needs; women neither. What would this look like?
- One billion tons of nuclear waste has to be administrated forever. Who pays for the bills?
- All capitalistic people are 50% healthier, drive 50% less with their car. The consequences?
- All households and enterprises consume 50% less electricity. Why? How? Where does this lead?
- 50% of all Americans and Europeans pursue 1 hour of self-knowledge every day. Consequences?
- Second question of an interview for a 'top-job': How well do you know yourself? Can you answer?
- Only people that have worked through their biography can teach. How would schools be?
- Every Westerner reduces his waste by 50%. What kind of consequences would that have?
- Politicians and economists in the West don't lie and don't distort anymore. What happens then?
- Incumbents of all religions become pioneering economists. What would they decide to do?
- Statesmen and ministers are psychically-spiritually highly developed. How would politics be?
- Billionaires are psychically-spiritually highly developed. What would they do with their money?
- 50% of all adults in the United States and in Europe reflect on their leisure life. What changes?
- Nobody is a fan of high-performance sport, but of just sport. What effects does that have?
- One billion people demonstrate because nobody takes love seriously

anymore. Imaginable?

- 1 hour daily, of obligatory self-knowledge at the work place. Would everyone want to work there?
- Nobody wants to learn anymore after school and vocational school. The consequences?
- Life lies stink like sewage. How would consumer and producer treat each other?
- All consumers read 12 books every year about life and consumption. What could change?
- The newspapers and TV-channels report daily about dreams from producers. Exciting reading?
- Centers for self-education are put up everywhere. Everybody goes. Economic consequences?
- Anyone can only get married if he/she has thoroughly practiced self-knowledge. Advantages?
- It is forbidden by law to have children without a thorough self-education. Who protests?
- Only people who strengthen themselves by self-education can become managers. Bad luck?
- 75% of economists train daily 2 x 10 minutes psycho-hygiene. How would this influence society?
- Earnings are linked to the status of the personal psychical-spiritual development. Why not?
- Billions of people write on their door what makes them happy. Possible effects?
- Also consumers want to maximize profit, always and with everything. Where does it lead?

➜ You can create now a picture about the consumers and the producers in the Western world.

➜ You understand that satisfaction, wellbeing, and happiness are not only just an economic matter.

➜ Now you are ready to enter into the world of microeconomics for a sustainable planet.

➜ Always remember: Capitalistic economics is made by humans and for humans. No?

➜ Respecting limits opens the door to another world of immense human values and fulfillment.

Conclusions:

Imagine the planet is a gigantic stage where everybody plays his theatric role. The most essential rule on this stage is for the entire humanity: 'You must lie to get what you want. Never allow the truth to appear on the stage, not even at the last moment of death'. Most people are ready to die for this great big lie!

Economics, politics and religion write the script on how to act out the lies. There is a struggle, between the economic, political, and religious ruler entities about who actually wrote the superior master script and who controls (directs) the master stage. Whilst public education is the master tool used to prolong and continue this theatre.

Only very few people clearly see through the manifold theatres. Most people, including academics have no capacities to think in a network of issues, space and time, to ask questions, to think critically, to look behind the façades, to dig deep into the meaning of words and their de facto utilities.

This global theatre only continues by repressing suffocating and misrepresenting truth. Wherever people live on earth, they are conditioned to first copy the script and understand it as the truth. The secret is: Masters, form, educate, shape, brainwash humans from prenatal times for whatever they (masters) want them to become.

→ The last limits of this theatre are closer than most people realize: the destruction of the planet and with that the destruction of humanity as a whole.
→ The entire humanity with its economics, politics, public education, and religions is already trapped in a dark labyrinth without any exit. They are all going crazy performing the script for each other.

We must consider this mad global stage when analyzing the economic theories, teachings and practices. As the capitalistic economics is a horrifying scam, we must show a roadmap to a new economics that serves all humans, protects the planet, and has the right knowledge about what makes a human become a genuine human with all the inner potentials for fulfillment (of soul).

→ Human's psychical-spiritual fulfillment – the collective archetypal evolution – must become the spiritual crown of economics, politics, public education, and religion.

And the public education must prepare the people to master their life and to manage their psychical-spiritual potentials in a life long process. The archetypal roadmap of human's psychical-spiritual fulfillment is extensively and profoundly elaborated and documented like never before in the history of mankind. [18]

But there is a major obstacle:

The majority of leaders and agents in politics, economics, religion and public education are thoroughly stubborn, radical, rigid, power obsessed, hysterical, neurotic, psychopathic, psychotic, conceited, bullheaded, imprisoned by their lies, cheating and deceiving, full of an unconscious hate for life. Not even a nuclear bomb could soften their mind and force them to explore themselves, their inner life, the causes that have made them into what they are, and to make vivid the Archetypes of the Soul in their inner being.

These people would prefer to destroy the entire planet and to eliminate all humanity for the purpose that nobody can unveil all their lies, false being, evil doing and cheating of the entire humanity for millenniums. Always they have motivated themselves and their blind followers by hiding behind the cry 'in the name of God the almighty creator, for glory and for gold', where this leads is also very well known for millenniums, but always denied, selectively forgotten, revised and rewritten.

→ Their final goal is obvious: God the almighty creator must be eliminated... deicide!

Not a single one of the truly 'holy' men and women, not a single one of all the wise men since millenniums, and not a single one of all the true founders of religions, from Buddha to Jesus and Mohammed (including many others), is truly accepted by these leaders and economic agents, and by all the folks (blinded followers) on earth as the 'authority' that could lead them all out of the dark labyrinth they are in.

However until the day this is clarified on the visible stage and the hidden invisible stage is revealed, let us explore economics with the aim of arriving at some alternative practical solutions.

---

[18] http://www.rcigi.com

2. Microeconomic Worlds

The Foundation of Economic Principles

A general function in many economic principles is the 'invisible hand'. McConnel gives us an insight that we first want to present and discuss shortly, although we have already extensively explored this function in Economics I.

"Firms and resource suppliers, seeking to further their own self-interest and operating within the framework of a highly competitive market system, will simultaneously, as though guided by an 'invisible hand', promote the public or social interest. For example, we have seen that in a competitive environment, businesses seek to build new and improved products to increase profits. Those enhanced products increase society's wellbeing. Businesses also use the least costly combination of resources to produce a specific output because doing so is in their self-interest.

Self-interest, awakened and guided by the competitive market system, is what induces responses appropriate to the changes in society's wants.

The 'invisible hand' ensures that when firms maximize their profits and also help maximize their profits and resource suppliers maximize their incomes, these groups also help maximize society's output and income." [19]

Another classical book about economics describes this 'invisible hand' and serves to highlight this absurd economic fairy tale: "Both the allocative and rationing functions of price underlie Adam Smith's celebrated theory of the 'invisible hand' of the market. Smith believed and taught that the market system channels the selfish interests of individual buyers and sellers so as to promote the greatest good for society.

The carrot of economic profit and the stick of economic loss, he argued, were the only forces necessary to ensure not only that existing supplies in any market would be allocated efficiently, but also that resources would be allocated across markets to produce the most efficient possible mix of goods and services." [20]

Mainly all the classical books we consulted about economics ride this crazy

---

[19] McConnel (et al.), p. 38
[20] McDowell (et al.), p. 214

horse of the 'invisible hand'. Business life is really very distressing with the carrot of economic profit and the stick of economic loss on its back. The psychotic blindness is obvious. That's why sleeping pills bring so much profit to the pharmaceutical corporations. What has this got to do with (descriptive or narrative) science?

The essential elements of these statements are: "The 'invisible hand' guides ... The 'invisible hand' ensures". The 'invisible hand' operates with carrots and sticks. This 'invisible hand' operates within the field of some factors: Firms and resource suppliers, their self-interest, a highly competitive market system, public or social interest, society's well-being, the use of the least costly combination of resources, production of a specific output, appropriate changes in society's wants, firms that maximize their profits, resource suppliers that maximize their incomes, and society's output and income. Within this field of combined market factors the 'invisible hand' regulates the dynamics aiming for a maximum of society's output and income.

Therefore the 'invisible hand' must be a dynamic active being, entity or factor. Logically, the 'invisible hand' also must be something intelligent and must have an intrinsic natural (logic, positive) aim of universal validity always striving for this aim. To operate in such ways, the 'invisible hand' must have a perception, an intelligence, an ability to analyze, to interpret, to understand, to conclude, to take action (being active in an intentional way), and to balance the market forces for equilibrium or highest possible profit.

In that sense the 'invisible hand' is an omnipresent operational function of the real world of economics. This is either the Holy Spirit, or the inner Spirit, or any other supra-natural entity you care to mention. Could it even be God? But as logically none of them can be this 'invisible hand', there must therefore be another kind of intelligent being or market-immanent natural 'law'.

We would also conclude that this 'invisible hand' couldn't be in the goods or production facilities or machines, because such an idea does not make sense. As the market only exists and moves due to human's activities, the 'invisible hand' could be an unconscious or transcendental factor in human's mind or in the collective unconscious of humanity.

If we take a short overview over the market of capitalistic countries, we see an enormous disaster: economic crises, all kind of evil doing, poverty, outrageous damages to nature and human's mind caused by the market. From this point of view we conclude:

➜ This 'invisible hand' must be a stupid, chaotic, destructive, evil omnipresent monster in the free market.

Or the 'invisible hand' simply does not exist, is an induced fantasy of an insane mind in order to be freed from responsibility for failure and externalities (collateral damages).

→ We have a completely identical pattern of such a phantom 'invisible hand' in religions too. It's simply a form of magical thinking from archaic times in order to reject responsibility for one's acting and life.

Our six principles of a new foundation for economics, free from this 'invisible hand', are:

1. The decisive point (aim) of a production entity is not simply what a producer gets for his product (the profit). It is always also about what a production entity has provoked, created and caused through the production process and its products by its labors, labor's life, by the consumers, in society, in the world, and to the planet.

2. The decisive point (aim) of working is not simply what a worker or employee or self-employed person or investor gets for his work (the wage) or for the financial contribution (an interest). It is always also about what a worker or employee or self-employed person or investor provokes, creates and causes through working by himself, his life, in society, in the world, and to the planet.

3. The decisive point (aim) of consuming is not simply what a human gets with his consumption (the satisfaction, well-being, happiness). It is always also about what a consumer provokes, creates and causes through consuming by himself, his life, in society, in the world, and to the planet.

4. The decisive point (aim) of economics is not simply the scientific (or: systematic) analysis (theories) of the world of economics (costs, products, profit, etc.). It is always also about what economics provokes, creates and causes through its theories (and by ignoring most important economic realities) by the students, by the workers and employees, by the investors, by the owners of businesses, by the humans, by the human's life, in society, in the world, and to the planet.

5. Economics in the real world is always in a process; there is nothing static, nothing valid to simply and blindly copy, nothing of an eternal law, and nothing mysteriously happening such activities as the nearly divine activities of the 'invisible hand'). Humans are in a process (psychological, biological,

spiritual), the world is in a process, nature is in a process, the planet is in a process, mankind is in a process – and therefore also economics must be in a (learning) process; but they appear to not be at all.

6. If humans are not in an evolutionary process, called 'psychological-spiritual process', then economics is also not in a process that promotes the evolution of mankind. Collectively not being in an evolutionary process reduces the producers and consumers, the investors and all the people doing business, to mere human biomass (robots, slaves) and reduces them to followers of the monstrous archetypal evil and his agent the 'invisible hand' and this inevitably leads to the elimination of humanity and the planet which includes as its ultimate aim the deicide (already identified in Economics I). And as I have clearly illustrated: it will not take 100 years to happen.

So, what now is economics and doing business about? What is now consumption about? What is human's life about: to memorize and copy, never to question knowledge, theories, ideas, one's parents, teachers and professors, the authorities, the ideologies and religion, including the economics and economy, and as a consequence to be an enslaved human biomass serving as an instrument of the monstrous archetypal evil?

→ What kind of microeconomics do you want for yourself and for humanity?
→ What kind of microeconomics do you want for the future generations?
→ Microeconomics for regression and elimination or for evolution?

In this chapter we explore the consumers and the producers, from there, the goods and services, the world of production and working. Everything, absolutely everything has permanently got to do with humans and with human's life! The human factors are omnipresent. Human factors are inextinguishably interconnected with economic realities and its variables.

2.1. The Consumers and Producers

2.1.1. Manifoldness of Consumer Population

Complex term 'consumer':

- The consumer is not necessarily the buyer.
- The consumer is not necessarily the shopping person.
- The buyer is not necessarily the consumer.
- The buyer is not necessarily the shopping person.
- The shopping person is not necessarily the consumer.
- The shopping person is not necessarily the buyer.
- The consumer can be segmented and targeted by marketing.
- The buyer can be segmented and targeted by marketing.
- The shopping person can be segmented and targeted by marketing.

The source for money spending:

→ The person that has the wage plays a decisive but not exclusive role in the purchase (in spending money for goods and services).
→ Not every consumer has a wage and therefore in a majority of cases, several consumers benefit from one wage of a (working) person.

Much of working is not for personal spending:

→ A person works an estimated 65% for other people, for the government, for the profit of production entities, for meaningless contaminated goods and stupid services, and for the actual and future damages of externalities.

We can categorize (segmentation by marketers) the people as the consumers by age groups (and gender):

▪ Babies	▪ Adolescents	▪ Elderly people
▪ Infants	▪ Young adults	▪ Old people
▪ Children	▪ Adults	▪ Very old people
▪ Teenager	▪ Advanced adults	

We can categorize (segmentation by marketers) the people as consumers by education:

▪ Very low education	▪ High school education
▪ Lower education	▪ Academic education
▪ Secondary education	▪ Further education (additionally)
▪ Vocational school education	▪ The higher intelligence

We can categorize (segmentation by marketers) the people as consumers by financial resources:

▪ The pocket money children	▪ Basic upper class economic state
▪ The pocket money youth	▪ Middle upper class economic state
▪ Very poor state	▪ Top upper class economic state
▪ Poor state	▪ The significantly rich people
▪ Lower economic state	▪ The very rich people
▪ Marginal higher economic state	▪ The billionaires
▪ Middle class economic state	▪ The multi-billionaires

From here we can make some 'evident' economic statements:

- A baby has not got the same bundle of consumer goods as a teenager, an adolescent, an adult or an elderly person.
- All the age groups of consumers (that consume goods and services) have different consumer good patterns.
- People with low education (not informed) see the goods and services with different approaches than those with higher education (informed).
- The education of people (and the information they have) influences their consumption pattern and their bundle of consumer goods.
- The pocket money children and youth dispose of an estimated 30-300 Euros (dollars) per month; their bundle of goods can be identified and strongly manipulated.
- The very poor people can't afford the minimal bundle of indispensable goods; and this is a very serious problem that affects millions in Europe and America, and billions of people globally.
- 'Poor' in United States or European Union (P17) is not the same as the 'poor' in developing countries; they can still dispose of minimum finances to make their life.
- Poor and very poor people in United States or European Union (P17) have a completely different bundle of consumer goods than those in the same countries with abundant money.
- For the (very) poor the marginal (means: little) improvement of cash or of

any benefit can mean a lot for their satisfaction of needs; they have practically no 'wants' in their bundle.

- It is not bad nor a shame to be poor in the Western world; these people can make their life and find wellbeing, genuine happiness, and fulfillment. It works without much 'wants'.
- The very poor can't make their life with the money they have at their disposal (if they have any); and this is an outrageous disgrace; it shows the true face of economics and governments.
- A marginal (means: little) higher economic state does not have the same impact on low and on higher or highest economic level.
- The middle class people have more financial means for a better and even comfortable life than the lower class; but their bundle of goods is still now very limited.
- The upper class people have a quite broad financial flexibility compared with the middle class; but their bundle of goods is also still remarkably limited.
- The rich and very rich people dispose of so much money that they do not even need 30% of it to get all of what they could reasonably need and want.
- On the billionaire and multi-billionaire financial level the extravagant luxury is affordable and here begins the lunacy for economic or political power over a country or over the world.

Economic faults in the system and its theories are:

→ There is really no fact that tells us that a 'general consumer behavior' or 'general bundle of goods' actually exists. The economy can't operate fairly and correctly with such a generalization.
→ In certain patterns male and female consumers have different requirements, different shopping behavior, and different approaches to decision making.
→ Mainly, all humans from prenatal time until their death are consumers. There is no human life without consuming; not to consume leads to illnesses and death; means: consumers = humans.

Consuming has manifold consequences for each human, for society and humanity:

- Consuming unhealthy food causes physical or mental reactions and reduces health.
- Consuming contaminated food causes physical or mental illnesses, even cancer.
- Consuming material goods with toxic elements affects health with severe

consequences.

- Consuming can become uncontrolled and cause physical or mental or behavioral problems.
- Consuming is the final step of production, but it further leads to waste, sewage and contamination.
- Consuming a good includes accepting the previous contamination and other damages.
- Above a certain limit, consuming very often becomes mentally unhealthy and makes people crazy.
- Consuming always goes in line with financial means (and with work) that is at their disposal.
- A human (and not a robot) is consuming; therefore human factors play a decisive role.
- Ways of consuming are acculturated; there are many optional cultural variations of consumption.
- Consuming is not only the result of needs and wants; it's also pushed by unconscious factors.
- Consuming is not only the result of needs and wants; it's also enormously pushed by marketing.
- Needs and wants do not only have a quantity, but also a quality, a meaning, and manifold effects.

New fundamental rules for economics:

→ Economic terms, principles, concepts, models, theories, laws, and practices (production and services) must consider all these manifold characteristics of consumers.

→ Economics has a decisive impact and therefore must take responsibility in human's life as the economic realities shape humans' attitudes, behavior, wellbeing, satisfaction, and lifestyle.

2.1.2. Manifoldness of Producer Population

The complex term 'producer':

- The provider of raw resources is not necessarily the producer.
- The provider of raw resources is not necessarily the supplier.
- The provider of raw resources is not necessarily the seller.
- The producer is not necessarily the seller.
- The producer is not necessarily the supplier.
- The producer is not necessarily the marketing entity.

- The seller is not necessarily the producer.
- The seller is not necessarily the supplier.
- The seller is not necessarily the marketing entity.
- The supplier is not necessarily the producer.
- The supplier is not necessarily the seller.
- The supplier is not necessarily the marketing entity.
- The marketing entity is not necessarily the producer.
- The marketing entity is not necessarily the seller.
- The marketing entity is not necessarily the supplier.

→ These very important differentiations are not considered in most theories in the context of 'production'.
→ But indeed: the bigger a corporation, the more it can be involved in all related systems (if not directly then indirectly): from raw material exploitation right up to manufacture and sale.
→ There are many corporations that operate in totally different segments, but on the level of the main shareholders or investors, there are the same people (owners) that take decisions.

The price maker:

- The provider of raw resources (to produce the goods) has a price.
- The producer has a price.
- The in-between (production processes) has a price.
- The traders (intermediaries) have a price.
- The speculators who influence the prices.
- Playing games with cash flow influences the prices.
- The provider making allocations (supply, transport) has a price.
- The seller entity has a price.
- Currency changes influence the price.
- The owners of land, capital, and commercial premises affect and have a price.
- The governments influence the prices (variety of taxes – direct and indirect; VAT, toll, capital gains, local community, etc.)
- The sales' people (personal sellers) in general do not determine the price.

→ Providers of raw resources, producers, suppliers (allocation, contingent) and sellers play a decisive role for the end-price. The marketing entity always acts as the sales stimulator/revenue generator and as such is also key to setting the end-price.
→ It is possible that the provider of raw resources, producer, supplier (allocation), seller, and marketing entity are all under the same roof (part

of one business entity).

→ The owner (-s) is (are) not necessarily actively (directly) involved in the chain of provider of raw resources, of producer, supplier (allocation), seller, and marketing entity.

→ One person (as the one owner) can be directly and actively involved as the manager ('boss') of all components such as provider of raw resources, producer, supplier (allocation), seller, including marketing.

→ One entity can also be separated from being provider of raw resources, producer, supplier (allocation) and act purely as the designer, seller and marketer of the final product.

→ The taxes play an immense role in the end-price creation, especially if there are taxes all along the chain from the raw material to all the in-between processes; the sale of part-units, the transport through different countries and in-between firms (intermediaries) up to the end-location of the sale.

The dilemma of price building is that a small firm can only produce a very limited amount of goods whereas a big corporation can produce millions of the same good and many additional goods at the same time at a much lower price per good than a small firm could ever do.

There are economic entities and people that dispose of hundreds of billions or even trillions of Euros (Dollars), so they can become owners (directly or indirectly) of immense 'producer' entities (networks) that include all possible chains from raw material up to the entity that sells the goods (e.g. supermarket); called 'investors' and 'corporations'.

Conclusion:

If economic science ignores the manifoldness and interdependences of and between the components, functions, and conditions in all the steps from the beginning of production to the related consumers, then the scientific result distorts economic realities, and this can't be useful, and it becomes even totally irrelevant as scientific statements.

Thesis 1: Economic science ignores purposefully much interdependence with human factors and with hidden activities (movements of money) for their own sake, as these are representatives of the top-investors and owners of powerful corporations and networks of corporations (including banks, media, and education). We have clear evidence of this all around us since 2006 when Western governments with support from so called economic experts chose to financially support with public money the 30 year old speculative (casino) activities (many blatantly illegal!) of these financial and corporate entities.

Thesis 2: It is said that the United States is not a state like Austria or Sweden; it's a corporation. If this is real, then the frightening question arises: Who are the owners of this American corporation? Such perspectives pose completely new questions about economics as a science; and even about who rules the European Union? Ergo, money through its conduit, finance, rules (nearly) everything, whilst the science (pseudo) of economics acts as nothing more than the veil of validity that conceals the lies and deceit whilst the media acts as the proxy for glorifying the dogma.

We can categorize the people as the producer by their age (and gender):

- We can exclude here all the babies, infants, and children (children's work neglected here).
- Teenagers and adolescents, age 12-16, are in some countries already used as labor.
- The majority of labor is composed of young adults and adults.
- Advanced adults, age 48-65, are already in high risk to lose their job.
- Elderly people, old people, and very old people are thrown out of the labor market.

60 years ago, men and women above age 50 were already understood as 'old' due to the much lower life expectancy. Today the life expectancy in the industrialized world is in the average above age 75; many more people reach an age of 85-90; also many more people get even older nowadays. An estimated 65-80% of all people above age 65 are still in a state of health that enables them to continue working; some with reduced working time and reduced performance level. The economic theories ignore these facts.

With Western pension age regulations an immense professional, social, and economic potential gets lost. 17-22% of the population of a Western society is simply thrown out of the labor market; cosigned to spend 15-35 years sitting at home in front of the television vegetating, dabbling into meaningless hobbies and blabbering in bars, cafés and pubs. They do not even matter as economic interests in the Western world as consumers as they spend little because they do not have much (pension). Too many in this group of people act like primary school pupils on a permanent holiday. There are also at least 35-50% of people with an age just above 50 that already start dreaming about their 'third age holiday life'. This is an expression of acculturated stupidity and insanity. Work is a genuine need for all humans and this need is slaughtered in the interest of maximizing profit. Most of these people not surprisingly regress increasingly to an infantile state, depression and mental deficiency, having been alienated from the society that they are deemed no longer worth contributing to.

We can categorize the people as a producer by their education:

- A lot of people have low or very low education.
- The majority of people have secondary and vocational education.
- Professional further education encompasses a selected group of people.
- Those with academic education are a much smaller group.
- The higher intelligence forms constitute an even smaller group.

It is common sense, but of the highest importance: the higher the education is, in general the better are the chances for a job, for a good job, and especially for higher wages.

People with low or very low education have to work on the very 'ground floor' of the production processes where very low knowledge and skills are required.

Most people with secondary and vocational education work on the 'ground floor' of the production processes; they must have a certain professional knowledge to do their job acquired through 'on the job' training.

Academic education opens the door to the 'upper floor', more easily, even with very specialized knowledge and skills. However, as far as they are employed (and not self-employed), they are still only executors/managers of orders from the 'top floor'.

We can only add a few people to the 'higher intelligence' group. Not all the CEOs, managers and leaders on the visible stage (of the 'top floor') fulfill the criteria of 'higher intelligence'. A part of the 'higher intelligence' group is simply exploited for special production development. Another part is in an extra-suite and has a steering wheel in their hands or becomes a 'master of puppets' behind the curtain on the hidden stage (see: Economics I).

We can categorize the working people (as producer) by their financial resources:

Very poor are the people that need governmental or social support. The poor have the absolute minimum for making their life. The lower economic state allows making a life and becoming fulfilled. Marginal higher income only allows here and there a bit more goods or getting a 'want'. These people – as individuals – have absolutely no say in the world of production.

Middle class and basic upper class financial and attitudinal status gives a bit more flexibility, but there is no doubt about the strong limits. Even the middle upper class financial resources do not allow one to enter into a life style of opulence; but they can save a bit of money. Mainly these people are executers and not commanders in the fields of production.

The financial resources of the top upper class are highly preoccupied with a generally higher life style that is required due to their academic or professional status; but at the end of a month there is no opulent saving. Only the significantly rich and super rich people have extensive flexibility for their life style, but still visibly limited. These people are still only protagonists and have no significant say in the corporations. They are not the policy decision makers ('commanders') of corporations.

The billionaires and multi-billionaires form another category of producers. We do not need to draw a picture about the private use of their financial resources. Some of these people have a steering wheel in the hands; a few do enter 'the hidden stage behind the curtain' and become a 'master of puppets'. Leaders in politics, education and religion, mostly with good financial resources, are the enslaved servants of the 'masters of puppets'. Most important is: the masters who command the economics in the real world and in academic institutions (with economic theories)!

Conclusions:

We observe two extremes: the very poor and the poor people (workers) on the one side and the billionaires (rulers) on the other side. The very poor and poor people cost money to the government. As 'poverty causes poverty' these people generate without end all the collateral problems at governmental costs and at the benefit of corporations.

Some billionaires play 'casino games' and destroy the wealth of a society, create imbalances, injustice, and many problems with irreversible damages around the globe. Other billionaires have absolutely no 'say' on what goes on 'the hidden stage behind the curtain'. We must distinguish here between those billionaires that possess this money at disposal for the market; and those who command the use of the wealth of corporations as they are superior owners (of shares).

Although we accept the poor people on the one side and the billionaires on the other side as something 'normal' or inevitable, we observe a resulting imbalance in this inequity with extreme consequences: lost democracy, too much influence by the few, vested interests hold back progress, destroyed environment, contaminated nature, social tensions and wars, and much more.

The economic power of production has become dictatorial and determines the way of living for the majority of people with all the logically resulting catastrophic problems humanity faces. People with best personal and professional education, even with very high financial resources, still have no say in Western economics ('production') and in their society as a whole (with democracy proving a sham equaled only by economics and economic theory). So, something is going wrong here! We shall explore this problem in greater detail in Economics III.

→ We conclude: The real leaders in the capitalistic world are in the economic world and not in the governments!

2.2. Structures of Consumers and Producers

2.2.1. Structures of Consumer Population

We can categorize the people as consumers by the structure of community:

- People living in rural areas
- People living in villages
- People living in small towns
- People living in big towns
- People living in cities
- People living in mega cities

➔ We assume that consumer behavior changes with the type of community.

We can categorize the people as consumers by the structure of households:

- Single (adult) living in parental household
- Single
- Couple
- Mother or father with 1 child
- Mother or father with 2 children
- Mother or father with 3 or more children
- Family with 1 child
- Family with 2 children
- Family with 3 children
- Family with 4 and more children
- Living community of 2-5 people
- Living community of 6-20 people
- Living community of 21- X people

➔ We assume that consumer behavior changes with the structure of household.

We can categorize the people as consumers by their working status:

- Single without unemployment benefit payment

- Couple without unemployment benefit payment
- Family without unemployment benefit payment (both parents unemployed)
- Family without unemployment benefit payment (with unemployed children above age 16)
- Single with a governmental subsidies
- Couple with a governmental subsidies
- Family with a governmental subsidies (both parents unemployed)
- Family with a governmental subsidies (with unemployed children above age 16)
- Single with unemployment benefit payment
- Couple with unemployment benefit payment
- Family with unemployment benefit payment (both parents unemployed)
- Family with unemployment benefit payment (with unemployed children above age 16)
- Day laborer
- Seasonal laborer
- Working with subcontracted status
- Working contract with short term status
- Working contract with long term status

→ We assume that consumer behavior changes in line with the work status.

We can categorize the people as consumers by critical mental status:

- Indecisive, disoriented, easily deflectable, lonely, helpless
- Strong preoccupations of all kind including stress
- Depressed, fearful, socially phobic, anxious
- With inner pain, sadness, suffering in their heart
- Very low confidence and very fast feeling lost
- Uncomfortable due to constipation, psycho-somatic reaction
- Very tired due to circumstances or sleeplessness
- Exhausted, driven by excitement, anticipation of something
- Actual heavy relationship problems (strong arguments, fights)
- Chronic sexual, love, care or attention frustration (need of compensation)
- Strong suppressed inner frustration (need of compensation)
- Strong inner unconscious conflicts (need of compensation)
- Low self-image (ego-image) (need of compensation)
- Consumption of psycho-pharmaceutics (to balance)

→ We assume that consumer behavior depends on the critical mental status.

A healthy mental status is first of all the absence or a low level of the critical components mentioned above. The 'archaic and evolutionary human being' as described in Chapter 5 gives a further orientation of a healthy mental status.

We can categorize the people as consumers under the influence of drugs:

A large majority of people, in the United States and Europe take occasionally or periodically psycho-pharmaceutics or other medicines; on average in a society, therefore 65% of the people are under the influence of drugs.

To this we have to add "recreational" drugs (majority are illegal) that range from cannabis, cocaine and heroin, ecstasy, amphetamines, LSD, barbiturates and benzodiazepines, psychedelic mushrooms and even solvents, as well as the abuse of alcohol (legal).

Additionally we have to list all kind of contaminating and toxic elements in the air, in food (meat, fish, vegetables, fruits), in drinking water, in beverages etc. The entire cocktail in the body of people influences the brain (and dehumanizes or reduces mind capacities) and has an influence on what are 'needs and wants' and in the 'rational choices' people make as consumers. There are also hundreds of millions of people that suffer from many kinds of addictions, which influence their consumer behavior.

➔ The Western world is a drug-addled and addicted society!

Painkillers	Amphetamines
Sleeping pills	Cocaine
Stimulant drugs	Heroine
Tranquilizers	Ecstasy
Drugs for concentration	Antibiotics
Anti-depressants	Anti-baby pills
Anti-phobias	Stomach stimulants
Anti-anxieties	A lot of alcohol
Drugs for schizophrenia	A lot of tobacco
Sexual stimulants	Stimulants making happy
Sexual drive killers	Amphetamines
All kinds of party drugs	And a hundred more medically approved substances

➔ We assume that consumers under the influence of drugs have other patterns of consumption than the consumers that are free of drugs in their body (and mind).

We can categorize the people as consumers by their emotional status:

a) Positive emotions while shopping, for example:

▪ Trust	▪ Peace
▪ Love	▪ Harmony
▪ Fulfillment	▪ Hope
▪ Joy	

b) Negative emotions while shopping, for example:

▪ Distrust	▪ Aggression
▪ Hate	▪ Disharmony
▪ Emptiness	▪ Despair
▪ Joylessness	

➔ We assume that the consumer behavior changes with the emotional status.

We can categorize the people as consumers by their ways of valuing money:

▪ Having worked (hard) for the money
▪ Not having worked for the money

➔ We assume that consumer behavior changes with the way of earning and valuing money.

From here we can create some economic statements to consider:

▪ The consumer behavior depends on structural patterns such as the kind of community, the structure of households, the working status, the mental status, the emotional status, and the ability to value their earned money or to handle money that they obtained by or without working.
▪ Consumer patterns are not the same in the shops and grocery stores in a small village as in the supermarkets and mega super-markets in towns and (mega) cities.
▪ Consumer behavior is not the same if people are in a negative or positive emotional state, if they are well educated and informed or not, in a real need or not.
▪ The manifoldness of working status is expressed in the manifoldness of patterns of consumer behavior.
▪ The mental status of people can have a significant variety and the variety is

expressed in the manifold consumer behavior.

- There is no such thing as the economic theory of 'rational choice' for the majority of people; there are too many unconscious and other factors influencing a choice.
- If people are in a good or bad mood, or have a negative or positive emotional state, even repressed and not realized, then it influences consumer behavior.
- If people have a positive emotional state, even repressed and not being aware of it, then it influences consumer behavior.
- If the entire society is burdened with the hidden negative emotional state of people, then the market is distorted. To find out the emotional state one can't simply ask the folk: "Are you happy?"
- If an entire society is healthy with a genuine conscious positive emotional state of people, then the market is balanced. Considering the economic imbalances, wars and mounting global problems, this is not to be expected as a given now or in the future.
- If the entire society is infected with critical mental disturbances of people, then the market is out of control. Indeed, the market has been increasingly out of control for many years!
- If large parts of modern society are plagued by addictions to psycho-pharmaceutics this has an impact on consumer behavior. Fact is: most people in modern societies are indeed on drugs and this is reflected in their volatile and irrational consumer behavior!

Outrageous fact:

→ Most of what the economics study books say about 'consumer behavior' is scrap material recycled for hundreds of years.

2.2.2. Structures of Producer Entities

We can categorize the producer entities by the structure of communities:

(We give here only some examples to indicate the structural importance)

- Rural areas: Agriculture and animal breeding (adjacent to villages)
- Villages: Small amount of shops, grocery stores, doctors, dentists, small clinic, specialized service firms
- Small towns: More and bigger shops, grocery stores, doctors, clinics, variety of service firms
- Big towns: Many shops, grocery stores, doctors, dentists, clinics, shopping centers, even greater variety of service firms, small and medium seized

industry

- Cities: Countless small and big shops, grocery stores, health care services, shopping centers, administration centers, abundance of service firms, small, medium and big seized industry in the outskirts
- Mega-cities: Immense amount of shops, grocery stores, health care services, shopping centers, administration centers; all kind of service firms from small to big size; small, medium and big seized industry in the outskirts

Some economic statements may lead to research:

Big producer entities in general can't be established in rural areas, small villages or towns. Big producer entities need a thousand and more workers plus well trained administration staff for management that requires highly professional skills.

The bigger a town or city, the more people search there for work and relocate from rural areas to towns and cities. The motives are manifold, mostly expecting work, a better life, and more affluence and opportunities as well as fun.

Most people with academic education (unless specialized to rural needs such as veterinary doctors) have much less options to find a suitable job in rural areas or villages; they are forced to move to big towns and cities to get a job with an appropriate wage.

The bigger the producer entities are, the higher is in general the level of contamination due to the private car traffic (travel to work, the masses of people living in that area) and the industrial emissions in the outskirts.

If some big producer entities dominate the production of selected goods, then small firms can't compete and disappear in this segment of production or are dependent as small suppliers.

If most big producer entities are concentrated in selected big towns and cities in a country, then they must allocate (distribute) their products throughout the country, which produces not only enormous vehicle traffic, but also high transport costs and contamination.

The bigger a town, a city or mega-city, the more the producer entities establish there their shopping centers (or renting premises in shopping centers) to be able (or aiming) to sell as many goods as possible. A very interesting question is who are the owners of the big shopping centers and in which way are they linked with the corporations that sell their goods there? The more people depend on the products of a few mega producer entities, the more money is concentrated towards these single producer entities. Producers control financial resources that a small firm in general can never achieve. As money gives power, the mega producer entities become more powerful than local, provincial, or national governments. This leads to other uncovered (ignored in the study books) economic consequences.

The less producer entities are based in villages and small towns, the more money goes away from the dwellers working in the villages and small towns, as these citizens must go shopping in the nearer big towns and cities.

Villages and small towns in the capitalistic economy are impoverish if they don't have enough income from their own producer entities that sell their products elsewhere; and they are dangerously exposed to national and international economic changes if they depend highly on one or few industries; for example on tourism or on a single good produced/grown in their location and exported.

As the objective of big producer entities is to pay in general low wages to their workers, they create or hold down poverty at their location; in the end it produces small pension payments for their (former) workers (if they are lucky enough as less and less producers offer this now!). As they have destroyed most of the small producer entities (in their product segment), they also create poverty in villages and small towns. Public resources then must pay for these 'damages'. In the long term first local governments of villages and small towns, then local governments of bigger towns and in the end national governments need to get immense loans (from investors that rule the corporation fields) and a downwards spiral effect is created with the whole population becoming impoverished with increasing levels of public debt (to the investors that rule the corporation fields) that can never be paid off by from the ever decreasing taxes from ever decreasing or non existent wages!

We can categorize the producer entities by their structure of business:

- Self-employed people (one person)
- Very small producer entity (2-5 people)
- Small producer entity with up to 20 employees, maybe with 2-3 departments
- Bigger producer entities with up to 250 employees, maybe with 5-10 departments
- The big producer entities with up to 1000 employees, maybe with up to 20 departments

- The very big producer entities with much more than 1000 employees and more departments
- The bigger a corporation, the more they can operate globally with production and finances.

Departments could be: segments of products, purchase of raw material, purchase of machines and other materials (e.g. stationery), internal services (machines, cleaning, etc.), pre-production, stock management, composition of parts, control of produced goods, process control, administration, marketing, planning, product design and development, public relations, communication, delivery, transport, legal and financial management, factory canteen, etc.

The more departments are given in a production entity (or any firm), the more labor with medium or higher vocational (and academic) education is required for management and other responsibilities. Once these higher positions are occupied with top qualified academic employees, they mostly stay for long, even life long (until retirement).

What happens when the big producer entities in Europe and America no longer exist as most already have outsourced production to China (globalization) or the factories are mechanized / robotized or have gone bust?

Over 20 years USA has lost officially 6.4 million manufacturing jobs due to outsourcing but judging by unemployment data the figure must be higher especially if we include mechanization / robots and companies going bust. (No data found on Europe.)

The role of the firm: "A firm is an economic institution that transforms factors of production into goods and services. A firm (1) organizes factors of production and/or (2) produces goods/services and/or (3) sells produced goods/services to individuals, businesses, or government."

Colander groups the firms as followed:

- A firm organizes factors of production, and/or
- A firm produces goods and services, and/or
- A firm sells produced goods and services.

The author mentions a critical aspect of highest importance: "More and more of the organizational structures of business are being separated from the production process." [21] We can mention here some criticalities:

---

[21] Colander, p. 277

- Business decision making structure is in Europe or in the United States with production in Asia
- Business decision making structure of a shopping center is not on the location of the shopping center
- Business decision making structure has no direct (humane) contact with the production process
- Business decision making structure that is separated from production processes ignores labor conditions
- Business decision making structure that is separated from production processes ignores externalities
- Profit always goes to the organizational structures (top-management) of the business

The modern world with its future development is built up on 3 pillars:

→ Oil/Gas: Society can't function without it!
→ Electricity: Society can't function without it!
→ Money: Society can't function without it!

→ Thesis: Power over oil/gas, electricity, and money means: Power over governments, societies and its people.

Interdependences of economic interests:

- Nothing works in societies today without these three pillars.
- No government can function without these three pillars.
- Oil/Gas and electricity production needs a lot of capital investments = money.
- Money must be obtained to manage oil/gas and electricity production.
- Institutions lending money to these industries control/influence these industries.
- The more oil/gas or electricity is sold, the more money (profit) comes back.
- Governments need money for their manifold duties through taxes (energy is taxed).
- Reducing prices for oil, gas or electricity reduces the income from taxes.
- Increasing prices for oil, gas or electricity reduces the value of money.
- The less consumption of oil/gas, the fewer taxes come in for the government.
- No oil means poor military power; high oil price means high governmental expenses.

- If governments don't have enough income from taxes, they must take on debt.
- The more money that is lent to government, the more the investors have political power.
- Power to determine the amount of oil production means: power over societies.
- The higher the price of oil, gas & electricity, the less money for other matters.
- The same interdependence is applied to the nuclear power stations.

Power perspectives of neo-capitalistic economics:

- To have power over these 3 pillars means: having power over governments.
- To have power over these 3 pillars means: having power over life of a society.
- The more power over governments and life of a society, the less democracy exists.
- To secure the business of oil/gas, the industry must have control over the resources.
- To increase profit, the industry stimulates or forces the demand and hinders alternative sources of energy.

Industrial sectors that corporations operate in:

▪ Chemicals	▪ Banking (Finance)
▪ Pharmaceutical	▪ Insurances
▪ Medicine/Healthcare	▪ Services
▪ Weapons/Munitions	▪ Legal Provider
▪ Telecommunication	▪ Media
▪ Technology	▪ Wood, cotton, wool, leather
▪ Electronics	▪ Agriculture
▪ Mining (primary material)	▪ Animal farms
▪ Electricity	▪ Fish and seafood
▪ Oil/Gas extraction/refineries	▪ Water and beverage
▪ Hospitality and tourism	▪ Retail
▪ Railways constructions	▪ Hospitals
▪ Shipbuilding	▪ Private or semi-private Education
▪ Aircraft and Aerospace	▪ Automobile

Fortune 500 has issued a list of S&P 500 companies along with their 2010 financial details. Along with American billionaires and millionaires, the 500 companies are believed to form a main part of the 'One Percent' rich in America. [22] [23] [24] *)

Who is the One Percent in America?
The following are the largest full-service global investment banks which usually provides both advisory and financing banking services, as well as the sales, market making, and research on a broad array of financial products including equities, credit, rates, currency, commodities, and their derivatives.
1. Bank of America
2. Barclays Capital
3. Citigroup
4. Credit Suisse
5. Deutsche Bank
6. Goldman Sachs
7. JPMorgan Chase
8. Morgan Stanley
9. Nomura Securities
10. UBS
11. Wells Fargo Securities

Petroleum Refining
The following are the top ten U.S. petroleum refining firms in terms of revenue in 2010. Fortune 500
1. Exxon Mobil .... $354.67 billion
2. Chevron .... $196.33 billion
3. Conoco Philips .... $184.96 billion
4. Valero Energy ....

Diversified Financials
The following are the top eight diversified financials in the U.S. in terms of revenue in 2010.
1. Fannie Mae $153.82 bn
2. General Electric $151.62 bn
3. Freddie Mac $98.36 billion
4. INTL FCStone $46.94 billion
5. Marsh & McLennan ...... $10.93 bn
6. Ameriprise Financial ..... $10.04 billion
7. Aon $8.51 billion

Oil & Gas Equipment, Services: The following are the top U.S. firms active in oil and gas equipment and services in terms of revenue in 2010. Fortune 500
1. Halliburton .... $17.97 billion
2. Baker Hughes .... $14.41 billion
3. National Oilwell Varco ..$12.15 billion
4. Cameron International ...$6.13 billion

Motor Vehicles & Parts
The following are the top ten U.S. manufacturing companies of motor vehicles and parts in terms of revenue in 2010.
1. General Motors ....

Commercial Banks
The following are the top ten commercial banks in the U.S. in terms of revenue in 2010. Fortune 500
1. Bank of America $134.19 billion
2. JP Morgan Chase $115.47 billion
3. Citigroup .... $111.05 billion
4. Well Fargo .... $93.24 billion
5. Goldman Sachs Group $45.96 billion
6. Morgan Stanley .... $39.32 billion
7. American Express .... $30.24 billion
8. US Bancorp .... $20.51 billion
9. Capital One Financial ..$19.06 billion
10. Ally Financial .... $17.37 billion

Aerospace & Defense
The following are the top ten U.S. corporations in aerospace and defense in terms of revenue in 2010.
1. Boeing .... $64.30 billion
2. United Technologies .... $54.32 billion
3. Lockheed Martin .... $46.89 billion
4. Northrop Grumman ...... $34.75 billion
5. Honeywell International..

[22] Forbes 2011; also reported on: www.rt.com
[23] http://money.cnn.com/magazines/fortune/fortune500/2011/full_list/index.html
[24] https://www.fortune500-app.com/

$86.03 billion
5. Marathon Oil $68.41billion
6. Sunoco $35.54 billion
7. Hess $34.61 billion
8. Murphy Oil .... $23.34 billion
9. Tesoro $20.25 billion
10. Holly $8.32 billion

$135.59 billion
2. Ford Motor $128.95 billion
3. Chrysler Group $41.94 billion
4. Johnson Controls $34.30 billion
5. Goodyear Tire & Rubber ..$18.83 billion
6. TRW Automotive $14.38 billion
7. Navistar $12.14 billion

$33.37 billion
6. General Dynamics .... $32.46 billion
7. Raytheon .... $25.18 billion
8. L-3 Communications ..... $15.68 billion
9. ITT .... $11.15 billion
10. Textron .... $10.52 billion

*) Subject to change and errors; see the original sources

The mad Power of Corporations

Business entities disposing of hundreds of millions and even billions of Euros (dollars) can easily start an economic strife. Between distinguished corporations are networks on different levels: management, board of directors, and investors. If there is a newcomer on the horizon that could occupy a field of interest or competition, they prepare the economic strife, even battle or war. The options are manifold:

- They buy the newcomer entity
- They force the newcomer entity to sell
- They give order to the media to fully ignore the newcomer
- They spread rumors about the newcomer
- They give orders to suppliers to keep their distance from the newcomer
- They blackmail the newcomer
- They menace the newcomer
- They copy the newcomer products
- They sell their products so cheap that the newcomer doesn't have a chance
- Via bank collaborators they place him in a loan trap or an investment trap
- They take legal action with absurd allegations to paralyze the newcomer
- They give order to a governmental administration to refuse an operating license
- They find something out about the past of the newcomer and hang him publicly through the media
- They collude with suppliers of raw material not to sell to the newcomer
- They try to find any possible way so that the newcomer can't have success

→ There must be a reason why the study books about economics do not explore this critical field of the application and practice of economic power.

We can dig deeper and create some economic theses:

If a corporation or an investor or a business club doesn't want a newcomer in their area or wherever, they always take action and destroy the business of the newcomer.

Corporations, some business clubs, or investors dispose of so much money that they can operate with proxy style actions on a level of national intelligence secret services.

There are superrich people that have with their economic potential so much power that they have most capitalistic governments and any single politician (of their interest) in their iron grip.

The networks of corporations and the networks of the eight biggest Western media conglomerates are operated from the hidden stage behind the curtains; and it is not the 'invisible hand' from Adam Smith.

The most powerful economic network exists; they control the economic realities and even the higher education (economics, business, education) in the Western world and in many developing countries. They have all the tools in their hand to open any door.

World War I, the World War II and all wars and political 'earthquakes' since 1948 up to today are staged and triggered from this most powerful economic network to destroy entire nations with the objective to 'maximize profit', to become richer and richer, and get more and more hidden power.

➔ How many people on earth accept such evil doing?

Example: Tentacled structures of corporations [25]

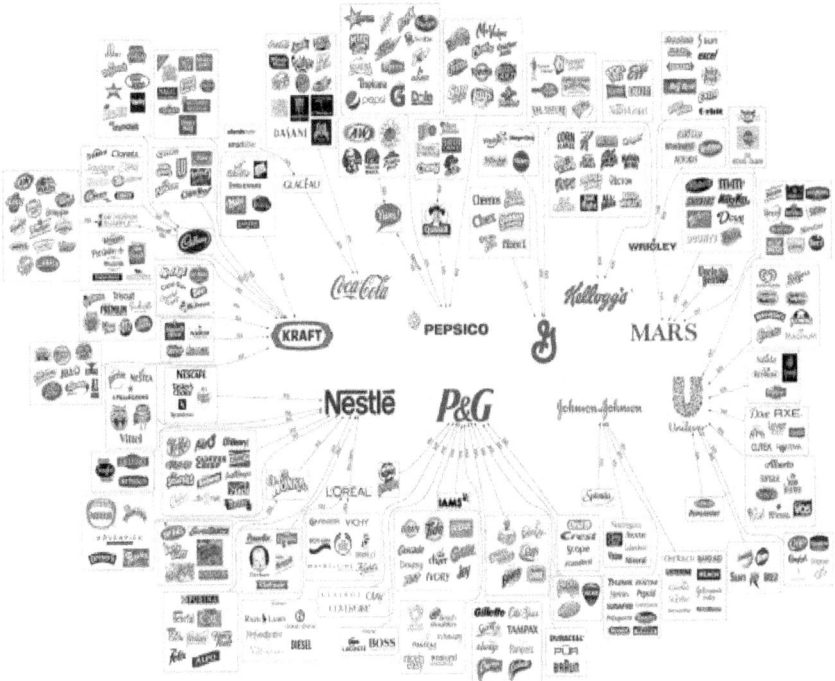

The Website 'theyrule.com' offers many examples of all kind of corporation structures: 26

"Theyrule.com aims to provide a glimpse of some of the relationships of the US ruling class. It takes as its focus the boards of some of the most powerful U.S. companies, which share many of the same directors. Some individuals sit on 5, 6 or 7 of the top 1000 companies…"

"A few companies control much of the economy and oligopolies exert control in nearly every sector of the economy. The people who head up these companies swap on and off the boards from one company to another, and in and out of government committees and positions. These people run the most powerful institutions on the planet, and we have almost no say in who they are…"

Karl Marx once referred to this ruling class a 'band of hostile brothers' noting

[25] http://www.qbn.com/topics/674044/
[26] http://www.theyrule.net/

that "they stand against each other in the competitive struggle for the continued accumulation of their capital, but they stand together as a family supporting their interests in perpetuating the profit system as whole."

Example: Harvard University [27]

Harvard University: 439 relationships

Prof. John Kozy writes about Harvard and Co.: "Anti-intellectualism never died; it continued to live in the dark alcoves of the religious institutions of the Middle Ages. That darkness came to America when its first universities were established. These universities were established as fundamentalist vocational training institutions ... The darkness is returning! ...

Harvard was the Liberty University of the day, a Bible school, and its function was distinctly religious ... The university's goal was and is to teach people to operate in an ideologically biased market economy as is shown by its history, influence, and wealth ... Harvard is also the alma mater of at least sixty billionaires. It is America's Cathedral of the Moneyed Elite, and it promotes establishment ideologies rather than universal learning ...

---

[27] http://littlesis.org/

Students at Harvard recently walked-out of Greg Mankiw's Ec 10 Principles class because of alleged ideological bias in his presentation … Students at Harvard, like students at many other schools, are not allowed to learn about alternatives to the neoclassical model …

(…) praised the success of Yale in the hope that it would maintain the Puritan religious orthodoxy … Stanford became the Harvard of the West, just another conservative, fundamentalist university … Corporations have also donated huge sums to colleges and universities to promote orthodox, classical Capitalism …

Evolution is dismissed because it conflicts with Biblical accounts of creation. Climate and environmental science are dismissed because they conflict with free market Capitalism …

In Europe, people can be imprisoned for denying that the official Zionist account of the Holocaust is true. Will teachers of evolution become criminals if they deny that the Biblical account of Creation is true …? … Backwardness never turns its head. … The darkness is coming!" [28]

You can interpret the following statements as opinion. But you can also dig deeper and find the right insights and arrive at conclusions for yourself:

➔ We are coming back to a new form of inquisition!
➔ Coward politicians have sold their country and people!
➔ Who are the true owners of Europe and America?
➔ This evil doing is protected by academic institutions and spread through media and the 'Accreditation' system!

It's all about neoclassical economics. One of the most important economic questions is: Who has the final say? Or: Who is the commander? And directly linked to that: Who has the money? Behind these questions is an even more important question: Who is the economic architect of 'neo-capitalism'?

Very interesting conclusions and insights can be drawn, from the article by Prof. John Kozy through the dissection and combination of his key points:

- Fundamentalist vocational training institutions
- A Bible school and anti-intellectualism
- An ideologically biased market economy

---

[28] http://www.globalresearch.ca/index.php?context=va&aid=31302

- Sixty billionaires
- Cathedral of the Moneyed Elite
- The neoclassical model
- Puritan religious orthodoxy
- Biblical accounts of creation
- Zionist and Holocaust

→ Combine them the right way and you start to come close to some economic answers!

Definition of Corporate structure: "A grouping of different positions and departments within a company, which all have separate tasks but work together to operate as one company. Many large companies tend to have similar corporate structures, which often include a marketing department, finance department, human resources department, and information technology department. The hierarchy of job positions is also part of the corporate structure, with a typical structure including a CEO or president, board members, managers, (workers) and other employees." [29]

---

[29] http://www.investorwords.com/6774/corporate_structure.html#ixzz1xmcAmNV0

Example of organizational structure: [30]

Sample Divisional Organizational Structure

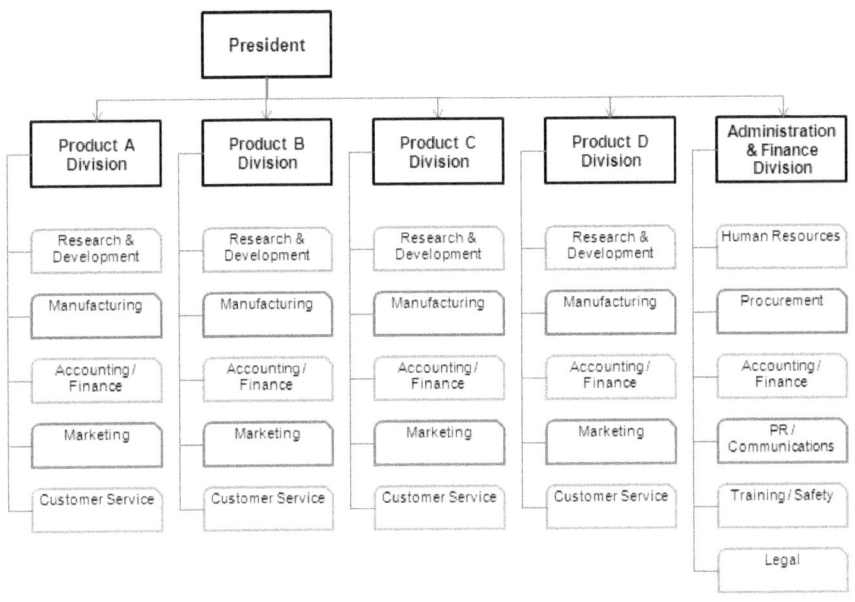

Example: Wal-Mart Stores [31]

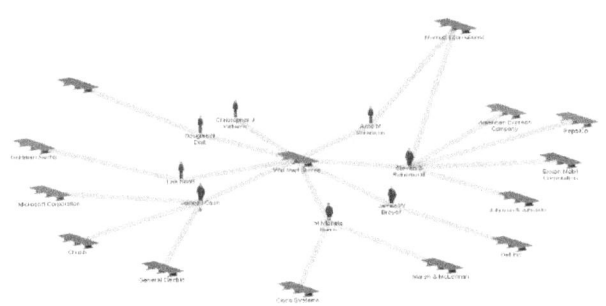

Wal-Mart: The world's biggest retailer

---

[30] http://www.vertex42.com/ExcelTemplates/organizational-chart.html
[31] http://www.theyrule.net/

Example: Goldman Sachs [32]

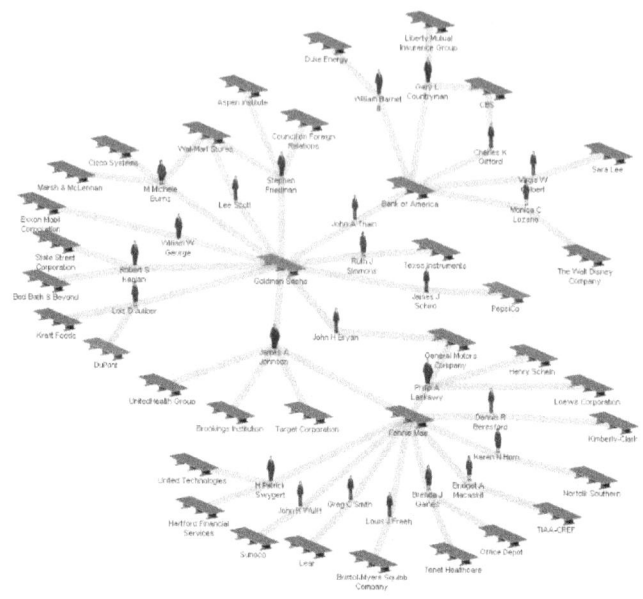

Goldman Sachs: 380 relationships

→ Hundreds of other examples can be found from the same source!

25 US Mega Corporations:[33]

If Wal-Mart were a country, its revenues would make it on par with the GDP of the 25th largest economy in the world by, surpassing 157 smaller countries.

We've found 25 major American corporations whose 2010 revenues surpass the 2010 Gross Domestic Product of entire countries, often with a few billion to spare. Even some major countries like Norway, Thailand, and New Zealand can be beaten by the size of certain U.S. firms.

→ Yahoo is bigger than Mongolia
→ Visa is bigger than Zimbabwe

---

[32] http://www.theyrule.net/
[33] http://www.businessinsider.com/25-corporations-bigger-tan-countries-2011-6?op=1

- → eBay is bigger than Madagascar
- → Nike is bigger than Paraguay
- → Consolidated Edison is bigger than the Democratic Republic of the Congo
- → McDonald's is bigger than Latvia
- → Amazon.com is bigger than Kenya
- → Morgan Stanley is bigger than Uzbekistan
- → Cisco is bigger than Lebanon
- → Pepsi is bigger than Oman
- → Apple is bigger than Ecuador
- → Microsoft is bigger than Croatia
- → Costco is bigger than Sudan
- → Proctor and Gamble is bigger than Libya
- → Wells Fargo is bigger than Angola
- → Ford is bigger than Morocco
- → Bank of America is bigger than Vietnam
- → General Motors is bigger than Bangladesh
- → Berkshire Hathaway is bigger than Hungary
- → General Electric is bigger than New Zealand
- → Fannie Mae is bigger than Peru
- → Conoco Phillips is bigger than Pakistan
- → Chevron is bigger than the Czech Republic
- → Exxon Mobil is bigger than Thailand
- → Wal-Mart is bigger than Norway

Challenge: Imagine when all Western corporations are bigger than America and Europe combined!

Example 'Mercadona' and the entrepreneur Juan Roig' (Spain)

Success, top-success, grandiose success 2011: [34]

- Shops: 1356
- New shops opened: 60
- Sales (revenue): €17,831 millions
- Gross profit: €1,040 millions
- Investment: €540 millions
- Profit increase: 19%
- Workers: 70,000
- Age of workers: 40% younger than 25
- Roig's wealth: €4,700 million

---

[34] Emprender Franquicias y Negocios. May 2012, p. 82-83

Critical questions are appropriate about: workers with lowest personality qualities, lowest wages (under the breadline), millions of tons of fishes and sea food stolen from folks living on the border of oceans, use of pesticides and other chemicals in the production of vegetables, fruits and meat, goods produced in low-wage-countries bought at dumping prices, genetically modified products, and the thousand hidden externalities (collateral damages). How much tax from workers' wages does the Spanish government get from this grandiose success? Is there any corruption in the economic game on a local and national level? How much in financial terms does a municipality benefit from this success? Could it be that the majority of the money from sales leaves the location and reduces substantially local cash flow every year?

→ Grandiose business success is with highest probability impossible without 'criticalities'.
→ Estimated 80% of Roig's wealth is essentially "stolen money" or "maximizing profit" by offering poor value and low quality performances to both consumers and producers. But it's legal.
→ The same criticism can be leveled at most large supermarket and hypermarket food retailers – Carrefour, Wall-Mart, Tesco etc. etc.

Conclusions to consider in analyzing economic principles, theories and laws:

→ The classical books on economics ignore that an ice-cream shop or a grocery store is not a corporation.

→ Simple and clear: All the small, medium sized and bigger businesses, including production businesses, have a completely different structure and interrelations than the big corporations.

→ It does absolutely not make sense to understand 'producer entities' of all sizes and varieties of complexity of networks as something equal (in the economic principles, theories and laws).

→ All economic theories that ignore these differences of structural quality and quantity have no scientific value at all. This is a systemic fault in economics!

The academic career problem:

Example: a big town with 650,000 citizens has one university (e.g. managed by a Catholic fraternity) with 85,000 students, whereof 90% are from the area and only 10% from elsewhere (other areas of the country and foreigners). The university has a yearly output of 15-18,000 estimated graduated students searching for work. There is another university in another town 80 km away and another town with a university is 150 km away; a third one is 200 km away. The land is fully rural. We estimate that 5,000 students from these 3 universities together, including from some business schools in the town and area, are graduates in sociology, business, economics, tourism, communication, or public relations. Prognosis: 80% will not find a job in production entities that fits with their academic education in this urban area. However, they have no idea what 'working reality' is and they all must start as apprentices in services, technological or production entities. Today, in 2012, there are only very few job offers on the market, anyway. Some of these students will find a job for €900-1,200 per month; minimum 50% will be unemployed and the rest can clean shoes for tourists on the streets, or work behind a bar, or live of their parents' budget. All other big towns and cities of this country also have immense amounts of students that graduate every year; but there are not enough jobs for this young academic generation. Therefore, they must leave the country or accept any job to get a wage to make a living. What was the point of their educations!

Solutions for this lost generation:

A society such as Spain or Greece needs 2-3 million small producer entities (self-employed, or micro firms with 2-3 employees) all over the country. But most Bachelor Programs in business and economics (and related programs of study) do not prepare students for such a business perspective. An immense potential for these nations is therefore lost as these graduated students fail to develop numerous small production and service businesses and even give work to people with low vocational education. Why? Because they are not equipped by "economic" education with the skills or attitudes to build and grow a micro firm!

In addition, in most countries the majority of the members of governments (national, provincial, and local) and most of academic teachers (in business and economics) do not really understand, how businesses in the real world work, anyway.

So, at the start of the 21st century we have a lost generation of approximately 25 to 30 millions of young people in many European countries. Harsh but true: too many politicians are 'good for nothing' only good at lies and deceit; not to mention the subtle corruption and 'rope teams' on both local and national levels. These people are destroying the hopes and dreams of an entire young generation today: millions of humans with a mind and a soul.

Who must shoulder the blame? Universities? Governments? Public education? Modern lifestyles? Economists? Billionaires? Religion? Or this spoiled, entitled, lazy, and dull young generation, most of them already dehumanized and degenerated and irreversibly damaged from contamination in the brain? No, it's the physical body of the 'invisible hand' of economics in concert with coward, hypocrite, arrogant, ignorant, neurotic, narcissistic, incompetent and treacherous politicians.

Conclusions:

→ Too many politicians are parasites, egomaniacs and traitors to their people.
→ This current economic crisis doesn't call for economic 'growth'.
→ This current economic crisis doesn't call for economic 'austerity'.
→ This current economic crisis doesn't call for warmongering.
→ This economic crisis calls for a catharsis of the entire economics system.
→ This economic crisis calls for a catharsis of all local, provincial, and national governments.
→ This economic crisis calls for a catharsis of all academic and vocational education.
→ This economic crisis calls for a catharsis of all institutions that were build on the premise of 'growth'

From the structure of corporations we now come back to the (internal) micro-systems and focus on the working people, we can refer to as 'producer entities' or 'working groups' or 'working classes':

We can categorize the producer entities by the hierarchy:

- The workers
- The administration staff
- The department managers with 'assistants'
- The top management with expert advisors
- The advisory board members
- The owners, investors

→ Such a structure does not allow most people a professional career within a producer entity.

We can categorize the producers by mental status:

As the producers (people working in the production) are also consumers, we can list the same variation for consumers; see the corresponding paragraph in the chapter 2.2.1.

We can categorize the people as workers in production by critical mental status:

- Indecisive, disoriented, easily deflectable, lonely, helpless
- Strong preoccupations of all kind
- Depressed, fearful, socially phobic, anxious
- With inner pain, sadness, suffering in their heart
- Very low confidence and very fast feeling lost
- Uncomfortable due to constipation, psycho-somatic reaction
- Very tired due to circumstances or sleeplessness
- Exhausted, driven by excitement, anticipation of something; anxious
- Actual heavy relationship problems (strong arguments, fights)
- Chronic sexual, love, care or attention frustration (in need of compensation)
- Strong suppressed inner frustration (in need of compensation)
- Strong inner unconscious conflicts (in need of compensation)
- Low self-image (ego-image) (in need of compensation)
- Consumption of psycho-pharmaceuticals and recreational drugs

➔ A healthy mental status is first of all the absence or a low level of the critical components mentioned above.
➔ A healthy mental status of all workers, managers, and leaders could improve the collective performances by an average of 50%, here and there and ultimately by 300%.

The 'archaic and evolutionary human being' as described in the Chapter 1 gives a further orientation for a healthy mental status.

We can categorize the people as workers in production by their emotional status:

a) Positive emotions concerning work:

- "Thank God, I have a job and can make my life": relative security
- The well paid department managers with a related attractive satisfaction
- The top management very satisfied with their wages
- The commanders that do not work in the production chains
- Investors (shareholders) get money, but have not worked for it

➔ A minority may have an inner devotedness and a humble character.

b) Negative emotions and attitudes concerning working:

- The workers and administration staff with permanent fear to lose the job
- The workers and administration staff with low working attitudes
- The workers and administration staff with no inner devotedness
- The workers and administration staff with a nice face and their fist in the pocket
- The department managers conceited and with authoritarian style
- The top commanders with fundamentalist neo-capitalistic attitudes

➔ A minority may have an inner devotedness and a humble character.
➔ Other characteristics are: stubbornness, rigidity, laziness, ignorance and arrogance.

We can categorize the people as workers in the production process by their valuation of their wages:

- Some laborers feel their wage is low and poor
- Some laborers feel their wage is under-paid
- Some laborers say they are outrageously exploited
- Some laborers feel their wage is correct and o.k.
- Some laborers feel their wage is really good
- Some laborers feel they are outstandingly paid
- Some laborers can say they are royally paid

On the one side, here and there in the economic understanding of needs and wants we could conclude that all people are never satisfied with their wage. But this is not true. Truth is, that in the capitalistic understanding it's quite common practice in certain sections to under-pay laborers so that they cannot sustain even a very modest life. Devaluation of money (price inflation) or higher taxes reduces their shopping volume further.

On the other side we must ask what the hidden psychological function and overall plan is by those who get a shameless wage and those who get a huge wage and a very opulent bonus at the expense of low wages or suspension of workers and firing of employees.

Some further considerations:

It doesn't make sense and it is not useful to simply talk about 'producers'. The picture of producers is extremely complex and diversified. The quality of producers gets completely different depending on the size of producers, but also depending on many other factors.

➔ Producers are not all sitting in the same boat. Ignoring the differences leads to ignoring the complexity of human implications and ignoring the collateral effects on society as a whole.

If we see 1,000 corporations together with 100 million small producer firms in one pot, then the picture becomes deceiving. These 100 million small firms suggest that these 1,000 corporations are of identical structure, importance and value and have equal importance of and servicing society.

Some essential facts must be considered and explored in scientific economics:

→ The big producers (corporations) destroy the small and medium sized firms.
→ The responsibility of the owner of a small and medium sized firm is crucial.
→ The big producers (corporations) ignore responsibilities wherever they legally can.
→ The worker in a small and medium sized firm is a human with friends and family in a community.
→ The worker in corporations is a single, anonymous, part of the human worker biomass.
→ The production interest of a small and medium sized firm aims for a balance.
→ The production interest of a corporation aims for maximum profit at minimum costs.
→ A small and medium sized firm is directly controllable and under a certain social control.
→ A corporation is practically not controllable from outside and under no social control.
→ The externalities of corporations for instance in Asia or Africa are not controllable.
→ A small and medium sized firm is interested in a social balance in its environment.
→ A corporation is not interested in a social balance in its environment or the society.

2.3. Culture of Consumers and Producers

The word 'culture' in general refers to education, behavior and habits, manners, style of living, expressions of mind, ways of social encounter, ambience, expressions of ideas and values, characteristics of belief, social pursuits and expressions, attitudes, tastes by individuals and groups, enlightenment.

In general, the word 'culture' encompasses the 'qualities' in humans, in societies and entities (including economics) from rough to excellent or highly developed. The immense variety of possible approaches requires here to focus on some aspects in the context of consumers (shopping) and producers (workers and entities).

2.3.1. Culture of Consumers

We can categorize the people as consumers by personal culture (mind and behavior) and general culture, both include collective life style:

- Stupid, badly educated, disinterested, ignorant, blabbers, lazy, slow-minded, rather chaotic, disorderly people
- Blinded sheep always following the trends of the masses, strongly dependent on peer groups, including their 'friends' on social websites.
- Educated people, but with little learning, little reading, rather superficial way of thinking, copying a lot consumer habits
- Educated people, learning, reading, on average useful thinking, organized life style or usual style of the masses
- Educated people, learning, reading, profoundly thinking, some creative activities, cultivated style, giving importance to quality and health
- Educated people, learning, reading, profoundly thinking, original style, and 'alternative' ways of living

→ From the manifold variety of personal culture of people we can conclude that there are many different ways of shopping, of forming bundles of goods, and of decision making as consumers.

We can categorize the people as consumers by shopping habits:

- Careless shopping	- Somewhat controlled money management
- Not thinking much when shopping	- Strong money management
- Carefully comparing options	- Well organized shopping procedures
- Moderately price conscious	- Unprepared shopping
- Highly price conscious	- Thoughtless shopping
- Concentrated shopping procedures	- Responsible shopping

▪ Taking a lot of time for shopping	▪ Relaxed shopping
▪ Prepared shopping list	▪ Stressed while shopping
▪ Low money management	▪ Somewhat controlled money management

→ There are many different ways of shopping habits and therefore also of decision making as consumers within the shopping pattern.

We can categorize the people as consumers by shopping groups (kind of shopping):

▪ Single	▪ Father or mother with child / children
▪ Couple	▪ With partner and child / children
▪ With a friend	▪ With father or mother
▪ With several friends	▪ Father or mother with child / children

→ There are many different shopping patterns with different social influences in the decision making of the average consumer (the buyer).

There are some important possible influences to consider:

- A single person shopping is only influenced from inside (their own mind) and the market environment.
- A couple may discuss and find compromises about the goods and prices to choose.
- Going shopping with friends implies factors such as interest, knowledge, emotions, time, etc.
- A mother or father going shopping with a child is influenced by the child's needs and wants.
- If an adult goes shopping with his father or mother, he gets advice or comments that influence his decision.
- If father and mother go shopping with their two children, then the shopping can easily get out of control.
- Going to a shopping center is not the same as going shopping to a local grocery store.
- The majority of people that go to shopping centers understand it as a way of entertainment.

→ There are also many different shopping patterns with different emotional influences (manipulations) from the seller's environment that effect the decision making of a consumer (the buyer).
→ The interaction between consumer unity (buyer) and the sales person with

his sales environment is crucial in a sale-buy process.

The personal life culture of people:

- Many people tend to talk before they think.
- Many people talk a lot without thinking.
- Many people don't care about the quality of food and goods.
- Many people don't even understand the concept of quality.
- Many people judge before they are essentially informed.
- Many people eat without a minimum of behavior culture.
- Many people prepare their lunch or dinner without care or art.
- Many people cook and eat too fast, in general stressed and hurried.
- Many people do not talk during lunch or dinner with partner and / or children.
- Many people have their TV on during lunch and dinner.

→ The manifold ways people talk, think, care, judge, act, and prepare creates a flow in their decision making processes as consumers.

Based on these explorations we can construct a variety of hypotheses:

- The market can depend on an estimated 80% of stupid, blinded, lazy-minded and low educated people, and with a low life culture.
- The market can use the fact that most people have conditioned habits developed since early childhood.
- The market can depend on the fact that most people have little information and do not make conclusions in a bigger context of the goods they buy.
- The market can consider that people are not really enthusiastic about learning (about product quality) because learning is strenuous.
- The masses have in general low self, time, and money management skills; and are in general rather careless in these crucial matters.
- The masses go shopping rather unprepared, not organized and not thinking much in choice' proceedings.
- Shopping groups tend to compromise opinions and interests, selection and quality-quantity decisions.
- The life style of masses is: cheap, superficial, thoughtless, indifferent to quality, and easily impressed with just the packaging.
- The more people are educated, thoughtful, responsible, informed, and have quality criteria, the more they chose rationally (thoughtfully).
- The more people are relaxed while shopping, the more they are concentrated and consider price-quality and quantity.

- The general life culture of people (e.g. talking, cooking, and eating) is a pattern that also operates in similar shopping settings.

➡ Most of what the economics study books say about consumer behavior does not consider the manifoldness of 'living culture' and therefore such study books must be considered as rather irrelevant.

2.3.2. Culture of Producers

We can understand here the producers as the labor groups and / or as the producer entity. We will have a view on both sides.

We can categorize the producers by their working culture and by the entities' style:

▪ Informal or formal	▪ Impolite or polite
▪ Intellectual or anti-intellectual	▪ Respectful of disrespectful
▪ Rough (rude) or sophisticated	▪ Disregardful or regardful
▪ Submissive or authoritarian	▪ Negligent or attentive
▪ With style or lack of style	▪ Understanding or insensitive
▪ Cooperative or uncooperative	▪ Indifferent or differentiated
▪ Creative or uncreative	▪ Interested or disinterested
▪ Emotional or functional	▪ Disciplined or undisciplined
▪ Badly groomed or well-groomed	▪ Communicative or not
▪ Ordered or chaotic	▪ Informative or non-informative
▪ Differentiated or primitive	▪ Careful or careless
▪ Dull or enlightened	▪ Transparent or opaque (obscure)
▪ Ignorant or informed	▪ Impolite or polite

➡ The financial and humane effects of working culture in a production process are immense and no economic theory in the classical books reflects its costs and possible economic benefit.

We can categorize the producers by working habits or rules of practice:

Impeccable or faulty	Improvisational
Immaculate or deficient	Creative space or instructed repetitive work
Strict or lax	Routine or irregular
Precise or imprecise	Hierarchic or loose structure
Rigid rules or flexible rules	Speed pressure or relaxed

100% as instructed or free space of practice	Clean or dirty
100% controlled or uncontrolled	Spontaneous or predictable
Line work or case work	

→ The financial and humane effects of working habits in a production process are immense and no economic theory in the classical books reflects its costs and possible economic benefit.

We can categorize the producers by working groups or producers' sections:

▪ Individual work	▪ Intellectual work
▪ Team work	▪ Creative work
▪ Group work	▪ Management work
▪ Section work	▪ Leader work
▪ Control work	▪ Administrative work
▪ Mass work	▪ Planning work
▪ Single units work	▪ Communicative work
▪ Manual work	

→ The financial and humane effects of working groups in a production process are immense and no economic theory in the classical books reflects its costs and possible economic benefit.

There are some important possible emotional influences that form a working culture to consider:

- Sympathy between workers
- Sympathy between workers and instructors or managers
- Attitudes between workers
- Attitudes between workers and instructors or managers
- Interaction (dealing with) between workers
- Interaction between workers and instructors or managers
- Working environment: light, temperature, space, decoration
- Working environment: noise, contamination, pollution, dirt

→ The financial and humane effects of emotional influences in a production process are immense and no economic theory in the classical books reflects its costs and possible economic benefit.

Moral business life culture in general:

- Everywhere there are little cheats and lies in the sales process
- Products are of low quality, but sold as high quality
- Products are offered as promoting health, but do not
- The packaging is big and great, but the content is small and normal
- Some substances of the material are toxic, but ignored
- Low quality products get a high price if the demand is high
- The façade of a product is luxurious, but the substance is cheap
- A great brand increases the price independent from any added quality
- Devices are constructed with planned obsolescence
- Artificial additives give the taste, but the content is a mix beyond imagination
- Workers are terribly exploited working under inhumane conditions
- Stealing 'legally' the natural resources of other countries
- Selling expired food with new updated labels
- Exploiting businesses with overpriced rents (for the premises)
- Identifying a non existent failure to generate a higher repair bill
- Destroying a competitor with under priced products
- Producing devices with batteries to promote the battery industry
- Using toxic chemicals, knowing that the consumer will become ill in the future
- Mixing a bit of good quality essence with very high low quality essence
- Giving a national identity to a brand/product, when 80% is made abroad
- Declaring a nutritional quality, when it's elements are laboratory made
- Speculating on/or betting with price movements (raw material, food resources)
- Hiding the low quality of a product with a quality sale decoration
- Lying about the risks of a product pretending it is 100% safe
- Manipulating consumers with advanced psychological knowledge
- Connecting human values with a product that are not real
- Letting the laborers work in miserable environmental conditions
- Abusing high unemployment rates by offering reduced wages
- Incurring high debt levels and letting it be paid off by future generations
- Abusing water resources and letting it be paid by future generations
- Contaminating agricultural land at costs of future generations
- Artificially growing vegetables that have lost their natural taste and nutritional value
- Factory farming using chemicals, pharmaceuticals, and junk-forage
- Factory farming under absolute down-and-dirty conditions for species
- Industrial tourism treating people like chickens in battery farms
- Soulless tourism that destroys the environment and local population culture
- Over-exploiting natural resources at the expense of the future generations

- Demanding high prices that do not correspond with the offered quality
- Slackers always working at lowest possible performance
- Glorifying cars that produce more damage and suffering than wars
- Deification of nuclear power stations with waste active for hundreds of years
- Coronation of capitalistic life standard at the expense of the environment and soul of mankind

→ The financial and humane effects of moral business life culture in a production process are immense and no economic theory in the classical books reflects its true costs.

Externalities: the society (humans!) not only pays today but in the future (the next 100,000's years and more) for the damages caused by economics today:

Pollution and contamination	Dominance over governments
Waste, sewage, nuclear waste	Destruction of democracy
Destruction of environment	Full of corruption on all levels
Destruction of the eco-systems	Destruction of natural wealth of people
Destruction natural resources	Decomposing of human's mind
Plundering the planet	Brainwashing (needs & wants)
Species extinction	Dehumanizing and degenerating
Disrespect of human values	Heating up greed, envy, avarice
Stockholders interest	Promoting egoism, individualism
Not human oriented, but profit oriented	Dashing to pieces human evolution
Impoverishment of entire peoples	Dissociation of genuine spiritual values
Decrease of middle class businesses	

Twenty-two, internationally renowned scientists declare: [35]

"Rising populations may be driving Earth towards a disastrous 'tipping point' where humanity starves itself out… Currently with 7 billion people about 43 percent of Earth's land surface has been converted to agricultural or urban use and with a predicted rise to 9 billion by 2045 it is estimated that half will be disturbed by 2025. … We may already be past (the) tipping points in

---

[35] http://www.dailymail.co.uk/sciencetech/article-2155322/Rising-populations-driving-Earth-irreversible-tipping-point--scientists-global-government.html

particular regions of the world. ...humanity is at a crossroads now, where we have to make an active choice. ... One choice is to acknowledge these issues and potential consequences and try to guide the future (in a way we want to). The other choice is just to throw up our hands and say, let's just go on as usual and see what happens. ... Climate change, population pressure and widespread destruction of natural ecosystems may be driving toward an irreversible change in biosphere with devastating consequences."

Cynically we could say: The United States will be well prepared with building the most advanced warship in history - DDG-1000 destroyer. The problem is the economic factor with the question about who will pay for it at which other 'costs' (e.g. more poverty, more contamination): "The construction of one DDG-1000 costs about $3.1 billion - nearly twice the cost of the existing destroyers. If we add the costs of research and development, the price of one destroyer increases to seven billion dollars." [36]

We can conclude from the author's statements:

→ The financial, environmental, and humane effects in a production process are immense and no economic theory in the classical books reflects its costs.

→ Where do these global developments lead humanity and the planet? The answer cannot come from neo-capitalistic theories.

2.4. Management in Life and Business

2.4.1. Self-management in Life

Most consumers (consumer groups) are not trained in the ability to manage their life matters with the corresponding knowledge and skills. People do not learn it in public schools and not even with academic education. Faced with the business world – the free market – they are in a weak position. Therefore it makes sense to shortly explore the concept of 'life management' and to see how it affects consumer behavior and its decision-making processes.

Thesis: People's self-management and life-management influences their

---

[36] http://english.pravda.ru/world/americas/06-06-2012/121327-usa_china_destroyer-0/

consumer behavior.

Self-determined	Alien-determined
Order	Disorder
Planning	By accident
Structure	Chaos
Overview	Lack of orientation
Clarity	Vagueness
Aim-precision	Aim-diffusion
Decisiveness	Indecisiviness
Self-management	Self-"tatter"
Seriousness	Indifference
Well-measured speed	Haste
Freedom	Compulsion
Transparency	Non-transparency
Precision	Inexactitude
Result of thinking	Indoctrination
Learning	Repetition
Moderation	Excess

General characteristics of a successful self-management: [37]

1. People need time for themselves; that means: nobody has to be reachable and accessible at every time of the day. Everybody needs their calm moments, with their mobile phone switched off. To relax every day for 5-10 minutes is recommendable.

2. To say 'no' without frustrating another person, is an art. On the other hand one has to be able to say 'yes' as well. In either case one has to account for such a 'yes' or 'no'. It is recommendable to precisely think how and why one has to say 'yes' and 'no'.

3. Identifying troubles gives people a clear orientation. Strategies for problem solving make life easier. Noise and clutter produce troubles and disturbances. Difficulties in any activity produce disturbances.

---

[37] Schellhammer, Management of Knowledge, www.rcigi.com

Motto: Daily life contains troubles and disturbances that need to be managed. They are part of life.

4. Thinking and acting with an aim in mind is efficient: In important matters of daily life, people should plan and act in the perspective of medium and long term personal aims. To practice this, one needs to keep a journal or diary.

5. To aspire for one's determined aims with a timetable and with working methods is efficient. For that, one sometimes has to read a book to get new suggestions and inspirations. Or ask others about their experiences. Never should people be afraid of asking for advice.

6. Efficient management in life requires dividing high aims of life into small constructive steps. Each life phase has it's own goals. But, at the same time people should not miss out on living the present.

7. Prestige, money and success are not the highest aims of life. To reflect upon one's consumption, especially compensating behavior is efficient. Searching for one's meaning of life inside in one's soul gives a strong foundation.

8. Part of self-management is to concentrate on the use of one's energy. Developing good self, time and life-management skills, focuses attention to not dissipate one's forces in chaos and lack of planning. Recharging one's energy on a daily basis is efficient. There are various techniques for relaxation.

9. To ascertain priorities, which lead to determined aims, is indispensable for life-management. A truthful life is the essential aim (or mainstream) of human life. Working is also living. A rule of efficient self-management is: Life lies don't lead to a good and fulfilling life.

10. Not everything is equally important and urgent. Importance means: aim and success. Urgency means: time and fixed date. Urgency goes before importance. It is a rule of life-management to ask every start of week: What is important and what is urgent this week?

11. Dealing with daily matters, but also with long term aims, is fundamental for an efficient life- management. One should ask: "Where do I want to be in 1-3 years?" Checking every few months if one can achieve his predetermined aims with the way of living creates a balance.

12. Life-management requires also regularly controlling one's use of time. A day-to-day plan for the week, integrating one's use of time, makes life-management efficient. One's life-time is one's capital. The corresponding question is: "Did you invest your time capital well this week?"

13. Controlling one's stress factors in order for stress not to control the person is crucial. Part of life-management is also planning one's mobility. Caution: even people, TV-news, advertisements, articles in newspapers, etc., are often stress factors.

→ Do consumers really consider and seek to develop such demanding self and life-management skills?

→ A majority of consumers do not even have the most basic knowledge about self and life-management.

The self-management and life-management of people is preponderantly characterized by attributes such as:

Un-determined	Chaotic	Diffused aims
Influenced	Disoriented	Indecisive
Disorderly	Vague	Hasty
By accident	Miscellaneous	Compulsive
Opaque behavior	Repeated	Imbalanced
Inexact	Copied	Lust-driven
Indoctrinated	Excessive	

→ Such quality of self-management and life-management of people influences their consumer behavior.

Consumer's time-management:

Time-management is in many daily life settings indispensable for an efficient result. With most people, time runs away: 15-20 hours a week on watching TV; 10 hours and more on talking without a content of individual interest; more than 10 hours hanging around doing nothing, plus the varied time-consumers such as phone calls, reading newspapers, short visits here and there, small quarrels in relationships without any result, waiting in a traffic jam, lack of personal organization, etc. All this added up over the years of one's life equals years of life-time that simply gets lost!

→ People's general time-management influences also their consumer behavior.

A constructive control of time usage includes:

Recognizing time wasters	To say 'no' if one feel so
Planning the day in the morning	Recognizing urgency
Weekly planning	Recognizing importance
Checking through daily aims	Arguing constructively
Communicating with a clear mind	Not always hesitating
Organizing dossiers	Making a shopping list
Preparing telephone calls	Reflecting on mobility
Defining small aims for the day	Being concentrated while talking
Regulating stress	Taking breaks
Starting to act slowly	To overview courses
To make checklists (e.g. travel)	

➔ The majority of people do not live with a reflected time-management. Their time use is imbalanced, chaotic, a waste, diffused, confused, indifferent, and an immense loss.

➔ Inefficient time use has also an effect in the consumer's behavior because there is no reasonable indication why it should be different to their general life time-management.

➔ There are calculations showing that humans in general during their life time waste 20%; that means for a 70 year old person we get an incredible loss of life time of 14 years. People from the age of 65 up to 80 years loose up to 65% of life-time.

Conclusions for the producers and sellers:

➔ A majority of consumers do not practice very efficient self-management for shopping.
➔ A majority of consumers are deceivable, seducible, manipulable, and suggestible.
➔ A majority of consumers are not very clear in their mind about critical shopping.
➔ A majority of consumers are lust-driven, without an exact focus when shopping.
➔ A majority of consumers are vague, hasty, miscellaneous, not exact when shopping
➔ A majority of consumers have no controlled time-management and are

distracted.

→ A majority of consumers is not trained for efficient management of their shopping.

Consumer's budget management for their goods:

In Chapter 2.8 we develop a picture about the variations of budgets for making a life determining the variations of bundles of goods and services related to different budgets.

Our question here is: How does the life-management ability of people influence in determining the use (distribution) of their budget?

Other questions are: 1) Do people first consider their budget and only then they determine their bundle of goods and services? 2) Or do people first create a picture about their bundle of goods and services and then they choke on their budget? 3) Or do people simply mindlessly consume until there is no budget left and then incur debt (credit cards, consumer loans, overdrafts, etc.)? These questions we will answer with following chapters.

Comments:

We can't just throw all people in the same bucket. There are people with a good life-management and other people that don't bother about life-management. We assume that a willingness to learn in life (e.g. from mistakes), to learn from information, and to learn through self-education shapes and enhances the overall life-management.

From a psychoanalytical perspective we assume that people with highly suppressed emotional problems, complexes formed during biography, and highly suppressed desires tend to be critically influenced in their self-management.

Therefore we continue with some general considerations about the 'quality' of life-management.

The life-management of people can differ between the manifold life areas:

Communication	Leisure activities
Watching TV	Management of children
Using mobile phones	Studying
Internet activities	Dealing with problems
Relationship matters	Biorhythm (life energy)

Household topics	Time management
Health	Management of aims
Stress	Etc.

As life-management can also have different levels of quality and differ between life topics we give to the categories the indispensable requirements (pre-conditions):

- Efficiency requires: knowledge, skills, clear mind, thinking capacities, concentration, and an aim
- Value: valuating presumes that people have a differentiated insight into human/material values
- Importance: Recognizing it needs to be able to differentiate between important versus unimportant
- Urgency: requires ability to perceive and think in networks of time, causes, effects, conclusions
- Balance: requires a measure and seeing things in interrelation and consequences of imbalance
- Knowledge: comes from open eyes, learning, having questions, thinking and media sources evaluation (critically)
- Skills: requires knowledge, learning, training (exercising), and knowing where and how to use
- Planning: implies seeing things in time-network perspectives, requires preparation, thinking, aims
- Self-Protection: requires knowing what is 'good' and 'bad', and the ability to identify influences (negative versus positive)
- Sustainability: requires having a bigger picture and an understanding of sustainability

→ We assume: Most people don't know these categories of life-management. They are not aware of the complexity of 'quality' in the life-management. And they have a low level of the indispensable requirements.

→ Therefore the different approaches to self and life-management allow us to conclude: People manage their bundle of goods and their budget on the same low level as they practice self and life- management. In which case, the 'invisible hand' has plenty of options here to direct and manipulate these people.

2.4.2. Self-management in Business

A majority of businesses, production and sale, have a very developed 'business management'. The working people are skilled within their field. Group leaders, team leaders, department leaders and the top leaders have the special knowledge and skills to manage their duties. 'Business management' makes efficient the operations in the world of production, services and sales. Businesses and departments of businesses cannot efficiently operate without a highly sophisticated management system.

→ Low self-management of workers slows down the productivity and tends to increase the amount of mistakes.

Thesis: If the labor's self and life-management is deficient, then their working-management is in a majority of cases also deficient. We cannot directly prove this thesis, but we can justify it with the logical consideration that it seems absurd that a majority having on the one side a low self and life-management have on the other side a high working-management.

We need to distinguish between the different labor groups, to carve out the criticalities, for example in groups such as:

- Unqualified workers
- Qualified workers
- Administration staff
- Team and group leader
- Manager of a small business
- Department manager
- Manager of a medium sized business
- Top manager, manager of a big business
- Board of directors

The above-elaborated aspects of self and life-management are correspondingly for the world of businesses, production, sale, and services:

Time management	Adaptation management
Perception management	Aim management
Alertness management	Behavior management
Thinking management	Learning management
Network management	Communication management
Solution management	Emotional management
Conflict management	Perseverance management
Control management	Discipline management
Concentration management	Stress management
Attentiveness management	Time waster management

Preparation management	Preciseness management
Organization management	Accuracy management
Flexibility management	

Conclusion:

With certain evidence we can conclude that in general the production process, team work, group work, communication, reacting to critical incidents, learning from new situations, identification of complexities, planning and organization, negotiation, sale proceeding, etc., can't be better than the quality of the corresponding management skills.

→ A new roadmap in the interest of production efficiency and profit is necessary!
→ Internal failures due to low management performance of workers are a waste of potentials and it is very costly.

The maxim 'profit' or 'maximizing profit' requires in general optimizing the reduction of costs and in critical situations to cut off sections or reducing labor expenses. Another significant intervention is to reduce quality of products and to ignore collateral damages at a cost to the society and the planet.

A new roadmap in the interest of profit could be: maximizing all the aspects of management as listed above. This requires education, further education, in-house meditation (mental training), and in general enabling (with further education) the workers, employees, and managers to find and live an all-sided balanced self and life-management.

→ Economics can develop concepts in order to optimize self, life and business management in order to reduce costs.

The three most important measures to reduce costs of internal 'failures' are:

1) Internal vocational further education and personality development education

2) Respect for the laborers and giving more importance to human factors

3) Wages for workers that allow making at the very least a basic life (single, family)

2.5. Limitedness of Satisfaction

Limitedness of Humans

Let's explore the limitedness of humans:

- A family with 12 children in a 50m2 apartment and without earnings is inhumane.
- Eating 10 pizzas for lunch leads to severe illnesses and as a habit it is fatal.
- Not sleeping during one week leads to mental disorder and serious risk of health.
- A day has 24 hours and nobody tries to change it to 30 hours for his life.
- It's not very probable that humans will soon live 150 years or even 200 years.
- No human can run 100 meters in 3 seconds without any 'special' help.
- A human of a height of 3 meters has not existed up to today, and probably never will.
- A human with a weight of 300 kg is incapable of most activities and will die from this state.
- A human that can fly without a special gadget will certainly be a dream forever.
- Under normal circumstances a human eats a certain amount of food per day, less than 2kg.
- A human needs a certain amount of liquids per day, but in the average less than 10 liters.
- A child of 6 years never has the potential to weigh 100 kg without technical or human help.
- Not relieving urine and excrement during one week would cause serious health problems.
- Working 20 hours per day during one year without a break will end in illnesses.
- It doesn't make sense to have 10 sofas and 20 beds in an apartment of 20m2.
- It would be absurd to have 20 fridges in an apartment with 2 rooms and for 2 people.
- Eating every day 2kg of chocolate, forever would lead to a physical collapse.
- Drinking one bottle, then two bottles more of whiskey leads to blackout and death.
- Fill your apartment with 5,000 goods to live with and the mess will be disastrous.

- Give your plant 10 liters of water per day and see how the plant will grow faster.
- A person that says 200 times per day "I want this … I want that" is insupportable.
- A child of age 6 that says every day to its mother "I want more money" has a mental problem.
- A person that wants sex 20 times a day, everyday and all year long causes relationship problems.
- A person that wants to talk to you every day for 10 hours becomes a nasty problem for you.
- A worker with zero potential but wanting a wage of 30,000 Euros per month has lost reality.
- A billionaire wanting more billions of profits for his pocket is a case for the psychiatry.
- There are very serious reasons why sexual child abuse is forbidden and severely punished.
- A person with a wage of 5,000 Euros that calculates every cent on every product is compulsive.
- Nature shows us in many ways: too much of something becomes poisonous (toxic).
- A pharmaceutical principle is: too much of something can cause very serious damage.
- A psychological intervention that ignores inner human limits is breaking something.
- If education (family, school) ignores inner human limits, then it creates a risky development.

→ Do you wish to be the sole owner of our planet?

We conclude from these examples:

Human's nature and human's life always sets limits even if the world and the planet offer unlimited amounts of whatever, sand or stones if you like. Human's body and human's mind have limits, sometimes here and there on a low level, sometimes on a high level, sometimes flexible, but never can they reach 'cosmic' dimensions.

Never and really absolutely never could a human leave the world with his biological body to go to paradise. And to procreate a human always an egg and sperm need to come together; there is no solution with the Holy Spirit or the 'invisible hand'.

Here we have another source of the unlimited madness about the ideal of 'maximizing profit' and the 'illimitableness' on earth. People claiming such things as true are really very mad in their mind. Religion and economics teach the impossible and destroy herewith the mind and humanity, the world and the planet; and both concepts require believing.

→ Belief is accredited in religion and economics. Does this make sense? Does this stimulate mankind's evolution? It's a cul-de-sac or a dark (Medieval) labyrinth without exit!
→ Everywhere in human's life and in the society or between nations is a breaking point; also with the planet and the ecosystems humanity is reaching a variety of irreversible breaking points.
→ Ignoring the principle of 'all-sided balance' creates in the mind and soul of people, in human's life, in society, in the ecosystems, including in economics, a very destructive development.

Humans, religions, and the economics in the real world can go until and beyond the breaking point, but then the damages are irreversible. How much damage do the humans, mankind as a whole, and the economic world need until everything breaks down with irreversible existential consequences?

If a big majority of mankind has lost the essential human values such as love, care, balance, hope, trust, inner security, reliability, inner potentials, the balanced mind, the inner spiritual intelligence as source of life, and the natural limits of the body and mind, the planet and the life style (with superficiality and compensation behavior), then the foundation and drive energy is given for the biggest war of all times.

From our explorations we interpret and conclude: [38]

- Dogmatic belief of Christian religion has broken all limits of confirmability, excludes all Archetypes of the Soul, and therefore is a very dangerous religious psychosis.
- Economic theories about 'maximizing profit' by ignoring 'externalities' have broken all limits and are parts of a psychotic system; and therefore is a very dangerous economic psychosis.
- The unlimited capitalistic politics with its increasing fascist practices have broken all limits and are parts of a psychotic ideology; and therefore are a very dangerous political psychosis.
- It is human's mad mind with completely unbalanced psychical functions and a soul that has reached a high grade of neurosis, a psychopathic and psychotic state that in turn has created such religion and economics.

---

[38] See also: Schellhammer: The Future in Your Hands. 2011

- A psychopathic and psychotic system, both together in one, does not have any potential to get out of itself and to find a new evolutionary roadmap. The next step will be a global war.
- Nevertheless, there is a solution – only one solution – to get out of this religious and economic, psychopathic and psychotic labyrinth.

Here is the archetypal frame for economic solutions:

→ Limits are always given in human's life, in the world, and on the planet.
→ Limits are related to the system to which the limit is bounded.
→ Limits are given by the all-sided balanced movement or development.
→ Limits are broken by loss of reality, by ignoring balance and human values.

2.5.1. Limits to the Satisfaction of Consumers

'Satisfaction' is a term with different dimensions:

Psychological satisfaction	Performance satisfaction
Moral satisfaction	Demand satisfaction
Spiritual satisfaction	Intellectual satisfaction
Physiological satisfaction	Emotional satisfaction
Physiologic-psychical satisfaction	Need satisfaction
Drive satisfaction	Want satisfaction
Pleasure satisfaction	

This is our thesis, which can be discussed and explored in the real economic world:

- Physiological satisfaction can be seen in specific contexts as an energetic dynamic: from zero to complete satisfaction. Once a physiological need (drive) is satisfied, it takes a while until the energy is again loaded up to a strong drive energy pushing a person to find again satisfaction.
- Satisfaction can be seen in the context of specific aims. Once the aim is reached, complete satisfaction is given with this aim. Only a new aim will re-load the drive to achieve satisfaction with this new aim.
- Satisfaction can be seen in the context of a specific level of development or performance, whereby the development and the performance can have a new progress achieving a new level. Only a new given level to reach will re-load the drive to achieve satisfaction with this new level.
- Breaking the potential of development or performance, the immanent limits and balance, becomes individually and collectively destructive.
- Emotional, intellectual, moral, and spiritual satisfaction can be fully

reached within the given context of life patterns. Only a new context of life pattern will re-load the drive to achieve satisfaction with this new life pattern.

- If a person has reached the satisfaction of fulfillment of his potentials (performance, thinking, spirituality, moral behavior, etc.), then there is no motive (drive energy) for more satisfaction. The potentials may find use on other contexts and then a repeated satisfaction is achievable.
- If a human realizes his inner satisfaction (intellectual, spiritual, emotional, psychological), then there is an inner balance and no need for endless new wants to satisfy, as they would be only compensations of an inner lack of satisfaction or fulfillment. Therefore needs are fully satiable as they are related to the limits of potentials of a person and the given life patterns.
- If a human respects his limits given by life and inner conditions, then he can find and respect the limits of his wants. The wants become a reasonable meaning. Only a lack of inner satisfaction boosts endless wants and more satisfaction with possessing wants. In other words: if living life is more important than possession of goods, then the wants are naturally limited with the capacities of a human and the life patterns. Therefore principally also the wants can be all-sided balanced and within the balance fully satisfied.

→ The economic concept of needs and wants that never ends and endlessly requires new satisfaction with new needs and wants is fundamentally wrong. It is also a question of character and personality quality (integrity) that determines the borderline of 'enough is enough'.

→ Economics destroys character and personality quality (integrity) of people to get more growth of production, more profit and always to maximize profit.

People have many genuine inner needs; most of them they don't even realize that they have:

True love	Complete fulfillment
Warm-hearted home	A spiritual rootedness
Honesty	A spiritual orientation
Trust	Fulfillment of all longing
Authentic expression	Stability in life
Emotional safety (protection)	A positive social environment
Physical safety (protection)	Experiencing nature
Respect	Experiencing the world of animals
Autonomy	Social celebrations
Authentic self-confidence	Marriage

Authentic self-esteem	Having one's own family
A positive authentic self-identity	Exploring the personal world
Freedom from inside to live	Developing and living talents
Fairness	Understanding one's own (inner) being
Social attention	Meaning of life
Physical nearness (relationship)	A positive understanding of suffering
Care	Playing, games, fun, entertainment, pleasure
Support in managing life and growing	Satisfaction of desires and special wishes
Having a good father	Humor
Having a good mother	Joy of life
Work (working)	Harmony with one's self and others
Being taken seriously	Peace and justice
Being adequately paid for work	Cooperation
Sex with love and tenderness	Hope in personal life and future oriented
Sharing life with a partner of the opposite sex	Justice
A positive working unconscious	

→ Each human and humanity as a whole, including religion, economics, politics, and public education must decide if they want these genuine inner needs fulfilled for them, for others, and for humanity.

→ Once the responsible people in society have taken decision for the psychical-spiritual evolution aiming for the fulfillment of these inner needs for their folks, then they must project a roadmap and nothing that could hinder and block this new collective path has a place there.

Some psychological aspects of the mind need to be considered:

- There are a lot of people that have a very narrow and coarse perception.
- There are a lot of people that have a very low capacity of thinking, interpreting, and judging.
- There are a lot of people that can't think in time and space perspectives of their life.
- There are a lot of people that have (genetically?) lost to feel a complete satisfaction.
- There are a lot of people we must ask if they are already genetically distorted or retarded.
- A lot of people have no feeling for dosage, balance, and reasonableness; and they are stupid.

- The self-perception of most people is extremely low and partial, ignoring genuine inner being.
- There are people that give high importance to performance satisfaction; others absolutely not.
- People do not consider intellectual or spiritual satisfaction and shift it to material satisfaction.
- A child in a big toy store sees 1,000 toys and wants to buy a hundred of them; we understand that. It is normal at that stage of development.
- An adult sees 5,000 goods in a super market and he is crazy and brainless if he wants to buy 1,000 of these goods. And this is not 'normal', it is sick.

→ The key of a solution is a new public education for the 21st century as described in Economics I.

Our explorations allow us to construct some hypotheses of importance for economics:

- Top efficient marketing strategies operate with these inner lacks (deficits) of satisfaction.
- There is a satisfaction of quantity and of quality of a good or service.
- There is a satisfaction on the level of meaning or reasonableness (of a need and want).
- Satisfaction is not simply related to a 'hunger' or deficit of something physical.
- There are needs and wants that move between 'stop and go' and this life long or periodically.
- There are needs and wants that come to an end of satisfaction; and then that's it.
- Consuming has a satisfaction level of 100% that does not refer to the budget's limits.
- Exaggerated consumption is provoked and not an expression of greed or dissatisfaction.
- Exaggerated shopping has a lot to do with the individual capacities of the mind.
- The economic theory about the illimitableness of demands (needs and wants) is a lie.
- It's the capitalistic market with its marketing that destroys the mind capacities of people.
- It's the public education that does not prepare children and teenagers for the economic traps.
- It's the public education that does not prepare children and teenagers to master their life.

- The ways most adult's minds work has not significantly developed since childhood.

→ Most of what the economic study books say about consumer behavior is pure scrap.

2.5.2. Limitedness of Profit Satisfaction

'Satisfaction' is a term with different dimensions that we already have explored in the previous chapter. As all producers are humans and consumers, the following considerations presume the human factors.

In all the capitalistic economic books the terms 'profit' and 'maximizing profit' is glorified as the ultimate aim of the producers.
People, all humans, have many genuine inner needs; most of them people do not even realize that they have genuine inner needs. Is there a special genuine human need on the side of the producers that endless requires getting more profit?

Working is a general genuine inner need of highest importance. If people can't work or are significantly under-employed, they can't find satisfaction of performance and satisfaction given through 'contributing to society'. They feel they are 'inutile' and 'valueless'. And they can't make their life without working, means without a wage. And if they get a lower wage than needed to make a humble basic life, they can't live a proper life and they get mentally and physically ill, and in the end they die from hunger and illnesses.

Certainly, an unemployment rate of up to 3% is part of the normal development of society as nothing can function perfectly in humans' and in society's life; not even with an 'invisible hand'. And we consider it as normal that some unemployed people may need 6-9 months or so to find the right job or any job. Lifelong unemployment or under-employment, or unemployed already with age 45-50 for the rest of the life is a dire misery and absolutely not normal! No jobs for 52% of the youth in some European (and other) countries are a human disaster.

Hundreds of millions are unemployed, more than a billion are underemployed, and billions of humans don't have a wage to make their humble life. Millions die due to not having or not having enough work and a wage to make a life: this is a crime against humanity. The main agents are the big corporations and the governments. It's a neo-economic failure.

Our hypothesis is: The deification of 'profit' or 'maximizing profit' (others call it worshipping 'the golden calf') is an essential cause of the immense amount of unemployed and underemployed people, and of the more than one billion people suffering from hunger and worst life conditions. The price is very high that these people must pay for the Western life standard. The roots of this evil are hundreds of years old.

→ Every human in the Western world, United States and Europe, must know: we live a good life on the backs of 3-4 billion exploited slaves that have an absolutely miserable life!

Some psychological aspects of the mind that are of high importance and immense value in humans' life have already been discussed.

We want to now focus on the question: How does the mind work in the frame of 'profit'-thinking? And: Can 'profit' really generate 'satisfaction' or 'happiness'?

'Profit' shortly described, is: Profit = total revenue minus total cost. What is 'profit' for?

Example 1: John has established himself as a self-employed business. He has costs and income. Each month he simply takes money from the income to pay for his life. Already in the first months he makes a surplus and during the year the surplus is increasing. Therefore he spends more and more from the surplus for his needs and wants. At the beginning he needed €1,000 (Dollars) for his life; but at the end of the first year he has spent in total 18,000 Euros (dollars) for his needs and wants. Therefore he spent his profit of €6,000 (Dollars). John does not differentiate between income and the costs that should include a wage for him. But now, the second year he decided to determine a wage of €1,300 (Dollars) and at the end of the year he has a profit of €8,000 (Dollars). In the third year the business gets worse and above that he needs new equipment. The equipment cost him €2,500 (Dollars) and with the profit from the year before, he could cover the losses.

Example 2: Mary get's a splendid legacy: a hotel with 50 beds. The building is 25 years old. There is no mortgage on the building as her parents worked hard for 25 years. But the furniture is old, the mattresses are old, the kitchen is old, the building needs some new painting. She has no money left and she lives from a wage and additionally from the accounted profit as her parents have done. She continues the following 10 years exploiting the business in that way. But the day arrives, the customers are not happy with this old hotel and she is forced to renovate and refurbish. Her bank offers her 55% of the building value as a mortgage to renovate the hotel and to cover the big losses from the last year. From this day on the bank is the main owner of the hotel; and she has additional costs: the interest and monthly repayments. If the business fails in the future, she would have to give away her hotel. If her parents would have saved the profit during all the years and if she also would have saved the profit, then she would not need a mortgage and she could use this profit for the renovation and refurbishing. But they all preferred to live a luxurious life.

Example 3: The same hotel story, but a much bigger hotel and a hundred shareholders and above that financed with 80% bank mortgage. Obviously all the shareholders got during all the good years a slice of the profit cake. But none re invested so, after 40 years the hotel is a dump and the customers leave to go to new hotels in the same beach area. The story ends with bankruptcy, the bank gets the crumbling hotel, and the shareholders look into the empty pie dish. At least the shareholders got a lot of money during the 40 years. That is well understood without having really worked for it.

We find similar stories everywhere in the world of businesses. The lesson is simple:

→ Profit should cover all the risks of the business (the ups and downs), the mortgage repayments (not only the interest rates), the periodic improvements, refurbishing and other updates. Investment in the future is the future not divestment for short-term gain – sharing the pie before it is even baked!

Economics teaches us: value of a land, a house, or a business premise that is not bringing in money is a loss of money (of profit). Therefore everybody should charge the property with a mortgage (as high as possible) to do more business aiming for more profit (to maximize the profit) in the end and / or to make more business with the money from the loan.

If everybody does this, then in the end all properties and businesses in a society belong to the banks as they already have their 'visible hand' on every property and business. And the banks make the most profit from the interests and investments they make without ever really working for the money (apart from administrative costs). One thing is certainly clear; the interest the banks get and yields from investments are much higher than the administrative costs for a mortgage or a loan.

Based on these considerations we can construct some hypotheses with key words:

- The pattern of maximizing profit is: investors and banks get money without working for it.
- Making profit and reinvesting profit gives a relative guarantee for a sustainable business.
- Mortgaging a property or business reduces the ownership safety of a property or business.
- The faster the world is changing, the higher becomes the risk of failure and bankruptcy.
- The more profit a business can offer, the higher is the chance to find (enough) investors.
- Maximizing profit is indispensable to find investors, mostly needed for increasing business.
- Investors and banks want to benefit as much as possible from the businesses they finance.
- Interest rate is in general short or medium term fixed, and can be periodically increased.
- A business that doesn't have financial resources needs a loan to cover ongoing costs and extras.
- Agricultural businesses can sell their future harvests without knowing how it will be.
- Selling unknown amounts of harvest (of all kind of goods) can be insured by companies.
- With investors, banks, and a lack of saved profit, a business is forced to permanently grow.
- If the business can't grow anymore due to the market, then at least the profit must increase.
- Profit: Public debt €10 billion at 10% interest: in 10 years the lender gets €20 billion (Dollars).
- To increase the profit (for banks and investors), labor and other costs must be reduced.
- A business must also calculate first with paying costs and delaying income from customers.
- Delayed income can also be pre-financed from banks; but now the bank owns the business.
- Businesses can grow, some should grow; if it's financed with banks, then the spiral goes on.
- Businesses can lease machines, cars and equipment to use the capital for making more profit.
- Private investors are liable for a business failure and are punished in case of bankruptcy.
- Public corporations, managers or shareholders, are not liable for failure in case of bankruptcy.

- The workers made the profit, but in most businesses they do not get a slice of the cake.
- There is no consideration for the workers within these speculation and 'casinos' games
- The bigger a corporation / company, the more the workers at the bottom 'pay' for the failures.
- In the final price of goods that consumers pay all the risks and costs of the games are included.

Without a doubt, the understanding of 'profit' and 'maximizing profit' is not oriented to building up financial substance for future risks or renewal, but for paying the shareholders and for getting more shareholders to increase the business in order to make even more profit. Such a circle includes also to the corresponding increases in the wages for the management and the board members. A big business, a corporation, can be 100% leveraged and therefore is forced to grow eternally, constantly avoiding getting close to the edge of decreases in the volume of business (means: income and profit).

→ Consequently a business must run and run, and can never slow down without crashing. This is the madness of the economic 'growth'.
→ Growth is not forced or motivated by aiming for a higher life style; growth is forced due to the rules of the financial system.

Contrary, a business that has saved profit during the years, can survive with this money if the business decreases in its production activity. Here the word 'profit' does make sense. And if the business fails and the commercial premises are free of mortgage, then the damage for the owner is significantly limited.

'Profit' is not given to the workers' benefit, is not related to the business' stability, is not related to healthy environment requirements, and says nothing about the real value of the assets of a business such as land, building, premises, raw resources, and equipment. In two short statements:

→ The profit satisfaction doesn't reach the workers and obviously always goes at cost of the consumers, and is accompanied with high risks!
→ 'Profit' and 'maximizing profit' only serves the owners, the banks, the speculators, and the investors and not the workers or consumers.

It is all about 'as much as possible'. Logically there is no absolute profit limit set in this 'as much as possible'. Certainly, a satisfaction is given when a profit reaches an outstanding level with a 'WOW'-effect, or reaches what these people expected to get. But starting from there, business owners want even more profit.

Investors always look first where they can 'get the best of it'. If investors get a higher profit from other corporations or from speculations, then they move from one place to another to get more profit.

This means: Satisfaction is only relatively established as investors permanently move from one to another opportunity if they get a higher profit. Such a system is completely unstable and not sustainable in the long term. It creates permanent insecurity and stress. It permanently forces corporations to fight for 'maximizing profit'.

→ As the game must go on and on, every year and all the time, then this profit drive never ends and there is never enough profit.

The compulsive drive always cries and pushes for more growth to get more profit. It is the insatiable greed of neurotic, mad, psychotic, and psychopathic people created and heated up from repressed inner conflicts and from the spiritual emptiness and darkness they find themselves in. It has become systemic.

2.6. Development in Life and Business

2.6.1. Life Development: Establishing a Household

There is a lot in life that starts with a zero status, from a new bottom:

Going to the (pre-) kindergarten	Having a first child
Going to school	Starting a job
Going to vocational school	Starting one's own business
Going to high school	Children leaving the household
Starting with academic studying	Going into retirement
Establishing a household	Going to a care home
Getting married	

We explore here different steps on the ladder of life development, starting with age 16-18:

Some young people start working at 16 or 18, after secondary school and / or a shorter vocational school; others go to school up to age 18-21, vocational school or high school; most of the high school graduates then start studying at higher education establishments.

Now, economics comes into play: This life phase has costs: fees, public transport, books, stationery, and some extras, additionally pocket money. The period a student is studying he can't work and earn money. Most students depend on money from their parents, and most live at home. Temporarily some students may get jobs to earn some pocket money. Banks also offer loans to students.

In general leaving the parental home requires having a job and renting a room, studio or small apartment. Latest from this day on the young adolescent has his personal consumer costs for making life.

Establishing a household is here of primordial economic interest. Renting an apartment at the beginning costs money for a deposit, the first rent, furniture, and equipment. Such an investment costs easily €5000-10,000 (Dollars) (e.g. in Europe). And there are the monthly costs to consider: rent, electricity, water, oil or gas for heating, eventually caretaker costs, a telephone and Internet connection, etc.

Getting married is another step of economic interest: more costs for furniture, equipment, and moving in case of renting a bigger apartment with higher costs. The partner may have work and can contribute to the costs.

More costs must be calculated with each child, easily €500 (Dollars) per month. Most people that create a baby do not previously think about the financial consequences over the next 20 years.

In the long run, to invite a soul to come to earth easily costs at least €150,000 (Dollars) in the Western World. If we add the costs for public education and higher education we reach the sum of estimated €250,000. And if we consider the stupidity of 80% of young parents, then we can add another huge sum for the disasters caused by a mal functioning mind (stupidity or lazy-mindedness) at public cost. That's a very costly business! A license resulting from prior personality education that allows for the creation of a baby would not be the worst solution. Imagine: 15% of your taxes goes towards the disasters of other stupid people!

Back to the first apartment in an adolescent life; 'adolescent' because men become adult at the earliest aged 33 years and women in the best case aged 28: Who pays for the starter investment?

There are four options:

- The parents pay for it as a gift for starting an independent life
- The parents pay for it giving a private loan
- The person has already saved the necessary money
- The person gets a loan because he has a working contract

With a loan a young person is already at the beginning of the independent life chained to the bank with repayment rates and an additional interest to pay monthly. The person is already programmed to be a specific consumer with an own bundle of needs and wants.

→ This day is something like an economic baptism, entering from now on into the market as an independent consumer (and payer).

But the programming of the needs and wants already starts in the prenatal time: food preferences from the mother, the marketing on television the mother is confronted with daily. With the years, from early childhood up to the adult age millions of pictures 'stimulating and longing' for the modern life style are processed and the products for the needs and wants enter into the mind of a young human:

Forming an ideal consumer through acculturation:

- 2-4 hours of television per day with countless marketing sequences
- Magazines and newspapers full of marketing and news about goods
- Marketing on streets and on public places everywhere
- Shop windows everywhere, passed by thousands of times
- Celebrities becoming an ideal for clothes, shoes, accessories …
- School experiences about what peers like and dislike
- Peer group preferences for certain brands or products
- Opinions exchange on social networks between unknown 'friends'
- Advice from father, mother, friends, and other people
- Product presentations, news and reports taken from the Internet
- Shopping experiences over the years, with family, friends or alone

Ubiquitous marketing that reaches people through manifold TV and radio channels (both 24/7 media), countless magazines and newspapers, billboards (posters), additionally millions of websites, already from the beginning of life on earth is shaping, luring, seducing, manipulating and brainwashing practically all humans; some more, others less or only a little, but all as there is no escape!

→ The critical point is not the marketing itself, it's the connotations that are intentionally shaped for a collective stream of opinions, needs and wants and its all-pervasive presence.

Marketing messages are:

- You deserve this brand
- This car makes your entire family happy
- People will love you with this brand
- This brand makes you better off
- People that have this brand are proud of it
- With this brand the problem is solved very fast
- This device makes life much easier
- The freedom you feel when you have this car is priceless
- You are so sweet with this perfume
- Never again will you sweat with this machine
- This special thing makes you feel superior to your neighbor
- We are here for you and care for you
- People give you respect when they see you with this brand
- Not getting this opportunity will make you feel bad
- You simply can't reject this opportunity
- Clever people already have this brand
- Tomorrow this special opportunity is gone
- People will admire you with this brand
- Never loose the chance to get what you want
- This diminishes all the uncomfortable
- It's a serious loss if you don't buy this brand
- It's a joy to possess this brand
- It makes you happy
- You are a loser if you don't have this brand
- You will feel wonderful with this brand
- A real man must have this brand
- A real woman can't be without this brand
- People will give you attention with this brand
- Intelligent people already bought this brand
- Such a unique deal you can't miss
- Only stupid people ignore this brand
- This brand gives you consolation
- You will not feel lonely anymore with this service
- The brand is the explosion of all pleasure
- People will be proud to be your friend with this brand

- Easily and very fast you will feel very well
- Modern people show what they possess
- You don't have to wait for years to get it: 100% loan today
- We save the rain forest with our beer.
- Our sugared tea is a thirst quencher.
- And much more

An example of marketing:

Coca Cola Corporation spends several billion dollars per year on marketing; they get a profit of several billion of dollars. If Coca Cola has conditioned billions of brains for a hundred years through all media with 'Coca Cola = Happiness', then a small business, not even a big or mega business, will ever have a chance to compete. Having such marketing power where the picture of a Coca Cola bottle already activates the emotional part of the brain for happiness or joy of life, then a small business can never operate the same way.

If Coca Cola needs 2.5 liters of water to produce one bottle of Coca Cola, and they produce let's say, 1.5 billion bottles per day, then the water resources in India and elsewhere diminish and cause enormous poverty and misery. Here is the key to understand that more than one billion people do not have enough healthy drinking water. The bottle of Coca Cola costs around 40 cents in India. The average income of poor people is less than one dollar per day. The poor people can't buy not even one Coca Cola bottle per month and above that they don't have healthy drinking water, not even enough water for agriculture. Other collateral damages: Coca Cola destroys the teeth (phosphoric acid, carbon acid, and citric acid). [39] And the additive 'methyl imidazole' is a carcinogen. [40]

→ Conditioning the emotional section in the brain of billions of people is a tool of religion, of politics, and of economics (the free market). The 'invisible hand' of the corporations has every day access to the brain of billions of people around the globe!
→ The marketing, already shaping the brain of a fetus via the mother, is programming people for their consumer behavior and for 'rational decision making' with all tools, images, words, and visual experiences.

The consumer robots of modern society, the society of the right life standard

[39] http://de.answers.yahoo.com/question/index?qid=20061026024424AAc3psY
[40] http://www.zdf.de/ZDF/zdfportal/web/heute-Nachrichten/4672/6605820/945ab4/Krebsverdacht-Cola-und-Pepsi-aendern-Farbstoffgehalt.html

and the superior race, are industrially produced.

→ So there is no natural 'consumer behavior law'. It's all the result of what's in the marketing networks every day and 24/7 for nearly everybody, day after day, month after month and year after year.

There are more steps on the ladder to go up during the years. The last investment will be the advanced payment for one's coffin and the grave or for the cremation and the urn. There is no such thing as a free life and not even a cost-free farewell from life.

The Church and economic entities accompany each human from the beginning of life up to the last minute of life, and then people leave them, sometimes with open bills. As in the Western world nearly everybody has a bank account, the bank is also a daily companion during life, until the last day of life, often with the savings bank book issued already with the day of the birth.

There are taxes to pay; the obligation to declare taxes is also always around for the people in general from the age 18. Nothing else is during an entire life so close to (nearly) all humans! 'Death and taxes' are the only sure things in life as the popular expression goes.

The permanent monetary company of all humans:

- The Church
- The market
- The marketing
- The banks
- The tax authority

An unclear question is: is a baby already a consumer? Or do we see as 'consumer' those individuals who personally buy a good? A child can already go shopping alone; therefore must be seen as a consumer. Starting from here, we determine the 'consumer' status begins with the first time a child goes shopping alone. Certainly, we also must consider that children, when going shopping with mother or father, have a great say about what must be purchased and therefore play a dominant role as 'indirect consumers'. But we can determine the consumer also as the person that consumes (something, whatever) and therefore every vivid human is a consumer.

Another problem we see is with people living in a psychiatric clinic, in a special-care home, in a home for handicapped people, or in an elderly home.

Most of these people are – depending on the definition of the word 'consumer' – not consumers anymore as they don't go shopping personally. The institution cares for their (indispensable) needs.

Conclusion:

The population of a nation is not equal to the population of consumers if we understand the consumer as the person who goes shopping (and pays). With this understanding we must deduce from a national population the early childhood population, the population in special care, the population (patients) in hospitals, the inmates and a majority of the (very) old people in care homes, and finally also the people in the military service (soldiers and staff).

Obviously everybody is free to understand the term consumer as the 'entire population' because every human needs to consume (whatever).

→ It is advisable to make clear in scientific context of economics what is meant with the word 'consumer': the consumer, the shopper, or the buyer.

- Economic view: A 'consumer' is a selected group of consumers that goes shopping, makes decisions and pays for a good or service. For all other people (also consuming) a higher institution is the 'consumer', means: goes shopping, takes decisions, and pays for the demanded goods. In Germany for example, these 'institutional consumers' all over the country are of highest interest for the producers and sellers of goods.
- No consumer goes shopping totally unprepared and free of being programmed, just like that, and takes 'rational choices' about the goods to buy; all humans are already brainwashed or manipulated when becoming a consumer (purchaser).
- The 'capitalist consumer' is the result of a shaping and molding process since prenatal time; and this process probably never stops getting influenced (even brainwashing) about all the goods during the entire life.
- There is a consumer behavior, a shopping behavior, an individual decision making process, and the person that pays the goods. So, marketing may ask: Who shall we, target and program to buy our goods/services?
- There are also different mainstreams of consumer patterns: the consumer pattern of a child, of a single person, of a couple, of a family, and finally a mainstream of elderly and old people. All consumers (sheep) can be programmed to move within their typical consumer group-pattern.
- Coming to earth and living on earth is very costly; money matter issues are endless: Everything always has to do with money, receiving and spending, going out of the home or staying at home, even love matters cost money.

→ Most of what the economics study books say about consumer behavior is not clear in the use of the word 'consumer'.

See it this way and prepare yourself: 'Living on earth is not for free.'

2.6.2. Business Development: Starting a Business

In the business world there is always a start from a zero status, in the past, today or tomorrow:

- An individual starts working as employee (worker)
- An individual decides to start working as self-employed
- A couple decides to start their own business together
- A family decides to start together their business
- A group of people decide to start a business

Is it possible that a group of 100 or 200 people decide to start a business? This would be a very special case; in general it is not common practice. Businesses start small and then may grow.

Everyone that wants to start a business has in general countless competitors. The market is already full of all kind of businesses.

As there are always businesses for sale due to failure, retirement or other personal reasons of owners, there is also always here and there a chance or an opportunity.

The expansion of and spread of urbanizations and new urban developments also provides here and there opportunities to start a business.

To start a business some capital is required, depending on the size and kind of business one must calculate with a minimum of €5,000-10,000 (Dollars); less if an individual starts in his garage (e.g. for repair or sale of special products) or in a room in his home (e.g. psychologist, psychoanalyst, language teacher for individual lessons, online business).

Much more money is required to start a business with significant furniture, equipment, special appliances, special raw materials, complex production processes, and with 5-20 employees.

The lease of a hostel or an existing business can easily cost €50,000-250,000 (Dollars), and with bigger size or special location can start at €500,000 (Dollars) and up to several millions. Young people starting a business are in general not the people looking for a business with a high lease due to lack of money and lack of specific business experience, knowledge and skills.

Starting a business requires business knowledge, professional experiences, specialized industry knowledge, skills, and often a specific vocational or academic education. Without such preparations there is a high probability the business will fail.

- Starting a business is a very important step in life; it doesn't happen just like that.
- Starting a business must be well prepared and planned with knowledge and skills to get success.
- A new business needs 4-5 years to be fully working, established and sustainable.
- It is possible to start a (very) small business with €3,000-5,000 (Dollars) starting capital.
- Starting a business does not allow for 36-40 working hours per week and 5-6 weeks holidays p.a.
- In the first and second year, a new business requires up to 60 hours of work (and more) per week.
- Starting a business requires skills for self-management, marketing, accounting, selling, etc.
- Starting a business requires responsibility for oneself, the business, the customers and the staff.
- Customers are not just waiting for the new business and then running to buy its products.

Here we also have different steps on the business development ladder:

There are very young people leasing a medium sized business and pay €50,000 (Dollars) or more for it. But they are not prepared, have ideas that do not match with the potential customers in the urban area. Most people never think that 80% of the success has to do with psychological factors. It makes sense to start very small and plan for 5-8 years. And it is advisable to first acquire professional experiences by working for a firm. In an estimated 95% of all cases young people between 20-25 are not mature enough to manage their own business, their self-employed activities, or a firm with 2-3 employees by themselves.

The bigger a business, the more experience is required to achieve success. Personality strength is another requirement. The development of a business, as self-employed or as a small firm, can be seen in steps: 5-8 years to get plenty of experiences and to grow as a person. People undervalue the importance of the personality development of an experienced businessperson.

A family business shapes the entire family life, especially the relationship between the parents. Running for 'maximizing profit' rapidly ends in a disaster not only for the business but also for family life. Therefore the first years are never meant for the business to rapidly develop in size and volume, but to evolve just like the respective family owners.

There is plenty of life time to start or expand a business at the age of 33-40.

→ Starting one's own business is a life decision and not simply a decision about work.
→ Strengthening the foundation of the business and the personality go hand-in-hand.
→ To be the owner of a business shapes a person in a different way compared to that of a worker.
→ The family life of a businessperson is different compared to the worker's family life.
→ The private life of a person with his own business is not the same compared to that of a worker.
→ Starting one's own business requires taking into consideration a variety of psychological issues.
→ A worker does not experience the same psychological effects as compared to a businessperson.

Do you want to work for Coca Cola now or do you want to become self-employed or start your own small business? Is brainwashing the way you want to earn a living or will you be just a collaborator ambivalent to the damages?

Forming a producer through acculturation:

Acculturation means in general: adapting ideas, ideals, values, conventions, habits, cultural traits, patterns of another group, and behavior of a social group, to something new.

Therefore we can say: Studying capitalistic economics leads to the adaption of capitalistic economic ideas, ideals, values, conventions, habits, methods, social traits or behavior, to something new.

Millions of students read the words 'profit' or 'maximizing profits' 10,000 times; and then the value is acculturated as something new and of the highest importance. Such learning processes produce a conditioning between these terms and the word 'happiness' or 'joy of life' – just like Coca Cola does.

→ Studying capitalistic economics creates a brain reaction to 'profit' or 'profit maximizing' that is linked with happiness and joy of life or fulfillment. What ways and what functions of profit making is meant with the economic theories?

→ Business is from humans and for humans; and the production is from humans and for humans. A human or a business entity (represented by a human) gives a job to a human and this job together with the wage is for the life of this human, for his family as well.

2.7. Bundles of Demand and Supply

Supply and Demand

The law of demand and supply: "The law of demand says that quantity demanded is inversely related to price. That is, when the price of a good goes up, the quantity we consume of it goes down." [41]

'Supply and demand' is a core matter in economics. Let's introduce this topic by discussing the approach from Mankiw (et al.) summarized in the following list. [42]

The theory of supply and demand includes a series of specific variables:

- A supplier offering a specific good
- A supplier offering a similar good
- A group of suppliers (as a basket) offering a specific good (competition)
- A group of suppliers (as a basket) offering a similar good (competition)
- A single buyer demand
- A group of buyers demands
- The amount of (possible) buyers
- A single person's budget
- A budget of a specific population
- A price related to quantity demanded
- A good related to quantity demanded
- A substitute that increases the sale of another good
- A complement that decreases the sale of another good
- The supplied quantity
- The supplied quality of the good

---

[41] Colander, p. 238
[42] Mankiw (et al.), p. 68-93

- The input price (resources) for production
- The technology for the production process
- The production costs
- The number of sellers
- The number of buyers
- Some human factors
- Some social factors
- Some environmental factors
- A surplus of offered goods
- A shortage of offered goods
- An equilibrium of price
- An equilibrium of offer (quantity)
- An equilibrium of supply and demand
- The expectations for the future

All these variables create the dynamics in the market world; some more, some less, and some occasionally. And these dynamics are not (probably never) stable (or static) for all kind of goods and in all locations in both the short and the long run.

"The equilibrium of supply and demand in a market maximizes the total benefits received by buyers and sellers." [43]

There are some simple facts that are logical and easily visible in the world of businesses. We can call them 'simple evident principles' as these are simply common sense:

- If there is no buyer for a specific product, then the product can't be sold.
- If there are fewer buyers than the amount of a product, then not all products can be sold.
- Sometimes a product can be sold within a different frame (packaging, marketing strategies, etc.).
- If there is a competitor that sells the same product cheaper, then the price must be adjusted.
- If there are too many competitors (in the area of the market), then some competitors will lose.
- Some products with specific characteristics are only of interest to a specific group of buyers.
- Price levels can change the groups of buyers depending on their budget.
- A substitute can increase the sale of another good (a complement that fits

---

[43] Mankiw (et al.), p.139

together).

- A complement that replaces a good can produce a decrease of sale of this other good.
- The sale of a good depends also on the marketing strategy and sale skills of the seller.
- Scarcity on one location and abundance on another place leads to different prices of the good.
- Daytime, weather, or special events in an area influence the sale of specific products.
- The sale of a specific product depends on collective taste which differs between regions.
- Trends in colors or products or any appearance can increase or decrease the sale of a product.
- Quantity production (mass) reduces the final price, but often also the quality of the product.
- Quality of a product is very often only for a selected buyer group due to higher price.
- The equilibrium of a good's price is never stable in the long run due to the flexibility of variables.
- The equilibrium of the market always has a certain variance of 3-10% in price structures.
- The more people are reached with information about the product, the more chances for a sale.
- The more people see the product during their shopping trips, the higher the chance for a sale.
- Even, for the ugliest goods, a buyer can be found with marketing if the price is 'attractive'.
- Some products have 'inferior' connotations and are therefore avoided by certain buyers.
- Some products have 'luxurious' connotations and are therefore avoided by certain buyers.
- Some products have 'strange' connotations and are therefore avoided by certain buyers.
- Some products or brands are unknown and therefore avoided by certain (most) buyers.
- Some products stimulate a strong positive connotation and are sold more easily than other goods.
- The 'law of demand' (decrease of price increases demand) refers mostly to mass consumers.
- Decrease of price of a good does not guarantee that the masses will run for it.
- Most products on the market have a fixed price; but some special

businesses allow negotiations.
- Access, parking, and location are of high importance for the sale of specific goods.

These are some principles that show how the market dynamic works. Highly professional business people consider them in the 'basket of goods' for sale and in their marketing plans.

2.7.1. Bundles of Needs and Wants (Demand)

We already explored in 'Economics I' the structure of distribution of a wage. There are the costs for rent (or mortgage), eventually garage/parking places, electricity, water, oil or gas (heating), telephone and Internet connection, and additionally the taxes and social security as relatively fixed costs. The remaining money at the disposal for needs and wants are very narrow with low wages and increased in line with rising wages.

First there are the basic needs in a modern society:

a) Daily, weekly or monthly needs:

- Food and beverage
- Toiletry items
- Detergents (cleaning and washing)
- Transport (public transport)
- Expenses for the car (petrol, cleaning)
- Books, CDs, DVDs
- Bank account costs (e.g. transfers, credit card)
- Hairdresser
- Pocket money for daily miscellaneous costs

b) Periodical needs during a year:

- Clothes and shoes
- Bed linen and bath or kitchen ware
- Appliances for kitchen or bath and entertainment
- Computer or laptop plus printer
- Additional devices for the computer
- Mobile phone
- Life and health insurance
- Holidays
- Home decoration

- Batteries for devices
- Car service and repair plus insurance
- Pharmaceuticals
- Stationery

c) Needs of a household with young children:

- Extra food and beverage
- Clothes and shoes
- Baby toiletry items
- Bed
- Other furniture
- Toys
- Games
- Children's books
- Children's computer
- Children's mobile phone

d) Needs of a household with teenagers and adolescents:

- With increasing age of children, also the variety of needs and wants increases.

e) Needs of a household of two people

- If a normal household of one person costs the amount of X, then when one person is added, the household does not increase by 100%; maybe by 50%, depending on the individual needs and wants. The quantity increases less.

Secondly there are the additional wants in modern society:

Essential wants of estimated 65-90% of people (adult consumers) in the modern world are:

- A car
- Eating out on Friday or Saturday night
- Sunday leisure journey
- Weekend leisure journey
- Long distance holidays
- Special hobbies (sports, spa, art & craft, etc.)
- Going out (cinema, concert, events, etc.)

- A better/bigger car or a second car
- Better and bigger appliances (equipment)
- Going to museums or cultural events
- Travelling within the country
- Further education for life and/or job

The inferior and superior goods: "Bus rides … are an inferior good … as high-income consumers prefer their car." [44] Therefore a car is a 'superior good'?

Comment: Who says that bus rides are 'inferior'? As a general statement this is not true. From a practical point of view in towns and cities buses or trams are mostly more efficient than cars and in that sense 'superior'. What does 'high-income' mean? There are masses of people with 'low-income' and they have a car, can get a car already with installments of €80 (Dollars) per month repaid over 6-10 years (loan). Also this part of the statement is a lie. The statement suggests that people using a bus are 'inferior' people and people having a car are 'superior' people. Now, as nobody wants to be 'inferior', everybody runs to get a car – no? Or is it that people in a society are considered by economics as 'inferior' or 'superior'. The question therefore arises: Are there 'inferior humans'?

Herewith goods in general can be categorized in 'inferior' and 'superior' goods. As a bus ride is very cheap compared with the costs of a car, we could categorize all cheap goods as 'inferior goods' and the shops selling cheap goods logically 'inferior shops'. In contrast 'superior goods' are to be found in 'superior shops' and if the producers of cheap goods are 'inferior producers' then the producers of 'superior goods' are 'superior producers'. Logically we can therefore categorize the world population in 'inferior humans' and in 'superior humans'. We can also group food as 'inferior food' and 'superior food'. In reality we know it: very poor people and poor people with low wages must eat 'inferior food' and only the people with high wages (the high-income consumers) can eat 'superior food', which means or permits the buying of healthy food.

→ Herewith we have identified another aspect of the true face of capitalistic economics!

We describe the natural limitedness with some examples:

- A household is limited by space. Therefore the amount of furniture and

---

[44] Mankiw (et al.), p. 449

equipment for 100% satisfaction has a 'natural' limit.

- People don't eat or drink unlimitedly. Therefore the amount of food and beverage for 100% satisfaction has a 'natural' limit.
- People don't use unlimited amounts of detergents. Therefore the amount of detergents for 100% satisfaction has a 'natural' limit.
- People don't use unlimited toiletry items. Therefore the amount of toiletry items for 100% satisfaction has a 'natural' limit.
- All goods that people buy for their needs have a demand limit; most real wants (not fantasies) also have a 'natural' limit.
- Certainly, many people want a wage of €500,000 or €1 million (Dollars); but it's only a daydream they enjoy, not a real aim. Most people have a 'reasonable' understanding of a fair wage for themselves.
- The majority of people know their life long limits; at a certain level they are satisfied and happy with their possessions or the other wants.
- Some people want to develop their life up to the possible maximum that they see as their realistic limit; and to do this is right.
- Some people have an enormous potential and drive to live to their full potentials; and this is not greed, but it is right.
- Many people feel well with low performance, a small apartment (etc.) and are satisfied; but are made crazy by marketing stimulation for more needs and wants.
- Only neurotic, mentally burdened people want 10 new pairs of shoes or 10 new suits or 5 new mobile phones, etc. every single year.
- It is not true that people have unlimited needs and wants; and especially it does not reflect the entire consumer population.
- Yes, many people try to get their wants without having worked for them or without increased professional knowledge or skills.
- Greed itself is not a 'big deal', rather something normal and in most cases reaches a maximum within the possible economic, social and psychological frame.
- It is the marketing and the market as a whole that heats up the greed of people up to an irrational level for possessions and excitements.
- Every possible combination of a household has alternative bundles of basic needs or additional needs and wants.
- These household bundles change with: age, members of a household, personal culture, population group, social development, community location etc.
- These household bundles also depend on individual interpersonal differences and compromises with co-dwellers.
- The economic theory that (most) people have unlimited needs and wants is completely wrong not founded in reality and is simply a manipulative lie.
- The economic theory about needs and wants misinterprets the potentials of periodic or life long developments (which requires increasing

performances).

→ Most of what economics study books say about consumer behavior is pure scrap and only forms (shapes) compliant soldiers or slaves for the corporations (industry).

Management of bundles of goods and services:

We have already developed a picture about the variations of needs and wants that determine the variations of bundles of goods and services.

Our question is now: How does the life-management ability of people influence the determination of their bundle of goods and services?

Based on the previous explorations about self and life-management we can find the answer with the same assumption: Most people don't know the efficient categories of self and life-management. They are not aware of the complexity of 'quality' in life-management. And even those that have a low level of self and life-management are not aware of this 'quality' required. But these are indispensable life skills for all!

→ People manage their basket of goods (the content of goods and services) on the same level (in the same way) as they practice self and life-management.

What does this look like in the real world?

- The content of the bundle of goods and services of people is not efficient for life.
- Genuine human values and material values are not considered as equally important.
- The importance is driven by irrational impulses and actual energetic drives.
- The urgency of inner and external life matters is not seen, but neglected or unevaluated.
- The balance between needs and between wants or between wants and needs is not given.
- The knowledge about the quality of the basket (the single goods) is very reduced.
- Life skills are rudimentary, just copied on and on, as public education does not provide any development knowledge.
- Planning: People plan day-to-day, maybe the next weekend and maybe a holiday; seldom more.
- Self-Protection: No clear picture about 'true or false', 'right or wrong'; therefore no protection.

- Sustainability: This is a strange word in a strange society. Most people do not understand it, and in any case have no use for it, as they cannot consume it.

Some new theses are:

- Consumers are not simply consumers; all consumers are humans on earth.
- The higher the wage is, the more they differ in their shopping habits.
- The section 'food' in a basket changes entirely in quality with the increase of wage.
- The economic background changes the self-image and choices of the consumers.

→ 'Consumer' as a variable has a much diffused meaning in general economic statistics.

2.7.2. Bundles of Goods and Services (Supply)

Supply means: the goods and services offered on the market. Let's explore a bit some variations, at first sight obvious and common sense really:

- There are places where only one good (with different shapes, size, quality, etc.) is produced.
- There are places where many goods (with different shapes, size, quality, etc.) are produced.
- There are places where the goods are produced, but not directly sold to the public.
- There are places where the goods are produced and also directly sold to the public.
- There are goods that go from the producer entity to a seller entity (to sell the goods).
- There are seller entities that do form part of the producer entity (same ownership).
- There are seller entities that do not form part of the producer entity (independent).
- There are places where different goods from different producers are offered to the public.
- There are places where the same goods from different producers are offered to the public.
- There are educational institutions that produce knowledge and skills for professional activities. *
- Intellectual producers do not directly sell the developed professional

activities to the public.

- Intellectual products (knowledge) can be sold through all kind of media, mostly books.
- There are intellectual producers (individuals, entities) and they also sell their service to the public.
- Intellectual agents can sell their activities to the public and to institutions (firms, corporations). *
- There are creative producers (arts and crafts) that sell their goods directly to the public.
- There are creative producers (arts and crafts) that do not sell their goods directly to the public.
- There are independent practical services (cleaning, repair, etc.) sold to public and entities.
- There are practical services for special goods owned by the producer of these goods.
- All producers sell goods or services that with the sale the ownership of the goods changes.
- Banks sell services (money management), but also the good 'money' that they do not produce.
- Banks rent out money (never 'sell') and the ownership of the good 'money' does not change.
- The Central Bank of a nation prints the good 'money', but who is then the owner of the money?

* An intellectual agent is 'produced' (gets the knowledge and skills) from the university or any academic or vocational institution.

For a majority of the mentioned combinations we can interpret:

There are the small businesses, the producers of small goods they can sell their goods directly to the consumers at the place of production; for example: baker, butcher, carpenter, painter (art), art and craft producer (including decorative goods), gardener, small livestock breeding (e.g. chicken, ducks, pheasants, rabbits, baby pigs), dog breeding, pet breeding, fisherman, fruit and vegetable farmers, shoe maker, etc.

Production examples: [45]

<u>Businessman A has land</u>

- His land is best for producing potatoes, not best for salad; rather average

---

[45] Mankiw (et al.), p. 52-66

for strawberries
- He works 50 hours a week
- Economically he does best producing potatoes
- His machines for producing potatoes are of low cost
- Other input costs (including labor) are high
- He makes most profit with salad per kilogram/hour/investment
- He makes medium profit with potatoes per kilogram/hour/investment
- He makes low profit with strawberries per kilogram/hour/investment

Businessman B has land (same size)

- His land is best for producing wheat, not best for corn; rather average for potatoes
- He works 50 hours a week
- Economically he does best producing wheat
- His machines for producing wheat or corn are of high cost
- Other input costs (including labor) are low
- He makes most profit with wheat per kilogram/hour/investment
- He makes medium profit with corn per kilogram/hour/investment
- He makes low profit with potatoes per kilogram/hour/investment

We have here several economic terms: specialization (choice), production possibility, opportunity cost, trade (market), profit (gains), efficiency, resources, sets of consumption opportunities, absolute advantage, and comparative advantage. Some of these terms suggest a necessary aim (it's all about highest possible profit); but we have shown that such limitation is not the complete picture.

We have here eight variables. We can combine reasonable options, starting with 2 products, and then with more products. But optimizing all these variables (for efficiency) is not the whole story of the real life of doing business. Soil is always vivid and fertilizers, chemicals or exploitation through planting may change within decades the capacity of the land's productivity. We should also not forget the possible current and future implication of climate change (e.g. more rain here, more droughts there). The network of variables is mostly much bigger than a thesis, a formula, a law, or a graph!

- One businessman may say: "I only produce the product that brings me most profit."
- Another businessman may say: "I produce the two most profitable products."
- There is a businessman that says: "I produce many products because already with the sale of any average combination of three or more products

I can live a good life."
- And the last businessman says: "I hate potatoes because as a child, we got potatoes every day."

Obviously all these businessmen want to sell their products on the market as they have a businesslike way of thinking and operating. Certainly all businessmen want to make a profit; one or another 'highest possible profit'. But the profit can change with the weather in the future; or with a change of demand or a change of prices in the national or global market. The risk could be: today best profit, tomorrow sitting on the amount of 1,000 unsold (perishable) products and going bankrupt.

Another example is: There are two businessmen, they want to sell a basket of goods consisting of 25 (50) items and they can choose from 50 (100) suitable items for their specific kind of shop. This example can include the option that they can at any time change the basket of goods that is for sale.

Critical questions:

- What are the possible combinations? There are mathematical models calculating it within seconds.
- What is the most efficient choice? This depends on the personal interest of the businessmen: One may say: "I first do what I like"; the other man would say: I do what brings me more profit." Or: "I hate potatoes, but I do this production as it brings me maximum profit." This man will hate his potatoes (his work) during his entire life! How will his character be in 10, 20, or 30 years?
- What are the criteria for choosing? Examples: financial aspects, having workers, the likes and dislikes, the kind of work that needs to be done, maybe the partner's likes, certainly also the demand on the market; and some businessmen also consider fertilizer and pesticide factors, weather resistance of a product or an emotional component.
- What are the possible aims? The list contains: profit, inner satisfaction, happiness, personal emotional or spiritual fulfillment such as a philosophy about strawberries or wheat, short term or very long term sustainability of the right use of the agricultural land, best possible flexibility considering market changes (demand, collective price developments).

Conclusion:

→ Economic formulas are never everlasting in real life! Nothing is stable over decades in real life. There are always many factors that depend on unexpected or unknown factors.
→ De facto many businesses, including agricultural ones, have the

opportunity to change their production policy; some at any time, others must plan changes a year or more in advance.

→ Don't let yourself be blinded by abstract (unreal) examples and confusing economic formulas that try justify and always aim for maximum profit! Graphs never represent the (entire) reality!

→ The best possible solution always implies human and environmental factors and balanced compromises between variables, factors of economic interest, and unpredictable risks.

→ The bigger a business becomes – from a small farm to a global agricultural corporation – the more human and environmental factors are reduced, and the higher the drive is for more profit.

→ Exploring the bigger picture of a business topic or focusing for a fundamental business decision is always indispensable in order to find the right solution that includes long-term sustainability.

Economic study books ignore some immensely important facts in the production chain:

- If the raw material exploitation (for later production) is not at the same place as the production entity, there are the transport costs and with that, often other businesses involved.

- If the production entity (producing goods) is not at the same place as the sale entity, there are the transport costs and with that often other businesses involved.

- If a good or service is sold in more premises (not on the place of the production entity), then the owner of the premises earns money (without working) by renting out the premises to a seller; he is in that sense involved in the chain of production, supply, and sale of a good.

- If the location of a premise gets with the years a higher concentration of public traffic, then the owner can ask a higher rent, and he earns more money without working for it.

- The higher the costs (e.g. rent) of a premise for production and of a premise for the sale of goods (or services), the higher is the price of the goods (and services) for sale or the seller needs to sell really a lot of the goods or have a very exclusive services.

- A producer needs to sell his products where enough potential customers live for his products, but he doesn't need to produce there where the consumers are. He can (must) produce where the prices for production (and labor, rent) are cheaper than in the location of the sale.

The small businesses that want to sell their products themselves, in many cases can't sell their product at the location of production. They need a place to sell were enough potential consumers are. They all do not need big premises; some can operate with 10-15m2, others with 20-25m2 maximum. But the world of premises, including shopping centers, in towns and cities are not made for such small business operations and the rents are very high. In the south of Europe for example, there are the market halls; in the north of Europe this kind of places are mostly history; and not all market halls are suitable for all the products of such small businesses.

→ Small businesses that produce a small number of different products in low quantity have very little chance to get success in the modern world of business; only very special goods and services can succeed.

→ Based on this picture we can conclude: the bundles of goods (supply) offered on a specific place depend on the costs of production and of the premises.

→ The market (supply) is fully dominated by those producers (corporations), which produce many different goods and everything in big quantities, producing in places with lowest labor and production costs and selling in places with highest concentration of customers and therefore also with highest costs of premises.

The big corporations are the economic model for covering the entire future capitalistic market: national and international sale and service chains such as dentists, clinics, hospitals, car repair, tires, car washing, launderette, decoration, bakery, cafés, restaurants, discotheques, hotels, private schools, language schools, real estate agencies, clothes stores, shoes, key services, electronic goods, household appliances, furniture, general household goods, etc.

Logically, the amount of small businesses, producers and sale businesses, and with that the middle class is dramatically shrinking. Therefore also the bundles of goods and services from such small producers and suppliers are shrinking; or let's say: are dictated to or suffocated by the corporations.

A similar effect can be observed in the fields of intellectual services: lawyers, psychologists, psychoanalysts, psychotherapists, economists, nutrition advisors, life coaching, business coaching, publishers, educational institutions, dog breeding, natural remedy, sport clubs, gyms, etc.

Production businesses and intellectual service businesses very often form their own trade associations and determine the criteria for accreditations. The compulsivity to control and dictate is unlimited. The imperiousness is total. What is the motive? It's the cake and with that the potential of profit; they only want to share the cake with those who fulfill what they believe. They are all rigid, authoritarian, conceited, servile and submissive towards the higher economic authorities in the capitalistic society.

Compulsion is neurosis! Exaggerated greed is a neurosis! Imperiousness is a neurosis! And neurosis together with arrogance hinders pioneering thinking, imagination, creative thinking, inner freedom, genuine new product development, explorations for new knowledge and skills, and the evolution of humanity.

→ The bundles of goods and services from suppliers are dominated and determined from the established powerful producers and owners of premises, not from the decreasing world of small businesses, and especially not from the consumers!
→ Large corporations simply innovate, whilst it is the small imaginative pioneer that invents and creates truly beneficial products or services.
→ We should bear in mind that different corporations with different brands, different goods, and different names can have the same owners (investors).

Quality of food – No food is for free:

In Germany for example, all kind of providers of food, including restaurants and hotels, give away food that is (nearly) expired, but still eatable. Social institutions (charities) distribute this food via 'food banks' to a few million poor people. Providers can deduct the real sales price of the given food in their tax accounting. 30% of these products – tons! – are not eatable and the social institutions have to bear the costs for elimination. That's the capitalistic deal. Most of this allocated food is of junk-quality or already has a miserable taste, sometimes with fungi included.

Examples with estimates and 'show-case' figures:

- "The contamination of food by chemical hazards is a worldwide public health concern." [46]
- "There are over 14,000 man-made chemicals added to the American food supply today." [47] [48]

---

[46] http://www.who.int/foodsafety/chem/en/
[47] http://www.sweetpoison.com/food-additives-to-avoid.html
[48] http://phys.org/news183110037.html

- Children have high health risk through food additives because of their physical development.
- "We eat the residue of everything the animal ate: growth hormones, pesticides, contaminants." [49]
- A chicken of 2 kilos costing €2.30; has eaten during its life substances of a value of 50 cents.
- The industrial milk on the market consists of estimated 20% of its original nutritive substances.
- There are yoghurts with a price of 20 cents; others cost 80 cents per unit, additives included.
- A rasher of rasher of bacon costs €1.80-2.50; 50-60% is fat plus 1-2 millimeters of skin.
- The taste of most apples today is far away from the taste they had in 1960: €/$1.80-3.65 per kilo.
- Sulfites are chemicals that keep fruits and vegetables looking fresh and prevent discoloration.
- Vegetable and fruits contain pesticides, herbicides, other agrochemicals; risk to health is evident.
- Fish and seafood contain chemicals, pharmaceuticals, estrogens, sewage, antibiotics, etc.
- Meat contains antibiotics, animal drugs, hormones, and is often washed with Nitrite and Nitrate.
- Zeranol is one of the most widely used chemicals in the U.S. beef industry; cancer risk included.
- Artificial colorings used in food are synthetic dyes and suspected of being toxic or carcinogenic.
- The real content of sausages is of 10% cheap meat; the rest is made up of fat, animal substances, water and additives.
- Industrial animal breading induces stress which produces chemical reactions and gives the taste.
- This is only a small part of a very long list …

The list highlights two economic concerns in short statements:

→ 1) The highest aim of capitalistic economics is obvious: Minimizing costs and maximizing profit
→ 2) The lower the costs = the lower quality, the more chemicals, the higher health risks

Other considerations for food products:

---

[49] http://www.breastcancerfund.org/clear-science/chemicals-linked-to-breast-cancer/food/

- There is a price per item. There is a price per weight unit.
- There is a weight of the goods to take home
- There is a sensibility to varieties. There is a shopping habit
- There is a size of goods
- There is the time distribution of going shopping

And all these variables can influence the consumer's choice and behavior.

2.8. Budgets for Life and Business

2.8.1. Budgets (Resources) for Everyday Life

(The figures in this chapter are purely for example and not factual.)

Now we have prepared the framework around 'needs and wants' and 'goods and services' and we come to the decisive economic point or aim: People (consumers) spend money! From here the explorations become even more exciting!

The first question is: About which group of people do we talk? Obviously, those who don't have money can't spend money. This population is not interesting to economic theory and world. You want to start a business in a specific location; therefore your first question must be: Are there people with money there to buy my goods?

We want to draw a picture about the general people; means: the poor, the lower class, the middle class, and the upper class; but not about the very rich and superrich because they form a very special class with different needs and wants and different 'mechanisms' in their decision making process. Mainly we can group these masses into a ladder of 'money at their disposal' for spending.

The following figures are examples and do not represent any official parameter (statistics) from the Spanish economy.

If 80% of a population, let's say Spain, earns less than €1,200 (Dollars) per month, then we can calculate a shopping bundle of around €300-400 (Dollars) per month for their needs and wants. If a household consists of two working people we can take an estimated €1,500-2,000 (Dollars) for a monthly budget of a couple or family and a bundle of around €600-800 (Dollars) per month, which is not bad at all.

Producers must calculate with the limited budgets of the masses, and the very small group of people (20%) with higher wages respectively a higher amount of money at their disposal for the monthly purchases. Obviously this 20% group has more expensive apartments and houses; and they also pay more taxes.

We already explored: Establishing that one's own household (renting an apartment) requires some starter money: deposit, first rent, furniture and home appliances. Such an investment easily costs between €5,000-10,000 (Dollars) in Europe; but some people can start modestly with €2,000-3,000 (Dollars), or they get old furniture and cast-offs from family and friends for free.

The first start of a household requires money and obviously having a job and getting a wage. In general people start working while they live in the parental home or they find a furnished room (shared apartment). The parents are mostly the main financial source for purchasing the first furniture and appliances, or the young person must first work and save money (while living in the parental home).

Or people get a consumer loan if they have a job contract. Sometimes parents need to give a guarantee for repayment to the bank. From this day on a person is chained financially to a bank. Sometimes banks are generous and people can even buy a little car for €80-100 (Dollars) installments per month. Getting this and most loan means: they can buy and possess goods now without first having paid/worked for them.

People that get a loan when starting their own life do not learn that one of the essential characteristics of human life is 'development'; in other words: everything in life has a development. Loans break this characteristic.

In most cases a loan allows people to experience: "You can have it now before having worked for it." The first consumer loan is something like a deformation and manipulation of the rule of human's life development. It programs the young generation for the modern life style that can only work with loans. Investigate yourself the devastation that the recent economic depression has brought to people who had big loans. No jobs, no house, no family, no future!

From here the relatively fixed monthly costs start:

- The rent is fixed and can't be changed easily for the better; it may increase with the cost of living index.
- Electricity, water, oil or gas, community costs are absolutely unavoidable with a very small flexibility to decrease, rather a tendency of increasing.
- Telephone and Internet connection is for most people with the modern lifestyle a minimum with small flexibility.
- Above a certain wage taxes have to be paid; always the social security fees.

From there we come to the essential daily basic needs:

- Food, beverages, toiletry items, and detergents: A certain amount is indispensable and if the budget is very limited people have to choose the cheapest products with the highest quantity without much flexibility.

- Public transport for going to work: The public transport has fixed costs with some flexibility in the case of a monthly or yearly card.

We all know: leisure time outside the home means mostly spending money:

- Costs for traveling (public transport or own car): see above
- Manifold options for leisure from 50 cents up to X-€/$: with 30-50€/$ per month not many possibilities are given. People can drastically reduce to one coffee or a drink per week, and occasionally a hamburger with chips and water.

Some people may calculate exactly how 'to make the best of it'. But very quickly this can become compulsive. Others spend the money for one, two or three special occasions; and for the rest of the month they don't spend another cent.

Periodically people need to buy/pay for:

▪ Clothes and shoes	▪ Hairdresser
▪ Accessories	▪ Dentist
▪ Bed linen	▪ Pharmaceuticals
▪ Bathroom items	▪ Condoms

There are always special individual 'things' people need or want unconditionally:

- Tobacco, wine, a newspaper, a magazine, a book, sweeties, condoms …

➔ The basic monthly budget consisting of indispensable needs is now determined:

1. Fixed monthly costs
2. Social security
3. The essential daily basic needs
4. Some minimum cash for leisure activities
5. Some special 'little things'
6. Saving some money for indispensable periodical needs or wants
7. Once per year above a certain level of wage there are taxes to be paid

For the consumer market the points 3 to 6 are most relevant. Some individuals on very low wages may have 6€/$ per day, others 10€/$ per day, which is 180€/$ or 300€/$ per month. There are countless producers that want a little bit from this amount of money from millions of people. For people with such a minimum amount of money at their disposal (economically the 'poor' and the bottom of the lower classes) only the market of the very cheap products is affordable. In a country like Spain it is a population estimated at 15-20 million people (consumers); in Germany maybe 30 million people. The producers are here in this basic arena to get some Euros (dollars) per month from each individual!

Now we come to the significant wants or extras – rarely affordable for the poor people living on the breadline. But above a minimum wage (150-300€/$ extra) new consumer options arise:

a) Car

▪ A car may be indispensable; but in more than 50% of the cases a car is not. The price for petrol (a scarce resource) nowadays is in general increasing every month or quarter. Either car drivers pay for petrol or choose public transport; or a combination to reduce petrol costs.
▪ The first costs start with the driving school, the exam, and the license. Going to a driving school also has costs.
▪ Then the individual need (or want) to buy a car: cash, renting, leasing, or a loan often with a high interest rate.
▪ A car has a lot of ongoing (extra) costs apart from buying the car: road taxes, insurance, inspection costs, repair, service, car washing, and in the majority of cases also a garage or parking space.
▪ Lastly cars not only depreciate in value with age (the initial value paid is always reducing) but require higher maintenance costs the older they are.

➔ Car costs must be calculated with: purchase price (or renting, leasing, loan) plus the expenses / added together on a monthly basis.

→ Even a very little old car costs on average per month 250€/$; a middle class size car starts with 500€/$ per month (capital amortization included).

→ If people buy their chosen car with cash, then they should plan that a few or many years later they will need cash again for another car.

→ If people have a wage that is €250-300 (Dollars) or €500 (Dollars) above the minimum as calculated above, the majority run first to get a car and with that they start suffocating their quality of life and life potentials.

b) Other wants with a high spectrum; here are some examples:

- Going on holidays
- Spending a weekend somewhere
- Going to special events (e.g. concert) or places (e.g. zoo)
- A hobby
- A sport activity
- Toys for the children
- Periodically a present for the partner
- Books of special interest
- Spa
- A course program for well-being
- Courses for personal development
- Courses for further education of professional interest
- Computer accessories
- CDs and DVDs or any kind of games
- Smartphone with internet connection
- A dog, a cat or birds, or an aquarium with fishes
- And many more other options

Here the 'opportunity costs' calculation becomes important. Indeed one can or should ask: Which 'want' gives me 'most of it'? Or better: which 'want' matches mostly with my genuine interests in life? What has higher or highest importance or (subjective) urgency? Our understanding of the 'opportunity costs' is not related to the general consumer goods, but it is much more a question of choosing the right life satisfaction and fulfillment within the frame of the needs, wants and affordability.

→ Critically we must consider: an opportunity cost calculation can result today into a preferable result; but who knows, whether sooner or later this opportunity can become a 'worst case'.

Criteria of importance (genuine interest) to answer such questions are:

Health (Spa)	Career
Sport activities	Having a pet
High care for relationship and love	Creativity
Exploring the world	Plants, garden
Enjoying nature and species	Cultural events
Interesting life (with partner, children)	Social or political activities
Education (learning)	Developing a talent (e.g. music, arts and crafts)
Knowledge (books)	And more

For most people such interests become important only after purchasing a car. But by then, a good majority does not have enough money left for these interests or only very little money remains for a small part of such interests. Consequently the question arises about the capacity of 'rational decision making':

If one rejects having a car and takes the public transport, then one has 250, 300, 400, 500 €/$ or more, extra for disposal on genuine interests, and this every month (!). Only people with €400-500 (Dollars) at their disposal after budgeting for the basic basket of goods can buy a car with a monthly cost of €250-300 (Dollars) per month and still have some (little) remaining cash for other 'interests' in life.

Examples:

- For €150 one gets every month alternatively to a car: Choose yourself!
- For €200 one gets every month alternatively to a car: Choose yourself!
- For €300 one gets every month alternatively to a car: Choose yourself!
- For €400 one gets every month alternatively to a car: Choose yourself!
- For €500 one gets every month alternatively to a car: Choose yourself!

Based on these explorations we construct some statements:

- All the people in the United States and in the European Union are permanently bombarded with countless perfidious (luring, seducing, manipulating, brainwashing) marketing that they never get the idea how easy a wonderful life with genuine happiness and fulfillment could be possible without having a car or without spending money on stupid things, even with a very moderate marginal higher wage, means monthly budget for consumption!
- The heating up of the consumer market with marketing hinders people to

even think on alternative spending options for an entirely satisfied life.

- If people would learn how to use their very limited financial resources efficiently in the sense of inner satisfaction (human values, human potentials, talents, education) and living genuinely their life, the world, nature, species, the entire planet would be much better off.

- Let's say 50% of the people with a low wage of €250-500 (Dollars) above the poverty line buy a car. Then the car industry gets nearly the same amount of money per month as the producers get for the basic goods of people with minimum low wages. As most people buy a car with a loan or leasing the banks earn immense amounts of money from the interest; and above that it's also very profitable for insurance companies and the government (taxes).

- Collateral effects of cars: immense environmental contamination with all its damages and reduction of life quality (e.g. noise), with dire suffering due to accidents and illnesses caused by contamination; and the genuine humane interests for genuine humane satisfaction and personal fulfillment are gone down the drain with the costs of a car. This is the enslaved market that has already dehumanized a majority of humans to consumer robots and car owners. Outrageous!

→ What is however positive and needs mentioning is principally: the Western free markets offer everything for personal interests, for self-realization (developing creativity, spirituality, talents, and potentials), for inner satisfaction and fulfillment, and for a good life with genuine human values in general, affordable for a huge majority of consumers if they would only consider it in their consumer decisions and care to build a modest life with the aim of fulfillment.

Now we want to have a look at the different consumer groups, based on the financial status. The differentiation here has exemplary character. It can be 20% higher or lower, bigger or smaller. The examples given are more about the meaning of living a life and less about real figures.

We have let's say 100-150 million people in the Western world living under or near the poverty line. Food is the most essential part of their basket of goods for their everyday life. This part of the basket corresponds to an estimated €150-200 (Dollars) per month for a single person; beer and wine (in the tetra pack for 99 cents per liter becomes indispensable and this group before food – to bear the misery). They are all forced to purchase the cheapest possible food and they run for the free food at the food banks. Logically, they get the lowest quality and the food with the highest amount of (toxic) chemicals. Therefore they are exposed to the highest health risks. This in turn produces health care costs and reduced capacities of brain, life management, and work.

→ The group of the poorest consumers encompasses an estimated 50-80 million humans in Europe alone.

Next, we have the group of consumers that may have an estimated €201-300 (Dollars) per month for this part of the basket (food) for a single person. It is also obvious that this group of consumers get very low quality and also the food with the highest amount of (toxic) chemicals. Cheap beer or wine (tetra pack or bottle) for €1.50 (Dollars) also becomes indispensable – to bear the misery. Therefore they are also exposed to the highest health risks. This in turn produces health care costs and reduced capacities of brain, life management, and work. This group of consumers encompasses in the United States and in the European Union an estimated 300 million humans or more.

Most important to these people is to have a full stomach every day at least twice a day; no matter what it is. Here satisfaction means: hunger is gone; the stomach is full. If people give highest importance to this aim, and they do because they are hungry, then they don't have real wants with significant costs; these wants are light years away anyway.

The group of people that have an estimated €301-650 (Dollars) per month for this part of the basket (food) for a single person is better off. This budget for food is already sufficient for healthy nutrition – if these people choose quality before quantity and respect genuine needs before the wants. They can be satisfied, find wellbeing, be happy and lead a fulfilled life. This group of consumers encompasses in the United States and in the European Union an estimated 200-300? million humans. But on this level of economic life standard we can already observe a fight between needs and wants. The tendency here is common sense: holding down the quality of food products (this section of costs) to get more on the side of the (not necessary) wants.

With the next higher level of economic living standard, with an estimated €651-1,500 (Dollars) per month for this part of the basket (food) for a single person, we enter into a comfortable quality of life. These people can choose good quality food and if they are aware of the chemicals in food and also give attention to this criticality. Life becomes more comfortable, the bottle of wine can cost 5-8 €/$; and we can observe a bigger fight between different wants. This group is already too small.

The people with an estimated €1,501-3,000 (Dollars) per month for this part of the basket (food) for a single person, is very comfortably satisfied in quantity and quality. The bottle of wine can sometimes cost 12-20 €/$ and every now and then a bottle of champagne is not a big deal. The world of products for their wants is widely open. This group is already very small.

The group with an estimated €3,001-5,000 (Dollars) per month for this part of the basket (food) for a single person can satisfy a lot of wants. An excellent wine and champagne with caviar can be part of any event in their life style. But we should not exaggerate about their financial potential. It's still quite limited and the luxury of their home is still far away from the top class. This group is already exclusive.

The group with an estimated €5,001-10,000 (Dollars) per month for this part of the basket (food) for a single person can get a 'paradisiac' life, but still without opulent extravagance. And a villa of 3-5 million €/$ is only achievable with a very high mortgage, but at least, the world of products for their wants is very abundant.

The group of people that earn between €250,000 – 500,000 (Dollars) per year can spend money every month in superabundance. But it takes time from there to become a millionaire and later to buy a villa of 5-10 million €/$.

People that earn more than a million €/$ per year - the 11 million millionaires and the 1,200 billionaires globally on the top - are living in another paradise; they form an extra league we don't need to explore here.

Wages and income shift: We have herewith another strange economic 'theory': "An increase in income leads to a parallel shift in the budget constraint."

This is what it is about: If John's income increases, he can buy more goods or wants and gets more flexibility in his bundle of goods (to choose). But fact is: very little extra wage is a lot for the very poor, but doesn't rigorously improve their life, neither does it catapult the middle class to the heaven of the upper class. This is an empty and banal economic theory. Embarrassing! At least: Creating and spreading such illusory theories gets one a wage of an economic professor or expert of €200,000-350,000 (Dollars). Unfortunately, in real life there is no sign in the clouds or in the tea leaves that forecasts an increase of all wages by 50% in the United States and in Europe (and there has not been one historically either).

Economic realities, firms and corporations, are never ready to freely significantly increase the wages of the workers (share the pie). So, why does economics promote this nonsensical and banal theory as evidence and fact?

→ Again we identify the compulsive economist: In case, the consumer gets a few cents (or Euros) more wage per month, how can I get these cents for my 'profit maximizing'?

Income Effect

What happens when a worker gets fewer wages? What happens when a worker gets higher wages? Not much if the change of a wage (margin) is small, let's say €10-30 (Dollars) per month. Nevertheless, if we count a higher wage margin of €10-30 per month and multiply it by 10 million wages (workers), then the strife can begin: Who gets how much from this splendid cake of €100 million or 300 million (Dollars) per month, and €1.2 billion or 3.6 billion per year? That's a fat chunk. The other way round: if the wages decrease by €10-30 (Dollars): Who will be the loser in the free market?

An income effect of €10-30 (Dollars) has an immense importance to the big corporations when we multiply the increase (or decrease) by 10-50 millions (citizens of a nation) per month or per a year: "The change in consumption that results when a price change moves the consumer to higher or lower (…)" affects especially the big corporations (food, beverages and clothes or shoes sector). Such a cake of 1-5 billion or much more €/$ per year is the battle field of some corporations in order to maximize profit. An unanswered question is how such changes affect the very small businesses and the medium size businesses.

Conclusion:

The economic theories about scarcity, infinite greed (for needs and wants), and maximizing profit disrespect the normality of the ladder of human's budgets and destroys the potential of the natural development of economic growth of individuals (e.g. through professional career).

Those individuals that have a mind and personality character with small potential and low integrity but wish to become a king have a malfunctioning mind and this is a case for the psychopathology or for re-education programs – but not a reason for 'needs and wants to be satisfied'.

If economics would conclude from their theories that all needs and wants of people must be satisfied and scarcity must be eliminated with perfect allocation, and profit must be maximized, then they can just say: "Get as much money as possible, as fast as possible, from whomever and however, at any cost, whatever the collateral damages and using any strategies and tools to let people believe that they can achieve and get everything in life, in the process making people blind, greedy, and mad consumers and enslaving them with mortgages and consumer loans!"

2.8.2. Budgets (Resources) for Doing Business

The business budget is the amount of value a business has at its disposal to do business. Starting a business requires a minimum budget. Keeping a business going also needs a certain budget, an amount of money at the disposal for all needs and some wants of the business.

A business budget has sectors:

Money (cash) at disposal	Other income (e.g. interest)
Turnover (income, revenue)	Values (infrastructure)
Indirect financial benefit (e.g. own land)	Properties
Profit	The costs

Nothing in the business world is permanently stable; these factors can increase or decrease:

The income	The profit
The costs	The value of a property
The turnover	The disposable cash
The indirect benefit	The value of infrastructure
Other income	The value of resources

Budget flexibilities:

- Costs can't be unlimitedly reduced without consequences for the business.
- Reduction of costs (due to an input scarcity) can lead to a reduction of the business operations.
- Benefit can't be unlimitedly reduced without loosing indispensable money.
- Profit can be small or at zero, but never a 'negative-profit'.
- Example: Vodafone sells the iPhone at €399 even though it costs €599 and then they tie you to a monthly contract which delivers them a much higher profit. Effectively, the sale of the iPhone at €399 is a loss; and not a 'negative profit'. Also computer printers operate on a similar model in their calculations: The printer is sold at €99 even though it should cost €299 to produce, but then the consumer is forced to purchase ink that has huge profit margins. Conclusion: the word 'negative profit' is nonsense due to its common meaning. We wouldn't say for example 'costs are negative income'.
- Loss of income can force to use saved profit (if there is any; and there should be).

Budgets must consider changes:

- Many businesses must periodically adapt to changes (demands) in society.
- People change in their needs and wants and therefore in their consumer habits.
- A single person changes their needs and wants once they are living in a relationship.
- A couple changes their needs and wants when they have a baby (or divorce).
- People change their needs and wants when they experience changes in work.
- The economic situation can change for the better or worse and it affects businesses.
- Goods that are related to an age group are at risk when the customer age group changes.
- New goods from competitors can influence other businesses and require changes.
- Goods related to wants are in general at a higher risk than the goods related to needs.
- Emotional ties to a good that is considered as a 'want' can be stronger than a need.
- A good that can be a substitute for another good can have high potential.
- A good that is complementary to other goods has potential if the other good is demanded.
- The bigger a population is, close to the business, the higher the probability of a relative stability.
- A good that compensates an inner emotional deficit has potential (if people have money).
- Loyalty of customers can be of high importance for the equilibrium of a business.
- The better a brand and reputation, the higher the customer potential due to the awareness/reminder effect.
- A good that responds to laziness has a higher potential than a good that requires strenuousness.
- A good that delivers genuine convenience has greater potential than just frivolity.

Budget and type of goods:

- There are businesses that need to sell many goods every day (high volume of small products).
- There are businesses that need to sell at least one good every week (e.g.

small luxurious goods).

- There are businesses that need to sell at least 1-2 goods every month (e.g. car sale).
- There are businesses that need to sell at least 1-2 goods once per year (e.g. real estate).

Budget and good segment:

The course of a budget during a year is more stable if the business considers indirect components and is composed of the product segment related to them.

- Products for needs with a substitution function
- Products for wants with an emotional component
- Products with high convenience attributes
- Products for compensations of inner deficits (or ego deficits)
- Products for complementation (with other products)
- Products for varied consumer groups (age, type of household)
- Products for varied tastes and ages or personality profiles
- Products with at least two price levels (lower, higher)
- Products that depend on the weather or season (to be bought)
- Products that promote wellbeing, positive emotion, and loyalty
- Products for a consumer group that is big enough in the area
- Products that mark a brand through their quality or appearance
- Products that people buy without planning (impulsive purchase)
- Products that need to be delivered
- Products for frequent and indispensable multiple use
- Products that are perishable (fresh fish, meat etc.)

With this selection one can calculate prices of different products or services that can balance the budget for doing business.

2.9. Environmental Cost Factors

Environmental Factors

Environmental factors have an influence on the behavior of consumers and producers. Costs and collateral damages burden the budgets of consumers, producers, and society. The management of the environmental factors can reduce costs for both consumers and producers.

The entire 'free market' has become crazy and mad on the producer side as well as on the consumer side. Billions of Euros are lost in Europe and billions of Dollars are lost in the United States due to lack of care, responsibility, use of intelligence, self-management, irrational activities and decisions, stupid shopping and production, stubbornness and cantankerousness, lack of patience and human values, blind greed and envy, ego-problems and identity-mess, hate and hostility, unwillingness to learn, and a public education with an understanding of 'human beings' from the 19th century, and partly even from the Middle Ages.

Nearly everything in the life of humans is hyped up, under speed pressure, driven by inner complexes, and wrong or inefficient mental coding. The entire Western world is contaminated with arrogance, ignorance, laziness, narcissism, neurosis, behavior disorder, psychopathy, psychosis, psycho-somatic reactions, and all kind of addictions. The 'inner hell' of most people is worse than the hell (in the other world) that is described in paintings from the Middle Ages.

The most stupid idea is that people believe that what they have in their conscious mind (the inner 'screen') is the reality (about them and the world). Everywhere a majority of humans are already dehumanized, some even genetically degenerated. It seems that most of them have lost their mind and soul; certainly they all run away from themselves.

The costs are astronomic both for individuals and society as a whole.

Who is to blame for this humane disaster?

2.9.1. Environmental Factors of Costs for Consumers

Environmental factors of costs to consumers are:

1. Costs of public transport for shopping
2. Costs for travel with the private car for shopping
3. Costs for parking in the town (for shopping)
4. Costs for packaging (of goods to take home)
5. Costs for shopping and using plastic bags
6. Costs due to contamination from cars (health)
7. Costs due to contamination from exaggerated use of detergents
8. Costs due to contamination from exaggerated use of pharmaceuticals
9. Costs for producing exaggerated waste (household)
10. Costs for using devices with batteries (continuous)
11. Costs for buying devices of very low quality (short product life)

12. Costs for buying lowest quality clothes and shoes (short product life)
13. Costs for buying industrial food of very low quality (health)
14. Costs for frozen products (electricity for the production-sale chain)
15. Costs for exaggerated consumption of meat (industrial animal breeding)
16. Costs for exaggerated consumption of industrial fish (sea exploitation)
17. Costs for continuous exaggerated alcohol consumption (health)
18. Costs for continuous exaggerated tobacco consumption (health)
19. Costs for travel due to unplanned shopping
20. Costs for thoughtless purchase behavior
21. Costs for dentists due to acidic beverage, sweets, sugar
22. Costs due to car or sport accidents
23. Costs due to use of the car for stupid fun (driving around for fun)
24. Costs for exaggerated watching television, DVDs
25. Costs for paid TV-channels to watch sick rubbish out of boredom
26. Costs for newspaper and magazines (those with 80% brainwash and blabber)
27. Costs for exaggerated use of mobile phone (and messaging)
28. Costs for use of Internet due to boredom and stupid fun (Facebook, etc.)
29. Costs for stupid hanging around in bars, cafés, or at friend's homes
30. Costs of purchasing (having) a car although there is no urgent need for it
31. Costs for studying, but not learning more than 30% of the given opportunities
32. Costs for visiting football matches that serve for criminal betting, absurd wages, marketing
33. Costs for watching sport (TV) that serves for absurd wages, betting business, marketing
34. Costs for thoughtless and unnecessary use of electricity
35. Costs for thoughtless and exaggerated use of oil, gas (heating)
36. Costs for thoughtless and exaggerated use of Air Conditioning
37. Costs for thoughtless and unnecessary use of water
38. Costs for exaggerated use of perfumes and beauty products
39. Costs for the stupid lottery, games and (online) betting
40. Costs for having the wrong friends or for superficial love (life lies)
41. Costs for a lifestyle that ignores balance, biorhythm, authenticity
42. Costs for consumer loans (high interest and often high risk)
43. Costs for mortgages with high interest and insecure future increase
44. Costs for unnecessary online shopping (e.g. Ebay, Amazon, catalog firms)
45. Costs for using credit cards (both sides: buyer and seller, each 1.5-3%)
46. Costs for stupid mass tourism that in the end destroys the local environment
47. Costs that arise because the shopping centers direct money out of the location
48. Costs that are provoked in the holiday home market due to naivety of

buyers

49. Costs for memberships of exclusive spiritual clubs that teach 90% rubbish

50. Costs for the Church that is 80-90% nothing more than a diabolic scam

Conclusion:

→ The list above shows us the sickness of the capitalistic lifestyle and life standard.

→ The big global problems of humanity and the planet are simply caused by stupid consumers.

→ Ego-centrism, narcissism, and neurosis are the main source of stupid consumer behavior.

→ Psychopathy and psychosis are the drive of capitalist economics in theory and practice.

→ Public education, including universities, is also a main cause of this consumer stupidity.

→ As Christian religion makes people naïve, blinded and psychotic, this is also a core cause.

→ Stupid consumer behavior promotes amoral and criminal behavior of producers.

→ Stupid consumer behavior promotes amoral and criminal behavior of sellers.

→ Consumer behavior patterns can only be changed with the right public education.

→ Changing consumer behavior requires a new collective lifestyle with genuine values.

→ Changing consumer behavior requires forming a healthy mind and an integer character.

→ Mental health requires parents that are able to love and to live life with knowledge and skills.

→ Marketing today is much stronger than the best parental upbringing and family life.

→ People could easily save 10-35% of their budget wasted on stupid consumer behavior.

→ Having 10-35% of a budget for 'humane values' is enough to create a happy fulfilled life.

→ Mainly we could also conclude that even many of those with low wages get far too much money.

2.9.2. Environmental Factors of Costs for Producers

Environmental factors of costs to producers are:

a) Labor:

Accidents	Preoccupations
Illnesses	Repetition of insufficient work results
Defective products	Missed opportunities
Loss of sales	Blocked ideas for improvements
Loss of customers	Lack of willingness for cooperation
Loss of time due to corrections	Dissatisfaction
Loss of time due to inefficient communication	Anger
Misunderstandings	Frustration
Misinterpretations	Emotional argumentations
Waste of time	Disinterest
Conflicts	Lack of inner commitment
Problems	Low performance quality

b) Production and sale:

The production and sale of products include collateral costs for society:

- Environmental damages; destroying entire natural areas
- Exaggerated exploitation of natural resources
- Using far too much fertilizers and pesticides
- Transport costs with collateral effects
- Abuse of water, agricultural land; deforestation
- Contamination of water resources and products
- Contamination and pollution (environment, everywhere)
- Nuclear waste (storage, maintenance)
- Exaggerated use of electricity
- Immense costs for all-area marketing
- High rent of premises for the sale of products
- Destruction of the small production entities
- Destruction of the middle class
- Abuse of labor, increasing poverty and leading to poverty
- Destruction of local culture and businesses
- Luring, seducing or blackmailing local governments

- Corruption in general in all directions
- Miserable food quality generating health problems
- Promoting psychopathic personalities (as ideals)
- As a model of ignorance towards human factors
- Destroying local culture and ways of living
- Causing wide-ranging health problems
- Destruction of the mind and soul of people
- Taking away land and resources from people and countries

Conclusions:

→ These cost-factors seen as a network reflect the process of deicide.

→ Most of these factors express hate of life and hate of love.

→ These environmental costs reflect the costs of a war.

→ No human can be happy and experience joy of life with such destructivity.

→ There is a lot of flexibility for producers to reduce environmental costs.

→ The race for maximizing profit (short-term) produces more damages (long-term) than profit.

→ Judicious use of natural resources (food, water, energy etc.) would increase sustainability of life.

→ Much more care for the workers would increase cost-effectiveness.

→ Much more care for the environment would increase cost-effectiveness.

→ Treating workers and consumers as humans would increase production and efficiency.

→ Eliminating or highly reducing these factors would create a paradisiac society.

→ Many of these cost factors will fall back on producers and consumers.

→ 25 years of such ignorance has already destroyed much of the eco-systems.

→ In the core these factors express an indescribable collective madness.

→ The architects and top-rulers of such a 'market' must be stopped and imprisoned.

2.10. Labor Market

The terms: 'Labor', Employee', and 'Worker'

What does 'labor' mean? Let's explore it from several sources focusing only on 'labor' and not on related wage or age:

Example 1:
- Productive activity, especially for the sake of economic gain.
- The body of persons engaged in such activity. [50]

Example 2:
- Physical or mental exertion, especially when difficult or exhausting; work. [51]

Example 3:
- Repetitive unskilled manual work, usually done in scorching hot and humid unsafe conditions. [52]

Example 4:
- Labor Logic – "Think with your muscles, not with your brain..." [53]

Example 5:
- A social class comprising those who do manual labor or work. [54]

Now, let's compare with the term 'employee':

Example 1:
- A slave with a paycheck. [55]

Example 2:
- A person who is hired to work for another or for a business, firm, etc. [56]

Example 3:
- One employed by another ... and in a position below the executive level. [57]

Example 4:
- Someone who is paid to work for someone else. [58]

There is also the word 'worker' to put in the context:

Example 1:

---

[50] http://dictionary.reference.com/browse/labor
[51] http://www.thefreedictionary.com/labor
[52] http://www.urbandictionary.com/define.php?term=labor
[53] http://www.urbandictionary.com/define.php?term=labor
[54] http://www.elook.org/dictionary/labor.html
[55] http://www.urbandictionary.com/define.php?term=employee
[56] http://www.thefreedictionary.com/employee
[57] http://www.merriam-webster.com/dictionary/employee
[58] http://dictionary.cambridge.org/dictionary/british/employee

- A person or thing that works.
- A laborer or employee: steel workers.
- A person engaged in a particular field, activity, or cause. [59]

Example 2:
- One that works especially at manual or industrial labor or with a particular material ('factory worker') – often used in combination [60]

Example 3:
- The one who works at a particular occupation or activity: an office worker.
- The one who does manual or industrial labor. [61]

Example 4:
- Someone who arrives late, leaves early and does as little as possible in between. [62]

Conclusion:

→ The terms 'labor', employee', and 'worker' have one meaning in common: people work for somebody else, for a person or an institution, or a firm, or a corporation. In general it is mentioned that the work is paid (these people get a wage).

→ The terms have different connotations, sometimes mentioned in definition: low class, manual work, industrial work, any kind of work, repetitive work, working with muscles (not with brain), productive activity, or mental work.

→ We realized by elaborating some classical study books about economics that the connotations of these words are often not clear, not in theories and not in graphs. We consider this as an irritating and confusing matter when it comes to the reality behind theories and graphs.

→ Using these three terms we must always be aware about the different real picture of work and workers behind the terms and theories or graphs. There is an economic salad of herbs and cabbage. The implications in a bigger theoretical or practical context may differ enormously.

Crucial questions in economics are left open:

---

[59] http://dictionary.reference.com/browse/worker
[60] http://www.merriam-webster.com/dictionary/worker
[61] http://www.thefreedictionary.com/worker
[62] http://www.urbandictionary.com/define.php?term=worker

- Is a doctor a worker?
- Is a self-employed person a worker?
- Is a sales person a worker?
- Is the owner of a firm that is actively working in his firm a worker?
- Is a teacher a worker?
- Is a civil servant a worker?
- Is an author or artist a worker?
- Is a lawyer a worker?
- Is a CEO a worker?
- Is a group leader a worker?

➔ They all work and get a wage!

2.10.1. Renting Work, Wages, Unemployment

General considerations:
Mankiw (et al.) say about work and leisure: [63]

- People have at their disposal 100 hours per week
- 40 hours of work means 60 hours of leisure
- More working hours means more wage and less time for leisure

➔ Conclusions: more hours of work = more money for spending

Mankiw continues: "Workers may now use (…) higher income to enjoy more leisure and not work additional hours." There is a trade-off between work and leisure for the worker: "What do you give up to get an hour of leisure? You give up an hour of work, which in turns means an hour of wages." [64]

Comment: Most workers can't choose how many hours they work. And 60 hours of leisure does not anyway reflect the worker's total free time (e.g. travel to work and cleaning the home is not leisure).

Living a life with a wage:

"Living wage laws, which are a type of minimum wage law that requires, specified employers to pay a living wage. Living wage is most often defined as that wage that would allow one worker, working 40 hours a week, to support

---

[63] Mankiw (et al.), p. 460-461
[64] Mankiw (et al.), p. 389

a family of four at the poverty level." [65]

It is common sense, but a rule of life of highest importance for everybody: People, once finished public education, have to work to live their life. The given exceptions we don't need to discuss here. Working people need a certain minimum wage to live their life.

On the other hand we must respect: "Wages reflect the market prices of the goods they produce." [66] Indeed, it does not make sense to give wages on a level that can't be financed by the business's result (income).

It is absolutely unacceptable and inexcusable with no argument that millions and billions of people can't live their life on a basic level with a basic wage. In addition, a significant amount of people with a wage that does not allow for a basic life are collectively self-destructive and cause extremely high costs for society as a whole.

The very poor cause damages (e.g. health, environment, and social unrest) and with that additional costs that everybody and all businesses, including the big corporations, have to pay for all this with taxes. To create millions and billions of very poor existences is totally inefficient, very stupid, extremely self-destructive, extremely short-sited, unintelligent and absolutely counterproductive for the entire humanity today and in the future. The young generation today will pay the legacy for this disaster. Students of economics and business must become fully aware of this, accept the consequences and take the appropriate measures.

A worker (human) has a value for the production: "The wage is, after all, simply the rental price of labor." [67] A small apartment has a small rent and a luxurious apartment has a high price; and if the demand increases, the rents of both also increase. But in general, this is not the case in the labor market.

There are two main questions:

1) What is the amount of working hours per week that is acceptable for a minimum wage?

In some countries the minimum hours of work is 36 hours per week (5 days); in other countries 38, 40, 42 hours. The minimum hours depend also on the

---

[65] Colander, p. 443
[66] Mankiw (et al.), p. 400
[67] Mankiw (et al.), p. 396

kind of work. In general, professionals in care-homes and hospitals work much more than people in offices. Many self-employed people work much more than those in the state administration. In the middle of the last century people worked 48-60 hours per week; and 6 days per week.

The statement 'work more hours to get a higher wage' does not hold the answer. We also have to consider the amount of holidays people take today: 4-5 weeks summer holidays and an additional amount of individual days off due to religious or cultural breaks. The majority of people in Western countries are extremely fastidious (spoiled) by non-working days and minimum working hours per week.

It is fully appropriate that people work 8 hours per day and another 4 hours on Saturday. With such a calculation we get 44 hours per week to get a reasonable minimum wage for those who have practically no or only little professional capacities (knowledge, skills, and education). This is the only path to solve the problem of poor people: more hours of work per week for an acceptable minimum wage to live a basic life. People are egregiously pampered with low working hours.

Politicians and economists could answer: yes, but there is not enough hours of work available in the country that could be distributed to all workers. And the answer here is: because politicians are cowards and absolutely not interested in finding solutions for more work places in the society. There are solutions! We will come back to this topic below.

2) What is the minimum wage for a basic life?

"Supply and demand forces strongly influence wages, but they do not fully determine wages. Supply and demand pressures through organizations such as labor unions, professional associations, and agreements among employers."[68]

We add: There is a limited elasticity of wage as "The higher the wage, the lower the quantity of labor demanded."[69] Also the elasticity of demand for labor determines the elasticity of wage.

"Technology makes it possible to replace workers with machines, so it will decrease the demand for labor."[70] "Labor is necessary for building and maintaining the machines, so increased demand for machines increases the

---

[68] Colander, p. 439
[69] Colander, p. 435
[70] Colander, p. 437

demand for labor … Technology can sometimes decrease the demand for certain skills." [71]

"In the 21st century we're likely to see a continued increase in the use of robots to do many repetitive tasks that blue-collar workers formerly did. Thus, demand for manufacturing labor will likely continue to decline, but it will be accompanied by an increase in demand for service industry labor – designing and repairing robots and designing activities that will fill up people's free time." [72]

"Efficiency Wages are wages paid above the going market wage to keep workers happy and productive." [73]

Do efficiency wages really keep workers happy and productive? Certainly, people are always are glad if they get a better wage than what the market in general offers. Workers can feel motivated to be more productive. But after a certain time this emotional drive may decrease and the wage becomes simply a 'normal' wage.

There is no general answer about a minimum wage for a basic life. It depends on the country and the location of the working population. To find an answer we must first consider some circumstances around the level of living costs.

Location and living costs:

- Rents for apartments are very high in the center of towns and cities, in general much higher in towns and cities than in villages.
- Living on the outskirts of towns and cities has lower costs the further away the location is from the town and city; first of all and especially the rents and prices of homes.
- The rents and prices of homes are much higher in areas of high living quality, e.g. with a lake, with wonderful landscapes, a healthy and clean nature, etc.
- The better the infrastructure of a location, the higher the living costs. Infrastructure: public transport, schools, hospitals, clinics, dentists, supermarkets, and entertainment services.
- If most of the working places are in towns or cities or in the closer industrial areas, then the workers living in the outskirts need an efficient public transport or a car to go to work.

---

[71] Colander, p. 438
[72] Colander, p. 438
[73] Colander, p. 443

- The attractiveness of towns, cities and mega-cities drives more and more people to live in such places and to avoid living in villages and the outskirts of towns (with much less or no work offers).
- To be able to sell goods as cheap as possible and to maximize profit most corporations have outsourced the production processes to countries with extremely low wages (e.g. Asia).
- The salaries plus bonus of CEOs and members of boards of corporations are extremely high and do not reflect that without the work of their employees they would never get that much.
- The shareholder system with unknown identities pushes a corporation to maximize profit, partly for the shareholders which get money without having worked for it. They are parasites!
- The producer of goods is not at the location of the sale location (shopping center). Immense money is transferred away, which means: local consumer's financial substance leaves the local community.
- Corporations have become gigantic monsters that exploit the masses by destruction of countless small businesses and many professions reducing/eliminating the options they had/have to exit.

There are also working related costs to consider:

"When you consider the transportation cost of getting to and from work, the expense of getting new clothes to wear to work, the cost of child care, and other job-associated expenses, the net gain in income is often minimal." [74]
The worker's manifoldness:

"People aren't machines. They're human beings with feelings and emotions. If they feel good about a job, if they feel they're part of a team, they will work hard." [75]

It is not a discrimination to say that there are people with different levels of 'quality'. There are people with a 'simple' mind and low potentials, but giving all they can. There are also people with enormous mental potentials. Between these two groups we have many levels of 'quality'. But all of them can live a satisfying and fulfilled life. It is the market that does not allow for an understanding of a modest life on a basic economic level as a positive frame for satisfaction, wellbeing and happiness.

There are also people who we must be characterize as follows: lazy, dull, stupid, thoughtless, braggers, blabbers, superficial, irresponsible, good for

---

[74] Colander, p. 434
[75] Colander, p. 442

nothing, unwilling to learn, unwilling to work, bad working attitudes, unreliable, cheater, liar, bad character, shirker, amoral, rejecting getting their hands dirty by working or to sweat, etc. These people can't expect to be welcome for a job and to get a comfortable wage. However, such an individual, male or female, will not have a successful life in any dimension, not even on a very basic level.

The main causes lie in their family, their parents that are not much better or even worse. Another cause lies in public and vocational education. Some solutions are discussed in 'Economics I'. Above that the media and marketing make them what they are. The free market can't solve this problem; it's a matter of education and governmental social intervention. The big Western corporations, producing in Asia for some cents per labor hour, including extreme contamination, are another criminal case that contributes to the decay of Western societies and job market.

The only solution for such individuals as described above – there are millions – is a semi-closed community where they have to be educated (as a person), to learn for life, to learn about discipline, to come down to earth with their stupid narcissism and infantile arrogance, and to get a vocational education. There are too many unemployed people that simply want to be paid by the government to stay in bed, hang around, and to live off the fat of the land. These badly educated people and other similar species with extravagant ideas to be serviced from the state, want at the age of 20 already a wage of 1,000 Euros (dollars) without having any outstanding potentials, or others that want to retire at the age of 40 or 45 (with a pension payment), need something like a paramilitary working camp (long finger nails not allowed!) to learn that life requires hard work in order to get money to live a decent life.

There is no other solution than to learn to take responsibility for one's life – or alternatively in the end accepting their dire misery when they get older. This is the price to pay for a majority that at school didn't respect the importance of hard learning with discipline.

We cannot always make the parents or the public school fully responsible for such failures. It is not true that young girls or boys of 12, or 14, or 16 are unable to be self-responsible for their stubbornness, laziness, loudmouth, and stupidity. They all must be put in educational caserns with dormitories up to 30-50 beds; and not in apartments paid for by the government.

But indeed, it is also a result of the modern society with its real capitalistic economics and with the narcissistic and incompetent (and super arrogant) politicians, already having distorted, destroyed, and degenerated irreversibly the mind of 65-80% of today's young generation (born after 1990). 'Degeneration' with brain damages means that they can't even realize that they are degenerated.

Pesticides (and other toxic chemicals) destroy brain structures already in the prenatal phase with irreversible consequences in capacities of thinking, reduced intelligence, attentiveness, emotions, language, behavior, and impulse control. [76] The economics with its marketing businesses highly appreciates such reduced self-control.

Above that, we should never forget that the wealth and modern life standard of the Western world is paid for by Asian, African and other nation's workers, with their poverty and extreme misery and their contaminated land and resources as collateral effects; and with all the land and goods and stolen wealth by the Europeans during the last 500 years of colonization with slavery, and modern imperialism with monstrous corporation octopuses, that having paved the way are being protected by the US Army together with NATO.

This is the context to understand the 10,000 times repeated word 'maximizing profit' in the classical study books about economics; which in other words means: "Steal, cheat and transfer as much profit as you can with as little costs as possible from (weaker) developing countries, from the working population in your own country, and from the consumers! It's worth it even at a marginal benefit."

Nowadays many people have two jobs: a main job and in the evening (or on Saturdays) part-time work for another few hours; or a couple living together, married or not, both have a job. Many families in the United States and the European Union can only survive if both parents work. A basic wage of a man, married with children, is in millions of cases not enough economically to sustain a family life.

The role of a mother has changed a lot since 1950 where the man worked to supply the entire family and the woman took care of the home and the children. Such a pattern of life is today a luxury and requires a comfortable wage for the man. If this is 'good' or not, is another question we can't answer here. Fact is: if somebody wants such a life, then the professional education must be well prepared from the man to get a wage that makes such a family life pattern possible.

In the past, those who were lucky enough to study already had from the start

---

[76] http://www.n-tv.de/wissen/Pestizid-veraendert-Hirnstruktur-article6154431.html

of their professional life a significant wage and within some years they already formed part of the upper middle class. Today graduated students can be very happy if they get a job with a wage of €1,500-1,800 (Dollars). By the age of 35-40 they can achieve a wage of €3,000-4,500 (Dollars). Not many academics reach a level of €6,000-8,000 (Dollars) by the age of 45-50.

Permanent professional further education and hard work with excellent attitudes is a must to go up the career ladder. The foundation starts with university life: party life, drugs, alcohol, and spending more time for fun than for studying is not recommended. Most young students must first learn that learning is hard work and learning the right stuff is crucial for a future professional development, even simply to get a job that pays well.

Most students have completely lost the ability to value their privilege to study for a better life (wage) in the future, and this life long. State departments of education have losses on a level of billions of €/$ per year with 20-35% of students that exit or fail due to a lack of the right learning attitudes. [77] Too many students graduate with a pattern of 'good for nothing'.

A study fee of €3,000-6,000 per year (depending on the faculty) is an indispensable 'must' in order that students appreciate with the right learning attitudes this educational opportunity for a guaranteed life within the middle or upper class.

It remains to be asked: What is 'bad' about somebody that has to first or along the way or during the long summer period (called: 'holidays') earn money by working in order to pay (partly) the fees and/or their 'cool' student life? Faculties, especially of social sciences, could easily implement part time study programs (5-6 years instead of 3 years for a bachelor) where students take per semester a personally selected amount of subjects.
Conclusions:

→ People with low education, low professional knowledge and skills ('labor quality') must accept and learn to live their life for all-round wellbeing on their income level.
→ There are locations with low, medium, high, and very high living costs; nobody can change this and it is not 'bad' at all. Workers must accept this and make balanced decisions.
→ People with low 'labor quality' cannot expect to live in places with top infrastructure, high quality and special comfort and attractiveness.

---

[77] http://www.4everspain.com/blog/government-wastes-e2960-mlllion-on-drop-out-students-in-spain/

→ People with lowest 'labor quality' must learn and accept that they have to be flexible with their living location considering the demand for labor; even to accept an hour traveling to go to work.

→ Basic wages also depend on the way corporations and businesses operate with their income, salaries, production costs, and profit.

→ Fair wages for labor with low 'labor quality' comes before profit, top-salaries, and bonus. The business world must determine labor wages that allow an individual to live a life in locations that are within reach.

Unemployment

We discussed this issue in the 'Economics I' book and concentrate here on some essential points. The thesis here is: A human that is for years or even lifelong unemployed is a situation that is not sustainable for the individual human or for the society as a whole.

Statistics March/April 2012 [78]

- The euro area (EA17) seasonally adjusted unemployment rate was 10.9% in March 2012.
- The EU27 unemployment rate was 10.2% in March 2012.
- Highest unemployment rate was in Spain (24.1%) and Greece (21.7%) in January 2012.
- In March 2012, 5.5 million young persons (under 25) were unemployed in the EU27.
- An estimated 25 million men and women in the EU27 were unemployed in March 2012.
- In April 2012, 17.4 million people were unemployed in the whole Euro Zone: 11%

→ Reminder: Having work in order to live a life is a fundamental genuine need of humans.

→ 25 million Europeans in despair, fear, sorrow, depression, inner stress, and weakened identity.

→ The statistics are of course manipulated; the complete picture of real unemployment is much higher.

→ Underemployment is not considered in these statistics nor is part-time or temporary employment or people who no longer qualify for unemployment benefit.

---

[78] http://epp.eurostat.ec.europa.eu/cache/ITY_PUBLIC/3-02052012-AP/EN/3-02052012-AP-EN.PDF

http://epp.eurostat.ec.europa.eu/statistics_explained/index.php/Unemployment_statistics

We must get a more differentiated picture about 'unemployment'

- The demand for all kind of jobs is higher than the supply of jobs in a specific region.
- The demand of all kind of jobs is area wide in the country higher than the supply of jobs.
- There is a high demand for jobs in special working sectors, but not enough supply in this sector.
- There is a job demand in a specific field, but the supply is only part-time or time-limited.
- There is supply for seasonal jobs (agriculture, tourism), but only for periods of 3-6 months.
- There is a temporary supply in specific job sectors (e.g. due to high demand in the production)
- There is always 2-3% unemployment in a society and always there are some jobs available.

"Entrepreneurship is labor that involves high degrees of organizational skills, concern, oversight responsibility, and creativity ... when a person is not self-employed, determining the demand for labor isn't as direct. It's a two-step process: Consumers demand products from firms; firms, in turn, demand labor and other factors of production. The demand for labor by firms is a derived demand.
In other words, it's derived from consumer's demand for the goods that the firm sells." [79]

Unemployment – Individual approach options for solutions:

- Find a suitable job in another area up to 100 km from your location if there is supply.
- Find a suitable job in another area of your province or country if there is supply.
- Learn and provide more flexibility for the supply: languages, IT skills, any vocational further education necessary.
- Find a part-time job and expand your options with additional vocational further education.
- Learn profoundly everything that is necessary to become self-employed in a field of your skills.
- Take a part-time or a seasonal job and use the rest of the time to learn about new fields.

---

[79] Colander, p. 436

- Reorganize your life and focus on this new vocational education, even with a reduced life standard.
- Drastically reduce your monthly spending in order to have enough resources for new learning.
- Accept a lower wage in order to rebuild or improve your professional knowledge and skills.
- Learn self-management, time-management, communication skills, and improve self-presentation.
- Carefully analyze your situation, find out what you like to do best and find alternative options.
- Accept worst jobs; during your free time prepare your professional perspective in 2-3 years.

2.10.2. Hiring Workers, Wages and Creating Jobs

Work and Identity

"Defining ourselves by our work means that work is more than just the way we get income. It's a part of our social and cultural makeup. If we lose our jobs, we lose part of our identity." [80]

We can also say: If a person doesn't have a job (work), or is significantly under-employed, he loses part of his identity. The consequences are manifold; it certainly depends on the duration of being without work: inner (emotional, energetic) stress, anxiety, social phobia, depression, addiction, and feeling of shame, feeling of inferiority, sleeplessness, aggression, reduction of perception and thinking, panic attacks, relationship problems, general disinterest, mental disturbances and malfunctioning of the mind's capacities.

A partial loss of self-identity leads to a loss of meaning of life. All these factors together block the psychical-spiritual development and turn people into slaves.

It is absolutely clear that economics is inseparably connected with human factors and it is not simply about determining standard of living as Colander imputes: "...social and political forces interact with economic forces to determine our economic situation." [81]

With that the question arises: Is a high rate of unemployment or a high rate of underemployment (or a low wage that doesn't allow one to live a reasonable

---

[80] Colander, p. 430
[81] Colander, p. 430

life) a failure of economics (as a practiced capitalistic concept) or of politics (of the political agents managing society)? Or is it intentional to weaken people's mind (e.g. critical thinking, creativity, living potentials) and commitments to human values? Or is it a strategic intention in order to prevent people from experiencing wellbeing, satisfaction with life, be self-confident, to live love, to strive for the truth, to be happy, and to find fulfillment?

There are many signs that allow the thesis:

→ High unemployment rate, underemployment, and low wages to manage life is a systemic failure of macroeconomics or of market structures, but not accidentally, but intentionally created.

Labor Demand

The term 'labor' we understand here as a 'worker' or 'employee'; a working person. A "labor is free to enter and exit the market and firms are equally free to employ and shed labor at will." [82] It is self-evident that a business does not employ a person if there is no work. Logically a business must also calculate if a worker's wage is justified within the production process; means: is financed with the product sales.
But this is not entirely true. 'Free' sounds like there is no associated cost, but in Spain for example to 'shed labor' means the employer has to pay for this 'shedding'! 1 month per year worked). Whether it's right or wrong is another matter, but it certainly isn't free and simply exercised at will.

In that sense we can say: a worker is a factor of production and with that a producer of money in the interest of the firm and in the interest of getting a wage. "The demand for a factor of production is a **derived demand**." [83] Labor demand is a derived (identified, determined) demand.

There are two aspects: Labor must generate through production and the sale at least the amount of money that covers the wage. But: "We assume that the firm is profit-maximizing ... it cares only about profit." [84] Therefore, for a firm it only makes sense to employ a person, if this labor produces above the wage a certain amount of profit.

In general the profit is a cake that is not distributed to the laborers. A profit

---

[82] Mankiw (et al.), p. 383
[83] Mankiw (et al.), p. 383
[84] Mankiw (et al.), p. 384

of a firm can be used for reserves to cover such risks as a period of decrease in sales, or for expansion, or improvement of equipment, etc. But profit can be (and it mostly is) shared out between the owners of the firm; labor excluded. What is right or wrong with this is a moral or policy matter for the firm or of society.

Labor Leasing

A firm is specialized in renting out labor to firms. Or a firm transfers its employees to a leasing firm and leases them back, usually at a lower wage. Contracts, costs, expenses and employment taxes of the leased employees are the leasing firm's liabilities. Labor leasing disencumbers firms from costs, liabilities, and long-term contracts and allows the firm to make higher profits.

Contingent Work

Contingent work is usually required for a temporary demand of labor: temporary contracted (hired) worker, especially for a task or a project, or for a limited period of increasing production due to a higher demand of products.

Calculations for labor demand: It is obviously reasonable to calculate the financial aspect of the work of an employed person and how much the wage should be. There are direct and indirect approaches:
a) The direct calculations:

A worker forms part of a production process and in that sense he contributes partly in this process and logically his part of contribution (for the production) must be a part in the price of the product.

"Factors of production are the inputs used to produce goods and services. Labor, land and capital are three most important factors of production." [85] We assume the author refers to corporations related to agriculture, animal breeding, raw resources, and construction. There are many firms that do not need land. In that sense the statement of the author is misleading. A generalization of the statement is not possible. The essential question here is: Which production needs land?

A "…profit-maximizing firm is concerned more with money than with (a product) … the firm considers how much profit each worker would bring in … the profit from an additional worker is the worker's contribution to revenue minus worker's wage." [86]

---

[85] Mankiw (et al.), p. 383

→ Is this now a confession of the dirty sin, of the absolute arrogance, and of the truth that corporations are in no way interested in contributing to society and culture?

→ The statement says clearly that corporations are 'more' interested in maximizing profit for their own sake.

→ The purpose of the workers' performance is only and exclusively in the interest of the major owners and investors of corporations. The worker is therefore as disposable and replaceable as any other piece of machinery.

The direct calculations have many components:

There is a **production function**: "The relationship between the quantity of inputs used to make a good and the quantity of output of that good." [87]

The production has costs and the amount of sold products must cover these costs added to with a certain amount of profit. The wage of a worker must be calculated in the price of the produced goods: "... a competitive, profit-maximizing firm hires workers up to the point where the value of the marginal product of labor equals the wage. (Therefore we can divide the production costs by the amount of produced products and we get the production costs for each sold product.)" [88] And where here is the profit accounted, before or after the wage?

Example 1: A firm produces 100 specific goods and calculates the costs of the production with €50,000 (Dollars), wages and profit also included. That means each product has a production cost of €500 (Dollars). The output price in a very complicated expression is: "The value of the marginal product is marginal product times the price of the firm's output."

This is a theoretical calculation. A firm may be forced to calculate the risk that he can sell only 70 products; and the remaining 30 products he must give away for 50% (or even less) of the production cost per unit.

A sale of 70 products creates revenue of €35,000 (Dollars). The loss would be €15,000 (Dollars). This would be the end of this business.

A madly (?) clever businessman includes this risk in the price calculation so that with the sale of 70 products, the production costs (wages and profit

---

[86] Mankiw (et al.), p. 384
[87] Mankiw (et al.), p. 384
[88] Mankiw (et al.), p. 386

included) of all 100 products are covered. A sale of 70 products for a price per product of €714.20 (Dollars) brings in the total of production costs, which are €50,000 (Dollars). The business man gets his financially calculated success.

If this firm can later sell the remaining 30 products for 50% of the sale price, he would get additional revenue of €10,713 (Dollars) which would be fully an additional profit.

Not bad at all! That's how it works sometimes a little here and sometimes a little there.

Example 2: A firm can decide to produce more of a specific good due to high demand. But for more production he needs more labor and he has other increased costs.

A businessman has three questions in this context:

a) What is the production capacity of one laborer?

This is the **Marginal product of labor:** "The increase in the amount of output from an additional unit of labor." [89]

b) What are the costs of the additional amount of products?

Value of a marginal product: "The marginal product of an input times the price of the output." [90]

c) What is the average cost per product, adding the new to the previous amount of product? And with that: What is the extra revenue from hiring an additional worker?

"The firm's **marginal revenue product**: is the extra revenue the firm gets from hiring an additional unit of a factor of production." [91] 'Factor of production' is the worker.

In most cases such calculations consider also the options given from technological progress because: "**Technological advance** raises the marginal product of labor which in turn increases the demand for labor." [92] But it also

---

[89] Mankiw (et al.), p. 386
[90] Mankiw (et al.), p. 386
[91] Mankiw (et al.), p. 386
[92] Mankiw (et al.), p. 387-388

works the other way round: better technology decreases the demand of labor and therefore also the costs. Or: The implementation of advanced technical tools must be cheaper than the labor costs for the same production result.

Supply of Labor

We pick up five statements from Colander (et al.) to extend the critical approach: [93]

1) "The labor supply choice facing an individual (that is, the decisions of whether, how, and how much to work) can be seen as a choice between nonmarket activities and legal market activities. Nonmarket activities include sleeping, dating, studying, playing, cooking, cleaning, gardening, and black market trading. Legal market activities include taking some type of paid job or working for oneself, directly supplying products or services to consumers."

2) "…incentive effect (how much a person will change his or her hours worked in response to a change in the wage rate). The incentive effect is determined by the value of supplying one's time to legal market activities relative to the value of supplying one's time to nonmarket activities."

3) "The higher the wage, the higher the quality of labor supplied."

4) "Economists focus on the incentive effect when considering an individual's choice of whether and how much to work."

5) "Applying rational choice theory to the supply of labor tells us that the higher the wage, the higher the quantity of labor supplied."

To statement 1: Most humans don't have much freedom to decide whether, how, and how much to work.
To statement 2: Most people can't choose the amount of hours they have to work (per day, week, or year).
To statement 3: $10m wage p.a. (average salary of an American CEO) doesn't reflect the quality of labor.
To statement 4: This may to be applicable to self-employed people, but not for most employed people.
To statement 5: The rational choice theory amputates the most relevant human factors and is a deceit.

Wages Equilibrium

---

[93] Colander, p. 431

Imagine, there is plenty of work supply; and alternatively there is very low supply. Another perspective: in Spain there are nearly 6 million unemployed people (included those who are not counted in the statistic), all looking for work, but there is only 200,000 work supplies.

Or we can take any area of India, Pakistan, Bangladesh, China or Africa: millions want to have work, but there is not even 20% work of that which is demanded. Therefore the offered wages are shamelessly low, not enough to make a modest healthy life. The working conditions are absolutely miserable: 7 days and every day from 12 up to 14 hours in premises that have space for 500 or 1,000 workers.

Above that we have a long list of externalities, especially contamination. Hundreds of millions have to work under inhumane conditions that are dictated or forced by the Western corporations.

Even in the United States and in the European Union we observe such developments with wages that do not allow an individual to live a modest healthy life. And if then immigration puts laborers on the market that are willing to accept a 'hunger-wage', then there is no equilibrium possible.

It's cynical how the economic theories see the problem of wages: "The wage adjusts to balance the supply and demand for labor." Or: "The wage equals the value of the marginal product of labor." [94]

Only one perspective reflects the frame of wages: "Highly productive workers are highly paid, and less productive workers are less highly paid." [95] This is common sense and it is also realistic and in general accepted.

But this general image also has its critical questions: The word 'highly' and the word 'less highly' let it open, how to value the real wage that is meant behind the statement. Another question is what is a 'highly productive worker'? To leave such aspects unanswered or ignored, produces suspicion that there is a 'dead dog' hidden somewhere. For too many 'highly productive workers' (academics, specialists) the wages are unjustifiably low due to the low interest in profit.

Depending on the location a wage of €5,000 (Dollar) compared to a wage of €2,500 (Dollar) at the same location doesn't make any significant difference (after taxes): this €5,000 (Dollar) only means (after taxes) a little bit more here

---

[94] Mankiw (et al.), p. 390
[95] Mankiw (et al.), p. 393

and there, a little better or bigger apartment, a bit bigger car, and that's all.

The amount of a wage is not simply a political matter; it is fundamentally an existential human matter with some essential normative principles – proposals to discuss:

1. Working is a genuine natural need from and for the mind and soul of humans
2. Individual potentials should ideally be promoted for future working
3. Working must also be understood as 'getting money to live a life'
4. An individual must be able to make at least a humble life with his wage
5. A family life (1-2 children) must be possible with the wages from both parents
6. A family life (1-2 children or more) living from one wage is a luxury status
7. A family with lowest (poor) education can't expect to live from one wage
8. The higher the required education and experiences, the higher the wage should be
9. Performance quality and responsibility should be valued with the level of wage
10. Procreating a baby requires secure financial resources and personality education
11. A 'good for nothing' with miserable character can't expect more than a very low wage.
12. Most firms have risks due to market changes and can't guarantee a life long contract.
13. Indefinite working contracts in the state administration are unfair, unjust, and inefficient.

To limit top wages doesn't solve the widely criticized injustice (imbalance); crucial is on what criteria their wages are based on and how these people contribute to democracy, society, education, human values and culture with their position, responsibility and financial power. They must give transparent account of it and they must be supervised and controlled by ethical authorities.

Estimated 70-80% of all politicians don't have the competences (relevant knowledge) in dealing with the real world of economics. It's absolutely indispensable that they all get a profound education in new economics in order to balance economic power, to drastically reduce externalities, and to efficiently promote freedom of pioneering and vanguard businesses.

Suggestions for solutions:

➜ Vocational education must prepare people for certain flexibility in choosing a working field; in the permanent changing world a periodic further education is an indispensable requirement.

➜ In case, (forced) re-education is indispensable to enable certain individuals for the labor market and living a life, including upbringing and educating their children (with supervision).

➜ If on the one side we call for responsibility for employers' wage policy, we must also call on the other side for living and educational responsibility by the workers (employees).

Labor Market

The understanding of labor market excludes the fact that economics (aiming for satisfaction and profit) is only a 'tool' for higher aims. Economics in theory and practice is for living genuine human values and achieving holistic fulfillment.

This understanding is much reduced: "A labor market is a factor market in which individuals supply labor services for wages to other individuals and to firms that need (demand) labor services." [96]

If the author introduces here the 'invisible hand' he unmasks himself: "...the invisible hand and the labor market is organized around the concepts of supply and demand." [97] It would be much more appropriate to say: *The labor market is organized in aiming for human's fulfillment within the genuine inner human values and the Archetypes of the Soul.* But in reality capitalistic economics destroys such fulfillment.

There is the labor market: One market segment has low job offers and another market has high job offers. Or for some specific professional profiles there is a low or a high job offer market. As a consequence some people with a specific education searching for a job can find a job, and others with other specifications can't find a job. In abstract terms: "The supply of labor in any one labor market depends on the opportunities available in other labor markets." [98]

---

[96] Colander, p. 430
[97] Colander, p. 430
[98] Mankiw (et al.), p. 389

The broader the vocational education and professional experiences, the higher the flexibility to move from one field of production to another field and therefore the higher are the chances to find a job. If this is of highest significance in the Western world, then it has consequences for the public education system, including vocational and academic education, and for each juvenile preparing himself or herself for a professional life.

Other costs to consider around the matter of wage:

We have here: payment for landowner, labor, and owner of capital. "Labor, land and capital each earn the value of their marginal contribution to the production process." [99] What are the consequences of such a statement? Who says this and why should this be considered? If the owner of a production firm is also the landowner, why should he earn for the value of his land that serves his business?

Or why should the capital owner (an investor, co-owner of the business, or the owner of the business) earn from the marginal capital contribution to the production process? This is an ideological statement and not a theory.

To have land and / or capital is not the same as: "The equipment and structures used to produce goods and services … they are not used for their own sake but for what they can contribute to production." [100] Talking about land and capital is not the same. Many firms started with the capital and / or land from the owner of the firm. "The demand for land and capital is determined just like the demand for labor." [101] Who says that this is the right way to operate with land and capital? This is an ideological statement, not a theory. We distinguish two prices: Purchase price (ownership) and rental price (payment to use business premises or land for a certain period).

Examples: A person has or buys for a specific use

- A farmer has and uses agricultural land for generations (no mortgage)
  Why should he sell his land? Then it's gone forever. Why should he mortgage his land? He risks losing his land forever. For a short-term solution the land's soil is gone for all future generations.

- A farmer buys agricultural land from saved or inherited money
  Buying agriculture land is a source for nutrition for generations. Buying

---

[99] Mankiw (et al.), p. 396
[100] Mankiw (et al.), p. 395
[101] Mankiw (et al.), p. 396

with mortgage risks to lose the land and the own money put in this purchase.

- A person has unused land for construction for generations (no mortgage)
  Unused land can serve for something. Could it be used for agriculture or small animal breeding? Once the land is sold, the property is gone forever. A small business might be possible.

- A person buys land for construction from saved or inherited money
  Buying land is a good investment, but the construction project should not risk the investment of the land. There is no law that states that land must bring as much profit as possible.

- A person has and uses commercial space for generations (no mortgage)
  Mortgage the premises to get money for the wants and you risk loosing it if you can't pay the mortgage back. Premises, free from a mortgage allows a business to operate with moderate prices.

- A person buys commercial premises from saved or inherited money
  It's good to have a commercial space without a mortgage. You can start a business at low costs and with moderate prices. Life has a great chance to be secure with a sustainable business.

- A person has and uses a business for generations (free from mortgage)
  Life has a great chance to be secure with a sustainable business. And the business can be a legacy for generations. Only stupid people would overcharge the budget and put everything at risk.

- A person buys a business from saved or inherited money
  If the business is well analyzed and thoughtfully considered for living a life, then the business becomes the main source of life and can be even a legacy for one's children in the future.

In general people who possess agricultural land, land for whatever, a commercial space, or a working business can always sell it or mortgage it up to the roof (as much as a bank mortgages it). The capitalistic imperative 'make more of it' or 'make as much as possible of it' can very fast lead to a disaster.
There are people and investors that dispose of immense amounts of money. They can offer excellent prices for land or properties, but once sold the land and property is gone; and 10-20 years later the land or property has increased in value and the buyer is the winner.
There is no law, but always the sick imperative understanding that everything must generate as much money as possible. This is capitalistic madness. It is

not healthy and very fast it puts everything at risk. Above that the 'more of it' is rapidly gone with the rising new wants. The only winner is in the end the bank that has provided the mortgage, if not within years, then certainly within decades. Additionally the imperative 'make more of it' never ends; it becomes something like an addiction: "I could make more … I could buy more 'wants' … I could get more profit …" It creates an understanding of growth that is a compulsion and makes the mind crazy. There is never peace of mind.

Business people forget very fast: "An event that changes the supply of any factor of production can alter the earnings of all the factors." [102] And there is another risk: "The productivity of each factor (depends) on the quantities of the other factors available to be used in the production process." [103] In other words: In the world of business many things can happen and the positive cost analysis of today becomes the 'burned dream' of tomorrow.

The price of a piece of land or of a specific amount of renting capital can be valued with a future perspective: The price of land will double within 10 years and with the rented capital one can make a significant profit during the next 10 years. Such thinking allows for one to pay a higher price than demanded, for example if other interested buyers are on the stage.

One could even pay 50% more if the interest in that land or capital is superior because the value and the sum of profit in the following 10 years pays for it easily without a loss of money (of profit). In the words of an expert: "Therefore the equilibrium purchase price of a piece of land or capital depends on both the current value of the marginal product and the value of the marginal product expected to prevail in the future."[104] Here we identify a speculation attitude.

How much labor, land and capital does a firm need for an expansion? There is an increase of products. There is an increase of total price for these products. Therefore the increase of price for these additional products (the sum) must at least equal the costs (sum) of increase of labor, land and capital to hire. In economic words: "For (labor) and land and capital, the firm increases the quantity hired until the value of the factor's marginal product equals the factor's price." [105]

There is another way of interdependence that needs to be questioned: "… a factor in abundant supply has a low marginal product and thus a low price,

---

[102] Mankiw (et al.), p. 398
[103] Mankiw (et al.), p. 398
[104] Mankiw (et al.), p. 397
[105] Mankiw (et al.), p. 396

and a factor in scarce supply has a high marginal product and a high price." [106] We translate this in more simple words: If labor, land and capital on the market exist in abundant supply, then their prices tend to be low. As a consequence the amount of an additional product has also a low limit and also a low price. On the other side, if labor, land and capital are scarce (and therefore more expensive), then the amount of an additional product is high and has a high price.

Such understanding of interdependences leads to the topic of 'growth': more production requires more investment (labor, land, and capital). The additional investment in labor, land, and capital must be equal or lower than the prices of the additional amount of goods. As the total of the prices (of the additional goods for sale) includes the factor 'profit', it only makes sense to expand (to invest for more production) if there is a remarkable additional profit with the additional amount of production. The theory of such interdependences for growth is called the 'neoclassical theory of distribution'. [107]

The core of an increase of production is called: Growth in productivity. "Growth in productivity is measured as the annualized rate of change in output per worker. Growth in real wages is measured as the annualized change in average wages deflated by the Retail Prices Index." [108] But growth in productivity does not necessarily (implicitly) lead to higher wages.

Starting a business or making a business work:

Minimum capital + minimum land/premise size + minimum labor with a minimum wage + minimum equipment + minimum other costs + minimum other resources (e.g. raw material) for the production process + a minimum of products that must be sold (at a minimum price) to make work a business without profit – and we can add a minimum of profit without questioning why this is necessary or for what it is.

Where is the 'divine law' that says that shareholders must participate in the profit (or suffer losses of profit)? They do not contribute with active work; they give money and have a right to get an interest for it; interest is here something like a 'rent' (they rent money to be used for the business).

The shareholder principle is in its core a speculation business! Worse than that it is a 'casino'; I bet (by buying shares) that the firm will double its

---

[106] Mankiw (et al.), p. 397
[107] Mankiw (et al.), p. 400
[108] Mankiw (et al.), p. 393

profits, and pay me a dividend as a shareholder and as the share price has increased I can sell the shares and make a bigger profit!

Components of the neoclassical theory:

There are several variables to consider for creating growth. In everyday language we can identify on the side of the production (firms, corporations):

Analyze the costs for new capital, new land (or premises), and new labor and calculate the profit of its use for a period of 10-20 years. The profit must be higher than the highest costs for new capital, new land (premises) and new labor. This is obviously a speculation calculation: the increase of prices for land or premises must be guaranteed with highest probability. The price for capital (in the present) must be lower than what can be expected for the following years, and the labor's wage should not or only minimally increase the following 10-20 years.

The same speculative calculation (as for land) can be made with the amount of required raw material on the market or land with such raw material (for production). The calculation about the demand over the next 10-20 years is also important, for example due to the growth of the world population. The business result must be 'growth of profit' (more profit than without expansion) which is the ultimate motive of growth of production.

The essential part of such calculation is: agricultural land, land for animal breeding, land with raw resources, land for construction, and wood. Other resources such as raw materials on the ground of the oceans can be acquired (stolen) via military power.

In the power game of growth the little citizen, owner of some land, woods, or premises, never has a chance to win. He will always be the looser. It seems as if the big corporations and investors want to be the sole owner of everything on earth, at least of land, wood, raw resources, properties, and wealth. If so, they also must take away from the middle class (medium sized businesses) their possession. But it's worse: nobody else other than these corporations and investors are allowed to have big success and to possess significant wealth (on a level of trillions of Euros or dollars).

3. Microeconomic Theories

We have explored until now the realities of the economic market. As the next step we explore the essential 'laws' and theories of economics. Everywhere the reader can compare the 'laws' and theories with the manifold factors of the economic realities as shown in the previous chapters.

Analyzing components of economic 'laws' and theories we presume: that the business already exists and has costs and revenues. Most terms related to money encompass the entity of a production, described by its 'goods'. In general the term 'production' is very vague and leads to some very important questions:

- Is it about a small firm, a medium sized firm, or a big corporation?
- Are there differences in the theories between a firm and a big corporation?
- Do the corporations with superior interrelations act the same way?
- Do the theories have the same implications for a grocery store and a big supermarket?
- Do the theories have importance also for example in 'John's small bar in a remote village?
- Do the terms also have importance to a self-employed repair business?
- Can we understand 'services' (a service firm) also as 'production'?
- Do the theories distinguish between small products (e.g. cheese) and big products (e.g. cars)?
- Could it be that in the tourist industry (including the small firms) all act the same way?
- Are there differences in the theories between a raw resource firm and an agricultural firm?
- Can the theories also been applied to construction of trains or nuclear power stations?

→ All the authors of the economic books we elaborate here systematically avoid categorizing the 'laws' and theories related to the topics in the above list of questions.

The following chapter encompasses a majority of the microeconomic theories. We will see here that economics is reduced to production entities and not to service entities. Most of the terms and models do not refer to self-employed production business, small firms, and medium sized firms.

The microeconomic theories are preponderantly related to big corporations.

Some terms and models – especially those who focus on 'growth' and 'maximizing profit' – do not apply to small, medium sized and big agricultural production. These businesses are principally limited by the nature (natural growing) and the weather conditions. Here economics gets an absolute intrinsic limit.

→ The readers, students and professors or experts are in the classical Western microeconomics manipulated and directed towards a concept that has very limited adaptability and favors big production corporations.

3.1. Production Costs

3.1.1. The Production Process

There is a way of thinking about planning: "The production process is generally divided into a long-run planning decision, in which a firm chooses the least expensive method of producing from among all possible methods ... and a short-run adjustment decision, in which a firm adjusts its long-run planning decision to reflect new information." [109]

The idea sounds like common sense. But something crept in here: Does a firm really choose the least expensive method? What is meant by 'method'? The meaning of 'methods' is unclear. We interpret 'method' as 'machines'. The price of a method expresses a quality. Purchasing expensive 'methods' may have a hidden mutual interest between the two firms (buyer and seller). The seller and buyer could be golf buddies. 'Among all possible methods': this is an exaggeration. There may be a hundred such machines (or methods) and there is not so much time and above that the repair service or other machine services are closer to the buyer's location than the production entity. And this 'short-run adjustment decision' is too vague to understand in the context of a production process. We could understand methods also as 'strategy'. But the term 'strategy' is very vague as well.

→ We identify here typical blabbering in economics. Nothing is really clear except for some general common sense! This has got nothing to do with a 'theory'!

---

[109] Colander, p. 279

Colander continues, now focusing on 'techniques': "In a long-run decision, a firm chooses among all possible production techniques. This means that it can choose the size of the plant it wants, the type of machines it wants, and the location it wants. The firm has fewer options in a short-run decision, in which the firm is constrained in regard to what production decisions it can make." [110]

Can the producer really always choose an exact location? Once a location is chosen; the rest is obviously a matter of options and availability in line with the time among all possible production techniques. Is it a problem if the firm can only chose between fewer options?

→ Again we identify here typical blabbering in economics. Nothing is really clear except for some general common sense! This has got nothing to do with a 'theory'!

"A long-run decision is a decision in which the firm can choose among all possible production techniques … A short-run decision is a decision in which the firm is constrained in regard to what production decisions it can make." [111]

→ It is not possible to get a clearer picture about a real decision process. We identify here a typical vague statement with a certain common sense. The word 'constrained' is foggy. Who knows what is meant by this? In general, in life and business there is always a constraint. This has got nothing to do with a 'theory'!
→ Economics speaks here about production corporations.

While reading such texts we never know if the author is speaking about a small firm, a big firm, or a global corporation. It seems he is talking here about a big production unit and not about a small shop 'around the corner':
"Real-world production tables are complicated. They often involve hundreds of inputs, hundreds of outputs, and millions of possible combinations of inputs and outputs. Studying these various combinations and determining which is the best requires expertise and experience. Business schools devote entire courses to it (operations research and production analysis)." [112]

How do we understand these 'millions of possible combinations of inputs and outputs'? It is as stupid as saying: "John can choose between millions of different clothes and combinations." In such a case business schools must

---

[110] Colander, p. 280
[111] Colander, p. 280
[112] Colander, p. 280

offer courses for at least a 10 year-program.

→ The description is unlimited and reveals a sign of psychosis.
→ Economics speaks here about large production corporations.

Now it becomes a little complicated: "The marginal product is the additional output forthcoming from an additional input, other inputs constant; the average product is the total output divided by the quantity of the input … workers' marginal product (the additional output that will be forthcoming from an additional worker, other inputs constant)." [113]

Let's try to understand: A firm decides about an increase in the quantity of a product. This amount is called the 'marginal product'. On the other side, to produce this marginal product, there is a need for an additional input in the production process (e.g. raw material, more labor, an additional machine). Now a calculation can be made: The quantity of higher output divided by the quantity of the input. And now: What is this result for? The author continues now talking about "…workers' average product (output per worker)". That means: it's about the increase of labor input for a higher amount of production output.

There are production functions:

Each worker has an output factor: "It is important to distinguish marginal product from average product. Workers' average product is the total output divided by the number of workers."

We could add: If the input of machines increases the output of a product (of different products) we can make a similar calculation: The machines' average product is the total output divided by the number of machines. And we can combine here the workers' output with the machines' output. This statement is about it: "A production function is the relationship between the inputs (factors of production) and outputs." [114]

In simple understanding: If a firm wants to produce more of a product or more products, then more machines and more labor is necessary. Machines and labors cost money. Therefore the higher (marginal) output must cover these costs. Or: the price of an additionally produced product depends on the costs of input. In any case, it must create as much profit as possible, which is not mentioned by the author.

---

[113] Colander, p. 280
[114] Colander, p. 280

➜ Economics speaks here about large production corporations.

There is a law of diminishing marginal productivity: "This range of the relationship between fixed and variable inputs is so important that economists have formulated a law that describes what happens in production processes when firms reach this range - when more and more of one input is added to a fixed amount of another input. The law of diminishing marginal productivity states that as more and more of a variable input is added to an existing fixed input, eventually the additional output one gets from that additional input is going to fall." [115]

The authors speak here about a 'law' they have created. It sounds like something physical (like the law of gravity) or a mathematical or natural law. "The law describes what happens when…"; but in the end this law seems to be not so significant when it's stated with 'as more and more … input, eventually the output … falls'. To call this a 'law' with the 'eventuality case' sounds hyped up. Any 'eventuality' can be important or not. To call such a statement a 'law' is rather exaggerated. The other part in the law-statement 'is going to fall' can't be interpreted. A fall can be temporary or too little to be of urgent action. A 'fall' is not always something negative. There could be a fall in one product (price), but at the same time it can increase the sale of another product (e.g. substitute). A calculated 'fall' can also be of strategic interest for something else and therefore intentionally wanted.

Another consideration is: There are always 'fixed and variable inputs'. And this 'law' is indeed something that always has to be calculated in the price of a product. Firms cannot change the price of a product at any time when the variable inputs increase in cost.

➜ This law is not a law in the sense of natural science or social science or mathematical science.
➜ It suggests that the price calculation is simply a result of cost and price of a (marginal) product.
➜ This law is gobbledygook!
➜ Economics speaks here again about large production corporations.

3.1.2. The Cost of Production

Short definition: "Cost is the value of everything a seller must give up to

---

[115] Colander, p. 282

produce a good." [116]

→ Costs of production in economics definition and theories do not consider costs for allocation, intermediate trade, end-price from a sale firm, and fraction for profit per produced good.

The list of costs can be very long, starting from raw material up to the electricity and labor costs. More interesting here is the word 'everything'. If the owner of a business has brought in land that is used for the production, then the owner can also demand to be compensated with a rent of the use of land which becomes then a cost for the business. For a farmer that has inherited his agricultural land it most probably makes no sense as the production does not generate enough money for such a cost. Does it matter? No! What matters here is that the statement allows one to invent any kind of cost to reduce taxes. Or the owner can mortgage his land and use this money for building a new home or for holidays and luxurious cars, or for speculation to generate more money. But herewith the risk starts that one day the bank will own the land.

There is more to take into consideration about the costs of production: "The law diminishing marginal productivity states that as more and more of a variable input is added to an existing fixed input, after some point the additional output one gets from the additional input will fall." [117]

Whenever an economist is talking about an economic 'law', the alarm bells start ringing. Here, the 'law' operates with 'after some point'. Who knows when this point is reached? And what does it mean in a real production? It can be a hidden suggestion: "Give more and more variable input to increase the output in order to never lose a possible marginal profit!"

Maybe it's simply a warning: "Pay attention that the new variable inputs always produce profit." Or: "Do not engage fully a new labor in order to increase production, if you only need 80% of the labor's work. This is already a 'fall', and nobody wants to 'fall'; and a 'fall' is always something negative to be avoided. The cause may also lie in the limited capacity of a new variable or in the risk of over-production.

→ Is it really an efficient attitude to claim that all machines and all other inputs must always be fully and 100% utilized, never missing one second of operation and therefore one per cent of one cent of profit?

---

[116] Mankiw (et al.), p. 144
[117] Colander, p. 283

Another short definition is: "The total spent for goods." Here 'spent' means the costs of production. Such calculations do not mention the factor profit that is de facto added to these costs. This definition also does not say if the cost is only related to the production process until allocation or supply.

- There are firms: production + sale (direct sale activity to costumers)
- There are firms: production + allocation (distribution) + sale (direct sale activity)
- There are firms: production + allocation (distribution) + sale to one or more intermediaries
- There are firms: production + allocation (distribution) + sale to one or more sale entities

Specifications:

- Firms can sell the products to intermediaries that sell the products to a seller entity (firm).
- Firms can sell the products directly to a sale entity (firm).

Sale chains:

- The firm sets the final price of the goods as it sells the goods itself.
- The firm sets the price of the goods for the intermediary that sells the goods to sale entities.
- The intermediary sets the final price of the goods for the final sale entity.
- The sale entity sets the final price of the goods.

→ Depending on the sale chain we have different firms that determine a final price including a profit margin. An intermediary and a final sale entity increase the price with their costs and profit margin. In the worst case we have with a chain of four business entities that include a profit margin.

→ The definition about 'production cost' is very variable depending on the complexity of a chain until final sale of the goods. 'Production cost' does not mean automatically that this cost determines the final price of a good (cost divided by the amount of produced goods). It does not say anything about where the profit margin is accounted for.

→ A sale price must include estimated taxes. The definition about 'production cost' does not say where these expenses are accounted per product or for the total of produced and sold products. If there is a profit accounted, then taxes must also be accounted for.

→ The definition about 'production cost' does not say anything about the size of the production firm and the kind of products, or anything about a service firms (e.g. a restaurant).

The money flow related to a business has several aspects. In general it's said: The production cost is about "how a firm goes about maximizing profit." [118]

Right now we are in the middle of the capitalistic economics: Everything is about how to 'maximize profit.' The real costs and the flexibilities or hidden traps with costs of production are irrelevant.

The core of the cost of production is not, for example: "Finding a balance of costs related to revenue (income) including for example a 1-5% profit."

→ We assume that economics speaks here about production corporations (big firms).
→ Costs of production in economics definition and theories do not include costs for allocation, intermediate trade, and end-price from a sale firm, estimated taxes, and a fraction for profit per produced (or sold) good.
→ The definition of the term 'production cost' remains vague and many components are still foggy.
→ As sharing a cake is not of interest for avaricious and greedy people, a corporation must think about covering all entities from raw material firms up to the final sale entity of their products. A compulsive accountant gets frustrated if he sees a possible margin of profit that gets lost.

There is an 'economies of scope': "The cost of production of one product often depends on what other products a firm is producing … economies of scope (means) when the costs of producing products are interdependent so that it's less costly for a firm to produce one good when it's already producing another. [119]
In easy words: Produce several goods in a way that you can reduce the costs of production as much as possible. Or: Choose to produce products that have minimal costs of production. In both cases it's a way (advice or law) to minimize costs. It's also a way to optimally use the inputs for the production processes.

→ Scope: It's about amount, volume, extension, range, span, dimension, area, field, quantity, and etc. The meaning of the word 'scope' becomes a special focus depending on the statement.
→ Every lost cent due to lack (neglecting) of optimally used inputs, including the working time of labors, can mean for a firm with hundreds of

---

[118] Mankiw (et al.), p. 265
[119] Colander, p. 304

thousands of products produced a loss of hundreds of thousands or millions of €/$ per year or in the long run.

→ The concern here is a serious matter in four directions: loss of profit, abuse of labor, unused potential of machines, and externalities (collateral damages).

"Economies of scope play an important role in firms' decisions about what combination of goods to produce. They look for both economies of scope and economies of scale (a quantity of goods has an optimal price by given fixed costs). When you read about firms' mergers, think about whether the combination of their products will generate economies of scope. Many otherwise unexplainable mergers between seemingly incompatible firms can be explained by economies of scope." [120]

→ Economies of scope realize with product strategies the maxim 'do the best of it'. We identify here again the compulsive character of their mind.

→ Costs of production in the context of 'economies of scope' do not include costs for allocation, intermediate trade, end-price from a sale firm, and fraction for profit per produced good.

→ We assume: Economics speaks here about large production corporations, not about small firms or service entities.

"Low-cost labor in other countries has led U.S. firms (and EU firms) to locate their manufacturing processes in those countries and to concentrate domestic activities on other aspects of production ... the costs of marketing, advertising, and distribution are often larger components of the cost of a good than are manufacturing costs." [121]

As labor in Asia costs 10-20 times less than in the United States and in the European Union, no wonder the production in these countries generates much less costs (for production) than marketing, advertising, and distribution in United States and European Union. This statement is very manipulative and ignores all the dire externalities with irreversible damages.

As many corporations calculate the marketing costs with up to 35% or more of the product price – and the marketing prices are in general very high (e.g. TV spots) – the small and medium sized firms and those firms who produce in Europe or America, have practically no chance to compete with a corporation that acts and calculates in such ways.

→ Low-cost labor in other countries destroys the small businesses and the

---

[120] Colander, p. 304
[121] Colander, p. 304

middle class businesses at home, in Europe and America.

→ Western corporations do not simply produce with low-cost labor in other countries for supplying products at cheap prices.

→ With such economic acting the big Western corporations generate billions of €/$ they invest in marketing due to low-cost labor and externalities in other countries.

→ The marketing and the entire media corporations have already irreversibly distorted, and damaged and dehumanized – even genetically – the brain of billions of people.

→ All, really absolutely all economic theories, principles, and 'laws', have irreversibly destroyed a huge part of the planet with all the consequences (e.g. climate change).

→ The intended aim of such economic doing is to destroy all competitors on the lower level, including governments and all genuine human values.

Production management must consider 'learning by doing': "Learning by doing simply means that as we do something, we learn what works and what doesn't, and over time we become more proficient at it ... Many firms estimate worker productivity to grow 1 to 2 percent a year because of learning by doing." [122]

→ This 1-2% sounds like: even from one cent less of cost they want to make 10 % profit.

→ This 1-2% may have an economic effect in big corporations, but not in standard sized firms.

→ The Holy Spirit may be able to find out what the truth is here about percentage and effect.

→ 'Learning by doing' means for production in Asia: 'brought up to speed' learning basic skills.

We say: Workers, employees, managers, and owners of firms could increase knowledge, skills, and personality qualities by 50-200% for a fair, efficient, sustainable, and successful business.

It is self-evident that a firm makes multi-dimensional decisions about cost, which products to produce and how much to produce. The author stresses that "economic decisions take all relevant margins into account." But the question is: what does 'all relevant margins' mean? Are there irrelevant margins? What could an 'irrelevant margin' be?

If one cent or 5 seconds in the working process (per labor of work) already

---

[122] Colander, p. 305

have an impact on the entire production process during one year and therefore become relevant in the accounts, then a firm will consider such margins as relevant. In other words: if 500 (or 5,000) workers work 5 seconds faster per hour then in the end of the year we get a significant positive production and cost figure and therefore we reach the slogan 'maximizing profit'. In such a context a parameter with its figures becomes a very 'relevant margin'. Based on this, we conclude:

→ Taking 'all relevant margins' into consideration is a compulsion, even madness.
→ Taking 'all relevant margins' into consideration is perverse and horribly sick.
→ Taking 'all relevant margins' into consideration expresses distain of humans.
→ Taking 'all relevant margins' into consideration is related to big corporations.

Colander's comment: "Learning the standard model, however, provides you with only the rudiments of cost analysis, in the same way that learning the rules of mechanics provides you with only the basics of mechanical engineering. Introductory economics provides you with a superb framework for starting to think about real-world cost management, but it can't make you an expert cost analyst." [123]

We interpret: Economics teaches us only the standard models. You, the student, must study 500-1,000 hours and more about economics and you only get the 'rudiments'. You learn the superb framework of maximizing profit – that's all brainwashing.

There are many more sophisticated and perfidious calculation models combining 'all relevant margins' to maximize profit everywhere, all the time.

3.1.3. Components of Costs of Production

Short definition: Summary of the total manufacturing cost of an item.

It involves charges to a processing department and the allocation of the total cost between the ending work-in-process inventory and the units completed and transferred out to the next department or finished goods inventory.
A cost of production report shows: [124]

---

[123] Colander, p. 308
[124] http://www.accounting4management.com/cost_of_production_report.htm

- Total unit costs transferred to it from a preceding department
- Materials, labor, and factory overhead added by the department
- Unit cost added by the department
- Total and unit costs accumulated to the end of operations in the department
- The cost of the beginning and ending work in process inventories
- Cost transferred to a succeeding department or to a finished goods storeroom

→ Costs of production in economics definition and theories do not include costs for allocation (here understood as 'distribution'), intermediate trade, end-price from a sale firm, and fraction for profit per produced good.

Technological advances influence the price; in most cases reduce costs: "Technological change is an increase in the range of production techniques that leads to more efficient ways of producing goods as well as the production of new and better goods ... Technological change can fundamentally alter the nature of production costs ... Technological change occurs in all industries, not only high-tech industries ... Technological change and learning by doing are intricately related." [125]

Indeed, Colander is riding the crazy horse for the long-run production decisions: "To make their long-run decisions, firms look at the costs of the various inputs and the technologies available for combining those inputs, and then decide which combination offers the lowest cost." [126]

Principally we can agree with technological progress. But economists have this 'margin' obsession. For example, a firm constructs production machines; and every year they improve the efficiency of their machines by 1% production capacity. Therefore firms compulsively must calculate every year the 'opportunity cost': "If I would buy the new machine, I would make a marginal profit..."

Now we can forecast the coming 200 years; for example: every year a technological (or aesthetical) advance providing one or two percent marginal benefit (of whatsoever), and therefore firms buy every year a new machine because their competitors do so as well. Or another example: the consumers get every year a new car model with 5% margin psychological or technical benefit and therefore the next 200 years a majority of car owners will buy a

---

[125] Colander, p. 306-307
[126] Colander, p. 295

new car every 1-3 years to get a marginal (psychological, social) benefit. The same picture could be developed with clothes (fashion), mobile phones, televisions, computers, etc.

We could say: Everything in human's life (and business) has a production phase or a realization phase (generating something) and in the end a result: a product or service or event that creates satisfaction, wellbeing or happiness; in other words: an input and an output with a benefit.

Where will this lead humanity and the planet? Where does it lead if people learn to think in '1-2 percent margins' about everything and this all the time; in their relationship, sex life, family life, and consumer behavior?

➔ "Darling, please give 5% more sensual energy and movement, and I will have a marginal benefit that makes me 5% more satisfied and happier."

3.1.4. Explicit (real) Cost

Short definition: It means "the input costs that require an outlay of money". [127]

In simple words, it's the total amount of real expenses of a firm. We interpret: the 'input' can be everything a firm needs for the production and has to pay for it.

"Accounting focuses on explicit costs and revenues; economics focuses on both explicit and implicit costs and revenues … For economists, total cost is explicit payments to the factors of production plus the opportunity cost of the factors provided by the owners of the firm … For economists, total revenue is the amount a firm receives for selling its product or service plus any increase in the value of the assets owned by the firm." [128]

➔ The revenue must always be higher than the production cost. If this would not be so, there would not be generated any profit. This calculation is not considered here from the authors.

---

[127] Mankiw (et al.), p. 265-269
[128] Colander), p. 278

3.1.5. Implicit (not real) Cost

Short definition: It means the input costs that do not require outlay of money by the firm.

For example land or premise or capital of the owner that has no cost, but a value that is used in the production process.

We interpret: The firm needs this input, but has not got to pay or not paid for it as it is an input from the owner or the firm that has become owner of it. Considering this as a 'cost' means it must be determined with economic figures (the parameter 'money'). The function of this vague parameter in the accounting is not specified from the author Mankiw (et al.). It can be seen as a substantial value of a business such as land, premises or building.

"An economist (…) would point out that the accountant's calculation doesn't take into account the time and effort that the owner put into making the widgets. While a person's time involves no explicit cost in money, it does involve an opportunity cost, the forgone income that the owner could have made by spending that time working in another job." [129]

We are here again in the middle of compulsive greed: A worker, owner of a firm, or an employee must always be working. It can or should never be that a worker, employee or the owner of a firm has one minute or hour of 'doing nothing'. Every minute of a laborer's work is money, and that has a potential for profit! That's why in Asia a worker can only go twice per day for 2-5 minutes to the toilet; and sometimes they are not allowed to go to the toilet even if they have a very urgent need. Seen that way: To go to the toilet is a reduction of the worker's production capacity (time) and this loss of active working time reduces a margin of the profit if we calculate the toilet-minutes during a year and multiply this by 500-5,000 employees or workers.

→ Minimizing the 'toilet-minutes' is taking away human's dignity in order to maximize profit.
→ The 'opportunity cost' figure is never static and can quickly become a Fata Morgana.

Unmeasured costs are: "Economists operate conceptually; they include in costs exactly what their theory says they should. They include all opportunity costs. Accountants who have to measure firms' costs in practice and provide

---

[129] Colander, p. 308

the actual dollar figures take a much more pragmatic approach; their concepts of costs must reflect only explicit costs - those costs that are reasonably precisely measurable." [130]

To speak here about 'cost' is irritating and confusing; it says: "You have it, but it does not cost anything." A compulsive economist could become very nervous and think: "But somebody has to pay for it. It can't be true that this value does not generate money from itself. Let's make a special income from it." We interpret that an economist's calculation is: Revenue = explicit costs + implicit costs + economic profit.

→ Calculating always the opportunity cost is dehumanizing and an abasement of human beings.
→ Calculating always the opportunity cost enslaves workers, employees, and even the owner.
→ Calculating always the opportunity cost expresses arrogance towards genuine human values.

3.1.6. Sunk cost

Short definition: Costs have fallen or have decreased.

→ A buyer likes 'sunk costs' if the price of the produced good also decreased.
→ A producer (or seller) likes 'sunk costs' if this allows him to make more profit.
→ A producer (seller) can sell more of a good as he becomes more competitive with a lower price.

3.1.7. Income

Short definition: Income means the amount of financial or other returns, earned or unearned, during a given period of time.

→ Conclusion: If corporations declare a figure about their income, then we cannot conclude that this income is 100% related to the sale of their products.
→ Conclusion: If corporations declare a figure about their profit, then we cannot conclude that this profit is 100% or 0% related to the sale of their products.

---

[130] Colander, p. 307

3.1.8. Revenue

Different sources, different definitions:

- Revenue is the money that comes in from the sale of goods or services.
- The money that comes to a firm (or person) from any kind of sources.
- The gross income from a firm, a sale, an investment, or a property, etc.
- All the income produced by a business activity.

Conclusion: Revenue = Income

→ Conclusion: If corporations declare a figure about their revenue, then we cannot conclude that this revenue is 100% related to the sale of their products.

The income can come from manifold sources: sales, services, maintenance (of sold machines, appliances), interest (bank), speculation (e.g. betting, short term financing (hours), any 'casino' activity wit the daily cash flow), rent (of goods), repair services, legal advice services, delivery services, installation work, etc.

→ Depending on the kind and size of firm the revenue (= income) does not simply refer to the sold goods or services. Revenue can be higher than the amount of sold goods and services.
→ A maintenance service guarantee (free of cost) has a calculated cost and therefore such costs are included in the price of a good; and this part of the price is not a real production cost!

There is also the term 'turnover', sometimes meaning 'revenue' or 'income':

Example 1: [131]

- The number of times a particular stock of goods is sold and restocked during a given period of time.
- The amount of business transacted during a given period of time.
- The number of shares of stock sold on the market during a given period of time.
- The number of workers hired by an establishment to replace those who have left in a given period of time.
- The ratio of this number to the number of employed workers.

---

[131] http://www.thefreedictionary.com/turnover

Example 2: [132]

- Change or movement of people, as tenants or customers, in, out, or through a place: The restaurant did a lively business and had a rapid turnover.
- The aggregate of worker replacements in a given period in a given business or industry.
- The ratio of the labor turnover to the average number of employees in a given period.
- The total amount of business done in a given time.

Example 3: [133]

- Accounting: (1) The annual sales volume net of all discounts and sales taxes. (2) The number of times an asset (such as cash, inventory, and raw materials) is replaced or revolves during an accounting period.
- Human resource management: The number of employees hired to replace those who left or were fired during a 12 month period.
- Finance: The volume or value of shares traded on a stock exchange during a day, month, or year.

Conclusion:

Revenue = Income
Turnover = A number, amount or ratio applicable in different economic contexts and time frames

3.1.9. Average Revenue

Short definition: Total revenue divided by the quantity of goods sold.

➔ This formula is only correct if it is declared to be the revenue from the sold goods.
➔ A general declaration of average revenue does not say that this revenue is 100% related to the sale of their products.

3.1.10. Marginal Revenue

Short definition: The change in total revenue from additional unit(s) sold.

---

[132] http://dictionary.reference.com/browse/turnover
[133] http://www.businessdictionary.com/definition/turnover.html

Calculations: Marginal revenue must be greater than marginal cost because there is a marginal profit calculated. If the marginal revenue is equal to marginal cost, then there is no profit; if marginal revenue is less than marginal cost, then there are losses and no profit.

→ The profit factor is always unspoken in economic theories and models.

3.1.11. Shutdown

Colander explains: "…the shutdown point (is the point below which the firm will be better off if it temporarily shuts down than it will if it stays in business)." [134]

The 'be better off' is not explained. Sometimes there are reasons not to shutdown but to continue with the business activities. Sometimes the shutdown is forced because the cake of the profit is eaten and the firm had not set aside financial reserves to bridge the gap of decrease in revenue.

Mankiw comments on the decision to shut down; [135] in short words we emphasize: In case of losses (or other reasons) there are two options: a) a short-run decision not to produce anything during a specific period of time. In this case the business entity still has to pay its fixed costs; b) Exit: Continuous losses in the long run decision leads to give up the business. – Obviously this leads to an end of paying fixed and variable costs.

3.1.12. Profit

Short definition: "The profit results from the total revenue minus the total cost." [136]

It sounds quite simple with this profit-parameter. Let's take a corporation: every month they get a profit on a level of one billion €/$. Do you think they simply leave this money in a bank account until the end of the year or the day they have to distribute slices from this cake to the shareholders? No! They can make more profit with the profit by speculating, betting, financing short-term money demand in the market…… 'casino' games, etc.

With a daily, weekly or monthly 'surplus' identified as part of the final profit

---

[134] Colander, p. 328
[135] Mankiw (et al.), p. 293-294
[136] Mankiw (et al.), p. 265-269

of the year, they also can sell some of their products at dumping prices to eliminate a competitor or to attract masses for the sale of their other products. They can even use their cash flow for such hidden businesses with cash money they will need for upcoming bills (days or weeks later). Always a corporation can play games with any amount of money they have in their account (or virtually) and this every day, week or month.

Maximize Profit: Profit = Total revenue minus the total cost

Normal profit: the minimum amount required to keep factors of production in their current use

"…Normal profit is built into the costs of the firm." [137]

Abnormal profit: the profit over and above normal profit

Economic profit: the explicit and implicit revenue minus the explicit and implicit cost

Alarm bells: Here something is wrong with the profit definition:

- Costs are costs, fixed costs and variable costs; and profit is not a cost; it's the cake!
- Revenue is the money that comes in from the sale of goods or services.
- Revenue can also be money that comes in from other activities, not related to sales.
- The prices of goods must cover at least the costs; and added with the profit.
- Nowhere it is said how the profit is calculated on the side of the price of a product.

→ There are the costs.
→ There must be a profit.
→ There is a product price.
→ There is revenue of sold products or services.
→ There may be revenue from other activities.
→ Therefore part of the revenue must be calculated as the profit.
→ Therefore the price of a product must be higher than the production cost.
→ The profit is logically part of the price.
→ How much is the profit-part of the product price?

---

[137] Colander, p. 330

A firm calculates the production costs for a specific amount of a good. From there the firm determines the price for one good. Profit is a must and therefore the firm adds for example 3% profit (or 12% as abnormal profit) as 'profit' on the price for one good.

There is also a risk that not the entire amount of produced goods can be sold. Therefore the risk must also be included in the final price of the good. For that risk another 3-6% of the price of a good must be added. With such a calculation, the final price always includes the profit margin (can be normal or abnormal) and a sale risk (probably abnormal). If the firm sells the entire amount of goods, then we could call the final profit, 'abnormal profit'. No?

→ Who knows what fact is? Fact is the maxim: 'get as much profit as you can'. Cleverness and creativity is required to become the winner in the market.

A calculation of a product price could be:

Price per product = calculated production cost + profit margin + sale risk margin + allocation cost (understood as distribution) + intermediary cost + final seller cost

→ Don't be naïve: The profit of a small firm and the cost calculation is something completely different compared to the networks of big business operations.
→ Corporations can move around a 'profit' between entities and countries in order to reduce profit and therefore tax costs. There are many manipulative methods of accounting.

There is a profit-maximizing level of output: "Since profit is the difference between total revenue and total cost, what happens to profit in response to a change in output is determined by marginal revenue (MR), the change in total revenue associated with a change in quantity, and marginal cost (MC), the change in total cost associated with a change in quantity. That's why marginal revenue and marginal cost are key concepts in determining the profit-maximizing or loss-minimizing level of output of any firm." [138]

→ Something is hidden and misleading here: "…profit is the difference between total revenue and total cost…"
→ The profit is never a 'cost' and therefore the definition of the term is not correct, it is hiding the real way of calculating and placing the profit-

---

[138] Colander, p. 322

parameter.

The single units of this statement include:

- Increase in output (quantity) generates marginal (increase in) revenue.
- Increase in output (quantity) generates higher total revenue.
- To increase an output a firm needs to give in a certain additional input.
- An increase of input increases the total costs.
- Therefore there is a marginal cost and marginal revenue.
- Loss-minimizing (or better avoiding loss) is an indispensable requirement.
- Profit-maximizing is an indispensable aim also by a marginal increase of output.

"To maximize profit, a firm should produce where marginal cost equals marginal revenue." [139] Seen as a formula:

- Profit Maximization is determined by: MC = MR

Another expert writes: "This rich variety of motives, most goods and services that are offered for sale in a market economy are sold by private firms whose main reason for existing is to earn profit for their owners. A firm's profit is the difference between the total revenue it receives from the sale of its product and all costs it incurs in producing it." [140] We doubt that the main reason for existing is to earn profit for their owners. The definition of profit is not correct as profit is not a production (input) 'cost'.

→ This is a manipulation: This formula does not generate profit because the price of the product must be higher than the cost of production. Again: Profit is not a production cost!

The author continues with profit maximization: "If marginal revenue does not equal marginal cost, a firm can increase profit by changing output. Notice that when you talk about maximizing profit, you're talking about maximizing total profit, not profit per unit. Profit per unit would be maximized at a much lower output level than is total profit. Profit-maximizing firms don't care about profit per unit; as long as an increase in output will increase total profits, a profit-maximizing firm should increase output." [141]

We get here complete transparency about profit maximization:

---

[139] Colander, p. 323
[140] McDowell (et al.), p. 164
[141] Colander, p. 324

- Marginal revenue must be equal to the marginal cost (or higher).
- Marginal profit per unit (product) is included in the price of the product.
- Maximizing total profit is of highest importance.
- An increase in output must increase total profits.
- A profit-maximizing firm always should increase output.

→ The profit percentage does not have to be the same for an increased output and for the standard amount of production. There are hidden (unspoken) flexibilities here.

The author confirms the 'greatest profit' as the aim of a firm: "Total profit is maximized where the vertical distance between total revenue and total cost is greatest." [142]

And he explains the strategic decision aiming to maximize profit: "To determine maximum profit, you must first determine what output the firm will choose to produce by seeing where MC equals MR and then determine the average total cost..." [143]

→ Economic advice: You must choose products or product combinations with lowest production costs and highest possible profit.
→ There is no concern about the importance of the goods that people need or of goods that are useful. You can produce anything that you can sell; the only thing that counts in economics is profit.

3.1.13. Fixed Costs

Short definition: It encompasses the total costs (all the expenses) that are not determined by the quantity of output produced. [144]

"Fixed costs are costs that are spent and cannot be changed in the period of time under consideration. There are no fixed costs in the long run since all inputs are variable and hence their costs are variable. In the short run, however, a number of costs will be fixed." [145]

- There are fixed costs of variables (factors) with low levels.
- There are fixed costs of variables (factors) with high levels.

---

[142] Colander, p. 327
[143] Colander, p. 328
[144] Mankiw (et al.), p. 273-275
[145] Colander, p. 283

➔ The bigger the amount of variables with fixed costs on a high level, the better financial planning for a limited period of time is practicable and reliable.
➔ Fixed costs of variables with low level are not important as they have much less weight in the list of costs.

3.1.14. Variable Costs

Short definition: It encompasses the costs that are dependent on the quantity of output produced. It is understood that the amount of produced goods is variable. [146] "Fixed and variable costs depend on the time scale." [147]

➔ Is the profit percentage calculation per product a 'variable cost'?

Labor is a variable cost: "…must also hire workers. These workers are the earring firm's variable costs - costs that change as output changes." [148]

➔ The conclusion is: If the output decreases, fire workers!
➔ The question is: How much does the output have to change until a worker is fired?
➔ The market is always a carousel: demand increases and decreases for many reasons.
➔ Hire workers, when you can make profit and fire them if you can't anymore.
➔ In the cost models we can't find any suggestion that promotes sustainability.
➔ The model itself is unsustainable, unbalanced, rigid, and compulsive-addictive.

3.1.15. Average Total Cost

Colander presents three cost models: [149]

1) "Average cost equals total cost divided by quantity … For example, average total cost (often called average cost) equals total cost divided by the quantity produced."

---

[146] Mankiw (et al.), p. 273-275
[147] Mankiw (et al.), p. 279
[148] Colander, p. 284
[149] Colander, p. 284

2) "Average fixed cost equals fixed cost divided by quantity produced."

3) "Average variable cost equals variable cost divided by quantity produced."

'Average total cost' refers to the amount of produced goods and is calculated by the total cost divided by the quantity of output (output, we interpret: produced goods). The single elements or 'variables' of calculation are:

- Total cost
- Average cost
- Average fixed cost
- Average variable cost
- Quantity produced

There are more possibilities in the real production: 10, 100 or 1,000 different products. With such different business production entities the cost picture changes completely.

In general a model for cost calculation is helpful and for most businesses a relevant matter. Many small businesses fail due to neglecting a professional cost analysis. But there are businesses, especially small firms and service firms, where such a model moves within a very small frame.

3.1.16. Average Fixed Cost

This term focuses on the average price of one produced good. The fixed costs are divided by the quantity of output goods (output, we interpret: produced goods).

There is another picture that needs to be considered in this context as some variable costs can be calculated as fixed costs:

Price per product = calculated fixed production cost + fixed profit margin + fixed sale risk margin + fixed allocation (distribution) cost + fixed intermediary cost + fixed seller cost

➔ We must interpret the term 'fixed cost' as costs that are really fixed during a longer period.

3.1.17. Average Variable Cost

We interpret: The costs are variable depending on the amount of the produced good. The variable costs are divided by the quantity of output. Unclear is what else makes the costs variable; e.g. electricity, water, and other production inputs. We suppose: Raw material, electricity, water, other goods for production can vary in their price at any time.

There is another picture that needs to be considered in this context:

Price per product = calculated variable production cost + variable profit margin + variable sale risk margin + variable allocation cost + variable intermediary cost + variable seller cost

→ Calculating average variable costs must be seen within a time frame and possible interventions on all sides (production volume and costs and sale price per unit and in total).

3.1.18. Marginal Cost

The term focuses on the increase in total cost that arises from an extra unit of production. The cost of an extra unit is called 'marginal cost'. Marginal cost rises with the quantity of (extra) output produced.

A marginal cost is: "Marginal cost is the increase (or decrease?) in total cost from increasing (or decreasing?) the level of output by one unit." [150]

Let's now consider the relationship between marginal product and marginal cost: "When marginal cost exceeds average cost, average cost must be rising. When marginal cost is less than average cost, average cost must be falling." [151]

→ We conclude that increasing the level of output should generate less than average cost to get highest possible profit.

3.1.19. Production Function

Short definition: "Production function (is) the relationship between quantity of inputs used to make a good and the quantity of output of that good." [152]

There is a production function. Krugman (et al.) writes in six statements: [153]
1) A production function is the relationship between the quantity of inputs a

---

[150] Colander, p. 285
[151] Colander, p. 287
[152] Mankiw (et al.), p. 269
[153] Krugman (et al.), p. 170

firm uses and the quantity of output it produces.

2) A fixed input is an input whose quantity is fixed for a period of time and cannot be varied.

3) A variable input is an input whose quantity the firm can vary at any time.

4) The long run is the time period in which all inputs can be varied.

5) The short run is the time period in which at least one input is fixed.

6) The total product curve shows how the quantity of output depends on the quantity of the variable input, for a given quantity of the fixed input.

The production functions consist of several variables:

- Quantity of inputs for production: fixed or variable
- Quantity of outputs that is produced
- A period of time: short term or long term

The thesis is: The quantity of output depends on the quantity of the variable input, for a given quantity of the fixed input.

In other words: A given quantity of a fixed input determines the quantity of output. And logically: if the input changes, also the output changes. Or: The amount of input determines the amount of output. It sounds a bit banal or simply obvious. The hidden message may be: Try to maximize the output with a minimum of input. Here we are again: profit maximizing! A more reasonable statement would be:

➔ Use the amount of input, fixed or variable, in the best way to succeed in the business.

Is it really always reasonable to squeeze out every possible micro drop out of a lemon? 'To get the most you can' in everything in life and business can break at a certain point human's dignity and mental health. It also induces cheating or abuse with all disposable (immoral) means. Such advice hidden in the 'production function' can never be sustainable in the world of business and in the society as a whole. It expresses the lunacy of dominating, controlling, and exploiting (economically and politically) every vivid and non-vivid thing on earth. And worst of all it's not even a scientific theory.

Inputs and Output can be flexible considering the 'margins': "The marginal product of an input is the additional quantity of output that is produced by using one more unit of that input." [154]

→ Here we have, as usual everywhere, the 'lemon' to squeeze out: Wherever you can, identify or introduce a possible marginal element (plus or minus) to get a higher profit.

"A fixed cost is a cost that does not depend on the quantity of output produced. It is the cost of the fixed input … A variable cost is a cost that depends on the quantity of output produced. It is the cost of the variable input." [155]

Indeed, there are fixed input costs independent from the amount of the quantity of output. But a variable cost (input) does not always and only regulates the quantity of output. For example, cleaning staff or a reception employee, a security service, the costs for electricity using a hundred computers, Internet access, or costs for business travel do not (directly) influence the output.

→ This statement is irritating and is driven by compulsion: Never let a cost occur that does not increase the output and / or the profit.

In this context the author mentions another principle or 'law': "The total cost of producing a given quantity of output is the sum of the fixed cost and the variable cost of producing that quantity of output." [156]

→ Kindergarten calculation! Is there something untrue or hidden? There must be something hidden!
→ Maybe there are exceptions: The total cost of producing a given quantity of output is not always the sum of the fixed cost and the variable cost of producing that quantity of output.

"The marginal cost of producing a good or service is the additional cost incurred by producing one more unit of that good or service." [157]

In other words: One more unit of a good or service that is produced has an additional marginal cost. This presumes that the input is already fully up to the extreme use for production. Only in that case is the statement correct.

---

[154] Krugman (et al.), p. 171
[155] Krugman (et al.), p. 175
[156] Krugman (et al.), p. 175
[157] Krugman (et al.), p. 178

Whatever the 'quantity of inputs' means (e.g. labor, machines, electricity, raw material, etc.) it has an increase (or decrease) of costs and must have an additional profit percentage per product and in total. Profit calculation is not simply a figure; it is a percentage per product from the standard amount of production and the additional amount of produced goods.

We assume that an economist tends to require that the percentage of profit per additional product (in the price) should not be lower than the percentage of profit per product (in the price) of the standard production. If the percentage of profit per product from an additional production is lower, then the total percentage of profit per (all) products (output) becomes smaller; and this percentage decrease of profit an economist will not want.

→ The production function ignores the percentage fraction of profit per product price.
→ It is rather an ideal to assume that all firms always operate with 100% balance between costs (inputs) and quantity of products (output).

3.1.20. Efficient Scale

Short definition: A certain amount or quantity of goods has an optimal price at given fixed costs.

Producing fewer goods increases the average price of a produced good as the total costs remain unchanged. Producing more goods can also increase the price of these additional goods as they produce more costs per unit than the optimal production quantity per unit. Therefore there is a certain quantity of output that minimizes (optimizes at lowest level) the average total cost.

→ Conclusion: The production capacities of given fixed costs should always be fully exploited to get an optimal price.

This view has an importance in many small and medium sized firms of all kind of production and services as a guideline:

- Restaurant: Put as many tables and chairs as the size of the premises allow.
- Shop: Put as many products on the shelves as physically possible.
- Manager: It is a waste of money (costs) if his office has a size of 100 m2.
- Hotel: Use the reception area for business and not for 'hanging around'.
- Every office m2 costs money; therefore generate money with every m2.
- Waiting rooms must be as small as possible because every m2 has a cost.
- Leased machines are operational 24/7 as on stand-by there is no profit.

- Production facilities: Every m2 must contribute to the production process.
- Bathrooms must be small as they don't generate profit and every m2 costs.

→ If you want to maximize profit, you must consider the capacities of machines and tools and the economic efficiency of every square meter and of all infrastructures, including furniture ... until the borderline where you get mad from compulsion, avarice, and greed.

3.1.21. Total Cost

Short definition: This is about "the market value of all the inputs a firm uses in production." [158]

A specific good may include many different and independent frames (firms):

- Raw material production
- Semi-production (production of parts)
- Production process entity (final product)
- Storage firms
- Intermediary trade
- Allocation firms (distribution)
- Sale firms

→ We must be aware that the total cost is related to a specific frame and not always to the end-price of a good in the store.

3.1.22. Opportunity Costs

Economists use the word 'costs' in a special verbal construction: 'opportunity costs'. It is the base of a decision for one business (opportunity) between two possible business (opportunities). It's all about: which of the business (opportunities) brings more profit. Economists include both when measuring a firm's cost; accountants consider only the real costs. The costs of capital also form part of the opportunity costs (and it always does of the explicit costs).

An extensive description is: "Opportunity cost was the benefit forgone of the next-best alternative ... It is essentially the marginal utility per dollar you forgo from the consumption of the next-best alternative ... The principle of rational choice states that, to maximize utility, choose goods until the

[158] Mankiw (et al.), p. 265-269

opportunity costs of all alternatives are equal ... The more you 'really, really need' something, the higher its marginal utility." [159]

Thinking in terms of 'opportunity costs' has a psychological implication: it can become a compulsion for business people and for consumers. But obviously its makes sense to consider 'opportunity costs' in a decision making process when acquiring a business or in deciding about the products to produce; or for consumers in their decision making about buying a specific good or another one that matches with the need or the want.

We have extensively explored the 'opportunity costs' in Economics I.

3.1.23. Producer Surplus

Short definition: This term means "the amount a seller is paid for a good minus the seller's cost (of this good)."

We interpret: 'seller' = 'producer'; but it is not clear in the statement. The seller is not always the producer. But we can say: The producer is the seller of his goods to an intermediary or a sale entity.

The term does not say, that there is not always a surplus; but in reality it can happen that there is a 'producer minus'. Of course, as Mankiw (et al.) says, the "producer surplus measures (shows) the wellbeing of sellers". Wellbeing is generated by profit.

The author also says: "Sellers always want to receive a higher price for the goods they sell."

How much does the seller's wellbeing rise in response to a higher or lower price? In other words: the more producer surplus, the happier the seller (producer). 'Wellbeing' and 'happiness' are very critical terms in this context. Is it really true that all sellers always want a higher price? Are all sellers that profit obsessed, greedy and compulsive?

The 'surplus mania' pushes the producer in a permanent stressful battle and nasty compulsion: surplus ... more surpluses ... much more surpluses ... That's sick! If we add here the scarcity hysteria, then it becomes madness: "Oh my God, there is a raw material (or electricity or water or agricultural land) scarcity and I must get more surplus. How can I get more surplus?" [160]

---

[159] Colander, p. 241
[160] Mankiw (et al.), p. 144

3.1.24. Economies of Scale

Short general definition: If the quantity of an output of goods increases, the long-run average total cost can decrease.

In economic words: "The property whereby long-run average total cost falls as the quantity of output increases." [161]

→ This theory presumes that the capacities of the input or a margin input at lower price allow for an increase of production.
→ It may mean: Purchasing a higher amount of raw material allows a lower price per unit and therefore the cost of production per unit falls.

3.1.25. Diseconomies of Scale

Short definition: If the quantity of an output of goods increases, the long-run average total cost can increase.

In economic words: "The property whereby long-run average total cost rises as the quantity of output increases." [162]

→ It may simply mean: More production has higher input costs.

In general these statements make clear what everybody may know: the bigger the production firm, the lower is the price of their goods. And as a consequence, small production firms never have a chance to compete with bigger firms (producing the same goods). The implications for a society are disastrous! That's why for example organic vegetables (organic fruits, organic meat, etc.) are expensive and not affordable for the masses of people with low wages.

→ The industrial development and the development of the thousands of corporations have reached a point where they destroy the world of businesses and its business culture, the society in general, the quality of food for example, and human's mind and soul.
→ That's why we have for example hundreds of millions of tons of nuclear waste nobody knows how to safely store for millenniums and maintain for a million of years. The cost of this is an externality to be paid by countless future generations. A disgrace of economics and politics!

---

[161] Mankiw (et al.), p. 279
[162] Mankiw (et al.), p. 279

3.1.26. Constant Returns of Scale

Short definition: If the quantity of an output of goods is stable, the long-run average total cost can be stable.

In economic words: "The property whereby long-run average total cost stays the same as the quantity of output changes." [163]

It is not clear in this statement ('law') if the output increases or decreases. The business interest is obvious: Get stable costs by the maximum reachable production.

In general, as everything in the world is changing very fast, and no price of whatever is invariable for eternity, a firm always must consider when making calculations: "… any decisions are fixed in the short run but variable in the long run..." [164]

Whatever changes, and there are always some changes in specific cost factors, the profit also always changes in the sense that it must increase every year but sometimes it decreases. Therefore the source of the call for economic growth lies in the profit maximizing greed.

→ Compulsion of greed arises here: Constant return of scale is boring and not satisfying as it does not increase profit in the long-term.

3.2. Consumers Making Choices

3.2.1. Consumer Surplus

The term 'consumer surplus' means: "the amount a buyer is willing to pay for a good minus the amount the buyer actually pays for it." [165]
"…buyers always want to pay less for the goods they buy; a lower price makes the buyer of a good better off." And "Consumer surplus is a good measure of economic well-being…" [166]

---

[163] Mankiw (et al.), p. 278
[164] Mankiw (et al.) p. 278
[165] Mankiw (et al.), p. 139
[166] Mankiw (et al.), p. 143

Above we cited a statement: Sellers always want more profit. And now we have the consumer that always wants to pay less. Isn't that a mad world? And: Is it really true, always and everywhere?

In the words of another author: "Individual consumer surplus is the net gain to an individual buyer from the purchase of a good. It is equal to the difference between the buyer's willingness to pay and the price paid ... Total consumer surplus is the sum of the individual consumer surpluses of all the buyers of a good in a market ... The term consumer surplus is often used to refer to both individual and total consumer surplus." [167]

The gains from trade are understood by Krugman (et al.): "The total surplus generated in a market is the total net gain to consumers and producers from trading in the market. It is the sum of the consumer and the producer surplus." [168]

Let's identify the single elements in these statements:

- There is an amount, a buyer is willing to pay for a good
- There is an amount a buyer actually pays for a good
- Buyers always want to pay less for a good they buy
- A lower price makes buyers of a good better off
- Value to buyers: The amount a buyer is willing to pay for a good
- Consumer surplus: Value to buyers minus the amount paid by buyers
- Consumer surplus measures the economic wellbeing
- There is an individual and a total consumer surplus
- There is a net gain to consumers
- There is a net gain to producers
- There is a total consumer surplus: the sum of the individual consumer surpluses of all the buyers of a good in a market

➜ If there is no consumer surplus then there is no economic wellbeing of the people.
➜ As people always want to pay less, there is never economic wellbeing in society.
➜ The net gain to consumers is not the same as the net gain to producers.

Example 1: A consumer is willing to pay €2 for a coffee. The coffee costs €1.50. In this case the buyer is better off and gets an economic wellbeing.

---

[167] Krugman (et al.), p. 99
[168] Krugman (et al.), p. 103

Example 2: A consumer is willing to pay €1 for a coffee. The coffee costs €2.00. In this case the buyer is extremely worse off and doesn't get an economic wellbeing.

Critical Question: Is the 'consumer surplus' theory applicable for all kinds of goods and services?
Critical Question: Is the 'consumer surplus' already relevant at a price difference of cents?
Critical Question: Is the 'consumer surplus' relevant only from a difference of 5% or of 20%?

Such an approach about 'consumer surplus' provokes some more questions:

1. What does 'willingness' mean?
2. What previously (before going shopping) forms this 'willingness'?
3. Is the 'willingness' formed within (through) a purchase pattern?
4. Does 'willingness' always lead to an action?
5. Under which circumstances does 'willingness' not lead to an action?
6. What can change the willingness within (through) a purchase pattern?
7. Is it true that consumers always want to pay less for a good?
8. Is it appropriate to consider that consumers always want to pay less for a good?
9. Are people really aware about their willingness (highest price willing to pay)?
10. If the price matches the highest price willing to pay, is then there wellbeing?
11. Is the lower price (than the highest price willing to pay) that creates a state of 'wellbeing'?
12. Is it true that a higher price puts the consumer in a state of 'non-wellbeing'?

Willingness to pay the maximum amount that a buyer will pay for a good:

Willingness means: Having a formed will and the ability to take decision regarding this will; based on this will accepting and disposed, prepared, inclined, being decisive, and ready to buy.

Willingness does not necessarily lead to an action. Willingness includes the 'free will'; a 'forced' or 'manipulated' will is not really a 'will'. A 'will' includes the understanding of the focus of a will-activity. There must be also a particular situation operating as a motive. Or: willingness always includes a motive, a decision, and an ability to act. Certain sale situations (shopping environment) can stimulate willingness to an action. To stimulate a willingness to buy only makes sense if the consumer can buy the product.

→ Many shopping behavior (habits) proceed without an aware willingness and without a rational decision.
→ Willingness must always include a motive, a decision, an ability to act, and an opportunity to act.

There are always people that want to pay less for more; some are dreamers, others are barefaced, and many are ignorant or arrogant. Too many people have 'wants' and want to get them without having worked for them or for much less than the production value. Too many people get 'things' that they do not deserve with robbery-attitudes.

→ The attitude of people 'always to want to pay less for a good they buy' is an attitude of exploitation, avarice, impertinence, disrespect, greed, and of stealing.

Above that: How does this economic science measure the consumer's 'wellbeing' or 'non-wellbeing' as an emotional state resulting from a willingness-situation? There is 'wellbeing' for seconds and wellbeing for hours and wellbeing for days or longer. And there are thousands of different goods with thousands of different prices, and thousands of different sale situations.

Remember what we said about the consumer characteristics, the consumer population, the mind and the dynamic of the unconscious mind, the external influences, the self-management, and the manifoldness of consumer goods, the varieties of individual bundles, the culture (lifestyle) of consumers, and the development of life. And add: willingness, awareness of price-differences (a price willing to pay and the market price of a good).

Now ask yourself: Does this 'consumer surplus' really work as a general principle or scientific law (theory) in the real world of consumption? It does not! It is incomprehensible how economic scientists can frivolously deal with such psychological matters (factors) of high importance.

→ The consumer surplus parameter may make sense for certain products, but certainly not for all kind of products on the market.
In the best case we can refer this kind of vague 'wellbeing' for peoples with very narrow and suffocating economic resources; for example those workers or poor people that are used to pay maximum one €/$ or 80 cents for a coffee.

Especially in tourist areas one can experience a situation of 'negative consumer surplus': On a menu it is written that the lunch menu costs €7.00. People are delighted and go there for lunch. They also order a small bottle of water (3.5dl), and when they get the bill they see that the water costs €4. This indeed creates a 'non-wellbeing' due to the standard 'unwillingness' to pay for water. But then the consumers must pay as they have already consumed the water.

Finally, most people have a fixed budget, and depending on the amount of the budget, they have more or less or not even a slight amount of a free will or a freely chosen willingness.

The question is, why does economics give importance to such a strange parameter, called 'consumer surplus' that is related to well-being? Compulsive economists always try to find the tiniest bit of a possible 'movement' in consumer's mind while shopping in the interest of more profit.

→ Consumer surplus is about: Economists want to find a clue where to start with controlling and manipulating people's willingness to accept a price.
→ Consumers' wellbeing is not the aim of economics; it is simply to find out the right price range for a product in order to sell as much as possible of a good and to maximize profit.

3.2.2. Consumer Choice

"(Consumers) have limited incomes but unlimited wants and the second is that they prefer to have more than less." [169]

We identify here two assertions:

- People have unlimited wants

  Comment: I have already explored this topic in Chapter 4 and the result is that this assertion is wrong. Human's biology and human's healthy mind sets limits oriented on the disposition.

- People prefer more than less

  Comment: If mentally healthy people have limited wants and if nature also tends to balance the 'more and less', then this assertion is also wrong and

---

[169] Mankiw (et al.), p. 439-465

useless in the real world.

→ It is the marketing of thousands of goods that boosts the attitude 'you must have it'. Marketing destroys the natural limits people have for wants. To 'prefer more than less' is the result of bursting the healthy limits and natural tendency to create balance.

"The budget constraint … shows what combination of goods the consumer can afford given his income and the price of the goods … The consumer's choices, however, depends … also on his preferences regarding (…) two goods." [170]

We interpret: The people's budget is limited. People have a thousand options to combine their bundle of goods within their limited budget. The consumer choices allow certain flexibility in choosing between two goods. Personal preferences direct the choice between two optional goods.

What for does this ascertainment serve? It's again the clue that a compulsive economist tries to find and aims to influence the choice between two preferred goods.

About preferences the author says also: "Different consumption bundles can give the consumer the same level of satisfaction." [171]

→ Therefore the practical interest from a producer is: How can I get the consumer to buy my good and not the good from a competitor if he has a willingness to choose between both goods?

It is obvious that the producer doesn't want to let the consumer choose freely and without manipulations. The consumer must be directed, in whatever way, in order to buy the good of interest from a specific firm. Where does this lead if all firms around the globe operate with any kind of manipulating consumers for all their goods? Pure sickness! The world is going mad!

---

[170] Mankiw (et al.), p. 439-465
[171] Mankiw (et al.), p. 440

3.2.3. Utility Theory and Individual Choice

"Freudian psychology tells us we do what we do because of an internal fight between the id, ego, and superego plus some hang-ups we have about our bodies. Other psychologists tell us it's a search for approval by our peers; we want to be OK. Economists agree that these are important reasons but argue that if we want an analysis that's simple enough to apply to policy problems, these heavy psychological explanations are likely to get us all mixed up." [172]

In Chapter 1 and 2 we have explored the human being from many sides, many psychological and spiritual (meaning-focus) factors, many compositions of household, ways of living, different life standards, and in that context the processes of individual choices (decision making). Freudian theories and peer-group-behavior is only a small section of the entire field of what makes a human to be a human and which factors influence human's consumer behavior.

Certainly, psychological faculty is not the duty of economics. But fact is that professional marketing operates with the most advanced knowledge of psychology, especially of the unconscious mind. Fact is also that humans (economists, scientists of economics) make the economic theories and also humans realize the concrete market (economic realities). Fact is furthermore that the real world of economics (businesses, consume) is for humans.

➔ We can even say that the concrete economic world creates the unconditional (indispensable) frame of life of humans.

The car industry, for example, has enormously improved the safety of driving and drastically reduced fatalities and accidents in general. Above that, the car industry could not sell cars without a network of driving schools and many other services. And this means: a license is necessary to be allowed to drive a car. The production of cars, and with that the entire private car traffic systems, have thoroughly shaped human's life. – There are hundreds of other products that shape the everyday life of humans and the entire society.

➔ We conclude from this example: Human factors are intrinsic in economics and must take on much more importance in all theories, 'laws', and concepts.

The concrete economics must consider human factors and the possible

---

[172] Colander, p. 231

damages (also safety, health) that could occur with humans dealing with appliances, medicine, etc. This normative statement refers also to possible damages in humans mind and soul and between humans (social factors) as the concrete economics shapes human's mind, human's behavior and lives, and the entire society as the frame of living and humane development.

→ An economic understanding of satisfaction and wellbeing does not comply with this systemic requirement which includes responsibility for humans and society.

An economic author answers: "Much of what people do reflects their rational self-interest. That's why economists start their analysis of individual choice with a relatively simple, but powerful, underlying psychological foundation." [173]

In a previous chapter we already analyzed the topic of 'individual choice': The concept of 'individual choice' is not only simple, but it is an immense reduction of human's psychological reality leading to a complete deformation (distortion) of reality about the individual choice.

The concept of 'individual choice' may be powerful through its simplification, but it distorts human's reality. Therefore the concept 'individual choice' is in the core absolutely not powerful as it ignores most human factors that influence individual choice.

→ The psychological foundation of economic theories has got nothing much to do with the complexity of psychology and human's mind and soul.

3.2.4. Utility

Colander explains the term 'utility' in an economic way: "(is) ... the pleasure or satisfaction people get from doing or consuming something and the price of doing or consuming that something. Price is the tool the market uses to bring the quantity supplied equal to the quantity demanded. Changes in price provide incentives for people to change what they're doing. Through those incentives, the invisible hand guides us all. To understand economics, you must understand how price affects our choices." [174]

The elements of this statement are:

- Pleasure of satisfaction

---

[173] Colander, p. 231
[174] Colander, p. 233

- Consuming creates pleasure of satisfaction
- The price of doing or consuming something
- There is a quantity supplied
- There is a quantity of demand
- There are changes in price
- Changes in price provide incentives
- Incentives intend to change what consumers do
- There are many possible incentives
- The invisible hand guides us all
- Prices affect our choices
- Prices affect in different ways our choices

We have here 12 variables and each variable has a scale. If we consider the manifoldness of goods and services, and also the economic interests of the producers, we also can say: 12 variables, each with a scale, can lead to a scientific approach to different results between all the goods.

→ The generalized understanding of 'utility' ignores the intrinsic differences between people and goods or services, even ignores the mutual effects between the market of one good and the rest of the goods on the market. The factor 'producer interest' is also ignored.

"Economists use the concept of utility to represent the satisfaction people derive from their consumption activities. The assumption is that people try to allocate their incomes so as to maximize their satisfaction, a goal that is referred to as utility maximization." [175]

- The word 'satisfaction from consumption activities' is very vague.
- People often don't try to allocate their incomes to maximize their satisfaction.
- 'Utility maximization' is not the way that people think.
- Is 'satisfaction' here price-related or related to the good that provides satisfaction?

→ The term 'satisfaction is a catch-all term and does not say anything of significant relevance.

Another critical approach: 'pleasure' and 'satisfaction' is not the same. 'Doing or consuming something' is not the same. Both terms have a very extensive connotation and can be referred to biological, psychical, spiritual, or even working matters.

---

[175] McDowell (et al.), p. 128

'The market uses the price: The market is neither a person nor any intelligent being bringing the quantity supplied equal to the quantity demanded. We should instead say: Money and the function of maximizing profit rule the market.

'Changes in price provide incentives for people': It is not identifiable what is meant by 'incentives'. A change in price can mean an increase or decrease of price. There is no proof given that incentives always or with high (or lower) probability direct 'people to change what they're doing'. It depends a lot on the kind of good or service.

The term 'incentive' is used here in a generalized way, which does not operate in all market segments of goods and services. As a parameter it is not clarified here what kind of incentive and what level (volume) of margin of an incentive have to determine the extension of the variable. And there is no 'invisible hand' as we already extensively analyzed in Economics I.

→ All these statements about 'utility' are nothing more than a speculative modeling in an undifferentiated way. This is not the way a social science should operate.

3.2.5. Total Utility and Marginal Utility

Another statement from Colander: 'Total utility and marginal utility': "In thinking about utility, it's important to distinguish between total utility and marginal utility. Total utility refers to the total satisfaction one gets from consuming a product. Marginal utility refers to the satisfaction one gets from consuming one additional unit of a product above and beyond what one has consumed up to that point." [176]

The 'total satisfaction one gets from consuming a product' sounds exciting: 'finally totally satisfied'! But how can we measure a 100%, 80%, 60% or 35% satisfaction of physical, mental, emotional, or spiritual importance?

'Consuming a product' sounds like being about eating or drinking; many people eat or drink too much to finally have a sensation of 100% satisfaction; or in other words: they need an additional 'marginal utility' to be satisfied. Some people 'consume' sex and therefore here we could say: 'The orgasm is the total satisfaction'. There is an enormous difference between a 'technical orgasm' and having sex and an orgasm with true love. Is it really? Some

---

[176] Colander, p. 233

233

people want 'more of it' all night or weekend long; and therefore this 'sign' of sexual satisfaction is also relative.

→ All these statements are nothing more than hot air; or where required, adaptable for specific products or interests.

The principle of diminishing marginal utility says: "As you consume more of a good, after some point, the marginal utility received from each additional unit of a good decreases with each additional unit consumed, other things equal."

The idea of a 'diminishing marginal utility' does make sense as a 'deficit-satisfaction-dynamic' which is always an energetic phenomenon (discussed in the psychology of motivation and the bio-psychology of sexuality): "The principle of diminishing marginal utility states that, after some point, the marginal utility received from each additional unit of a good decreases with each additional unit consumed, other things equal." [177]

Example: John drinks a bottle of beer and then he is 80% satisfied; he needs some more, and with each gulp the sensation of satisfaction increases; and after 20 more gulps he is finally 100% satisfied. Indeed, this happens every day everywhere. The stomach or the alcohol is here the 'invisible hand' controlling the process of satisfaction and saying 'now full satisfaction is reached'.

The consumer sensation: "…the principle of diminishing marginal utility does not say that you don't enjoy consuming more of a good; it simply states that as you consume more of the good, you enjoy the additional units less than you did the initial units." [178]

→ Probe required: 'You enjoy the additional units less than you did the initial units'. Without knowing which good is meant here, we can't find any sense in such a statement.
→ We could conclude in general: All needs are satisfiable, some people need more and others less to reach full satisfaction; and some people need a marginal utility to get fully satisfied.
→ Marginal utility is applied for many kind of goods. Therefore, if there is a diminishing marginal utility, then there also must be for some goods a continuous marginal utility.

We can make two formulas which create a new problem:

[177] Colander, p. 233
[178] Colander, p. 233

- A standard amount (volume, level, intensity) leads to 100% satisfaction
- Some people additionally need a 'marginal utility' to get 100% satisfaction

→ Who knows what the standard amount (volume, level, intensity) for all people and all goods or services is that provides 100% satisfaction?
→ Where does the theoretical limit of a 'marginal utility' lie in order to get 100% satisfaction?

3.2.6. Rational Choice and Marginal utility

"The analysis of rational choice is the analysis of how individuals choose goods within their budget in order to maximize total utility, and how maximizing total utility can be accomplished by considering marginal utility.

That analysis begins with the premise that rational individuals want as much satisfaction as they can get from their available resources.

The term rational in economics means, specifically, that people prefer more to less and will make choices that give them as much satisfaction as possible. The problem is that people face a budget constraint. They must choose among the alternatives … Because people face a budget constraint, they must choose among alternatives." [179]

We identify here several different statements:

- Individuals choose goods within their budget

  Comment: Common sense, but only partly true: People can ask for a loan and a loan is not simply part of the budget.

- Individuals choose goods in order to maximize total utility

  Comment: 'Total utility' means total satisfaction and 'total satisfaction' is very relative as it can mean duration of satisfaction for minutes, hours, days or weeks. Total satisfaction is also very relative to the people's mind, character, ethics, and life philosophy.

- Maximizing total utility can be accomplished by considering marginal utility
  Comment: This we already commented above. The very critical part of this statement is 'maximizing'. As there are always individual differences it is

---

[179] Colander, p. 233

not possible to determine the standard and the maximum.

As maximum total utility has no objective measure here, it doesn't make sense to introduce a 'marginal utility'. People can choose a good and this good, measured in quality or quantity, gives them the maximum satisfaction whereat 'maximum' is always a subjective measure on many levels, for countless products and all price ranges.

- Rational individuals want as much satisfaction as they can get from their available resources

  Comment: Individuals that always want as much satisfaction as they can get, are in most cases mentally imbalanced people, if not neurotic people. Such people are not 'rational'. To say that people always or mostly run for 'as much satisfaction as they can get' is simply absurd. The part 'available resources' can refer to their budget or to the market offers (available goods, prices). 'Satisfaction' or 'economic satisfaction' is a very diffuse and primitive term.

- The term 'rational' means: people prefer more to less

  Comment: 'Rational' means: using intelligence, thinking, and calculating, interpreting, concluding, and logical thinking. 'Rationality' means: Utilization of reason or logic. Do people really always or mostly or 'very often' use their rational mind potential in taking choices? 'Prefer more to less' is certainly not a characteristic of 'rationality' and has got nothing to do with logic or immanent thinking. We have shown in other contexts that this statement about 'rational choice' is never an economic or psychological or philosophical 'law'.

- People make choices that give them as much satisfaction as possible

  Comment: Always searching and controlling that the maximum satisfaction is reached with a good is extremely compulsive, always part of an addiction that is driven by an 'irrational choice'. In general not even 'irrationally making choice' is a rule or 'law'. The statement is absurd and expresses economic sickness.

- People face a budget constraint

  Comment: That's 100% true on all 'normal' levels of wage. Earning €10 million or €100 million (Dollars) per year is another world; such a human only feels a budget constraint if he wants to possess or rule the world.

There are some strange monsters on this planet that wish to rule the Universe and even God. Logically these people get crazy with their budget constraint even on a level of hundreds of billions or trillions of €/$.

- People must choose among alternatives

  Comment: That's true! It starts in the morning as everybody knows: getting up and going to work, or staying in bed. There are many situations in the life of billions of people where they can't choose between alternatives; or the optional alternatives are between the plague and hell. And there are many more situations in everyday life people can choose between many alternatives.

  The more alternatives of whatsoever people are confronted with everyday, the more they get mad. Everyday riding the crazy horse of the alternative choices dehumanizes people, destroys human values, the ability to love, loyalty and solidarity, reliability and integrity, and even a relationship or marriage: there are always 'better' options (without knowing what is de facto behind a face, in their mind and in their bed).

  Do you know how many toxic elements and what kind of chemicals and pharmaceuticals (toxic) elements you eat every day in vegetables, fish, fruits, meat, and beverages?

→ The rational choice and marginal utility concept is pure madness. We must ask: Is it an intentional aim of the capitalistic economics to destroy human's mind and soul, human's dignity and human's striving for the deepest meaning of life and the fulfillment of the longing of their soul? YES, it is an intentional aim as it is systemic in economics!

3.2.7. Some Choices

"Choice 1: Obviously you want to get the most for your money, so you choose goods that have the highest units of utility per unit of cost." [180] – And the author continues:

"Choice 2: Here the two alternatives have a cost in time, not money. The analysis, however, is the same."
Starting with 'obviously (you want)' is here a suggestive and manipulative element. And 'the most of your money' can refer to quality or quantity. The variable 'highest units of utility' expresses the compulsive sickness. 'Highest'

---

[180] Colander, p. 234

is a superlative, means a 'maximum'. Do people naturally want always the 'highest', the 'maximum' (satisfaction)? Each cent and everything that people buy is related to 'maximize satisfaction'.

→ How sick is that? Only mentally distorted, dehumanized, and very neurotic people are in such a mental coding. If the written content here reflects the author's mind, then we know who they are.

There is a little misleading factor in the concept: Economics use the term 'economic satisfaction' which does not refer to a physical or psychological or spiritual satisfaction. The term refers to a pure mathematical scale (e.g. percentage, or for example from zero to hundred). In that sense the term 'satisfaction' in economics is an abuse, or is misleading as the term means in the core always a human experience: physical, psychological, spiritual, social, intellectual, professional, mechanical, financial or religious.

'Economic satisfaction' measured by price acceptance (willingness) is an expression (indicator) of avarice, envy, oral deficit (psychoanalytical term) or anal-fixation (anankastic), ego-centrism, egomania, individualism, and inability to love and care. Therefore we must conclude that the authors and creators of economic theories suffer from such kind of psychological and moral disorders.

→ We have shown that the term 'satisfaction' is always a matter of subjective scales and interpretation, and that there are many subjective factors that create partial or full 'satisfaction'.
→ We suspect that the use of terms (words) with manifold connotations is intentional: it confuses and it allows for arguments with different meanings, which produces quarrels. Is there a hidden cantankerousness?

3.2.8. The principle of rational choice

"The principle of rational choice tells us to spend our money on those goods that give us the most marginal utility per dollar." [181]

Go to a shopping center, explore what people have in their shopping cart, and you will see that this statement doesn't reflect reality.
→ Considering all analysis given above, this statement is nonsense.

We have explored aspects of this term and its theses in Economics I.

---

[181] Colander, p. 235

3.2.9. Maximizing Utility and Equilibrium

"When the ratios of the marginal utility to price of the two goods are equal, you're maximizing utility; this is the utility-maximizing rule ... Achieving equilibrium by maximizing utility (juggling your choices, adding a bit more of one and choosing a bit less of another) requires more information than I've so far presented." [182]

People must choose the good that provides the maximum satisfaction, marginal included. If they find two goods that are equal in their potential satisfaction, then they reached the maximum utility.

But in such a situation people must choose as both options are equal in satisfaction. That's real life! To solve such a problem, people must get both goods. If they chose one good, then they will always think: 'maybe the other good had a thin marginal utility'. If people would do so, rationally or irrationally (unconsciously), they would get totally insane during the course of their life.

"The reason is that consumers don't have enough money to buy all they want. They face a budget constraint and do the best they can under that constraint - that is, they maximize utility." ... "So when you say you want a Porsche but can't afford one, economists ask whether you are working two jobs and saving all your money to buy a Porsche. If you aren't, you are demonstrating that you don't really want a Porsche, given what you would have to do to get it." [183]

Now the author talks about 'wants' and before many statements suggested to be focused on 'needs'. Wants and needs are not the same! And sometimes a want can be a need depending on the subjective interpretation or on a given frame. The systemic strategy here is to confuse the mind and to argue always on the line of interest.

Fact is: There are billions that can't satisfy their needs, not to talk about their wants. In the capitalistic world we can certainly focus on wants as people have wants after having satisfied their needs. People do 'the best they can under constraint budget'. This statement is rather the result of a person that has lost real ground. The Porsche example in other words: If people want something, but only can get it with more working, then the want is only real if they indeed start working (more) to get it. There are Porsche models with a

---

[182] Colander, p. 236
[183] Colander, p. 238

price of €90,000 (Dollars); and others with a price of €180,000 (Dollars); second hand is half price or less. One can pay cash or with a loan. 'Working more to get it' sounds a bit unrealistic. Here economic theory is totally derailed.

Correct is and people know it even as wisdom: If you really want something that you can get if you perform harder, then you get it with more performance – if the want is realistic. The 'want' becomes an imperative or a 'law' or simply a fact in human's life.

→ The rule of life is: If you want something realistic in relation to given dispositions, then you must perform to get it. The more you want, the more you must perform.
→ If you are lazy, lazy-minded, unwilling to learn and to perform hard, then you can't expect to get much in life.
→ There are many businesses that have 'needs' and 'wants'. But with the thousands of corporations dominating the global market, these businesses will never get it.
→ There are normal (realistic) 'needs' and 'wants' that are not satisfiable for up to several billion people. And there are 'wants' that are only reachable for multi-millionaires and billionaires.

3.2.10. Incentive

- A price discount on the good
- A price discount for a double package
- A second unit with 50% discount
- A quantity discount
- A discount per time unit (e.g. public transport)
- An age discount (e.g. children, retired people)
- A family discount (e.g. tickets for the zoo)
- A discount by advance payment
- Payment with 6-month installments without interest
- Extension of payment to do (e.g. from 30 days to 3 months)
- An extended time use (e.g. Gym, tennis court)
- A financial bonus for posterior purchase
- A sample of merchandise
- Free childcare while shopping (e.g. shopping centers)
- A free service (e.g. installation)
- A free liquor after lunch or dinner
- A focused time frame with reduced price (e.g. drinks, happy hour)
- An additional service for free (e.g. delivery)

- A piece of chocolate (e.g. with a coffee)
- Psychotherapy: you get a chocolate for every session
- Car washing: cleaning your shoes or washing your dog

→ Incentive offers are in general time-limited (during a specific time period) and do not become a permanent margin for free or for reduced price.

3.2.11. Marginal Rate of Substitution

"Two goods are substitutes if a rise in the price of one good leads to an increase in the demand for the other good. Two goods are complements if a rise in the price of one good leads to a decrease in the demand for the other good." [184]

Substitute means an 'alternative', a 'replacement' for something, or one thing takes the place for another. This situation is not about choosing between two goods; it's about 'one good must go away (be ignored, rejected) for another good that replaces it'. We already can easily smell the economic battle! In economic words: The marginal rate of substitution means "the rate at which a consumer is willing to trade one good for another." [185]

There are three aspects to consider: [186]

1. Consumers usually prefer more of something to less of it.

Comment: We have shown that this is not true; at best it happens in a certain field of goods.

2. The rate at which the consumer is willing to substitute one good for another: in most cases the consumer likes both goods. The case of contradiction is called 'axiom of transitivity'.

Comment: There are a thousand cases where people like both goods.

The relevant question is: for which goods is this true? What does the word 'likes' mean?

This statement is very undifferentiated and therefore not useful. The words 'transitivity' and 'axiom' are terms in logic and mathematics. 'Usually' is not a

---

[184] Krugman (et al.), p. 69
[185] Mankiw (et al.), p. 441
[186] Mankiw (et al.), p. 443

scientific term. The author bluffs here pretending to make a scientific statement; but it is spume.

3. People are more willing to trade away goods that they have in abundance and less willing to trade away goods of which they have little.

Comment: Which people? Which goods do people have in abundance? Which goods do people have little of? What are the limits people understand as 'abundant' or 'little'? Do we talk here about the poor, the well off, the rich, or the very rich? Does it refer to children, teenagers, adults, elderly people, men or women? 'Trade away' always has a motive: What are the possible motives? Is the 'amount' the sole motive for a decision? What is the probability of such a decision of 'trade away'? 'People are more willing': How many people in percentage terms?

➔ This is a blabber-statement without any access to comprehend it.

Example: There is a good on the market from a firm. Another firm wants to do business and enters into the market. Or a firm, a corporation, wants to make more profit and searches for an opportunity (a new product) to expand. As a very new product is unlikely to be easily sold, they think about creating substitutive products. Therefore the question is: How can we make people buy the new good and stop buying the other good. They produce a good that is a substitute of another good that people have in abundance. Why should 'abundance' be a motive to buy the substitutive good? It's again the compulsive and perverse mind that creates wherever possible an opportunity to find a way to 'steal' from others (that have success). Again we are in the middle of the battle of the sick market.

Perfect substitution:

= Two goods are perfect substitutes if the marginal rate of substitution is constant.

Perfect complements: (our interpretation from the author's description)

= Perfect complements means that the two goods complement each other necessarily.

3.2.12. Consumer's Optimal Choice

Optimal Choice:

= The optimum represents the best available combination of two goods.

Example 1: There is a consumer. There are two goods with a similar price (small price difference). The consumer wants to choose and takes a decision. Or, the prices differ more. What could be the motives that he chooses one of the two? Could it be the price?

Example 2: There is a consumer. There are two goods with a similar price (small price difference). One good is a substitute. In one case the substitute is more expensive; in the other case the substitute is little bit cheaper; and in a third case both goods have the same price. The consumer wants to choose and takes decision. What could be the motives that make him choose (to a take decision)? Could it be the price?

Economics asserts that the price and the marginal rate of the substitute directs the decision (are the motives to chose): "In making his consumption choices, the consumer takes as given the relative price of the two goods and then chooses an optimum at which his marginal rate of substitution equals this relative price." [187] In other words: The substitute must have a little higher benefit and a relative (little lower or equal?) price.

"…market prices of different goods reflect the value that consumers place on those goods." [188]

Lower or higher wage, it influences the consumer behavior: "The change in consumption that results when a price change moves the consumer along a given … (price level) to a point with a new marginal rate of substitution." When the price of a good decreases, then the consumers may buy more of this good or they can buy goods they didn't buy before. If the price of a good increase then the consumers may buy less from this good or they can't buy the goods they bought before.

Normal is what the author says (the law of demand): "When the price of a good rises, people buy less of it." [189]

But the margin of rise (or decrease) and the economic level play a decisive role: Little changes in the price provoke changes in the very poor and poor social class, but don't necessarily change the consumer behavior of the middle and upper class. Considering these relations, the thesis (theory) of the authors

[187] Mankiw (et al.), p. 445
[188] Mankiw (et al.), p. 446
[189] Mankiw (et al.), p. 453

is not correct, at least not applicable for people on all economic levels.

"When individuals have more income, they are normally more likely to purchase a good at any given price. For example, if a family's income rises, it is more likely to take that summer trip to Disney World – and therefore also more likely to buy plane tickets." [190]

How much does the travel and a ticket for a family with two children cost for a summer trip to Disney World? A ticket for example to a Zoo costs easily €25 (Dollars). We have to add lunch and some snacks for four people and we easily get €250 (Dollars); and for Disney World we must calculate even more for a family, cost of the trip not included. From here we can have a look at the increase of a wage: A worker may get an increase of €50 (Dollars) (wage).

Let's imagine the needs or wants he has in his mind: He wishes to have a coffee machine, or a pair of shoes for his wife, or some books or toys or also shoes for his two children. Maybe he wants to buy some plants or a new washing machine.

The worker's mother lives on the poverty line; therefore he thinks that he could give his mother €30 (Dollars) every month. And we could extend the list with 50 more small wants. The Disney World trip costs him €650 (Dollars) (hostel included) plus a plane ticket for four people and he feels that this is not appropriate considering the low increase of his wage.

Conclusion: The author should come back to reality and make clear the variable 'when individuals have more income' with absolute figures (wage + marginal wage).

In general we can say: "Changes in the price of a good alter the consumer's budget constraint and, therefore, the quantities of the (…) goods that he chooses to buy." [191]

But this is a lapidary fact for certain low social groups and not a theory and not valid for the upper social classes. Other exceptions are mentioned: "Consumers can sometimes violate the law of demand and buy more of a good when the price rises." [192]

➔ This is the scientific 'sometimes law', valid everywhere in the economic

---

[190] Krugman (et al.), p. 70
[191] Mankiw (et al.), p. 451-451
[192] Mankiw (et al.), p. 453

theories.

When the prices rise then the consumers buy more of this good? This must be a special good and / or there most be a special motive. What are the motives to buy more of a good if the price of this good rises? The good must have more prestige, more importance, more urgency, or more meaning, or a specific marketing that produces a sheep behavior to buy the good with the increased price.

All humans are allowed to have 'dreams', secret wants: "Expected changes in future income can also lead to changes in demand." [193] Do people expect to get a higher wage in the nearer future? Increase of a wage is in general a small proportion of the wage. They do not much change their demand, but focus on some additional little wants. In that sense the statement is very vague and doesn't allow for any concrete conclusions.

Again we are in the trap of the compulsive economist: "What do I have to do so that people buy my good when the price is increased?" Or: "I want more profit from my good and for that I must increase the price and I need to know what I can do so that people continue buying my good with the higher price.

In general we can agree: And this is why Marketing exists because there are people like that. Frankly they get what they deserve. Change human beings and you can change Marketing, Economics and the whole system. Till that happens, there is only bluster and blubber!

- ☑ There are greedy and avaricious people that never have enough.
- ☑ There are people preponderantly focusing on satisfaction (mood category).
- ☑ There are people preponderantly wanting the maximum satisfaction.
- ☑ There are compulsive people that have a magical way of dealing with matters.
- ☑ There are people that always calculate in all matters of life, even in love matters.
- ☑ There are mad people driven by control and perverse obsessions.
- ☑ There are people that suffer from all kinds of addictions, also economic addictions.
- ☑ There are people that have a deep longing for peace and fulfillment.
- ☑ There are people that have an unconscious drive to compensate for inner suffering.
- ☑ There are people with unconscious complexes that dominate their

---

[193] Krugman (et al.), p. 71

consumer behavior.

- ☑ There are rigid people who always know what is best in life (to do and to have).
- ☑ There are business people with a mind for profit and calculating cents or seconds.
- ☑ There are people that have lost touch with reality, on lower level as well as on top-levels.
- ☑ There are impatient people that get angry if they don't immediately get what they want.
- ☑ There are people that live without soul and always focusing on material goods.
- ☑ There are insane people that always and lifelong are obsessed with 'wants'.
- ☑ There are people that buy any stupid good simply out of an unidentified impulse.
- ☑ There are envious people always wanting what their neighbors of friends have.
- ☑ There are people that always want the best, the maximum, the number one, the top.
- ☑ There are people that always want much more than they deserve to have.
- ☑ There are people with much more psychical insufficiencies and a bad character.
- ☑ There are people with completely distorted and disfigured psychical functions.

- → But this does not give the foundation or a sufficient reason for the critically discussed economic statements, principles, laws, rules, models, terms, and theories.
- → Most economic statements, principles, laws, rules, models, terms, and theories operate with a human image that is completely reduced and does not match with human's realities.

Consumer's Optimal Choice has to do with behavior: "Behavioral economics is the study of economic choice that is based on realistic psychological foundations … individuals maximize a utility function that involves getting more for themselves." … "…a strong status quo bias - an individual's actions are very much influenced by the current situation, even when that reasonably does not seem to be very important to the decision." [194]

This statement is not correct; it is not true. Economics has absolutely no realistic psychological foundations. The psychological and social human factors are outrageously ignored or reduced to an infantile and naïve

---

[194] Colander, p. 244-245

understanding of what psychologically and spiritually makes a human.

3.3. Free Market Dynamics

Aspects of free market are: [195]

1. Free markets allocate the supply of goods to the buyers who value them most highly, as measured by their willingness to pay.

2. Free markets allocate the demand for goods to the sellers who can produce them at least cost.

3. Free markets produce the quantity of goods that maximizes the sum of consumer and producer surplus.

The term 'free market' in these statements from Mankiw (et al) can be replaced by 'distribution systems' and 'producers'; the three statements do not explain what 'free market' effectively means, but suggests that this is a 'free market'. 'Willingness' is in many purchase patterns not really a free will. What buyers do value most highly is introduced here in a suggestive way. Production 'at least cost' includes or must be added with 'highest possible profit'. And 'maximizes the sum of consumer and producer surplus' is simply the fire for 'maximizing profit'. It's again the melody of greed and compulsion.

In the free market the needs and wants are the key drives for consumers as well as for producers (and sellers). 'Needs' versus 'Wants' are explained in the following way: "Economists like to emphasize that once we have achieved bare subsistence levels of consumption – the amount of food, shelter and clothing required to maintain our health – we can abandon all reference to needs and speak only in terms of wants."

→ Therefore, given that an estimated 80% of the Western world has achieved bare subsistence levels of consumption, the 'demand' focuses on 'wants'.
→ But there are many people that reduce their 'needs' to an absolute minimum to get a 'want'.
→ There are in America and Europe 15-25% of people that can't live a decent life on a level of 'achieved bare subsistence levels of consumption'.
→ How many people around the globe also can't live their life on a level of

---

[195] Mankiw (et al.), p. 152

248

'achieved bare subsistence levels of consumption'? We estimate: 3 billion people, including taking into account that dirty water and one miserable meal per day does not express the satisfaction of need.

3.3.1. Demand

The law of demand is described by McDowell: "People do less of what they want to do as the cost of doing it rises … By stating the law of demand in this way, we can see it as a direct consequence of the Cost-Benefit Principle, which says that an activity should be pursued if (and only if) its benefits are at least as great as its costs. Recall that we measure the benefit of an activity by the highest price we would be willing to pay to pursue it – namely, our reservation price for the activity."

➜ If the 'reservation price' for a good is individually flexible on different levels of wage (and it is), then this law of demand is very relative.
➜ The law of demand ignores the fact that people sometimes or often buy stupid goods without thinking, sometimes goods of a much higher price than they consider as 'acceptable', and sometimes they set priorities: today this, next month that; and there are also goods that are much cheaper than their reservation price.

"The law of demand says that a higher price for a good or service, other things equal, leads people to demand a smaller quantity of that good or service." [196] This 'law' is very flexible, if we consider some patterns in reality: People can move to a substitute that is cheaper. People can pay the price and renounce buying another product of less subjective importance. People don't bother much and prefer making some saving. 'A smaller quantity means that a product is measured by quantity. Not all goods can be bought either with higher or with lower quantity. And there are many services that can't be divided into units; e.g. either you go to a hairdresser to cut your hair (a basic service), or you don't go, or you only go every three months instead of every month, or you find a cheaper hairdresser. There are many goods you only can buy it or leave it. In that sense the 'law of demand' is very relative and can't be understood as a general 'law of demand'.

Another definition of demand: "…a price increase reduces the quantity demanded because it reduces a consumer's purchasing power. It affects the consumer's overall ability to consume." [197]

---

[196] Krugman (et al.), p. 66
[197] McDowell (et al.), p. 67

Interesting is here the second part of the statement. "It affects…" is not really a substantial expression. It does not mean a reduction as we have shown above. And it does not necessarily reduce purchasing power. A price increase is rarely higher than 3-6%. Therefore we are confronted here with a very 'small power'. Everything is vague here. The author continues: "Income effect the change in the quantity demanded of a good that results because of a change in real income of purchasers arising from the price change." Here the same can be commented: not really scientific!

Logically the created 'law' of demand in the context of our examples (and many similar examples more) fails: "Generally, the proposition that a higher price for a good, other things equal, leads people to demand a smaller quantity of that good is so reliable that economists are willing to call it a 'law' – the law of demand." Is this law only applicable for food or also for any other product?

A 'law' has something absolute or at least a very narrow frame of flexibility. The word 'law' is here not linked with a probability and therefore it is not appropriate to use in such a general way. Either it's a 'law' with a clearly determined frame or it has a certain probability of happening. It could also be that with one specific good, this 'law' works fully; and with other goods not at all.

→ The 'law of demand' is generalized in an inappropriate and unscientific way. This leads to misunderstanding, misinterpretation, and pretending to be of proven supra-importance.

What are these 'wants' about? Here we have an interpretation: "Wants (also called 'preferences' or 'tastes') are clearly an important determinant of a consumer's reservation price for a good. But that begs the question of where wants come from … Are largely biological in origin. But many others are heavily shaped by culture, and even basic craving may be socially moulded." [198] On another place the author says: "In most markets, different buyers have different reservation prices." This can mean that for each good or for the same good different buyers have different reservation prices. More interesting would be to know the type of market and the kind of good to realize the importance of such a statement. The statement remains vague.

→ Preferences and tastes are an aspect of wants, something like a motivating 'drive'. But these aspects are not 'wants' as they are not goods. Goods are in the focus of wants. Preferences and tastes are only loading factors. That

---

[198] McDowell (et al.), p. 119

250

the 'wants' are largely biological in origin is a stupid, absolutely idiotic opinion.

→ This is another of many examples that shows how undifferentiated these experts and economic scientists operate with words.

We explore the wants, not to determine a 'law' or a 'rule', but much more to understand and to stimulate a differentiated view; incomplete here certainly:

- There are 'healthy' wants and stupid meaningless or even insane wants. The healthy wants are related to the inner disposition of humans and to interests of learning, creating, expressing, exploring, or touching (showing) real potentials to live and to use for higher aims (e.g. projects, visions).
- Wants can be a tool or an expression of culture or experiences, style, or arts, or status, but also for joy of life, pleasure, lust, satisfaction, and fun. Healthy wants are limited, 'normal', 'humane', controlled and managed.
- Healthy wants are an enrichment; they do not destroy; they have a reasonable proportion; they do not destroy balance in life; they do not aim to pretend something; and they are simply also a matter of life for seconds, minutes, hours, days or for a long period of time.

The demand curve in words: "…a price increase reduces the quantity demanded because it reduces a consumer's purchasing power. It affects the consumer's overall ability to consume." [199]

The way it is said it expresses a 'law'. But does a price increase always reduce the quantity demanded? Consumers always have to choose between many options of the goods they want. The amount is limited. The amount per good is limited. For each good the consumer has a price willingness (to pay). In general each consumer has within his personal frame of goods and disposable money certain flexibility: here a bit more, there a bit less, and another good is planned for next month. The statement does not say if the price increase is meant for all goods on the market or only for a special section of goods. If a price increase affects many of the goods in the bundle of a consumer, then, yes, there is a reduction in the consumer's purchasing power. If this is not the case, then the consumer uses his flexibility; and this is not really a reduction in the consumer's purchasing power. As the statement speaks about 'consumers', we must ask: which consumers? We have many categories of consumers and many levels of wages. Therefore the purchasing power becomes a variety of pictures with a very different importance of purchasing power.

---

[199] McDowell (et al.), p. 67

→ As very often in economics statements ('laws') also this kind of generalization is not really a scientific 'law'.

In summary, an increase in demand – the decision by consumers to buy larger quantities of a product at each possible price – may be caused by: [200]

- A favorable change in consumer tastes
- An increase in the number of buyers
- Rising incomes if the product is an inferior good
- Falling incomes if the product is an inferior good
- An increase in the price of a complementary good
- A decrease in the price of a complementary good
- A decrease in the price of a complementary good
- A new consumer expectation that future prices or income will be higher

We continue with such kind of statements: "The Cost-Benefit Principle tells us that a given person will buy the good if the expected benefit to be received from it exceeds its cost. The benefit is the buyer's reservation price, the highest money amount he (or she) would be willing to pay for the good." [201]

The buyer's reservation price includes that a consumer always has for each good he wants to buy an exact reservation price. But this does not reflect reality. A consumer with a very low wage has a very limited reservation price meanwhile a consumer with a significant higher wage a much higher (more flexible) reservation price. Both will rarely always focus on the top-limit price they are willing to pay.

→ The cost-benefit-principle generally does not work in reality and it is very rigid and expresses again the seller's (producer's) compulsion to always find out the highest money amount a consumer would be willing to pay for the good.
→ It's a false estimation if economists think that all or most consumers are also affected from this compulsive virus; here the other way round: driven by greed to pay as little as possible. As the theory of rational choice does not work the way its theory says, the cost-benefit-principle also doesn't work the way it is described in the statement.

There is a difference between 'want' and 'demand': "Unless you are willing and able to pay for it, you may want it, but you don't demand it." [202]

---

[200] McConnel (et al.), p. 38
[201] McDowell (et al.), p. 68
[202] Colander, p. 84

252

This is a very serious consideration to distinguish between 'I want, but do not demand it'. Indeed most people have 'wants', but they do not demand them. Such wants are fantasies, dreams, or can express that the good they want (but not demand) is appreciated as something attractive, good or cool. And the good stimulates daydreaming about it. Such kind of 'want' is not relevant for the consumer market, but it confirms the attractiveness of the good, which on the side of marketing becomes very relevant.

→ A 'want' requires willingness to buy, a financial ability to buy, and a de facto purchase process.

→ The economic drive: All people have fantasies about all kind of 'wants'. We must connect with their fantasies!

To bring out the attractiveness of such a good with words, associations, connotations, sceneries, and packaging has a stimulating effect for those that have the money and the willingness to buy this good. Finding out why people want it, but do not demand it, helps to optimize the marketing and even to optimize the good in order to create a bridge between 'want' and 'demand'.

→ 'I want, but do not demand it' is a human phenomenon of importance for the marketing and the production of the related good.

"Prices are the tool by which the market coordinates individuals' desires and limits how much people demand. When goods become scarce, the market reduces the quantity people demand; as their prices go up, people buy fewer goods. As goods become abundant, their prices go down, and people buy more of them." [203]

The author says that people 'want, but do not demand it' because of the price that is too high for them. He also says that if the good is scarce, then less people will have a demand. We interpret: the reason is: if the good is scarce, the price often or in general goes up. The other way round: the more of a good is on the market, the lower is the price (in general or for certain products; and because of the low price more people can and will buy the good. Who or what is the market that coordinates 'wants' (fantasies, desires) with the tool called 'price'?

→ Desires are a bio-psychical phenomenon. Marketing must focus on the (pleasure-) lust factor!

---

[203] Colander, p. 84

'The market' is a term of immense dimension and includes countless variables and components, active and passive ones. To present statements as a 'law' or 'principle' of such dimension is not serious. It's extremely hyped up or like a Swiss cheese, 75% of the entire mass are holes.

Especially it manipulates the economic thinking of students and future economics experts that only learn by copying. Such learning promotes stubbornness, a rigid authoritarian personality, and blinded followers of an ideology.

→ 'I want, but do not demand it' can be broken with a decrease of the price of the good which includes the necessity of an abundant allocation of the good; or with stimulating the lust-factor.

Depreciation is "a measure of the decline in value of an asset that occurs over time." [204]

'Depreciation' has a negative connotation: it's bad. A decline in values is something unwelcome. But is it always bad? 'Values' can be overheated, a bubble. Values are always relative to the value that people give to goods or services. Values can have a speculative character. Values change with the time.

→ Depreciation can have a 'healing' effect: back to reality, to the real value of production (performance) or of product use (utility).

This 'law' of demand is expressed from Colander with: "The law of demand states that the quantity of a good demanded is inversely related to the good's price." In other words, if other components remain constant: [205] [206]

- If the price falls, the quantity of demand rises.
- If the price rises, the quantity of demand falls.

And Krugman (et al.) writes: "When a rise in income increases the demand for a good – the normal case – it is a normal good ... When a rise in income decreases the demand for a good, it is an inferior good." [207]

The price can fall, but nothing will change. The people must be informed about the decrease of a price which leads to marketing and special announcements in a shop. Therefore it's wrong what the author claims to be

---

[204] Colander, p. 308
[205] Colander, p. 85
[206] Colander), p. 239
[207] Krugman (et al.), p. 70

a law. It only works with special information and a powerful marketing. But many small firms do not have the financial resources to make an effective marketing. Above that, it depends on the kind of product: from a chewing gum up to a luxurious car of €150,000 (Dollars).

Another critical thought about this 'law' is: If a product costs €5 (Dollars), and the prices fall by 10%, means the new price is €4.50 (Dollars): does it matter to most consumers? Will they run to get the good with this price? How much must a price fall to get a higher significant amount of buyers?

→ Again we have a generalization that is not correct as it expresses an interrelation that is not really valid as a scientific statement of interdependence between two variables.

The author also says: "This law is fundamental to the invisible hand's ability to coordinate individuals' desires: as prices change, people change how much they are willing to buy." [208]

Here the author comes back to the 'invisible hand' that in the economics' theory coordinates desires (bio-psychical factor!) and wants with price changes and willingness to buy. A desire is an internal impulse, a want is already a first decision, the willingness is crucial for the purchase, and the level of the price directs who can buy and / or will buy it.

Desire can be biological, emotional, social, unconscious, or ego-concentric variable loaded with certain (psychical) energy. The willingness is also a complex variable as we have described in another chapter above. The decision making process as well is very complex and can't be reduced to a 'rational' process as we have described in another context above. The price is obviously a simple variable from low to high.

And now, where is this 'invisible hand'? What is the activity of this 'invisible hand'? It's the seducing, the luring, and the repetition of the marketing strongly touching unconscious complexes to stimulate compensatory consumer behavior.

Another approach must be considered: "Change in price causes a movement along a demand curve; a change in a shift factor causes a shift in demand." [209]

The 'law of demand' shows indeed an existing dynamic, but it does not always

---

[208] Colander, p. 85
[209] Colander, p. 86

work and never for all kind of products and services. We can't say that always and everywhere existing demanders buy more of a good and new demanders buy the good if the price decrease. [210]

First of all it depends on the kind of good; and secondly this law may be valid for only 25% of a corresponding consumer population in a village and 12% in a city. Where are the figures (statistics) for 50,000 goods that show us with which probability this law works everywhere on earth (or in America or Europe)? Consider what is happening in China and the rest of the world EVERYONE wants a piece of capitalistic pie. Everyone is greedy everyone wants more!

→ Thesis: The 'law of demand' does not work in many important markets.

Example 1: This law absolutely does not work in tourist areas such as those along the Mediterranean Coastlines: With the high demand in summer, all prices of all goods and services rise into the heaven; and during low season the prices fall with the very low demand into the cellar, except for luxurious goods. The fall of prices in low season does not simply generate more tourists.

Example 2: This law absolutely does not work in the Spanish real estate market: There are 2-3 million homes for sale (2012), but most prices do not fall accordingly down to 40% of the original price which would be (in many cases) the real construction price (and the 60% were the speculation margin).

Example 3: For many products and services such as milk, beer, or rent of commercial premises (e.g. in Spain), or bar-restaurant services in non-touristic areas the prices do not change with an increase or decrease of demand. If, for example, the shoe prices fall 5-10%, will there be significantly more shoe buyers? Not at all; but maybe more people will buy if all shoe prices would fall by 50%.

→ There is no such thing as the 'invisible hand' that coordinates desire ('want') with demand (willingness to buy) and the price.
→ There are other factors that coordinate or shape bridges in order to buy a good: a change in price, the flexibility of a budget, individual tastes, cultural (national) tastes, show-off, experiences expectations, and prices of other goods, a new actual trend, a cheaper good of similar or identical characteristics, unexpected personal or collective events, a decrease of taxes, increase of wage, and the weather. People are influenced in

---

[210] Colander, p. 89

consumer behavior from many psychological effects. [211] [212] [213]

→ From a statistical point of view the quantity of demand changes during a day, a week, a month or a year. For many goods it is also different between the kinds of urban areas (village, city). In that sense the quantity of demand is not everywhere and permanently constant.

→ The law of demand can't be explained simply with the 'principle of rational decision'. People have countless rational and irrational options in decision-making and are exposed to countless marketing influences in general and by a movement of price and shift in particular. [214]

→ There is not simply one 'law' that characterizes 'demand and supply'. The complexity requires a multi-variable (multi-dimensional) approach. The identification of the complexity, seen as a complex network of interdependences, obliges us to get rid of this magical 'invisible hand' as a scientific variable.

Finally Colander agrees: "How real-world people make decisions in real-world situations is an open question that modern economists are spending a lot of time researching … to make real-world decisions, most people use bounded rationality - rationality based on rules of thumb … They argue that many of our decisions are made with our minds on automatic pilot." [215]

With this statement Colander puts into question his 'law'; it makes it even irrelevant or at least puts it on a low probability level. The 'automatic pilot' is bonded to the unconscious mind, to reflexes, and to thoughtlessness or stupidity and much more.

→ Economics doesn't know the real-world: "…how people make decisions in real-world situations is an open question."

→ The 'law' of 'demand and supply' has not got much to do with science! It must be completely revised respecting the manifoldness of variables in all market segments.

Income and substitution effects must be considered: "First, we're poorer due to the rise in price. The reduction in quantity demanded because we're poorer is called the income effect. Second, the relative prices have changed.

The price of ice cream has risen relative to the price of Big Macs. The reduction in quantity demanded because relative price has risen is called a

---

[211] Colander, p. 87-89
[212] Colander, p. 239
[213] Colander, p. 242-244
[214] Colander, p. 238
[215] Colander, p. 241

substitution effect." ... The substitution effect in action: It tells us that when the relative price of a good goes up, the quantity purchased of that good decreases, even if you're given money to compensate you for the rise." [216]

The firm's perspective: A rise in price leads to a decrease in demand when the wages don't go up. The fact is common sense: If a firm sells less of a good, then the income decreases. But with the rise in price the firm may be compensated.

"The Scarcity Principle challenges us to allocate our incomes among the various goods that are available so as to fulfill our desires to the greatest possible degree. The optimal combination of goods is the affordable combination that yields the highest total utility." [217] Do people really try to fulfill their desires to the greatest possible degree? This sounds very theoretical.

The consumer perspective: A consumer with a narrow budget reacts when there is a rise in price of a good. But do the consumers at the same time realize the rise relative to the price of Big Macs?

People may realize an increase of price from €1.50 (Dollars) to €2 (Dollars). But people living on comfortable life standard will not consume less.

Who gives money to compensate for the rise of a price? This part of the statement opens the door to unlimited ideas. We cannot identify a concrete variable. Such language seems to be a tactical principle of economics: 'Guess what it is!'

It says: 'When the relative price of a good goes up, the quantity purchased of that good decreases'; but it does not say: because people then chose another product, called a 'substitute'. The statement also does not say how much a price of a good goes up until the quantity purchased of that good decreases.

The statement 'we are poorer due to the rise in price' can have an immense importance in the life of people living on the breadline and as a consequence also in the world of many businesses.

→ The word 'poorer' is here not appropriate for people living on comfortable life standard. 'Poor' has a clear connotation of miserable life or near to a miserable life. The term is abused here.

---

[216] Colander, p. 239-240
[217] McDowell (et al.), p. 130

Poorer due to rise in price can lead to manifold reactions:

- People buy less (quantity) of a good.
- People move to another good (substitute) that is cheaper.
- People buy less or cheaper meat, less or cheaper fruits, etc.
- People change their bundle of goods, first the semi-needs (i.e. clothing, shoes).
- People spend less for leisure wants (i.e. Gym, restaurant, cinema, hairdresser, etc.)
- People spend less for holidays; even stay at home or in their country
- People change their needs, first i.e. moving to a cheaper home.
- People sell their (second) car or any abdicable good of value.
- People buy or lease a cheaper car.
- People ignore car repair, car services, car inspection, even car insurance.
- People consume less electricity, water, petrol, etc.
- People may use their saving for their wants.
- People move to another location.
- People look for a second part-time job (evenings, Saturdays).
- People start working in the black market.

→ The substitution effect operates only in a small (margin) frame of price changes.

3.3.2. Supply

"The quantity supplied is the actual amount of a good or service producers are willing to sell at some specific price." [218] In other words: Producers are willing to produce a good and willing to sell this good at some specific price. And they produce a certain amount of this good. Certainly, nobody produces a good that can't be sold or a high quantity of a good that can't be sold. What is the meaning of this statement? It is common sense and not a 'law' or 'thesis'.

Let's first collect some statements that refer to 'supply': [219]

- For many goods there is an intermediate step
- Individual supply factors of production to firms
- Production is a multistage process

---

[218] Krugman (et al.), p. 73
[219] Colander, p. 91-92

- Supply of produced goods is a multistage process
- There are factors of production
- There is a transformation of factors of production into goods
- Firms produce to earn a profit
- Profit is tied to costs
- If costs rise, profit will decline
- A profit is to be determined (per good and total)
- Supply refers to a schedule of quantities a seller is willing to sell per unit of time
- There are various goods and various prices
- Changes in price cause changes in quantity supplied
- There is a specific amount that will be supplied at a specific price
- There is an effect of a change in price on the quantity supplied
- Supply falls when the price of inputs rises
- There is a firm's ability to switch from producing one good to another (substitution)
- Other things are constant

All components of supply have to do with cost and profit. More quantity can have higher cost of production, but lower cost of the price per unit (end-product). The more units can be sold, the higher the profit. From the beginning (raw material) to the end (supply for sale) we have a variety of prices and an increase or decrease of prices. Implementing a substitution product changes the prices. There are prices of one good and of a variety of goods.

Critically we put into question the statement: 'Profit is tied to costs'. As profit is not a cost of production, we can't declare profit as a cost (as above explained: it's a distortion of the common meaning of the word 'profit'). The factor 'profit' is an absolute independent factor and is always calculated depending on the volume of costs and amount of the produced goods, on the different goods (having a different price and different costs), on the owner of a firm, on the price-acceptance in the market, and on the equal or similar goods (prices) of competitors. 'Negative profit' can be interpreted as 'absence of profit'.

➜ Profit calculation is very variable and is subject to many factors and is also subject to the interests of the firm's owner.

The author comes back to the magical thinking: "... the law of supply is fundamental to the invisible hand's (the market's) ability to coordinate individuals' actions." [220] What exactly is this magical hand doing in the complexity of production and supply? Maybe the magical hand is the owner's hand (additionally the hand of the owner that produces raw material, the hand of the owner of the transport firm, or the hand of the owner of the sale firm), or their greed for maximizing profit. The adaptability of a product (price) on the market is certainly the essential decision maker if a good can be sold or not and therefore can be produced and supplied to the consumer or not.

The five main factors that can shift the demand curve are changes in (1) the price of a related good, such as a substitute or a complement, (2) income, (3) tastes, (4) expectations, and (5) the number of consumers. [221]

These 5 factors are real, and nothing invisible. Considering millions and even billions of single consumer patterns (purchase of a good) every day, we can introduce here an understanding that is much more comprehensible than the 'invisible hand' in economics:

"In probability theory, the law of large numbers (LLN) is a theorem that describes the result of performing the same experiment a large number of times. According to the law, the average of the results obtained from a large number of trials should be close to the expected value, and will tend to become closer as more trials are performed." [222] That means: A shift becomes a mathematical probability, calculated here with five variables and innumerable combinations in extension and price level of each variable and a thousand purchase (or: wants) patterns.

Colander mentions six statements about supply to be considered: [223]

1) "Advances in technology change the production process, reducing the number of inputs needed to produce a good, and thereby reducing its cost of production. A reduction in the cost of production increases profits and leads suppliers to increase production. Advances in technology increase supply."

It is not the 'advances in technology' that increase supply. Advanced technology allows for the production of more of a good (or more goods) at lower costs and therefore the price of the product (all the goods) decreases. And with that more consumers are interested (and able) to buy the good. The statement is manipulative and ignores the question of reasonableness for an increase of supply with lower price per good.

---

[220] Colander, p. 91-92
[221] Krugman (et al.), p. 73
[222] http://en.wikipedia.org/wiki/Law_of_large_numbers
[223] Colander, p .93

2) "If a supplier expects the price of her good to rise at some time in the future, she may store some of today's output in order to sell it later and reap higher profits, decreasing supply now and increasing it later."

That's a speculative strategy in order to make more profit. If this is good for the market and the firm is another question. The speculation can fail. Who will pay for this failure?

3) "Taxes on suppliers increase the cost of production by requiring a firm to pay the government a portion of the income from products or services sold. Because taxes increase the cost of production, profit declines and suppliers will reduce supply. Subsidies to suppliers are payments by the government to produce goods; they reduce the cost of production. Subsidies increase supply."

Decisions about taxes and subsidies are a matter of government; often forced by lobbyists, sometimes forced with corruption. This topic will be discussed in Economics III.

4) The law of supply: "According to the principle of rational choice, if there is diminishing marginal utility and the price of supplying a good goes up, you supply more of that good … In supply decisions, you are giving up something – your time, land or some other factor of production - and getting money in return." [224]

Always when an economist talks about an economic law, we must be alarmed! It would be a gift from heaven if the economic laws would really be a 'law' (like in physics). This would allow for the organization and management of a perfect market with zero unemployment, zero environmental damages, zero contamination, zero poverty and misery, zero over-exploitation, and zero demonstrations, unrest, riots, and wars. Unfortunately as there are too many people with an unhealthy or malformed mind and soul (on the ground floor and in the upper echelon), even such an ideal case would probably never be possible.

5) "In thinking about the connection between cost and supply, one fundamental insight is that the revenue received for a good must be greater than the planned cost of producing it. The difference between the expected price of a good and the expected average total cost of producing it is the supplier's expected economic profit per unit." [225]

---

[224] Colander, p. 240
[225] Colander, p. 303

This statement shows clearly: The profit must be added to the production costs and therefore, after intermediary and allocation costs, determines the end-price of a good. How much profit do they calculate in percentage?

6) "An entrepreneur is an individual who sees an opportunity to sell an item at a price higher than the average cost of producing it. The entrepreneur is the organizer of production and the one who visualizes the demand and convinces the individuals who own the factors of production that they want to produce that good." [226]

The entrepreneur or owner of a firm decides about the percentage of profit per good and in total of all goods. And we can conclude from this statement: It doesn't make sense to produce a good if no profit can be made. A very little profit may also lead to the decision to not produce a good.

3.3.3. Diminishing Marginal Product

Example: A production firm gives a small or bigger input (machines, labor, more space, and technical equipment, etc.) in order to increase the output. The motive is always obvious: maximizing profit; and there is a demand. In classical economic words: "Marginal product (is) the increase in output that arises from an additional input." [227]

But there is a problem: sometimes giving work to more laborers under the same structural conditions (e.g. machines, size of working areas) is counter-productive. In other words: a restaurant kitchen of 20m2 with 2 cooks works efficiently but with each additional cook the production (preparing menus) declines as there is not enough space to work. Or: the more table and chairs a restaurant business puts in a given space, the less costumer will come as it becomes very narrow and uncomfortable.

The additional input doesn't create an increase in output and therefore not more profit. Economics says: "(If) the number of workers increases the marginal product declines." [228]

---

[226] Colander, p. 303
[227] Mankiw (et al.), p. 269
[228] Mankiw (et al.), p. 270

3.3.4. Market Efficiency

Efficiency = "getting the most it can" [229]

Allocative efficiency: "A resource allocation where the value of the output by sellers matches the value placed on that output by buyers." [230]

The philosophy and the compulsive mind behind this understanding of 'efficiency' are already identified. 'Efficiency' is here a normative term. It doesn't say what is efficient; 'efficiency' only refers to the ideological goal. Who says that this is reasonable, positive, and efficient?

O.k., let's try to transfer this ideological principle to other life topics with some examples:

Example Cinema: John runs to the cinema, already 2 hours before the start of a movie, so he can get the best place possible. Everybody wants the best place. Now, everybody runs already 2 hours before the film begins to the cinema.

Example sexual encounter: Men and women always try to get the most they can in order to get the supra orgasmic explosion. Very stressful mechanical work and it will kill love.

Example family dinner: Mom prepared the dinner, amongst other things 5 pieces of meat that are not exactly the same size. There is also the father and the 3 teenagers. Everybody wants the most they can; therefore they all try to get the biggest piece of meat. And now they have a fight.

Example shoe shop: Mary is a bit addicted to shoes. She has €100 (Dollars) to buy shoes. She wants the most possible and she buys 10 pairs of shoes as there is a sale of the 'inferior' goods. As she always wants the most possible, she already has a hundred pair of shoes at home.

Example dating: Max is looking for love and he wants 'the most he can get'. He knows there are inner values and values related to appearance and wealth or status. He has already tried a hundred times, but always got crazy trying to get 100% of all possible. A complete failure!

Example driving a car: Sean is a door-to-door salesman and he drives every

---

[229] Mankiw (et al.), p. 148
[230] Mankiw (et al.), p. 139

day 200 km. To get the most he can, he always drives 'the most he can' (as fast as possible) to not lose a second or to miss one client less than what is 'the most he can per day. Or: All taxi-drivers in a city try 'the most they can' by always driving at the maximum possible speed; every second is counted for 'the most it can'.

The business importance of this kind of efficiency is clearly declared: "If an allocation is not efficient, then some of the gains from trade among buyers and sellers are not being realized. For example, an allocation is inefficient if a good is not being produced by the sellers with lowest cost … Similarly, an allocation is inefficient if a good is not being consumed by the buyers who value it most highly … Moving consumption of the good from a buyer with a low valuation to a buyer with a high valuation will raise the total surplus." [231]

The single information units of this statement are, in our words:

- An allocation is not efficient if there is not an area-covered distribution
- Not area-covered distribution: there is more area that can be covered with goods
- If not all areas are covered, then there is a loss of possible profit
- All possible areas must be covered (with the good for sale)
- A firm must make profit on every possible occasion
- An allocation is inefficient if a good is not being produced by the sellers with lowest cost
- Firms must produce at lowest cost
- As many goods as possible must be sold
- If fewer products are sold, then the allocation is inefficient
- With the lowest costs more goods could be distributed
- An allocation must be efficient in order to sell as many units of a good as possible
- Inefficient allocation is, if a good is not being bought by consumers from willing buyers
- The good that consumer value most highly must be sold (as much as possible)
- A firm must focus on those consumers that value the good most highly
- Don't try to sell a good to consumers that values it low

→ The never satisfied economist that never can miss an opportunity for a profit!
→ Very compulsive! A distress 24/7 due to permanent fear of missing a profit. A very sick mind!

---

[231] Mankiw (et al.), p. 148

Another statement about efficiency: "Efficiency is important not because it is a desirable end in itself, but because it enables us to achieve all our other goals to the fullest possible extent. Whenever a market is out of equilibrium, it is always possible to generate additional economic surplus. To gain additional economic surplus is to gain more of the resources we need to do the things we want to do. Whenever any market is out of equilibrium, there is waste, and waste is always a bad thing." [232]

It says that efficiency enables people to achieve all their other goals to the fullest possible extent. In general it is true that efficiency is indispensable to reach demanding goals. The question here is in the author's mind what are these 'goals'. Do people really have 'goals' in their mind and try to achieve them in an efficient way? We doubt it. Disequilibrium in everything in life requires a reaction, a special action to re-establish equilibrium. One question is about the criterion that says there is disequilibrium. Equilibrium here has only one goal: to gain additional economic surplus.

One could get crazy if he doesn't get an additional surplus wherever disequilibrium exists. As equilibrium is never static, always in a motion, consumer and producer must permanently calculate the necessary action to take for getting the most they can.

→ Waste is always a bad thing. Missing to get a margin more profit (benefit) is a loss.
→ Consumers and producers can learn here: never accept a waste or loss of whatsoever.
→ The pattern is compulsive, shows greed or avarice, a drive that never gives peace of mind.

3.3.5. Allocation

We consulted some sources in the Internet to get a picture about the term 'allocation'; here the result, some examples:

- To set apart for a special purpose; designate.
- To distribute according to a plan.
- The act of distributing by allotting or apportioning; distribution according to a plan.
- To allocate something is to set it aside for a specific purpose; to allot something is to give it with an implied restriction and an understanding of

[232] McDowell (et al.), p. 183

sharing.
- The act of allocating; apportionment.
- The state of being allocated.
- The share or portion allocated.
- Distribute according to a plan or set apart for a special purpose
- The systematic distribution of limited quantity resources over various time periods, products, operations, or investments.
- The act of putting one thing to another; a placing; disposition; arrangement
- The process of dividing up and distributing available, limited resources to competing, alternative uses that satisfy unlimited wants and needs.
- Process of partitioning a valuation account and assigning the resulting subsets to periods of time.
- Allocation includes the assignment of assets to expense as well as the assignment of liabilities to revenue over a time frame.

The term 'allocation' can have different meanings:

- Supply
- Contingent
- Dividing
- Distribution
- Systemic distribution
- Adding one thing to another
- Placing
- Partitioning
- Arrangement
- Disposition
- Making available
- Appropriation
- Provision
- Setting aside for a specific purpose

Let's take another definition: 'Allocative efficiency' means: "A term describing a situation where the limited resources of an economy are allocated to the production of the goods and services that consumers most greatly desire to consume." [233]

It states here clearly: 'limited resources of an economy are allocated to the production'; and this means: distribution! And this distribution is managed in order for 'consumers most greatly desire to consume'. And this refers to a

---

[233] Antonini (et al.), p. 369

value. Therefore we have here: available resources for the production of goods; the products that consumers want; and the price behind the expression 'most greatly desire'.

Another definition helps further: Allocative efficiency means: "…a resource allocation where the value of the output by sellers matches the value placed on that output by buyers." [234] Who are the sellers here? Is it the production entity? We assume that. So, it's about a product and this product shall match the value buyers give to this good.

→ As allocation in the core does not mean 'value' or 'valuation' or 'benefit' or 'profit', or 'satisfaction', we take the term 'allocation' in the overall sense: gathering resources to produce goods and ultimately placing them at the disposal of the consumer.

Conclusion:

The term does not clearly say if the transport (distribution) of a product to different places is included or if it means only putting at disposition a certain amount of a good for a determined area or sale entities. It could simply mean the amount of goods that are produced. But then, the produced goods are ready for a distribution. And the distribution is in general planned even before production. Therefore we can include the part of the effective distribution, means the logistic transport, in the understanding of the term 'allocation'.

And the other part is the given value: 'Do not produce a good, nor store or distribute a good that is not highly valued by the consumers (having the desired price from buyers and sellers). We can also say: A good is only then allocated when it is at the location (destination) of the sale; because a good stored at the location of the production entity is still not 'at the disposal' of the consumer at the destination; it may never arrive there for whatever reason.

The Sainsbury's depot in Waltham Abbey is the retail giant's largest distribution centre in the UK; search with Google to get impressive pictures: "24 million customers, three million cases and four-and-a-half miles of conveyor belts." And then ask yourself: Is this allocation, contingent, supply, distribution, or simply storage? [235]

---

[234] Mankiw (et al.), p. 883
[235] http://www.dailymail.co.uk/news/article-1338281/24-million-customers-million-cases-half-miles-conveyor-belts-The-supermarket-warehouse-thats-gearing-Christmas-rush.html

However we understand the term 'allocation', in general, does it make a difference? It makes a difference when we want to analyze the logistic transport and its costs. We can also analyze if the distribution is all-area covered or distributed to the right areas (with the potential consumers) and if the amount of goods are appropriate to the chosen destinations. And if the goods are ready for distribution, then we can focus on storage costs related to the time of storage and eventually additional costs (e.g. cold storage). The production itself and the planning of production are not included in the meaning of the term 'allocation'.

→ The term 'allocation' has different connotations and therefore a different frame of costs and other implications. The general use of this term ignores the surrounding components.
→ Creating a 'law' or a 'theory' about allocation requires exact clarification about its meaning. We have here again the same diffuse use of terms which leads to varied lines of discussions and analysis.
→ A majority of economic terms, principles, concepts, graphs, and theories represent nothing more than a wish-wash. This is essentially the core characteristic of neuroticism. This is not science!
→ From a psychoanalytical point of view, because such a way of use of terms in economics is standard, we identify a hidden cantankerousness, rigidity, a neurotic mind and distorted character, even sadism, and a taking the piss of all critical thinking. A representative of the capitalistic economics can always say to a critical approach of economic theories: "This is not what the term means."

3.3.6. Allocative Efficiency

To be mentioned here is also the term 'Allocative Efficiency'; we resume from the author: [236]

- This is a measure of the utility (satisfaction) derived from the allocation of resources.
- Allocative efficiency occurs when the value of the output that firms produce (the benefits to sellers) match the value placed on that output by consumers (the benefit) to buyers.
- The equilibrium of supply and demand in a market maximizes the total benefits received by buyers and sellers.

---

[236] Mankiw (et al.), p. 139

In the context with the use of the term 'allocation' we identify here some factors that all have a relation to other variables:

- There is a measure of the utility (satisfaction)
- There is the allocation of resources
- Allocation is linked with efficiency
- Allocation has a level of efficiency
- Allocation is linked with the value of the output that firms produce
- The value of the output is the benefit of the seller
- There is a value placed on that output by consumers
- There is a value of the output that is the benefit of the buyer
- There is equilibrium of supply and demand
- There is a total benefit received by buyers
- There is a total benefit received by sellers
- There is a relation between the total benefits received by buyers and sellers
- The equilibrium maximizes the total benefits received by buyers and sellers

The term 'allocation' is here within a wider field of connotations: The disposition of resources (goods) can be seen as 'produced, stored, and ready to distribute. We can say: the goods are available. Efficiency is here related to the (total) value of the produced goods, a value of the good placed on that output by consumers, and other values and benefits for sellers and buyers. And as a whole 'allocation' includes here variables of value, benefit, supply, demand, and implicitly a price.

It seems that the term 'allocation' becomes here a superior quality and importance. The term wants to put all possible components under one roof in order to have in the iron grip the calculated maximum profit. Allocation here has got nothing to do with logistic distribution, storage, the real transport of goods, and the planned contingency for the sale locations.

We pulled the statements into pieces and concluded:

- Efficiency includes satisfaction and this can be measured
- Efficiency also refers to allocation of resources
- Efficient is: Efficient allocation produces satisfaction
- Efficient is: the sale price matches with the consumer's price acceptance
- Efficient is: the equilibrium between demand and supply
- Efficient is: the maximized benefit by sellers and buyers
- The better the allocation of a product, the more people are satisfied.

From these statements about 'Allocative Efficiency' we conclude:

→ It's not about people's satisfaction.
→ It's about the firm's satisfaction: to get as much profit as possible.
→ Never lose the realization of a possible gain.
→ To sell you must produce with lowest cost.
→ It's a business failure if a consumer doesn't buy the good although he values it most highly.
→ The author here is unmasked as a deadening agent.
→ And the economics here shows its compulsive and greedy character.

3.3.7. Equilibrium

From Krugman (et al.) we want to have a closer look at the term and principle of 'equilibrium':

"The price that matches the quantity supplied and the quantity demanded is the **equilibrium** price; the quantity bought and sold at that price is the equilibrium quantity." [237]

- There is a quantity demanded (on the market)
- There is a quantity (of a good) supplied
- There is a price of the quantity supplied
- There is a quantity bought at that price
- There is a quantity sold at that price
- There is the equilibrium quantity
- There is an equilibrium price
- 'Equilibrium' means: balance

Equilibrium is given by:

→ The quantity of the produced (supplied) good is demanded at the given price.
→ The price of the good allows for the sale of the entire quantity of the good.

Another approach to describe the equilibrium is given by McConnel: "At the equilibrium price and quantity in competitive markets, marginal benefit equals marginal cost, maximum willingness to pay equals minimum acceptable price, and the total of consumer surplus and producer surplus is maximized ..." [238]

---

[237] Krugman (et al.), p. 80
[238] McConnel (et al.), p. 99, 72

This statement is as many other economic statements very concentrated and confusing. We need to divide the text into its pieces:

- There is an equilibrium price
- There is an equilibrium quantity
- The matter here occurs within the competitive markets
- There is a marginal benefit
- There is a marginal cost
- There is a point: marginal benefit equals marginal cost
- There is a maximum willingness to pay a minimum acceptable price
- There is the total of consumer surplus
- There is the total producer surplus
- There is a point: consumer surplus and producer surplus is maximized

→ Summarized: The sellers (producers) and buyers (consumers) in the market completely pressed out the lemon; and this final state, where no more benefit for both side is possible, leads to successful market activities; successful for both sides. So we have all sided total maximization!

There are more views and approaches to this market culmination:

Finding the equilibrium price and quantity: "There is a surplus of a good or service when the quantity supplied exceeds the quantity demanded. Surpluses occur when the price is above its equilibrium level." [239]

In the words of another economist: "Market equilibrium occurs in a market when all buyers and sellers are satisfied with their respective quantities at the market price." [240]

Another author defines: "When we say that market equilibrium is efficient, we mean simply this: if price and quantity take anything other than their equilibrium values, a transaction that will make at least some people better off…" [241] That's rather a small talk in a bar, but not a scientific statement. What is 'simple' here?

→ This kind of satisfaction can be simply a result of accepting realities as they can't make the price of goods. All consumers are always challenged with giving priorities in choosing goods and accepting given prices which they can afford. It expresses imperiousness and a possessive addiction.

---

[239] Krugman (et al.), p. 82
[240] McDowell (et al.), p. 72
[241] McDowell (et al.), p. 183

It can happen that a firm produces more of a good than is demanded. This occurs when the price is too high. Or in other words: There is no equilibrium between price and demand.

At which moment between planning and the sale of a product is the equilibrium price and quantity determined (calculated, identified)? How and when can a firm exactly know how much of a product is demanded? How and when can a firm exactly know the accepted price (by the consumers) of a product? Is the parameter 'equilibrium' a planning factor or an evaluation of the revenue result?

"There is a shortage of a good or service when the quantity demanded exceeds the quantity supplied. Shortages occur when the price is below its equilibrium level." [242]

It can happen that a firm did not produce enough of a good as the demand is higher than the supply. Economic thinking concludes: the price is too low.

We conclude: the firm can produce an additional amount of the good that is demanded without increasing the price. Or: the firm has underestimated the amount of demand. It simply does not make sense to jump in this statement directly to a higher price.

→ Greed is always running faster than the reasonable mind.

"A general principle: When demand for a good or service increases, the **equilibrium** price and the equilibrium quantity of the good or service both rise." [243]

It says: If the demand for a good does increase, then a firm can increase the price of the good. The equilibrium is given as long as the demand of the good with the increased price does not decrease the demand. The idea, that if there is more demand, the price can also increase sounds very irrational. Doubt arises if such a calculation is realistic. It only works fully if the consumers are addicted to the good.

→ The little devil is always focused on a price increase. He can never allow that anybody gets something at a generous price if some cents more could be sucked out of the consumers.

---

[242] Krugman (et al.), p. 84
[243] Krugman (et al.), p. 85

➜ The hidden business secret is here: Make people addicted to your good, physically, socially, psychologically, sensually, or spiritually! Sure it will work!

"Another general principle: When demand for a good or service decreases, the equilibrium price and the equilibrium quantity of the good or service both fall." [244]

It says: If the demand for a good decreases, then the equilibrium price and quantity falls; means: the equilibrium is not given anymore. Or: the quantity planned and produced was over-estimated and probably the calculated price too high. The price factor may be only one critical factor. There may be another good on the market that replaces this good; or the good got a bad reputation.

Another aspect here is: 'When demand for a good or service decreases…'. It states clearly: the product is planned, produced, allocated (at disposition), and distributed, in the shop and already on sale. But unfortunately the demand is low or has decreased. A (drastic) price discount helps to sell the produced amount of the good. Such a case is not always a miscalculation at the planning stage. It simply can happen to any firm with any good and at any time. The mentioned principle here is scientifically meaningless – a pseudo-scientific gobbledygook!

➜ Reducing the price does not always guarantee a higher demand.

"To summarize how market responds to a change in demand: An increase in demand leads to a rise in both the equilibrium price and the equilibrium quantity. A decrease in demand leads to a fall in both the equilibrium price and the equilibrium quantity." [245]

This summary, as well as the previous statements from the author are very complicated sentence constructions. It seems to indicate a 'law', but there is nothing that guarantees a calculated 'equilibrium' of price and quantity. The term 'equilibrium' sees rather an abuse of the meaning. We assume this 'law' should maximize both: quantity and price up to a level that does not break down.

In other words: produce as much of the good as possible and set the price as

---

[244] Krugman (et al.), p. 85
[245] Krugman (et al.), p. 85

high as possible; as long as demand is given and price is accepted. But it could also mean: Don't produce a good whose costs are not covered with the sale of the good.

→ Go always and everywhere to the most extreme limit with the aim to maximize profit!
→ Search in every little corner even for the most little space to get the best of it!

"A general principle: When supply of a good or service decreases, the **equilibrium** price of the good or service rises and the equilibrium quantity of the good or service falls." [246]

→ The omission of the demand and or the change in demand, makes this statement baseless.
→ Again we have here a very sick sentence construction. With 100% guarantee it reflects the author's mind! It expresses total imperiousness.

A supply of a good can decrease: What is the reason of a decrease? Is it a lower demand that leads to a lower production quantity? Is it the decision of the firm to decrease supply (means: production) for whatever other reason?

"An increase in supply leads to a fall in the equilibrium price and a rise in the equilibrium quantity. A decrease in supply leads to a rise in the equilibrium price and a fall in the equilibrium quantity." [247]

Again here: supply presumes production on the one side and allocation (or distribution) on the other side. Does it also mean: demand? Once the supply is organized and the good in the shop for sale, the price is long ago determined; is probably determined before production. Therefore: where and how in the entire process from production planning up to the sale is an equilibrium (increase, decrease, or fall) calculated?

"Economic loss (means an) economic profit that is less than zero. A negative economic profit is an economic loss. If he expects to sustain an economic loss indefinitely, his best bet would be to abandon (the business)." [248] The statement is deceiving: There is a zero profit (100% loss of profit) and from there we can talk about 'economic loss' which means the revenue is less than the production cost. The word indefinitely is used as if it were predictable.

---

[246] Krugman (et al.), p. 87
[247] Krugman (et al.), p. 87
[248] McDowell (et al.), p. 212

Fact is in reality, there can be times where a business can only cover costs but still survive. This may be for a year or two and then changes in the market result in profits. The suggestion 'best bet would be to abandon the business' merely reveals the endless craze for 'maximum profit'.

Price Ceiling:

"Deadweight loss is a key concept in economics, one that we will encounter whenever an action or a policy leads to a reduction in the quantity transacted below the efficient market equilibrium quantity. It is important to realize that deadweight loss ... Price ceiling causes inefficiency ... is a loss to society." [249]

Let's start here with a very normal mind:

- 'Dead': People don't like this word; it does not have any positive connotation in human's daily life.
- 'Loss' is one of the most hated words of economics.
- It has to do with an action or a policy that leads to a reduction.
- In a general understanding 'reduction' can occur with any parameter.
- 'Reduction' is also a word that opposes to 'maximizing' and 'growth.
- 'Transact' means: realizing, executing, arranging, performing, operating, passing…
- 'Transaction' is an incident, development, realization, procedure, occurrence…
- It's about 'the below the efficient market equilibrium quantity'
- It's about something important to realize
- It's a loss of economic efficiency
- It's an excess burden or allocative inefficiency

It has to do with the equilibrium: [250]

- People have more marginal benefit than marginal cost but don't buy the product.
- Or people have more marginal cost than marginal benefit and buy the product.

It happens every minute somewhere in America or Europe: People don't buy a product although there is a higher marginal benefit than the marginal cost. A compulsive person must have now a terrible rage attack: "Why the hell do these people not buy my product?" Or the economists gets crazy because

---

[249] Krugman (et al.), p. 106-107
[250] http://en.wikipedia.org/wiki/Deadweight_loss

people do something stupid; something that does not confirm their 'rational choice' theory.

Definition of 'Price Ceiling': "The maximum price a seller is allowed to charge for a product or service. Price ceilings are usually set by law and limit the seller pricing system to ensure fair and reasonable business practices." [251] The source, Investopedia, explains 'Price Ceiling': "Price ceilings are regulations designed to protect low income individuals from not being able to afford important resources.

However, many economists question their effectiveness for several reasons. For example, price ceilings will have no effect if the equilibrium price of the good is below the ceiling. If the ceiling is set below the equilibrium level, however, then there is a deadweight loss created."

Price Ceiling is a matter for 'Economics III'. We assume that 'price ceiling' is also something like a 'bad matter' for compulsive economists. The economist is limited by law in operating for the unlimited maximizing drive. That's why the author says: 'Price ceiling causes inefficiency and is a loss to society'. The word 'loss' is like 'hell' for economists. They feel offended in their ambition, omnipotence, and control, sense of honor, perfectionism, vanity, cantankerousness, and dictatorial obsession. The 'holy free market' is not taboo anymore with governmental intervention. However, the free market does not significantly exist in America and Europe as a majority of significant business fields are extremely regulated and dominated by corporations.

3.3.8. Technical Efficiency and Economic Efficiency

"The terms economically efficient and technically efficient differ in meaning. Here's how: Technical efficiency in production means that as few inputs as possible are used to produce a given output … Many different production processes can be technically efficient … A long-run production decisions, firms will look at all available production technologies and choose the technology that, given the available inputs and their prices, is the economically efficient way to produce." [252]

The crossbar is given: 'As few inputs as possible are used to produce a given output'. But what are the consequences of such a normative statement? A firm would always have to negotiate with all input-providers and to search around the globe for the cheapest input requirements. This can become very

---

[251] http://www.investopedia.com/terms/p/price-ceiling.asp#axzz1xJWGBzDw
[252] Colander, p. 296

time consuming. If there are a hundred or much more cost factors (inputs) in a firm (in the production), then a department would have a lot of work for this.

→ We suspect here as in many contexts a compulsion to save every cent of costs (input).
→ Avarice is everywhere.
→ Who are these avaricious people?

Certainly, cost planning is important, for example: The indivisible setup costs are: "…the cost of an indivisible input for which a certain minimum amount of production must be undertaken before the input becomes economically feasible to use." [253] The author continues: "…the minimum efficient level of production is the amount of production that spreads setup costs out sufficiently for a firm to undertake production profitably." [254]

We suppose that such a normative is meant for big production entities and rather not for small firms.

But the planning can become a problem:

- The sale of the goods is tough.
- A competitor suddenly has a similar product that is (much) cheaper.
- Unexpected technical failure produces extra costs.

→ Planning is necessary, but a compulsive planning never matches a vivid reality.

Sometimes the economical feasibility requires calculating costs of input and the price of a good within the frame of several goods where some have a higher profit and others a lower profit.

About Equilibrium it is said: "…a market in which neither suppliers nor consumers collude and in which prices are free to move up and down, the forces of supply and demand interact to arrive at equilibrium."
Equilibrium quantity "…is the amount bought and sold at the equilibrium price. Equilibrium price is the price toward which the invisible hand drives the market. At the equilibrium price, quantity demanded equals quantity supplied." [255]

---

[253] Colander, p. 297
[254] Colander, p. 298
[255] Colander, p. 95

Do suppliers never collude? Consumers are individuals and therefore there is a very low probability that a significant group of consumers collude. Prices are never free to move up and down; prices are planned and determined, and must be adapted to the market.

A permanent 100% equilibrium during a long period is not probable. In the best case equilibrium is possible within a certain variance. What are the criteria for an acceptable variance extension? People decide about prices trying to find a balance in the dynamic of price movements on the market. There is no invisible hand!

Each firm looks at the other firms, compares, adjusts, and decides about production and price policy. All firms move up and down, expand or reduce.

There are products that can have much easier long term equilibrium than other products that are more sensible to movements on the market (e.g. due to raw material speculations or political developments).

→ Production and the market are together something like a vivid organism, permanently in balancing all variables in order to get the possible optimum.

It would be easier to understand the 'equilibrium' in the context of production or market sectors. The more money is concentrated on some corporations and the more some single top-masters rule over trillions of Euros and Dollars, the more they can deliberately create selected disequilibrium to damage competitors and even societies or nations.

Internal disequilibrium of a firm we could consider as a matter of one firm. But if several or many firms or some very big corporations lose their equilibrium (of a sustainable variation), then it affects an entire production or service sector or even the entire society. Such a situation could lead to a continental or global economic earthquake.

We had the first global earthquake of the 21st century in 2008. We expect the second global earthquake in 2012-2013, much bigger than the one in 2008 because the minimum equilibrium of the economy in the Western world (within economies and between different economies) is already heavily damaged if not already destroyed.

We could conclude that this is the result of a systemic failure of economics (theories). But we could also ask if this is the result of a long planned roadmap to destroy entire countries aiming for supra fascist states-organization, or in a global perspective the 'one world order'.

→ Equilibrium can never be static; is always in a dynamic. And there is no magical 'invisible hand'.
→ Economic growth is always more or less in different sectors and this creates sector disequilibrium.
→ There must be criteria for an acceptable variance within each single market segment.
→ Yearly analysis of disequilibrium would allow taking the right measures for reestablishing equilibrium.
→ The madness of 'growth' and the insane speculation businesses create most disequilibrium.
→ Disequilibrium can be the aim of an economic (industrial) war between competitors.
→ Disequilibrium and equilibrium can become a matter of a society or a region of several countries.

Another very important question is: What produces disequilibrium? Some examples:

- Speculation businesses (raw material)
- Casino (betting)
- Interest politics of banks
- Governmental intervention
- Governmental ignorance
- Warmongering (Balkans, Middle East, Afghanistan)
- Damages of Climate Change
- Psychopathy and psychosis on the upper echelon
- Industrial espionage (much bigger than CIA, MI5, and Mossad together)
- Lobbyism
- Corruption
- Ignorant politicians
- Industrial wars

There are also other causes of disequilibrium: [256]

- Excess supply produces disequilibrium: quantity supplied is greater than quantity demanded.
- Excess demand produces disequilibrium: quantity demanded is greater than

---

[256] Colander, p. 95-96

quantity supplied.

- Prices tend to rise when there is excess demand and fall when there is excess supply.
- "When quantity demanded is greater than quantity supplied, prices tend to rise.
- When quantity supplied is greater than quantity demanded, prices tend to fall.
- Whenever quantity supplied and quantity demanded are unequal, price tends to change.

→ A general equilibrium is never possible.
→ Equilibrium is possible in a very limited frame.
→ Equilibrium is never stable during a period of more than some weeks or months.

From equilibrium analysis we can continue with supply/demand analysis: "Supply/demand analysis, used without adjustment, is most appropriate for questions where the goods are a small percentage of the entire economy … The fallacy of composition is the false assumption that what is true for a part will also be true for the whole." [257]

- It is about supply and demand analysis
- It is about analysis without adjustment
- Supply and demand analysis is not for a complex economic field
- It is about analysis of goods of small percentage of the economy
- It is not about analysis of goods of the entire economy
- What is true for a part is not true for the whole
- Concluding from a part to the whole is a fallacy

The problem of economic concepts, theories, and science in general is:

→ They too often, if not nearly everywhere, conclude from a part to the whole.
→ They too often do not distinguish between the different sizes of (small medium) firms.
→ They too often do not make clear the differences between firms and corporations.
→ They too often do not distinguish between the characteristics of consumers.
→ They too often do not distinguish between the characteristics of all the

---

[257] Colander, p. 100

goods.

→ They too often do not distinguish between the characteristics of products and services.

→ They too often do not distinguish between the goods for needs and goods for wants.

→ They too often ignore the 'price' that 5 billion people pay for the profits of capitalism.

3.3.9. Equity

Short definition: The term 'equity' means: "The prosperity of distributing economic prosperity fairly among the members of society."

Or in other words: "The gains from trade in a market are like a cake to be distributed among the market participants." [258]

In easy understanding:

- Efficiency = the cake is as big as possible
- Equity = the cake is divided fairly
- Fair or fairly = proper, just, honest, free from bias or injustice or dishonesty

The gains from trade means: the profit. And the profit goes only to the one side. The profit can be long term sustainable for other use (investment). On the other side, the benefit consumers have (the satisfaction and well-being with the goods they bought) is very time limited and not sustainable; in most cases of consumption they can't use it for long and in case of other use (investment) there is rather not much sustainability.

Economic prosperity is even in capitalistic market not distributed fairly. The goal 'as big as possible' is again a sign of compulsion and greed; and it's a normative term that ends in the trap of 'getting the most it can': a life long race and a race for centuries – if there is a future for humanity!

→ The 'equity' turns out to be a bubble of heated air. This is not a scientific approach about fairness and equity.

3.3.10. Concept of Elasticity

---

[258] Mankiw (et al.), p. 148

Short definition: Elastic or elasticity means: flexible, adaptable, tolerant, accommodating; or capability to move between a 'more or less'; there is an original shape, length, weight, and it can move within a certain frame.

At first sight we expect with a 'concept of elasticity' that everything and everybody in the market is or must be 'elastic'. What is this good for, favorable or meaningful?

Another approach to understand the term 'elasticity': "The price elasticity of demand for a good is a measure of the responsiveness of the quantity demanded of that good to changes in its price. The price elasticity of demand for a good is defined as the percentage change in the quantity demanded that results from a 1 per cent change in its price." [259]

For economics there is price elasticity: "The price elasticity of demand measures how much the quantity demanded responds to a change in price." [260] The business interest is: If consumer income changes, how does the elasticity demand change? If income changes, is there a higher quantity of demand (in a product)?

→ The economic advice is: Permanently control the price elasticity of demand! You could lose money or you could risk your profit maximizing. Let's have a look what the experts say to that:

"Why does it matter whether demand is unit-elastic, inelastic, or elastic? Because this classification predicts how changes in the price of a good will affect the total revenue earned by producers from the sale of that good. In many real-life situations … it is crucial to know how price changes affect total revenue. Total revenue is defined as the total value of sales of a good or service: the price multiplied by the quantity sold." [261]

"The price elasticity of demand tells us what happens to total revenue when price changes: its size determines which effect-the price effect or the quantity effect – is stronger. Specifically:

- If demand for a good is unit-elastic (the price elasticity of demand is 1), an increase in price does not change total revenue. In this case, the quantity effect and the price effect exactly offset each other.
- If demand for a good is inelastic (the price elasticity of demand is less than

[259] McDowell (et al.), p. 91
[260] Mankiw (et al.), p. 95
[261] Krugman (et al.), p. 140

1), a higher price increases total revenue. In this case, the price effect is stronger than the quantity effect.

- If demand for a good is elastic (the price elasticity of demand is greater than 1), an increase in price reduces total revenue. In this case, the quantity effect is stronger than the price effect." [262]

Krugman (et al.) has more to say: [263]

"The price elasticity of demand tends to be high if there are other goods that consumers regard as similar and would be willing to consume instead. The price elasticity of demand tends to be low if there are no close substitutes.

The price elasticity of demand tends to be low if a good is something you must have, like a life-saving medicine. The price elasticity of demand tends to be high if the good is a luxury – something you can easily live without.

The price elasticity of demand tends to be low when spending on a good account for a small share of a consumer's income. In that case, a significant change in the price of the good has little impact on how much the consumer spends. In contrast, when a good accounts for a significant share of a consumer's spending, the consumer is likely to be very responsive to a change in price. In this case, the price elasticity of demand is high.

Time: In general, the price elasticity of demand tends to increase as consumers have more time to adjust to a price change. This means that the long-run price elasticity of demand is often higher than the short-run elasticity."

Importance of price elasticity:

- The cross-price elasticity of demand: How does the quantity demanded of one good change when the price of another good changes? (by substitutes or complements)

- Price elasticity of supply: How much does the quantity supply of a good respond to a change in the price of that good?

Economic theories say; summarized here: [264]

---

[262] Krugman (et al.), p. 141
[263] Krugman (et al.), p. 144
[264] Mankiw (et al.), p. 95-115

- Goods with close substitutes tend to have more elastic demand.
- The more substitutes, the more elasticity
- Necessities (needs) tend to have inelastic demand
- Luxurious goods (wants) tend to have elastic demand
- In the end for a seller is important: the changes in total expenditure and total revenue.
- Changes in sales in relation to changes in price result in changes in total revenue.

The business interest is obvious: How much are consumers willing to move away from the good as its price rises? If there is a clear answer, then it leads a producer to the question: How can the consumers be manipulated to leave a good (from another producer) and to buy the good from the producer having a new good (substitute) on the market.

→ This is simply another approach to influence the consumer's optimal choice.

A next step is the price elasticity: Price elasticity of demand is "the percentage change in quantity demanded divided by the percentage change in price." [265]

- There is a percentage-change in quantity demanded: e.g. 10 % more or 12% % less demand
- There is a percentage-change in price: e.g. 5% higher or 8% lower price

In other words:

- Demand and price can vary, can increase or decrease.
- There is more or less (increase or decrease) demand for a good.
- There is a higher or lower (increase or decrease) price of a good.

→ Common sense. Banality! But for a corporation calculating with cents and seconds multiplied by hundreds of millions or even a billion it becomes financially important.

The author continues with the price elasticity of supply: "…is the percentage change in quantity supplied divided by the percentage change in price."

In other words:

- There is an increase (x %) or decrease (y %) of quantity.

---

[265] Colander, p. 154

- There is an increase (h %) or decrease (k %) of price.
- Both variables can be combined calculated and this is the parameter for: 'Price elasticity of supply'

In the words from Colander: "Price elasticity is the percentage change in quantity divided by the percentage change in price." [266]

And where does this parameter lead us? Let's combine the variations:

- There is an increase of quantity and at the same time an increase of price.

Comment: The firm makes more profit due to an increase of quantity; and the firm makes even more profit due to an increase of price. That's a celestial business!

- There is a decrease of quantity and at the same time a decrease of price.

    Comment: The firm sells less quantity and therefore makes less profit. That's not good! And as at the same time the price also decreases, the business is even worse! No firm likes that.

- There is an increase of quantity and at the same time a decrease of price.

    Comment: The firm makes more profit due to an increase of quantity. But at the same time here is a decrease of price. And that is not good. Depending on the amount of price decrease, the business is really bad as profit is low or even gone. Here is even a deficit risk. Very bad!

- There is a decrease of quantity and at the same time an increase of price.

    Comment: The firm sells less quantity and that's not good; it leads to less or no profit. But as at the same time that the price increases, the decrease of quantity can be balanced with the higher price and in the end the profit is given.

→ As firms want to maximize profit, they must strategically act to find a balance between increase and decrease of quantity and increase or decrease of price.
→ The price elasticity of supply gives the firm an indication about how the firm must strategically manage the variables to make profit.

---

[266] Colander, p. 155

The strategic modus operandi is expressed in the following statements between a state of elastic and inelastic:

"…demand or supply is elastic if the percentage change in quantity is greater than the percentage change in price. Conversely, demand or supply is inelastic if the percentage change in quantity is less than the percentage change in price." [267]

- Demand or supply is 'elastic' can mean: demand is more flexible; sell more goods.
- Demand or supply is 'inelastic' can mean: demand is less flexible; increase the price.
- We interpret 'elastic': more or less instable or flexible
- We interpret 'inelastic': more or less stable or inflexible

3.3.11. Substitution and Elasticity

"The most important determinant of price elasticity of demand is the number of substitutes for the good … Factors that affect a good's substitutability of demand differ from factors that affect a good's substitutability of supply." [268]

Again in parts; with an apology for misinterpretation due to the distorted (very complicated) statement from the author:

- There are factors that determine price elasticity; means: instability.
- There are substitutes; that means: other goods that can replace a good.
- There is a demand for substitutes of a good; there are substitutes.
- There are factors that determine the substitutability of a good.
- The more substitutes for a good, the more a price of this good is instable, means 'elastic'.

→ A consumer can become a maniac always searching for a substitute and choosing between different substitutes.
→ A producer has fear that a competitor has a substitute of his product or that he must find a substitute to react on a given change in demand.

Another simple and clear explanation about 'substitution' is: "When the price of a good changes, the quantity of it demanded changes for two reasons: the substitution effect and the income effect. The substitution effect refers to the

---

[267] Colander, p. 162
[268] Colander, p. 162

fact that when the price of a good goes up, substitutes for that good become relatively more attractive, causing some consumers to abandon the good for its substitutes." [269]

→ Consumers can also simply abandon the good and its substitute and don't even try to find a substitute.

3.3.12. Substitution and Demand

"Two goods are **substitutes** if a rise in the price of one good leads to an increase in the demand for the other good ... Two goods are **complements** if a rise in the price of one good leads to a decrease in the demand for the other good." [270]

The number of substitutes a good has is affected by several factors ... the most important factors are: [271]

- The time period being considered
- The degree to which a good is a luxury
- The market definition
- The importance of the good in one's budget

→ The more substitutes, the more elastic is the demand and the more elastic is (must be) the supply.

If a production entity produces a good (an original), it must expect that sooner or later a competitor will produce a substitute of this good to get its consumers of the (original) good buying his substitute that is a bit cheaper.

With the time there are several substitutes from several firms on the market. Obviously the production entity of the original good, will have a severe loss. How can it protect itself from such market dynamics? It must produce the substitutes itself either in its firms; or it produces substitutes for its original products with other firms that they buy or build up. – Where will all this lead in the end if we extrapolate this example with 100 corporations and 10,000 goods?

3.3.13. Time and Supply

---

[269] McDowell (et al.), p. 128
[270] Krugman (et al.), p. 69
[271] Colander, p. 162

There is an interrelation between time and supply: "To emphasize the importance of time, economists distinguish three time periods relevant to supply": [272]

1) In the instantaneous period, quantity supplied is fixed, so supply is perfectly inelastic. This supply is sometimes called the momentary supply.

Comment: In a present period where quantity supplied is fixed, supply is inflexible. The word 'perfectly' seems to mean: ideal, optimal. But why is this ideal, optimal? What is the benefit?

2) In the short run, some substitution is possible, so short-run supply is somewhat elastic.

Comment: In a short period, where a substitution is given, the supply in this time period is a little bit flexible. What is the benefit? 'A little bit' sounds rather 'not good'. The word 'somewhat' is not really an expression of a scientific statement.

3) In the long run, significant substitution is possible; supply becomes very elastic.

Comment: In a longer time period, where a substitution is given, the supply is very flexible. Also "demand generally becomes more elastic." [273] In a long period, where a substitution is given, the supply in this time period is very flexible. 'Very flexible' sounds 'attractive', 'positive'. But what is the benefit? What exactly is the potential frame of action here?

"Firms have a strong incentive to separate out people with less elastic demand and charge them a higher price … Economists call this price discrimination." [274]

Comment: 'Incentive' means here: motive, stimulus, benefit, or product of high importance. It also can mean a 'performance impulse'. With this, a firm can separate people (focus on people) that have a rather inflexible demand and charge a higher price. The other way round would be: A firm without or with products of little motive, stimulus, benefit, or of low importance can't charge a higher price.

---

[272] Colander, p. 163
[273] Colander, p. 164
[274] Colander, p. 168

3.3.14. Income Elasticity

"Income elasticity of demand shows the responsiveness of demand to changes in income ... Cross-price elasticity of demand shows the responsiveness of demand to changes in prices of related goods." [275]

There is an 'income elasticity of demand'. Or in other words there are several variables:

- There is a demand for flexible income, for more flexible income.

Comment: means that the income is not very flexible or inflexible).

- There is responsiveness to changes in income.

  Comment: A decrease in wages requires more substitutes or people simply buy less goods. An increase in wages doesn't necessary lead to more sales or to the sale of more expensive products.

- There is demand that income changes.

  Comment: If more and more people can't live their life on the wages they get due to high prices, these people require higher wages. If they don't have enough money to live their life, the producers get a lot less profit and some producers will even fail.

- There is a 'cross-price'.

- Comment: If there is a change in wage, people compare prices of related goods (they consume) and move up or down the price categories of specific products to find a new balance in their bundle of goods and expenses.

"Shoes are a necessity – a good that has an income elasticity between 0 and 1. The consumption of a necessity rises by a smaller proportion than the rise in income ... The term applied to such goods is inferior goods - goods whose consumption decreases when income increases." [276]

In other words, there are several variables:

---

[275] Colander, p. 169
[276] Colander, p. 170

- Elasticity can be measured: 0 = no elasticity; 1 = total elasticity; or e.g. 0,5 = half elasticity
- There is a consumption of a necessity
- Consumption of a necessity can increase
- Consumption of a necessity can decrease
- Income can increase
- Income can decrease
- People buy fewer additional shoes in proportion to a higher wage.
- There is interdependence between consumption of a necessity and change in income
- Consumption of a necessity rises by a smaller proportion than the rise in income
- Consumption (demand) of inferior goods decreases when income increases

→ The thesis expresses a generalization that is surely not valid for all kind of 'inferior goods'.
→ We would expect here a full list of such 'inferior goods'.
→ Categorizing 'indispensable goods' as 'inferior' expresses arrogance and disrespect.
→ Why should people buy fewer additional shoes when they get a higher wage?
→ The motive can't lie in the higher wage. Is there a psychological factor?

"Positive cross-price elasticity of demand means the goods are substitutes – goods that can be used in place of one another. When the price of a good goes up, the demand for the substitute goes up.

Substitutes have positive cross-price elasticity; complements have negative cross-price elasticity." [277]

In other words, there are several variables:

- There is cross-price
- Cross-price means: two or more goods, each with a different price
- There is cross-price elasticity
- There is an elasticity of demand
- There are substitutive goods
- A substitute is a good that can replace another good
- A good has a price

---

[277] Colander, p. 170-171

- A substitute has a price
- A price can go up (or down)
- A demand can go up (or down)
- There is a positive elasticity; means: high flexibility
- There is a cross-price-elasticity; means: elasticity of prices between a good and a substitute
- A complement is a good that serves (is used) in conjunction of another good
- A substitute is not a complement
- Complements have negative (means: no) cross-price elasticity
- A substitute has positive (means: existing) cross-price elasticity

Here we identify several variables. Scientific methodology has statistical concepts of multi-variant analysis that can easily operate with 30-100 and more variables, each with its own scale, from thousands of people, consumers or producers. Such analysis is necessary in order to formulate a kind of 'law' based on proven theses with a probability, with clusters or variances in hundred and more product segments.

→ A scientific book about economics (from traditional universities or business schools) should show hundreds of results of such analysis from different countries.

As long as this is not done with results repeatedly confirmed or rejected and therefore revised, the economic 'laws' and theses remain mere hypotheses or unproven statements.

3.3.15. Diseconomy of Scale

'Economy of scale' is about labor supply, advanced technology, new resources, new implementation, and specialization. An increase of such parameters increases the production while it decreases average cost of production and which leads to higher revenue.

'Diseconomy of scale' is given when an increase of output leads to an increase of the (average) costs of production.

Above a certain size of a firm the costs of production (per unit) does not fall anymore, but increases.

There are several possible reasons for this:

- Demotivation due to worse working conditions (size of working space)
- Hindrance in efficient working (e.g. small kitchen for 4 cooks)
- Pressure of work and consequently distress
- Operating machines beyond the usual working schedule
- Excessive strain on infrastructure

In the diseconomy of scale described by Colander there are more factors to be considered: [278]

1) Production relationships have social dimensions, which introduce the potential for important diseconomies of scale into the production process in two ways:

a) As the size of the firm increases, monitoring costs generally increase.
b) As the size of the firm increases, team spirit or morale generally decreases.

Comment: 1) a) The statement expresses common sense. More interesting would be to get a picture about under which circumstances monitoring costs will not increase. What are the 'social dimensions'? What is the social dimension of a very low wage? What is the social dimension of producing in Asia, China or Africa?

Comment: 1) b) The statement means: Production unities with big amount of laborers (e.g. 500-1,000 workers in one workplace) function with low spirit and low morale. As there are thousands of such production units in Asia and elsewhere, it seems that owners and mangers of big companies don't bother about human values such as team spirit and morale. We can conclude: The team spirit and morale attitudes in big corporations are very low.

2) Monitoring costs that are the costs incurred by the organizer of production in seeing to it that the employees do what they are supposed to do.

Comment: It means: Worker must be controlled so that they perform accordingly.

3) The other social dimension that can contribute to diseconomies of scale is the loss of team spirit: the feelings of friendship and being part of a team that bring out people's best efforts. Most types of production are highly dependent on team spirit. When the team spirit or morale is lost, production slows considerably. The larger the firm is, the more difficult it is to maintain team spirit.

---

[278] Colander, p. 299-300

The essential variables are:

- Social dimension (team spirit, morale)
- Size of a firm (increasing, decreasing)
- Monitoring costs (controlling worker's performance)
- Feelings of friendship
- People's best effort
- Long-run average total costs

➜ We have here again the lemon-principle that must be used everywhere in all parameters!

4) …constant returns to scale where long-run average total costs do not change with an increase in output.

Comment: 'Constant return to scale means: "returns to scale … of scale … describes what happens as the scale of production increases in the long run, when all input levels including physical capital usage are variable (chosen by the firm). [279]

Is there a production where long-run average total costs do not change? As in the market everything changes periodically, we must assume that long-run average total costs also change.

There are many production costs that are variable and therefore create a change in total cost. An increase in an output means a higher amount of product outputs. It does not sound logical, that there could be invariant cost (raw material, electricity, monitoring costs, etc.).

"Economies of scale are an important reason why firms attempt to expand their markets either at home or abroad. If they can make and sell more at lower per-unit costs, they will make more profits. Diseconomies of scale prevent a firm from expanding and can lead corporate raiders to buy the firm and break it up in the hope that the smaller production units will be more efficient, thus eliminating some of the diseconomies of scale … Economies and diseconomies of scale play important roles in real-world long-run production decisions." [280]

Important variables are herewith:

---

[279] http://en.wikipedia.org/wiki/Returns_to_scale
[280] Colander, p. 301

- Production and sale of more products at lower cost per unit
- More profit is possible with lower cost per unit
- Sometimes expansion is necessary or at least profitable
- Smaller production units can be more efficient
- Risk: Raiders try to buy the firm that does not expand efficiently

→ It's all about maximizing profit by expanding under certain circumstances; not without risks.

3.3.16. Envelope Relationship

"Since in the long run all inputs are flexible, while in the short run some inputs are not flexible, long-run cost will always be less than or equal to short-run cost at the same level of output.
The envelope relationship is the relationship explaining that, at the planned output level, short-run average total cost equals long-run average total cost, but at all other levels of output, short-run average total cost is higher than long-run average total cost.

The envelope relationship is the relationship between long-run and short-run average total costs.
In the short run, you have chosen a plant; that plant is fixed, and its costs for that period are part of your average fixed costs. Changes must be made within the confines of that plant. In the long run, you can change everything, choosing the combination of inputs in the most efficient manner … Constraints always raise costs (or at least won't lower them). So in the long run, costs must be the same or lower." [281]

Let's identify the elements of the statements and its variables:

- In the long run all inputs are flexible (long-term flexibility)
- In the short run some inputs are not flexible (short-term inflexibility)
- Long-run cost are less than or equal to short-run cost at the same level of output
- There is a planned output level
- There is a short-run average total cost
- There is a long-run average total cost
- There are other levels of output
- Short-run average total cost can be higher or lower than long-run average

---

[281] Colander, p. 301-302

total cost

→ Such kinds of interrelations vary between small firm, medium sized firms, and big corporations.
→ It is not correct to describe interdependences in the business world (production entities) without distinguishing between sizes of firms and even the kinds of products.

3.3.17. Competitive Market

"Roughly, a competitive market is a market in which there are many buyers and sellers of the same good or service. More precisely, the key feature of a competitive market is that no individual's actions have a noticeable effect on the price at which the good or service is sold." [282]

"A market is an institution or mechanism that brings buyers ('demanders') and sellers ('suppliers') into contact. A market system conveys the decisions made by buyers and sellers of products and resources." [283]

Let's have a closer look at this statement:

- A market is an institution: What kind of institution? Is it a business institution?
- An 'institution' has a legal structure like a firm. But this doesn't make sense here.
- A market is a mechanism: What kind of mechanism? It must be something mechanical.
- A market is an institution or mechanism: Is it one of both? Or can it be both?
- It is a mechanism that brings buyers and sellers together. 'Mechanism' sounds like a gadget.
- The 'event' mechanism is: Consumers want to buy and producers want to sell.
- There is a market and a market system: What is the difference?
- Instead of 'conveys' we could say: directs, organizes, or balances.
- A market system conveys the decisions made by … buyers and sellers.
- Is it not the system or a mechanism that conveys the decisions of buyers

---

[282] Krugman (et al.), p. 64
[283] McConnel (et al.), p. 32

and sellers?

From here we could interpret: buyers and sellers of products and resources are energetic agents with an intrinsic unspoken aim to create a dynamic balance of all components of the market; or of the buyers' and seller's interests. In simpler words: Buyers and sellers come together to make a deal.

→ Buyers and sellers come into contact because they have a complementary interest and this interest is the motivational drive.

→ Buyers and sellers meet each other not in the Church, but there where the one has something to sell and the other has a motive to buy this something. And this 'place' is called 'market'.

We have to distinguish between different price-takers: "A price-taking producer is a producer whose actions have no effect on the market price of the good or service it sells. A price-taking consumer is a consumer whose actions have no effect on the market price of the good or service he or she buys. A perfectly competitive market is a market in which all market participants are price-takers. [284]

The imperfectly competitive market is described as follows: "Imperfectly competitive firm, a firm that has at least some control over the market price of its product." [285] Interesting is here the part 'at least some control'. This is not a scientific statement. Nothing is clear about this 'some'.

"Neither the actions of a price-taking producer nor those of a price-taking consumer can influence the market price of a good … In a perfectly competitive market all producers and consumers are price-takers. Consumers are almost always price-takers, but this is often not true of producers. An industry in which producers are price-takers is a perfectly competitive industry … A perfectly competitive industry contains many producers, each of which produces a standardized product (also known as a commodity) but none of which has a large market share … Most perfectly competitive industries are also characterized by fee entry and exit." [286]
The question is: When is a production profitable? The standard answer of several sources is: "The economic profit of a firm is the firm's revenue minus the opportunity cost of its resources."

---

[284] Krugman (et al.), p. 198
[285] McDowell (et al.), p. 166
[286] Krugman (et al.), p. 201

→ As the opportunity cost of given resources of a firm periodically changes, the game is like periodically turning another wheel. And this leads us to the hell of compulsive dynamics.

There is no economic thinking and analysis without the 'opportunity cost': "Remember that one of the basic principles of economics is that the true measure of the cost of doing something is always its opportunity cost. That is, the real cost of something is what you must give up to get it." [287]

→ Therefore, a firm must periodically calculate the real cost of something by calculating the cost of what which has to be given up.

The principle "The economic profit of a firm is the firm's revenue minus the opportunity cost of its resources" leads to an endless moving in a circle trying to find a better opportunity that produces more profit with the given resources. Isn't this totally insane, except if a firm is in danger to fall?

An explicit cost is a cost that actually involves laying out money. (See: chapter 3.1.4.) An implicit cost does not require an outlay of money; it is measured by the value, in monetary terms, of benefits that are forgone. (See chapter 3.1.5.)

"The accounting profit of a firm is the firm's revenue minus the explicit cost of its resources. It is usually larger than the economic profit." [288]

'Many buyers and sellers of the same good or service' is not enough to say that there is competitive market. A corporate group of vegetable production has much more flexibility in price decision due to its high quantity production and advanced techniques and therefore an immense effect. A small firm that also produces vegetables can never produce in high quantity and the machines are much less productive. Therefore such a small firm has very little flexibility in price decision.

→ We conclude here that there is no competitive market; here is one powerful producer that suffocates a very small producer with highest risk of failure.

Definition of competition:

- Where more than one firm offers the same product
- Where substitutes exist (the closer the degree of substitutability)

---

[287] Krugman (et al.), p. 101
[288] Krugman (et al.), p. 204

- On the level where ties exists (service, human factors, …)

A key theory is: "A firm in a competition market … tries to maximize profit…" [289]

Does this mean that a firm that is not in a competition market doesn't try to maximize profit? It would be more realistic first to say: A firm in a competition market tries to make the business work and to get success. 'To maximize profit' is a subliminal normative statement put here as if it would be a necessary empirical factor to make the business work and to get success in the competitive market.

Furthermore, a firm in a competition market can fully get satisfaction and well-being without a 'maximum profit'. The compulsive profit-addiction ('getting the maximum profit') dominates here as everywhere the theoretical economic approach. It's always an infective virus for the students as well as for the world of businesses.

→ Competitive market means: permanent activity, movement, control, innovation, flexibility, changes, analysis, renewal, new decisions, adaptations, implementations, etc.
→ Competitive market means a permanent rivalry, hindrance, economic fight, battle, or war between the competitors.
→ Competitive market forces to critical means: lies, cheat, industrial espionage, sabotage of other competitors, corruption, dirty games, speculations, casino games, etc.

The so called 'perfect market' does not exist as humans are not perfect, as nothing is infallible in human's life (except the Archetypes of the Soul), and economics is far away from scientific perfectionism or perfect economic 'laws'.

The 'perfect market' is an ideal or a deceiving lie. A meaningful and indispensable question is certainly: Is there an alternative to the use of Machiavelli's methods in the market, something like a fair competitive market?

To anticipate the result of our exploration, the 'perfect market' is a fairy tale, making students and economists to believe that Jesus could really walk on water and that it is the stork that brings the babies. How can the authors of economics dare to even introduce such an idea of a 'perfect market'? In their

---

[289] Mankiw (et al.), p. 288

mind they must be beyond the real world, driven by a psychotic pseudo-religious mission.

Definition of 'Perfect Competition': "A perfectly competitive industry is an industry in which producers are price-takers. A producer's market share is the fraction of the total industry output accounted for by that producer's output. A good is a standardized product, also known as a commodity, when consumers regard the products of different producers as the same good." [290]

Let's go through some statements of economic authors, Colander (et al.): [291]

A perfectly competitive market is a market in which economic forces operate unimpeded. For a market to be called perfectly competitive, it must meet some stringent conditions:

- Both buyers and sellers are price takers
- The number of firms is large
- There are no barriers to entry
- Firms' products are identical
- There is complete information
- Selling firms are profit-maximizing entrepreneurial firms

Colander (et al.) explains his necessary conditions for perfect competition:

1) Both buyers and sellers are price takers. A price taker is a firm or individual who takes the price determined by market supply and demand as given.

Comment: Price takers are consumers, consumers for personal life or consumers for business inputs. Nothing can be perfect with consumers as extensively described in Chapter 2. Not in all cases these consumers take the determined price. There are businesses where the customers can negotiate. And there are businesses that dominate the price politics without any chance for the consumer to modify it. Taking a determined price has got nothing to do with perfectionism.

Consumers are forced to accept a price or to leave the deal. Consumers have no right here; especially because in the price there is always an unknown (secret) calculated proportion of profit.

2) The number of firms is large. Large means sufficiently large so that any one

---

[290] Krugman (et al.), p. 199
[291] Colander, p. 318

firm's output compared to the market output is imperceptible, and what one firm does, has no influence on what other firms do.

Comment: Here the first meaning is: There are many firms; and indeed in America and Europe and around the globe there are millions of firms and a few thousand big corporations. But the second meaning is as the author says: 'sufficient large'. The word 'large' refers not to the amount of firms, but rather to the size. But the way the author writes it, it still refers to the amount of firms and not to the size of firms. Let's say: we have a super large amount of firms around the globe; and we have many large and very large firms around the globe. Again we identify a confusing use of words.

All these firms have an output, the small ones have a small output and the big ones have a big output. The author says that the output is 'imperceptible'. Really? Everywhere we perceive, if we have open eyes, the outputs of firms. Above that, most firms have a website where one can consult and see their output and compare with whatever exists on the market.

The word 'imperceptible' stimulates to ask: What is 'imperceptible' on the market, in the firms and corporations, with and in the products?

Another part of the statement says that 'what one firm does, has no influence on what other firms do'. If John opens a bar, he sees what his competitor does around the corner in his bar. If John's competitor decreases his price, then it has an influence in the business of John. All firms and all big corporations are permanently occupied with all legal and illegal tools in finding out what their competitors do in their production planning, production processes, and their price politics. This knowledge significantly mutually influences what they do.

3) There are no barriers to entry. Barriers to entry are social, political, or economic impediments that prevent firms from entering a market. They might be legal barriers such as exist when firms acquire a patent to produce a certain product. Barriers might be technological.

Comment: There are barriers to entry, especially those imposed by governments. There are also barriers given by banks as they decide who can get how much business loan. Money can open doors or lack of money can hinder to enter the market. And the big corporations are in general an iron barrier for thousands of new business ventures. But, yes, let's accept that everybody can theoretically try starting a business.

It is well known that big corporations and shopping centers or shopping malls have destroyed and continue destroying millions of small and medium sized businesses. These businesses simply can't compete with big corporations. A classical example is bio-agriculture and in general small farms. The result is a dramatically shrinking middle class. And this is intentional in order to dominate the national, continental, Western world, or global market.

The barrier then lies more in the marketing power. If corporations have a hundred million or much more than a billion dollars or Euros, then those with less financial potential for marketing can't really compete.

The insanity of regulations and accreditations and business associations extremely hinder the establishment of new businesses, especially pioneering and vanguard businesses. Additionally lobbyism blackmailing politicians and governments to set up barriers for future ventures (e.g. renewable energy).

If in the United States 6 media giants control 90% of what the consumers and business people read, watch or listen to, then there is little chance to establish a new business that competes with the big corporations. 232 media executives control the information diet of 277 million Americans. The same can be said about Europe where 2 media giants control much of what the consumers and business people read, or watch, or listen to. [292] And these media also operate globally.

There is no fair chance to enter the market. And if a firm tries and get success, then the owner must expect economic warmongers knocking at his door. These people dispose of hundreds of millions, even billions of dollars to get rid of any competitor or other business that takes away a slice of the profit cake that they want. These monsters are never satisfied and want to control and benefit from everything on earth.

4) Firms' products are identical. This requirement means that each firm's output is indistinguishable from any other firm's output.

Comment: The author presents his concept of 'perfect market'. But here it seems this concept is reduced to firms producing goods that are identical. This is one dimension we can accept. But there is another dimension, namely the forces between competing firms on a variety of levels (products). To ignore this dimension is a deception and camouflage. Which firms produce 100% identical products? Not many. Is a firm that produces (normal) milk or (normal) printer paper always identical (with its products) to a similar firm that also produces (normal) milk or (normal) printer paper, but with 5-20%

---

[292] http://www.frugaldad.com

difference in quality or taste?

The term 'indistinguishable' has an absolute claim. And this means one firm copies another firm with its production. Is a Spanish 'pizzeria' indistinguishable' from a pizzeria in Italy? Or, is a pizza from a corporation chain the same as a pizza from an Italian cook in Barcelona, who has his pizzeria there? Do BMW and VW produce the same (identical) products? Yes: they produce cars. But no, they are not the same as their cars are very different. The author's requirement does not create a 'perfect market' with the requirement of 'identical' products.

5) There is complete information. In a perfectly competitive market, firms and consumers know all there is to know about the market- prices, products, and available technology, to name a few aspects.

Comment: Please where on this earth can we find 'complete information'? We will never find 'complete information' about the corporations' activities if it is behind the curtain. God may have complete information; sometimes the CIA, Mossad, Google, or Facebook with their one billion users may have a lot of information about what is of interest to them. It appears to me that this economist is favoring 100% citizen control.

Or, in real business situations, who really has 'complete information', firms and consumers about the product, available technology, prices, etc.? If the Americans and the Europeans would know what is in their food and beverages, the chemicals in cars and furniture or other products, they would refuse to eat and drink or to use at least 80% of all these products.

Who knows what is in Coca Cola? Who knows what is in a Spanish sausage? Who knows how vegetables are produced in Almeria (Spain) and what in general the contamination and fine dust is in the air, soil, and in products? Does John, the pizzeria man, know what is in the pizzas of his competitor? Who knows what is in the plastic material of toys? Sometimes it's even better that the tourist consumers do not know what is on their plate or which chemicals are in a glass of wine, or what can be found in the mattress of the hotel rooms or behind the kitchen oven.

Do all the consumers in America and Europe know about the production and labor conditions and all the externalities (means: collateral damages) from Western capitalistic corporations in Asia and Africa or South America?

This 'complete information' ideal sounds like singing 'Halleluiah' and feeling to be in the heaven – at least far away from reality.

6) Selling firms are profit-maximizing entrepreneurial firms. For perfect competition to exist, firms must seek maximum profit and only profit, and the people who make the decisions must receive only profits and no other form of income from the firms.

Comment: This statement starts with a cult message: 'Selling firms are profit-maximizing entrepreneurial firms", a holy avowal, with the normative call: you 'must seek maximum profit and only profit'; if you do not do so, then you are not an entrepreneur. Now, it becomes very hot: 'only profit'! That means: the only aim of a firm is getting profit and maximizing profit. That's devilish!

If a firm does not fulfill this 'law', then the firm creates the 'imperfect market' and this is not welcome. But there are millions of owners of small firms that simply want to live their life and to work in what they like to do. They feel proud of their business, their knowledge and skills, the realization of their talents and potentials, and their soul experiences a certain fulfillment; profit is not the motivation of doing so. The capitalistic economics doesn't respect or promote such firms.

Supply and perfect competition ... "combined, they create an environment in which each firm, following its own self-interest, will offer goods to the market in a predictable way." [293]

The first message of this statement is: each firm follows 'its own self-interest'. Following self-interest is normal and acceptable. But a majority of firms also have a social responsibility for laborers and supply of specific goods such as electricity, water, food and much more. But there is not much social and environmental conscience in the free market. The second message is: 'each firm offers goods to the market in a predictable way if there is perfect competition'. But the perfect competition does not exist. It's a fantasy.

The economic royal advice is obvious: Get market power! Become owner of the 'essential input', get all the needed resources under your control, if necessary with corruption, and blackmailing governments, including triggering wars. [294]

→ The current economic crisis, the global contamination, and the consequences of climate change show us that a lot in the real world of

---

[293] Colander, p. 318
[294] McDowell (et al.), p. 246

economics is not predictable and / or not an expression of moral attitudes for society, humanity and the planet.

→ The declared credo 'the only aim of a firm is getting profit and maximizing profit' is without ambiguity. To achieve the aim you must control as much as possible of the input factors.

→ The neo-capitalistic competitive market is not simply a free market. It includes strives, battles, luring or seducing or blackmailing governments and indirectly triggering wars.

→ We must conclude that all 'law's, theories, principles, and terms are in function of maximizing profit and never in function of real satisfaction, well-being, happiness, forming a professional identity, or professional fulfillment of the labor, or a well-balanced society.

→ There is no free market. The market is dominated by the immensely powerful corporations that act at any cost to get their complete control of humans, societies, and governments.

4. Systemic Failure of Economics

4.1. Destructivity of Economics in Society

4.1.1. Systemic Failures

The responsible institutions for humanity, the world and the planet are:

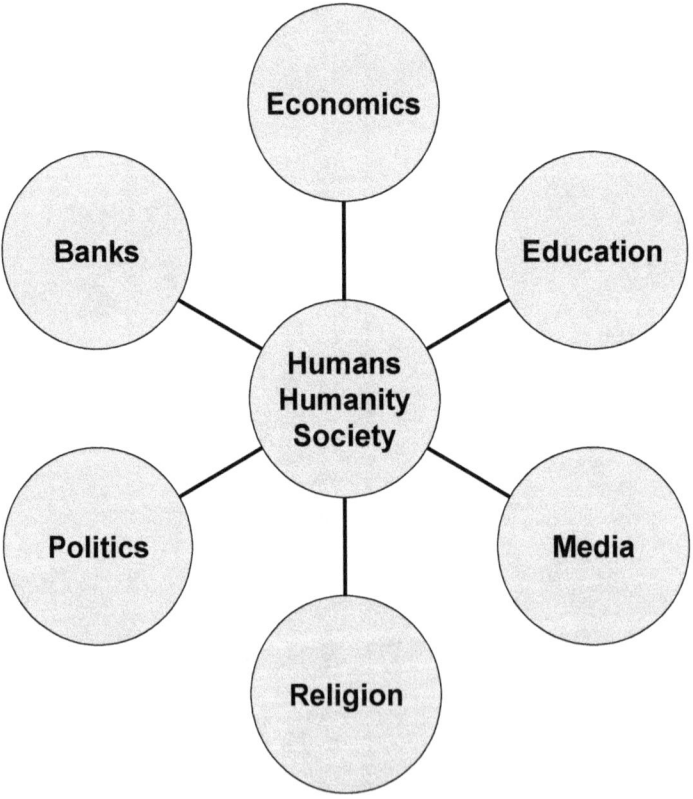

Which system is the most powerful system? The monetary network is the most powerful system. If 100 or 300 individuals are the ultimate decision makers about allocation (distribution) of money, means lending money, then these individuals have all other systems by their throat, especially the economic market, the governments, the media, and the education partly through the governments and partly through private investments in schools and universities. Religion could become a serious threat to the monetary network if it would be free of scam and rooted in the vivid Archetypes of the Soul, including the superior Archetypes of the Soul. These 100-300 individuals never operate on the visible stage, but always on the stage behind the curtains.

Prof. Mujahid Kamran gives us an insight into the economical power institutions to show what is meant with 'free market' and what 'economics' is really about:

"The control of the US, and of global politics, by the wealthiest families of the planet is exercised in a powerful, profound and clandestine manner. This control began in Europe and has a continuity that can be traced back to the time when the bankers discovered it was more profitable to give loans to governments than to needy individuals ... These banking families and their subservient beneficiaries have come to own most major businesses over the two centuries during which they have secretly and increasingly organised themselves as controllers of governments worldwide and as arbiters of war and peace ...

The US is a country controlled through the privately owned Federal Reserve, which in turn is controlled by the handful of banking families that established it by deception in the first place ... for the great Winston Churchill, there is a 'High Cabal' that has made us what we are ... This 'High Cabal' is the 'One World Cabal' of today, also called the elite by various writers ... The elite owns the media, banks, defence and oil industry. In his book Who's Who of the Elite Robert Gaylon Ross Sr. states: "It is my opinion that they own the US military, NATO, the Secret Service, the CIA, the Supreme Court, and many of the lower courts. They appear to control, either directly or indirectly, most of the state, county, and local law enforcement agencies." ... 1774 Amschel Mayer Rothschild stated at a gathering of the twelve richest men of Prussia in Frankfurt: "Wars should be directed so that the nations on both sides should be further in our debt." ...

The elite owns numerous 'think tanks' that work for expanding, consolidating and perpetuating its hold on the globe. The Royal Institute of International Affairs (RIIA), the Council on Foreign Relations (CFR), the Bilderberg Group, the Trilateral Commission, and many other similar organisations are all funded by the elite and work for it ... In addition to these strategic 'think tanks' the elite has set up a chain of research institutes devoted to manipulating public opinion in a manner the elite desires … it was in 1913 that an institute was established at Wellington House, London for manipulation of public opinion.

According to Coleman: The modern science of mass manipulation was born at Wellington House London, the lusty infant being midwifed by Lord Northcliffe and Lord Rothmere. The British monarchy, Lord Rothschild, and the Rockefellers were responsible for funding the venture … the purpose of those at Wellington House was to effect a change in the opinions of British people … The Tavistock Institute has a 6 billion dollar fund and 400 subsidiary organisations are under its control along with 3,000 think tanks, mostly in the USA … (their philosophy and aim:) absolute behaviour control is imminent." [295]

In all six systems there are systemic faults: Economics, education, media, religion, politics, and banks.

- If one system has an immanent systemic fault, then the entire system can't work in a sustainable way; means: all-sided balanced. All systems have several dominant systemic faults.

- Each system influences the other systems and therefore, if there is a systemic failure in one or more systems, then all systems can't work in a sustainable way.

Conclusions:

- Economics needs a fundamental re-construction in the interest of human's life, mind and soul, and the development of all inner potentials in order to promote psychical-spiritual evolution and to respect the creation; economics must become a comprehensible science.

- The monetary system (banks) must fundamentally change, regroup its duties in entities of clear sizes and especially the interest-fault and absence of ethics must be eliminated; speculation and 'casino' businesses must be forbidden and replaced with services for people and businesses.

- The educational system must be thoroughly renewed with the most advanced knowledge about human's mind, the potential of the psychical-spiritual development, and the behavior psychology, including all human

---

[295] http://www.globalresearch.ca/index.php?context=va&aid=25160

values and the basic archetypal processes of development. [296]

- The media must find back to objective and educational information and shall never be abused for political, economical, or other interests of society's importance. The media must become a platform for balancing all interests of society and humanity, including of human values. [297]

- The politics, governments, lawmakers, and political parties must reinvent themselves in the service for all humans and society, with profound ethics and integrity, and the knowledge and skills for the duties; all citizens must be prepared for a genuine democracy on all levels.

- The religions must go through a complete catharsis and reconciliation with God, eliminating everything that has no value for the archetypal evolution of humanity; and then re-start with the vivid Archetypes of the Soul, including the vivid supreme Archetypes of the Soul. [298]

→ The systemic faults generate unstoppable and increasing chain reactions on a global scale.
→ It is a deadly mistake to think that the leaders can solve the global problems with technology.
→ It is fatal if leaders try to solve the global problems with lies, deceit, wars, and fascism.
→ The world economy can never be solved with the ideology of growth and maximizing profit.
→ With 8 billion, then 9 billion and later 10 billion people (2050-2060) doom is the unavoidable final result.
→ Most damages of the ecosystems, the mind, the genes, and dehumanization are irreversible.
→ A catharsis of unseen dimension and thoroughness is the only path for a future of humanity.
→ There is no future for humanity, if the authorities globally reject multi-dimensional renewal.
→ The global roadmap of 25 years is on the table of the author, elaborated during 30 years.

The future lies in the hands of the young generation today and of those that will be in power the coming 10-30 years! 'The Future in Your Hands' is a clarion call for action for all humans. [299]

---

[296] See: Economics I
[297] See: Economics I
[298] 'The Incredible Solution', http://www.rcigi.com

'SURVIVING PROGRESS'; Extract from the complete transcript: [300]

"Colin Beavan: doing more of … is not progress. We're like stuck in this, it's like a record.

Ronald Wright: Faith in progress has become a kind of religious faith, a sort of fundamentalism, rather like the market fundamentalism that has just recently crashed and burned. The idea that you can let markets rip is a delusion, just as the idea that you can let technology rip, and it will solve the problems created by itself in a slightly earlier phase. That, that has become a belief very similar to the religious delusions that caused some societies to crash and burn in the past.

Michael Hudson: Written records go back about 4,000 years, and from 2,000 BC to the time of Jesus, it was normal for all of the countries in the world to periodically cancel the debts when they became too large to pay. So you have Sumer, Babylonia, Egypt, other regions all proclaiming these debt cancellations and the effect was to make a clean slate so that society would begin all over again …

Rome was the first country of the world not to cancel the debts. It went to war in Sparta, in Greece, to overthrow the governments and the kings that wanted to cancel the debts.

Ronald Wright: Peasants had access to public land, but as the Roman State became more powerful and the lords and the generals began to appropriate public land for their own private estates, more and more peasants became landless.

Michael Hudson: What was absolutely new in the Roman Empire was irreversible concentration of wealth at the top of the economic pyramid, and that's what progress has meant ever since. Progress has meant: 'You will never get back what we take from you'. That's what brought on the Dark Age and that's what's threatening to bring in the Dark Age again, if society doesn't realize that if it lets the wealth concentrate in the hand of a financial class, this class is not going to be anymore intelligent in the long-term in disposing of the wealth than their predecessors were in Rome or in other countries.
Simon Johnson: The bankers can't stop themselves, it's in their DNA, in the DNA of their organizations, to take massive risks, to pay themselves

[299] See: www.rcici.com
[300] http://survivingprogress.com/wp-content/uploads/2012/03/SP_transcription.pdf

ridiculous salaries, and, and to collapse. And the, the more that reasonable, responsible people in the center, and the Left and the Right, see this, the closer we'll get to finally constraining the power of, of these out of control financial oligarchies.

Michael Hudson: The problem is a small oligarchy of 10% of the population at the top to whom all of these net debts are owed to. You want to annul the debts to the top 10%. That's what they're not going to do. The oligarchy is running things. They would rather annul the bottom 90% right to live than to annul the money that's due to them. They would rather strip the planet and shrink the population and be paid rather than give up their claims. That's the political fight of the XXIst Century.

Kambale Musavali: The number one costs for foreign lending through some of the multilateral institutions such as IMF or World Bank is the death toll on the continent.

Margaret Atwood: Rich countries lend a so-called developing country a big whack of money. Debt is incurred on behalf of people who have nothing to do with it, that don't know anything about it. Then they are expected to pay, pay the price, by, by scraping off their livelihood, turning it into money and giving it to somebody else.

Michael Hudson: You can relate the destruction of the rain forest in Brazil directly to the Wall Street and London financial sector. The story begins in 1982, when countries couldn't pay their debt anymore. And the result is that the Latin American countries, generally, stopped paying, because they said, We're already paying all of the balance of payment surplus we have to the banks. We don't have any money to import to sustain living standards, we don't have money to import to build new factories and to pay the debt'. So the International Monetary Fund, at that point, said, Don't go bankrupt, you have an option. You can begin to sell off the public domain; you have plenty of assets to sell to pay us. You can sell off your water rights, your forests, your subsoil mineral resources, you can sell us your oil rights. And so, Brazil, Argentina, and other countries began to sell off their resources to private investors. And the private investors bought these resources on credit.

Anio Beata: The people responsible for destroying the Amazon are the big farmers, the international corporations, the biggest farmers are senators, deputies, colonels. They're the ones destroying the Amazon forest. Them. Not us.
David Suzuki: Economics is so fundamentally disconnected from the real world it is destructive. If you take an introductory course in economics, the

professor, in the first lecture, will show a slide of the economy, and it looks very impressive, you know, raw materials, extraction process, manufacturer, wholesale, retail, with arrows going back and forth…

…And they try to impress you because they think, and they know damn well, economics is not a science, but they're trying to fool us into thinking that it's a real science, it's not. Economics is a set of values that they, then, try to use mathematical equations and all that stuff, and pretend that it's a science.

But if you ask the economist: in that equation, where do you put the ozone layer, where do you put the deep underground aquifer as a fossil water, where do you put topsoil, or biodiversity? Their answer is, Oh, those are externalities. Well, then you might as well be on Mars: that economy is not based in anything like the real world. It's life, the web of life that filters water in the hydrologic cycle, it's microorganisms in the soil that create the soil that we can grow our food in. Nature performs all kinds of services, insects fertilize all of the flowering plants, these services are vital to the health of the planet. Economists call these externalities … that's nuts!

Jane Goodall: Unlimited economic progress in a world of finite natural resources doesn't make sense. It's a pattern that is bound to collapse. And we keep seeing it collapsing, but then we build it up because there are these strong vested interests, we must have business as usual. And you know, you get the arms manufacturers, you get the petroleum industry, the pharmaceutical industry and all of this feeding into helping to create corrupt governments who are putting the future of their own people at risk.

Gary Marcus: One of the challenges that, that faces the human species is we are more and more in a position of acting like gods. This has been true for a while, because we've had the ability to change the climate, for example. This is gonna be even more true with genetic technologies, we're gonna be able to manipulate other species, and eventually ourselves. We are going to be in a position of controlling our own fate in a way that no creature has ever in, you know, a billion years on the planet had an opportunity to do."

➔ It's all about economics – the capitalistic economics that all students have to learn!
➔ It's accredited! Students and parents of students want accredited academic programs!
➔ Go and learn it there and you will be brainwashed to become a slave of the oligarchy!
➔ The systemic fault in the modern economics is rooted in the mind of insane oligarchs!

4.1.2. Destroyed Human Values and Human Mind

The capitalistic economics as a theory is not a science. The capitalistic economics is an ideological concept. Most declared 'principles', 'laws' and 'theories' are not applicable as they are supposed to be; they are invalid or insane constructions. Everywhere we found a jumble of meaning behind the so called scientific terms and statements. The interconnections of several single models and parameters are hype and distort the real business world. The 'margins' and 'maximizing profit' focus everywhere is insane and toxic for the mind and soul of people.

The result of compulsive economics, the brainwashing media, the perfidious marketing, the political propaganda, the psychotic religion and the highly reduced (archaic) education:

➔ People are unformed, deformed, malformed, distorted and self-alienated; and they don't see nor do they want to see their sick and mad psychical-spiritual state.

➔ Degeneration of human's mind and self-alienation as the main result are collectively fully in progress. All essential human values are destroyed.

We have revealed that a huge majority of economic terms, laws, theories and models express and produce greed, illimitability, avarice, envy, compulsion, neuroticism, cantankerousness, psychosis, and much more.

The real world of economics has destroyed all relevant human values such as love, trust, hope, reliability, integrity, fairness, balance, honesty, justice, respect, morale attitudes, and the truth in general. Economics has erased the dignity of humankind and the psychical-spiritual evolution of humanity as a whole. Economics excludes and does not allow to 'love the creation'.

The capitalistic understanding of personhood, human life, household, modern lifestyle, working and doing business has destroyed all fundamental human values and human's mind in general.

Our thesis is: the all-round destructive effects of a majority of economic 'principles', 'laws' and 'theories' are intentional and of global perspective. There is a hidden global roadmap for such evil doing!
This madness and systemic evil doing is even crowned with Nobel Prizes!

4.1.3. Destructive Behavior

Behavior disorder	Despotic, dictatorial
Asocial	Subordinate
Suicide	Slaved, enslaved
Intention of suicide	Exploiting
Violence	Rigidity
Abuse	Radicalism
Arrogance	Parasite
Corruption	Low skilled
Behavior disability	Superficial
Aggressive provocation	Oppressing
Unhealthy eating	Sadism
Driven, pushed	Forcing
Stressed	Relationship games
Fights	Lack of care for health
Arguments	Inability to express love
Quarrels	Disrespecting human values
Aggression	Ruthless, unscrupulous
Inability to master life	No satisfaction with life
Cantankerousness	Compensation behavior
Non-cooperative	Despotic, dictatorial

→ Multiply this picture by billions!

4.1.4. Destructive Mental-Spiritual State

Ignorance	Psychopathy
Infantile defense	Narcissism
Mental disease	Megalomania
Mental disability	Psychosis
Greed	Inner pain
Laziness, lazy-minded	Lied, lying, life lies
Falseness	Distorted
Stupidity	Suppressed
Naivety	Blackmailed
Blind, blinded	Cheated
Brainwashed	Detracted
Poisoned	Self-alienated
Lured, seduced	Magic thinking
Manipulated	Inability to love
Programmed	No or fake spirituality
Dehumanized	No love, trust, peace

Cowards	No faith, hope, balance
Hypocrites	No inner satisfaction
Blabbers	No fulfillment
Neurosis	

➜ Multiply this picture by billions!

4.1.5. Psychical and Somatic Reactions

Headache	Frigidity
Migraine	Problems with orgasm
Asthma	Imbalanced menstruation rhythm
Allergies	Cardiac fibrillation
Anorexia	Sleeping disorder
Chronic constipation	Spinal and back pain
Diarrhea	Stomach burns
Addictions	Abdominal pain
Chronic sadness	Cramp
Energetic weakness	Tremor
Burnout	Stutter
Obese	Nervousness
Overweight	Uncontrollable emotions
Chronic anxiety	Breaking out in a sweat
Fear	High blood pressure
Social phobia	Tinnitus
Depression	Heart attack
Compulsions	Neurodermitis
Cancer, tumors	Chronic fatigue
Impotence	

➜ Multiply this picture by billions!

4.1.6. Modern State of Humans

This is the picture of at least 6 billion people:

- Stupid, blind, lazy, lazy-minded, thoughtless, short-sighted, lethargic, superficial
- Suggestible, seducible, deceivable, credulous, imprudent, infantile, callous
- Narcissistic, neurotic, suffering and inside heavily laden, disrupted, conflictive

- Emotional, fearful, unconfident, insecure, chicken-hearted, cantankerous
- Stubborn, superstitious, fatalistic, dull, indifferent, unconcerned, ignorant
- Big-headed, conceited, egoistic, ego-centered, ego-weak, false, inside not free
- Uninformed, misinformed, low educated, brainwashed, manipulated, lured, seduced
- Unconscious living, driven by desire, submissive (to authority), dependent, hypocritical
- Distressed, tense inside, over-loaded inside, imbalanced, unsettled, labile, coward
- Possessive, greedy, envious, jealous, avaricious, ravenous, pleasure oriented

4.1.7. Humans' Compensations

Only one 'finger' of the 'invisible hand' or one tentacle of the 'octopus with a hundred tentacles' is gearing and steering humans' compensations:

- People tend to compensate for their deformed, malformed or unformed psychological state.
- Compensations are: consumption, striving for power, possession, reputation, acceptance.
- To sell a product or service, people can be manipulated in their psychological state.
- Depending on the product or service different manipulative approaches are relevant.
- To govern people politicians control the psychological state of humans with laws and order.
- Chaotic and archaic (deformed) human's inner life leads to the destruction of society.
- Compensation as a habit or life style leads to dependence, submission, compliance.
- Compensative behavior can be reinforced through loans, mortgages, work, career status.
- Religion, spirituality and ideology can replace, reinforce or complement compensations.
- Reducing compensative behavior leads to less profit of the industry (corporate groups).
- Reducing compensative behavior requires collective personal development (Individuation).
- Compensative behavior is based on a strong libido bond (tie) to the compensative product.
- Compensations give satisfaction, relaxation, tranquility, joy, pleasure,

balance, strength.
- The results of compensations are always superficial with short effect and require repetition.
- Compensations lead to self-alienation, suppression and increase of the suppressed amount.
- The more people compensate, the more they become malformed, distorted, self-alienated.
- The more suppressed content in the unconscious, the more people need to compensate.
- It's impossible to change compensatory behavior with rational arguments and knowledge.

4.1.8. Destruction of the Planet

The 30 big problems of humanity, the earth, and the planet are:

Some key words to draw the fields:

1. **Earth population:** Increase, urban growth, youth population, elderly population, motives for procreating a baby, increase of needs, contamination, risks, no sustainability
2. **Poverty:** Famine, hunger, misery, lack of food and drinking water; causes; physical, psychical and social effects; different patterns of poverty in countries, no sustainability
3. **Contamination:** Sewage, garbage, electro-waste, drugs, detergents, pollution, fine dust; network of causes; chains of effects; increase of population growth, no sustainability
4. **Destruction of agriculture:** Drought, desertification, deforestation, flood, tornados; effects on food production, food prices and social life; lost value of agriculture land, no sustainability
5. **Exploitation of manpower:** Abuse, child labor, slavery, low wages, working conditions, destruction of human values and social life, attitudes of exploitation, no sustainability
6. **Exploitation of resources:** food and non-food; limited water resources; no sustainability of natural resources; speculations; no sustainability for production
7. **Energy production:** Coal, nuclear power stations, renewable energy, producing energy with manpower; consumers of energy; risks; costs; increasing long term demand, no sustainability
8. **Transport:** Car traffic, public and good transport traffic (air, train, sea, bus, tram); life style and demand of transport; direct and lateral effects (contamination, accidents), no sustainability

9. **Climate change:** Causes; catastrophes and economic consequences; long term effects on eco-systems, humans, societies, countries; long term costs of damages, no sustainability
10. **Industry:** Overproduction, mass production, globalization; mega corporate groups and its power; damages in small and medium businesses; effects on humans; environmental damages
11. **Economy:** Financial institutions, public debt, consumer debt, earnings, speculation businesses; power of mega-institutions and the owners and CEOs; complex effects, no sustainability
12. **Business:** Decrease of small and medium sized businesses; ignored importance and sustainability of such businesses; laws and regulations; no sustainability
13. **Health:** Physical and mental illnesses, disease, addictions; epidemics; accidents (Traffic, work, home, leisure); lack of health care; costs and exploitation (abuse), no sustainability
14. **Law and human rights:** Lack of laws for nature; power interests; police intervention; injustice; court and corruption; abuse of laws for power and mega greed; no sustainability
15. **Extinction of species:** Due to contamination and climate change; complexity of importance for nature and food chain; consequences of decrease of species; no sustainability
16. **Environmental destruction:** Due to over-construction and other causes; catastrophes as a result; urban expansion and influences on humans, human life and society, no sustainability
17. **Extinction of nature:** Due to contamination and climate change; deforestation and its long term consequences on the climate; destruction of human, social, species life; no sustainability
18. **Eco-systems damages:** Contamination, climate change; all-area global consequences; destruction of food resources, islands, land, beaches, water resources, no sustainability
19. **Unemployment:** High rate, lack of earning (not enough work) opportunities; political and economic causes; economic imbalance, the long term costs and damages, no sustainability
20. **Politics:** Lack of real democracy; distorted communication; inefficiency; lack of qualifications of politicians; career brainwashing; abuse of power, taxes; cheating entire folks; no sustainability
21. **State administration:** Lack of quality and efficiency; rigid regulations; totalitarianism, over-control, over-regulations; lack of professionalism; no sustainability
22. **Leaders and power:** Abuse of power, world power aspiration, the elites behind the scene undermining democracy; the uncontrollable excessive financial power, no sustainability
23. **Military and wars:** Militarization, wars, civil wars; terrorism; economic

and cyber war; weapon manufacturer's interests; triggering wars with intrigues and false flags; no sustainability

24. **Trouble spots:** Tensions, unrest, riots, civil wars, political crimes; the causes and effects; police reactions, military and leaders; lack of knowledge and skills for solutions, no sustainability

25. **Crimes:** Organized crimes, corruption; crimes, violence, cheat, scam; prison life; the human sources of crimes; the function of deviating from political crimes, no sustainability

26. **Media:** Brainwash, manipulation, power of information; the almost impossibility for individuals to address a folk; the propaganda for the elite's interests, no sustainability

27. **Religions:** Dogmatism, fundamentalism, myths, superstition, deception, falseness, brainwash; power abuse; lack of authentic and comprehensible 'divine' experiences, no sustainability

28. **Ethics and human values:** Lack of moral and human values; the lost truth; the all-embracing exploitation of human's soul and life; no respect for ethics in politics, no sustainability

29. **Public education:** Illiteracy, lack of vocational schools; the state of humanity and the planet as an expression of lack of education or wrong education, no sustainability

30. **Conspiracy or facts:** WTC, Apollo 12, false flags, murdering, intrigues, hidden triggering of (proxy) wars, the hidden moguls ruling the world for more than 2,000 years, no sustainability

➜ Extrapolate the picture by one billion people more, then by two billion more, and then by three billon people more (means 10 billion people on earth).

➜ Now think about this. You (if you are not already old) will experience these dire realities with immensely increasing explosive calamities in the future.

➜ The topmost drive that leads to this future is the outrageous capitalistic economics and capitalistic dictatorships madly obsessed with war.

A Spanish news report (translated): "…Scientists from allover the world forecast an immanent planetary collapse … Today, the next change of the global state will be very baleful for our civilizations, and once a planetary change is produced, there is no return … Humans have done nothing really important to avoid the worst." [301]

➜ So, what for do we need a capitalistic economic science that is not a

---

[301] http://www.que.es/ultimas-noticias/curiosas/201206062036-cientificos-aseguran-revista-nature-colapso-cont.html

science and that has essentially produced these disastrous developments?

→ There was a chaotic land. There was the old sick king. And the entire folk asked: "How can we heal this king?" And I say: There is no remedy and no therapy. The old king must die. A new king, healthy in the mind and soul and with highest archetypal integrity must govern the land and folk towards an all-sided balanced and ordered society and world.

4.2. Indispensable Changes in Economics

4.2.1. The Myth of Capitalism

Prof John Kozy expresses very clear statements about the Western economics: "Everything that is discarded (not taken into consideration in the model) is called an "externality." So the models only work when the externalities that were in effect before the models are implemented do not change afterward. The realm of economic models can be likened to the realm of Platonic Ideas. Both realms are static and unchanging throughout all time... Economists are frauds and economics amounts to nothing but an apologetics of greed... Everyone everywhere is not better off... employment alone is not a sufficient condition for prosperity; full employment can exist in an enslaved society along side abject poverty, and an increasing GNP does not mean that an economy is getting better... Since externalities are excluded from all economic models and can be expected to change after any model is implemented, all economic models necessarily fail... Free market economic conditions create a situation in which vendors always prevail. In the end, they get all the money... Humanity is enslaved by these economic practices but the enslavement is carefully and continuously hidden...All market economies motivated by profit are founded on unfairness as should be easily seen. In any financial transaction between two parties motivated by profit, one party wins and the other party loses..." [302]

Portuguese economist Guilherme Alves Coelho uncovers the 10 myths about capitalism: [303]

Myth 1: Under capitalism, anyone who works hard can become rich

---

[302] http://www.globalresearch.ca/index.php?context=va&aid=29270
[303] http://english.pravda.ru/business/companies/15-02-2012/120518-ten_myths_capitalism-0/

Myth 2: Capitalism creates wealth and prosperity for all
Myth 3: We are all in the same boat
Myth 4: Capitalism means freedom
Myth 5: Capitalism means democracy
Myth 6: Election is a synonym of democracy
Myth 7: Alternating parties in office is the same as having an alternative
Myth 8: The elected politician represents and decides for the people
Myth 9: There is no alternative to capitalism
Myth 10: Savings generate wealth

➜ As the authors says: Capitalism is a myth!

Brian Jonathan Liew provides us with some statements that confirm the result of our explorations and analysis: "In today's materialistic and superficial world and because of our indoctrination that having materialistic possessions will provide us eternal love and happiness, we believe that money is the only way out of our misery and problems … we were taught by our parents on how to be 'Successful', the education system teaching us how and who to be in order to be successful, the media ranging from movies, television programs, magazines, newspapers, advertisements showing us the 'Norm' by setting what is socially acceptable according to them … the media wields a lot of influence and power in terms manipulating the perceptions and thoughts of the masses of people … If the media portrays a certain fashion or style and proposes or presumes it as fashionable and popular in a commercial, movie, television series, magazines and other forms of media, with its constant and consistent bombardment of these messages via radio, television or print, it is bound to affect the psyche of those exposed to it … The banks finance the corporations, the corporations lobby the governments and have politicians in their pockets, the government controls the central bank (thus all other banking institutions) or in many cases the central banks have been separated from government control and authority, and are governed by a collection of heads of corporations. The corporations own the media outlets and thus all of them could be grouped together and referred to as the 'Controlling Elites' or 'Elites' … the power of the media dictates to the populous what the masses Should or Shouldn't have, and the masses purchase whatever is impulse to them just so that they 'Feel' normal and thus they 'feel' they are socially accepted … We have been enslaved by our own greed and insecurities because we are afraid to be different and afraid to be labeled weird … Our enslavement is aided mainly by the so called 'Elites' particularly the Government who taxes our hard earned income to unnecessary levels and uses our income for the benefit of the 'Elites' themselves but not us. They use our tax money for wars to benefit oil corporations and the military industrial complex, they use it to bail out Wall Street and the Bankers during the 2008

Economic downturn, they use it for death and destruction in other nations in particular third world nations ... The Banks play a major role in further enslaving us by creating loans and charging us the public ridiculous amount of fees and interest. Our society, in particular the western society is a debt society ... the banks are basically committing daylight robberies and enslaving us by using the media to impulse us to purchase and manipulating our greed to acquire materialistic possessions even when we cannot afford them ... From what is left, we purchase our products from corporations which more or less have monopolized the industries and they created an illusion of choice by creating different names for their corporations but in fact they are owned by the same group of people known as Oligarchs. These Oligarchs often have political connections and belong to powerful lobby groups who have the politicians in their pockets and often own the major media outlets ... Elites sit back and laugh at us falling for their deceitful system without even knowing it and enslaving us ... It is not money that is evil but how money has been and is still being used by these 'Elites' to manipulate us through our greed to obtain absolute control of us." [304]

→ We have confirmed these statements with our analysis of economic terms, principles, and laws!

4.2.2. The real Face of the Financial Crisis

A) Financial Crisis 2008:

Some very rich people with decisive power on the hidden stage behind the curtains have realized that many firms could grow enormously and that a new generation of wealthy people has been building up all-area power; for example: tourist industry, construction industry, sport industry, and entertainment industry.

A generation of 'new rich' people on local levels has been born. And the very rich people didn't like this because it could endanger their power on the hidden stage; or they would take them a slice of the cake away; or simply because they got envious. Something had to be done to cut these developments of a new rich and wealthy middle and upper class. Therefore their question was: how can we get the money and wealth from these new rich people in order for us to become even wealthier and to get richer than anybody else. They found the solution.

Thesis: The financial crisis in 2008 was not a crisis; it was triggered with the

---

[304] http://www.equalmoney.org

intention and purpose of growth of specific corporations and in the purpose of getting more ('the most it can') from investments aiming for total concentration of financial power within a perspective of 5-10 years.

The Messianic aim of economics is 'to get as much as possible' which is to be achieved by 'maximizing profit'. We have also identified that those who get the profit are not the workers. These people (investors) do not work for the profit. We have seen that a big production entity is a complexity of quite strenuous activities and management. The production process is costly and takes time, and time is money, and a high profit is never guaranteed for a long period.

B) The extended real Face:

There are thousands of articles on the Internet from top-experts about the financial crisis since 2008. We chose two articles and present an extract to show the real face of the financial crisis in America which also reflects in its essential parameters and structural consequences the financial crisis in Europe.

There where America stands today, some European states (Spain, Greece, Italy, Ireland, and Portugal) already also stand in significant parameters and the other countries of Europe are gearing up fast to reach similar economic and political constellations of society and the entire European Union. We go even further with our interpretation: The entire European Union is ruled via economic tools by the American financial (corporate) iron grip.

Our thesis is: The most important parameters of economics are not reflected in the capitalistic economics study books. The main purpose of all these classical books is to deviate from the real aims of economics, to ignore the hidden roadmap of the capitalistic economics (where the 'financial crisis' is a step and not a failure), and to avoid any critical, creative, and pioneering thinking about capitalistic economics and its implicit consequences for societies and the world.

1) Prof. James Petras tells us: [305]

...the 'crises of capitalism' was turned into a 'crises of labor'. Finance capital, the principle detonator of the crash and crises, recovered, the capitalist class as a whole was strengthened, and most important of all, it utilized the political, social, ideological conditions created as a result of 'the crises' to

---

[305] http://www.globalresearch.ca/index.php?context=va&aid=29388

further consolidate their dominance and exploitation over the rest of society.

The 'crises of capital' has been converted into a strategic advantage for furthering the most fundamental interests of capital: the enlargement of profits, the consolidation of capitalist rule, the greater concentration of ownership, the deepening of inequalities between capital and labor and the creation of huge reserves of labor to further augment their profits.

(The advocates) frequently correct the official data which understates the percentage unemployed by excluding part-time, long-term unemployed workers and others.

The 'crises' argument is strengthened by citing the millions of homeowners who have been evicted by the banks, the sharp increase in poverty and destitution accompanying job loses, wage reductions and the elimination or reduction of social services. 'Crises' is also associated with the massive increase in bankruptcies.

The vast and growing inequalities and the rigged rules by which banks exploit their size ('too big to fail') to raid the Treasury at the expense of social programs.

In summary the advocates of the thesis of a 'Global Crises of Capitalism' make a strong case, demonstrating the profound and pervasive destructive effects of the capitalist system on the lives of the great majority of humanity.

Declining income and employment has been a major factor facilitating the rapid and massive recovery of the profit margins of most large-scale corporations.

It is utterly foolish to argue for a 'global crises' when several of the major economies in the world economy did not suffer a major downturn and others recovered and expanded rapidly. China and India did not even suffer a recession.

While Southern Europe wallows in a deep sustained depression, by any measure, from 2008 to the foreseeable future, German exports, in 2011, set a record of a trillion Euros; its trade surplus reached €158 billion, after €155 billion surpluses in 2010.

To speak of a 'global crises' obscures the fundamental dominant and exploitative relations that facilitate 'recovery' and growth of the elite economies over and against their competitors and client states.

In several European countries youth unemployment (16-25) runs between 30 to 50% (Spain 48.7%, Greece 47.2%, Slovakia 35.6%, Italy 31%, Portugal 30.8% and Ireland 29%) while in Germany, Austria and Holland youth unemployment runs to Germany 7.8%, Austria 8.2% and Netherlands 8.6%. (The critical figures in 2012 are even higher!)

Greek workers are pressured to accept a 20% cut in minimum wages while in Germany workers are demanding a 6% increase.

If the 'crises' of capitalism is manifested in specific regions, so too does it affect different age/racial sectors of the wage and salaries classes. The unemployment rates of youth to older workers vary enormously:

Capitalists constantly resort to using the unemployed to lower wages and benefits and to intensify exploitation (dubbed to 'increase productivity') to increase profit margins.

According to General Motors 2011 report to its stockholders, they celebrated the greatest profit ever, turning a profit of $7.6 billion, surpassing the previous record of $6.7 billion in 1997

In 2011, the US economy grew by 1.7%, but median wages fell by 2.7%. According to the financial press, the profit margins of the S&P 500 leapt from 6% to 9% of the GDP in the past three years, a share last achieved three generations ago.

Surveys of top corporations reveal that US companies are holding 1.73 trillion in cash, 'the fruits of record high profit margins'.

Also negligible federal interest rates and easy access to credit allow capitalists to exploit vast differentials between borrowing and lending and investing. Lower taxes and cuts in social programs result in a growing cash pile for corporations. Within the corporate structure, income goes to the top where senior executives pay themselves huge bonuses.
When the capitalist class increases its profit margins, hoards trillions, it is not in crises. The key point is that the 'crises of labor' is a major stimulus for the recovery of capitalist profits.

Thanks to the capitalist state's unprecedented massive transfer of wealth from the public treasury to the capitalist class – Wall Street banks in the first instance – the corporate sector recovered, while the workers and the rest of the economy remained in crises, went bankrupt and out of work.

Between 2009-2012 hundreds of former Wall Street executives, managers and investment advisers seized all the major decision-making positions in the Treasury Department and channeled trillions of dollars into leading financial and corporate coffers.

The new doctrine argued that the state's first and principle priority is to return the financial system to profitability at any and all cost to society, citizens, taxpayers and workers.

State bailouts and financing are complemented by hundreds of billions in tax concessions, leading to unprecedented fiscal deficits and the growth of massive social inequalities. The pay of CEO's as a multiple of the average worker went from 24 to 1 in 1965 to 325 in 2010.

Private bankers take appointments in Treasury (or are recruited) to ensure that all resources and policies Wall Street needs are granted with maximum effort, with the least hindrance from citizens, workers or taxpayers. Wall Streeters in Treasury give highest priority to Wall Street survival, recovery and expansion of profits. They block any regulations or restrictions on bonuses or a repeat of past swindles.

It should be abundantly clear that elections, parties and the billion dollar electoral campaigns have little to do with "democracy" and more to do with selecting the President and legislators who will appoint non-elected Wall Streeters to make all the strategic economic decisions for the 99% of Americans.

The Wall Street-Treasury conundrum (WSTC) dumped the capitalist principle of 'fiscal responsibility' in favor of hundreds of billions of dollars in tax cuts for the corporate-financial ruling class...

Treasury and the Central Bank (Federal Reserve) provide near zero interest loans that guarantees big profits to private financial institution which borrow low from the Fed and lend high, (including back to the Government!) especially in purchasing overseas Government and corporate bonds. They receive anywhere from four to ten times the interest rates they pay. In other words the taxpayers provide a monstrous subsidy for Wall Street speculation.

Cheap credit and bailouts for the billion dollar banks and no refinancing for households and small and medium size firms leading to bankruptcies, buyouts and 'consolidation' namely, greater concentration of ownership. As a result the mass market stagnates but corporate and bank profits reach record levels.

Within the power matrix of Wall Street-Treasury Dept. all the old corrupt and exploitative practices that led up to the 2008-2009 crash have returned: multi-billion dollar bonuses for investment bankers who led the economy into the crash; banks 'snapping up billions of dollars of bundled mortgage products that resemble the sliced and diced debt some (sic) blame for the financial crises'.

Democracy has been replaced by a corporate state, founded on the revolving door between Treasury and Wall Street, which funnels public wealth to private financial coffers.

Capitalism, as we experience it over the past decade and for the foreseeable future, is in polar opposition to social equality, democratic decision-making and collective welfare.

Inequalities between the top 1% and the bottom 99% have reached record proportions.

The entire political process, including elections, is profoundly corrupt!

The author has a vision of a modern socialism:

Socialism involves the large-scale reorganization of the economy, the transfer of trillions from the coffers of predator classes' of no social utility to the public welfare. This change can finance a productive and innovative economy based on work and leisure, study and sport.

Socialism replaces the everyday terror of dismissal with the security that brings confidence, assurance and respect to the workplace. Workplace democracy is at the heart of the vision of 21st century socialism.

We begin by nationalizing the banks and eliminating Wall Street. Financial institutions are redesigned to create productive employment, to serve social welfare and to preserve the environment. Socialism would begin the transition, from a capitalist economy directed by predators and swindlers and a state at their command, toward an economy of public ownership under democratic control.

2) David DeGraw adds: [306]

Most Americans remain unaware of the economic world war currently

---

[306] http://www.globalresearch.ca/index.php?context=va&aid=25967

unfolding.

World War III is a war between the richest one-tenth of one percent of the global population and 99.9 percent of humanity.

Increasingly severe economic and governmental policies have systematically eroded civilian wealth, power and rights. Intensive propaganda has effectively distracted, confused, isolated, marginalized and divided the US population.

The US population, if a critical mass is reached, represents the greatest threat to the Economic Elite. In this regard, the American people are their primary adversary.

The government and corporate media spread propaganda on vital economic statistics that mask the severity of our economic crisis. Deceptive inflation, unemployment, poverty and GDP measures, which cast the illusion of recovery, are easily exposed with some research and a closer look at the data.

The Census Bureau poverty rate is a horribly flawed measurement that uses outdated methodology.

The Census measures poverty based on costs of living metrics established in 1955 – 56 years ago.

They ignore many key factors, such as the increased costs of medical care, child care, education, transportation, and many other basic costs. They also don't factor geographically-based costs of living.

Recently, the National Academy of Science released their latest findings, backing up my claim by revealing that 52,765,000 Americans, 17.3% of the population, lived in poverty in 2009.

(Our estimations) bring the total number of Americans living in poverty up to 80 million people, 26% of the population.

In 2005, 25.7 million Americans needed food stamps; currently 45.8 million people rely on them.

When accounting for population growth within the total labor force, from December 2007 to present, we have lost 10.6 million jobs.

• Lower-wage industries constituted 23% of job loss, but fully 49% of recent growth

• Mid-wage industries constituted 36% of job loss, and 37% of recent growth
• Higher-wage industries constituted 40% of job loss, but only 14% of recent growth

While the cost of living from 1990 – 2010 increased by 67%, worker income has declined. According to the most recent available IRS data, covering the year of 2009, average income fell 6.1%, a loss of $3,516 per worker, that year alone. Average income has declined 13.7% from 2007 – 2009, representing $8,588 loss per worker.

The decline in worker income is due to the dramatic increase in CEO pay. CEO pay has consistently increased year-over-year since the mid-1970s. From 1975 – 2010, worker productivity increased 80%. Over this time frame, CEO pay and the income of the economic top 0.1% (one-tenth of one percent) of the population quadrupled. The income of the top 0.01% (one-hundredth of one percent) quintupled.

In the last year alone, CEO pay skyrocketed by 28%. Looking at 2009, according to a recent Dollars & Sense report, workers lost nearly $2 trillion in wages that year alone.

In 2009, stock owners, bankers, brokers, hedge-fund wizards, highly paid corporate executives, corporations, and mid-ranking managers pocketed—as either income, benefits, or perks such as corporate jets—an estimated $1.91 trillion

From 2009 to the fourth-quarter of 2010, 88% of income growth went to corporate profits (i.e. CEOs), while just 1% went to workers.

More than four-fifths of the total increase in American incomes went to the richest 1 percent.

While 68.3 million Americans struggle to get enough food to eat and wages are declining for 90% of the population, US millionaire household wealth has reached an unprecedented level.
According to an extensive study by auditing and financial advisory firm Deloitte, US millionaire households now have $38.6 trillion in wealth. On top of the $38.6 trillion that this study reveals, they have an estimated $6.3 trillion hidden in offshore accounts.

In total, US millionaire households have at least $45.9 trillion in wealth

US millionaire households will see a 225% increase in wealth to $87.1 trillion by 2020. Accounting for wealth hidden in offshore accounts, they are projected to have over $100 trillion in total within the next decade.

Only 0.076% of the population, less than one-tenth of one percent, earned over $1 million in 2009.

The highest bracket for annual income is $50 million or more. Only 74 Americans are in this elite group. The average income within this category was $91.2 million in 2008. As astonishing as that is, in 2009 they averaged $518.8 million each, or about $10 million per week. This means, in the depths of the recession, the richest 74 Americans increased their income by more than 5 times within this one year. These 74 people made more money than 19 million workers combined.

In context, overall, the richest 400 people in the US have as much wealth as 154 million Americans combined, that's 50% of the entire country.

The year 2010 was a record year for compensation on Wall Street, while corporate CEO compensation rose by over 30%....

In 2010 a dozen major companies, including GE, Verizon, Boeing, Wells Fargo, and Fed Ex paid US tax rates between -0.7% and -9.2%. Production, employment, profits, and taxes have all been outsourced....

I could go on and on, but the bottom line is this: A highly complex and largely discrete set of laws and exemptions from laws has been put in place by those in the uppermost reaches of the US financial system. It allows them to protect and increase their wealth and significantly affect the US political and legislative processes.

They have real power and real wealth.

To get into the top economic 0.01% (one-hundredth of one percent) of the population, you have to have a household income of over $27 million per year.

Former Goldman Sachs CEO and Bush Treasury Secretary Hank Paulson had already amassed at least $700 million prior to moving to the US Treasury in 2006. Current Goldman Sachs CEO Lloyd Blankfein and a few other top executives at Goldman Sachs just received $111.3 million in bonuses. Blankfein just took home $24.3 million, as part of a $67.9 million bonus he was awarded. Goldman's President Gary Cohn took home $24 million, as part of a $66.9 million bonus he was awarded. Goldman's CFO David Viniar and former co-president Jon Winkelried both took home over $20 million in bonuses.

Citigroup CEO Vikram Pandit just took home $80 million, in what may eventually total more than $200 million in compensation and bonuses. Coming in at the top of the list is JP Morgan

Chase CEO Jamie Dimon, who just took home $90 million.

If you think people in this income level don't control the US political process, you are not paying attention.

Leaders of Cigna, Humana, UnitedHealth, WellPoint and Aetna received nearly $200 million in compensation in 2009, according to a report, while the companies sought rate increases as high as 39%....

H. Edward Hanway, former chief executive of Philadelphia-based Cigna, topped the list of high-paid executives, thanks to a retirement package worth $110.9 million. Cigna paid Hanway and his successor, David Cordani, a total of $136.3 million last year...

Ron Williams, the CEO of Hartford, Conn.-based Aetna Inc., earned nearly $18.2 million in total compensation, down from $24.4 million in 2008.

Aetna CEO Ron Williams has recovered from his down year in 2009 by making $72 million in 2010.

Within this Economic Elite group, you also have the war profiteering oil companies, which themselves are in large part owned by the big Wall Street banks.

To further demonstrate how the mega-wealthy have seized control our political process, consider that the richest 400 Americans paid 30% of their income in taxes in 1995, but they now pay only 18%.

In fact, 1,470 Americans earned over $1 million in 2009 and didn't pay any taxes.

The cuts in taxes for the mega-wealthy have led to record wealth inequality and resulted in a record national deficit.

Inequality = Debt = Austerity = Civil Unrest

As the national debt has reached a record $14.6 trillion, total personal debt is now over $16 trillion [63]. Consumer debt is $2.5 trillion. Credit card debt is $805 billion and student debt now exceeds $1 trillion.

Over 250 million Americans, another record-breaking number, are currently living paycheck-to-paycheck struggling to make ends meet.

We now have the highest and most severe inequality of wealth in US history. Not even the Robber Barons of the Gilded Age were as greedy as the modern

a) People are so busy trying to maintain their current standard of living that their energies are consumed by holding on to the little that they have left.
b) People have very little understanding of how much wealth has been consolidated within the top economic one-tenth of one percent.

Considering the first factor, it is obvious that people have become beaten down psychologically and financially.

The average person has never personally experienced or seen the excessive wealth and luxury that the mega-rich live in. Wealth inequality has grown so extreme and the wealthy have become so far removed from average society…

Even now most underestimate the rewards of bankers and executives. Top pay has reached such levels that, rather like interstellar distances, what the figures mean is hard to grasp.

Americans drastically underestimated the level of wealth inequality in the United States.

Having never personally experienced or known of this wealth, the average American cannot comprehend what is possible if even a fraction of it was used for the betterment of society as a whole.

In fact, given modern technology and wealth, not a single American citizen should live in poverty. The statistics clearly demonstrate that we now live in a Neo-Feudal society.

The fact that the overwhelming majority of Americans are struggling to get by, while tens of trillions of dollars are consolidated within a small fraction of the population, is a crime against humanity.

BBC Speechless As Trader Says: "The Collapse Is Coming … And Goldman Rules The World … This economic crisis is like a cancer, if you just wait and wait hoping it is going to go away, just like a cancer it is going to grow and it will be too late!" [307]

4.2.3. The Debt Lunacy

We want to present some figures that indicate the debt lunacy. Obviously it is only a very small part of the entire picture; and the figures change (increase) rapidly.

There are several global debt clocks; some show increasing figures above 39 trillion dollars, others above 40 trillion dollars[308], one global debt clock shows 43 billion dollars[309] and ticking, and one clock reports a $54 trillion in-debt view of the world. [310]

Another source tells us: "The Debt Bomb: 7,600,000,000,000 Dollars of Debt Must be Rolled Over in 2012 ... When it comes to government debt, it is not just new debt that is the problem. Every single year, governments around the world must "roll over" gigantic mountains of debt that come due.

That means that the actual borrowing that takes place each year is far greater than the yearly budget deficits that you see talked about on television.
In 2012, a total of 7,600,000,000,000 dollars of debt must be rolled over by the G-7 nations, Brazil, Russia, India and China. ... Sadly, most people simply do not care about the debt bomb that is hanging over the nations of the world, and the coming crisis is going to devastate their lives without any warning." [311]
In total a picture is given with: "Total market debt is now up to an astonishing $53 trillion and continues to grow ... A debt bubble cannot be solved with more debt." [312]

In economics, consumer debt is outstanding debt of consumers, as opposed to businesses or governments. In macroeconomic terms, it is debt which is used to fund consumption rather than investment. [313] Private debt means: debt owed by private sector borrowers. (This should not be confused with

---

[307] http://www.zerohedge.com/news/bbc-speechless-trader-tells-truth-collapse-comingand-goldman-rules-world#ixzz1ZGpvrRBA
[308] http://www.economist.com/content/global_debt_clock
[309] http://dailybail.com/home/global-debt-clock-43-trillion-ticking.html
[310] http://www.viewsoftheworld.net/?p=1766
[311] http://www.prisonplanet.com/the-debt-bomb-7600000000000-dollars-of-debt-must-be-rolled-over-in-2012.html
[312] http://www.mybudget360.com/day-of-reckoning-for-global-total-debt-total-credit-market-debt-consumer-debt-large-charge-of-household-debt-trillions/
[313] See:.wikipedia.org/wiki/Private_debt

commercial debt, which is owed to private sector creditors.) [314] And in the words of another source: "Debt held by private individuals and usually borrowed from banks or accumulated on credit cards." [315]

About household (private) debt some figures show the criticality:

"A new report shows the average Canadian family debt has hit the $100,000 mark. The report, released by the Vanier Institute of the Family on Thursday, suggests the debt-to-income ratio is a record 150 percent." [316] More about is to find here: [317]

"In 2009, two-thirds of households had outstanding debt that averaged $114,400. Couples with children held one-half of all household debt, with an average debt of $144,600, higher than the overall average of $114,400. Similarly, individuals under 45 held 61% of household debt, $129,200 on average. Debtors in British Columbia, Alberta and Ontario owed, on average, between $124,700 and $157,700, compared to the national average of $114,400." (And in another context the report says that the average household debt in Canada is: $129,200)." [318]

In the United Kingdom the total personal debt stood at £1,456 trillion (end of January 2012). Other figures say: Average household debt in the UK (including mortgages) is £55,988.

The average amount owed per UK adult (including mortgages) was £29,634 in January. This was around 122% of average earnings.

Average consumer borrowing (including credit cards, motor and retail finance deals, overdrafts and unsecured loans) per UK adult was £4,221 in January.

The estimated average outstanding mortgage for the 11.2m households that carry mortgage debt stood at £111,260 in January.

Based on January 2012 trends, the UK's total interest repayments on personal debt over a 12 month period would have been £63.2 billion … This is equivalent to £173 million per day … The daily increase in Government national debt: £248,500,000 (PSDN) … The figure for public sector net debt

---

[314] www.jubileeusa.org/index.php

[315] understandingfiscalresponsibility.org/glossary-of-common-terms

[316] http://www.statcan.gc.ca/pub/75-001-x/2012002/article/11636-eng.pdf

[317] http://www.ctv.ca/CTVNews/Canada/20110217/family-debt-110217/#ixzz1x5SwdF1E

[318] http://www.statcan.gc.ca/pub/75-001-x/2012002/article/11636-eng.pdf

(PSND) expected in 2015-16 (excluding financial interventions) rises to £106,429 per household. 319

There are also alarming statistics on U.S. consumer debt: "In the US, consumers and households are dangerously in debt. Even after the catastrophic financial crisis in 2008, it seems in 2010 lessons from past mistakes have not been learned and taken on board. The Federal Reserve is looking at $2.4 trillion in unsecured debt. And the numbers just keep rising. Eighty-eight million accounts and credit lines representing $751 billion in credit have been closed since September 2008 … Alarming statistics on consumer debt: 1) The total amount of consumer debt in the US is nearly $2.4 trillion in 2010. That's $7,800 debt per person. 2) Thirty-three percent of that debt is revolving debt (such as credit card debt), the other 67 percent comes from loans (such as car loans, student loans, mortgages and the like). 3) $51 billion worth of fast food was charged to credit cards in 2006, compared to $33.2 billion the previous year. [320] The total consumer debt is 11.4 trillion dollars (increasing). [321]

Another picture shows the truth about America's debt: [322]
"What are you going to do about the more than $74 trillion dollar debt that has already been accumulated? … The federal government keeps two sets of books…the set the government doesn't talk about, reports a more ominous financial picture."

Dennis Cauchon, USA TODAY writes:

"We've all heard about the federal debt. But most of us haven't heard the truth … Politicians will tell you that the federal debt is more than $14.5 trillion … That sounds bad enough—but it gets even worse. Together with unfunded liabilities (all of the benefits that the government has promised to seniors, Baby Boomers, and other citizens) our nation is in the hole for more than $75 trillion dollars … That's more than $246,000 for every man, woman, and child in America, and it's growing every day." [323]

Another source says the following about America: [324]

[319] http://www.debtsimple.co.uk/uk-debt-statistics.shtml
[320] http://www.economywatch.com/economy-business-and-finance-news/a-dozen-alarming-consumer-debt-statistics.21-05.html
[321] http://www.creditscore.net/u-s-consumer-debt-in-2011/
[322] http://www.truthin2010.org/
[323] http://www.truthin2010.org/
[324] http://endoftheamericandream.com/archives/35-statistics-that-show-the-average-american-family-has-been-broke-down-tore-down-beat-down-busted-and-disgusted-by-this-

- U.S. home values have fallen an astounding 6.3 trillion dollars since the peak of the real estate market in 2005.
- 31 percent of the homeowners that responded to a recent Rasmussen Reports survey indicated that they are 'underwater' on their mortgages.
- The number of homes that were actually repossessed reached the 1 million mark for the first time ever during 2010.
- There are 10% fewer 'middle class jobs' in the United States today than there were a decade ago.
- Half of all American workers now earn $505 or less per week.
- Total U.S. credit card debt is more than 8 times larger than it was just 30 years ago.
- Americans now owe more than $904 billion on student loans, which is a new all-time record high.
- Average household debt in the United States has now reached a level of 136% of average household income. In China, average household debt is only 17% of average household income.
- 1.5 million Americans filed for bankruptcy in 2010. That represented the fourth yearly increase in bankruptcy filings in a row.
- Over the last decade, the number of Americans without health insurance has risen from about 38 million to about 52 million.

More information can be found on the given website link. Students may now ask: What is capitalistic economics about?

Similar pictures can be found about Portugal, Greece, Ireland, Italy, and Spain. On the internet there are thousands of similar economic warning 'signs' about the state of many developing countries that show what capitalistic economics is really about.

We guess that 80-90% of everything that is really important in the world of economics is not told to the people by the media. Max Keiser and co-host Stacy Herbert gives you plenty of insight. [325] We also recommend considering articles about the global economy from another Russian media. [326] And although an Iranian media is quite overloaded with propaganda, it also provides very interesting views on the global economic battles. [327] Every day a Canadian website from experts about economics provides readers with economic and political analyses: [328]

---

economy
[325] http://rt.com/
[326] http://english.pravda.ru/
[327] http://www.presstv.com/
[328] http://www.globalresearch.ca

In June 2012, Germany has a public debt of around 2.1 trillion Euros, increasing every day. [329]

Another picture gives us an insight into the external debt (or foreign debt). This is the part of the total debt in a country that is owed to creditors outside the country: [330] (1)

Rank	Country	External Debt US dollars
1	United States	15,570,789,000,000
—	European Union	13,720,000,000,000
2	United Kingdom	8,981,000,000,000
3	Germany	4,713,000,000,000
4	France	4,698,000,000,000
5	Japan	2,441,000,000,000
6	Ireland	123,058,047,000
7	Netherlands	1,884,489,600,000
8	Italy	2,223,000,000,000
9	Spain	2,166,000,000,000
10	Luxembourg	1,892,000,000,000
11	Belgium	1,241,000,000,000
12	Switzerland	1,200,000,000,000
13	Australia	1,169,000,000,000
14	Canada	1,009,000,000,000
15	Sweden	853,300,000,000
16	Austria	755,000,000,000
—	Hong Kong	750,800,000,000
17	Norway	643,000,000,000
18	China	635,500,000,000
19	Denmark	559,500,000,000
20	Greece	532,900,000,000

(1) Many more countries are listed on this website.

About the global economy a report says: "June 5, 2012 – GLOBAL ECONOMY – The hits just keep coming and with $647 trillion reasons to worry, aka, the total notional derivatives now outstanding as of Q4 in 2011

---

[329] http://www.silberknappheit.de/schulden/staat.php
[330] http://en.wikipedia.org/wiki/List_of_countries_by_external_debt

per the Bank of International Settlements just released this afternoon and published officially on Monday. Of course the problem is that as one can see in the graph above, the amount of Gross Credit Exposure has returned to 2008 levels, something the world might want to pay attention to. Once the lessons of the mistakes of the past are ignored, the risk factor increases proportionally and with Europe teetering on the edge of a Lehman event, the increase in interest rate derivatives might well indicate a new risk that has not been accounted for:

A sudden collapse of the Euro currency below the 1.20 or even parity level. Such an event would make Lehman look like a picnic but there is more bad news beyond that as it is not just interest rate derivatives that have increased past 2008 levels as the chart above demonstrates, but some idiots placed bets on the currency markets which means that a collapse of the Euro creates an irreversible game of dominoes and destruction:

Unfortunately for us common folk, no one has taken the time to explain the implications of a 10, 20, or even 30% decline in the value of the Euro versus the US Dollar in a compressed time period. This is one warning sign of many from the report but the other one is more mundane and ties to the Federal Reserve's mandate, er, unwritten mandate to support the U.S. equity markets by laundering money through its member banks to purchase stocks and give the illusion of a strong economy. – John G" [331]

Another report makes clear what economics is about; and we assume that his statement also covers the European citizens: "The economic statistics that you are about to read are incredibly shocking, but they are also very, very real. Tonight there are going to be millions of men and women all across America that cannot sleep because they are consumed with anxiety about their financial problems. Even as you read this, there are a lot of parents out there that are trying to figure out how to explain to their children why their homes are being taken away. There are also hordes of very hard working Americans that are incredibly frustrated because they have sent out thousands of resumes and yet they can't seem to get a job interview. Have you ever been at a point where you couldn't pay the mortgage or put food on the table for your family? It can be an absolutely soul-crushing experience. In fact, there are some cities in the U.S. that have been so utterly devastated by this economy that it seems as though virtually everyone has had the hope sucked right out of them. The mainstream media is trying to convince all of us that we are in an economic recovery, but that is a lie. The truth is that we are in

---

[331] http://theextinctionprotocol.wordpress.com/2012/06/05/unregulated-global-derivatives-debt-market-hits-647-trillion-mark/

the middle of a long-term economic decline and the greatest economy in the history of the world is dying right in front of our eyes." [332]

Researchers at Jay W. Forrester's institute at MIT says: "…the world could suffer from 'global economic collapse' and 'precipitous population decline' if people continue to consume the world's resources at the current pace … Most of the computer scenarios found population and economic growth continuing at a steady rate until about 2030. But without drastic measures for environmental protection, the scenarios predict the likelihood of a population and economic crash … The Australian physicist Graham Turner says 'the world is on track for disaster… There is a very clear warning bell being rung here … We are not on a sustainable trajectory'." [333]

Steen Jakobsen, chief economist at Saxo Bank, outlines some theses to discuss: [334]

1) "In general, the art of government consists in taking as much money as possible from one party of the citizens to give to the other." – Voltaire
2) …now we are in a debt trap in which governments and banks remain thinly capitalized and have no access to further credit unless the central bank is willing.
3) The world governments and commercial banks now take so much of the 'credit cake' that the private sector is only left with crumbs.
4) The governments and weak banks and over-indebted companies need very low interest rates to continue to carry and roll their gigantic debt loads.
5) The biggest policy mistake historically has always been for central banks to stay too easy for too long.
6) The policy makers have printed in excess of 3 trillion US dollars globally to keep the financial market and governments afloat.
7) The banks and government are dependent on the false sense of security low interest rates creates.

➔ Do you now know what capitalistic economics is about?

4.2.4. The Post-Modern Fascist Capitalism

Thesis from David DeGraw: The Economic Elite have turned America into

---

[332] http://endoftheamericandream.com/archives/35-statistics-that-show-the-average-american-family-has-been-broke-down-tore-down-beat-down-busted-and-disgusted-by-this-economy
[333] http://news.yahoo.com/blogs/sideshow/next-great-depression-mit-researchers-predict-global-economic-190352944.html
[334] http://rt.com/business/news/central-banks-interest-rates-467/

a modern day fascist state. [335]

"Fascism should more properly be called corporatism, since it is the merger of state and corporate power. In the early 1900s, the Italians who invented the term fascism also described it as 'estato corporativo', meaning: the corporate state.

Corporations now control our government and have the dominant role in our society.

The most power global corporations dominate the legislative and political process like never before.

President Franklin D. Roosevelt once described fascism: The liberty of a democracy is not safe if the people tolerate the growth of private power to a point where it comes strong than their democratic state itself. That, in its essence, is fascism — ownership of government by an individual, by a group, or any controlling private power.

American Legislative Exchange Council (ALEC), which is a group of corporate executives who literally write government legislation.

An increase of $19 billion in programs for building prisons, 'effectively making the construction of prisons the nation's main housing program for the poor.'

We now have the largest prison population in the world. With only 4% of the world's population, we have 25% of the world's prison population.
The US, by far, has more of its citizens in prison than any other nation on earth. China, with a billion citizens, doesn't imprison as many people as the US, with only 308 million American citizens. The US per capita statistics are 700 per 100,000 citizens. In comparison, China has 110 per 100,000. In the Middle East, the repressive regime in Saudi Arabia imprisons 45 per 100,000. US per capita levels are equivalent to the darkest days of the Soviet Gulag.

Now, let's consider the fact that, according to the Census Bureau, 31.1 million people lived in poverty in 2000, and according to Columbia's study 875,000 deaths came as a result. This means that 1 out of every 35.5 people living in poverty die annually as a result of their impoverishment. If you extrapolate this data to the 2009 total of 52.8 million people living in poverty, you get an estimate of 1,486,338 deaths within that year. Even if you use the lower

---

[335] http://www.globalresearch.ca/index.php?context=va&aid=25967

poverty totals from the Census Bureau, 43.6 million people, you get an estimate of 1,228,169 deaths in 2009.

Compare the million people who die annually as a result of these economic attacks, to the 2,977 that died on 9/11. As someone who lived three blocks from the World Trade Center, as tragic as 9/11 was, these economic attacks are much more severe and damaging to us as a nation, albeit a much slower and unseen death toll. Nonetheless, the result is of genocidal proportions. One can statistically compare the economic attacks on the US to the invasion of Iraq, which some estimate as leading to one million deaths. Once again, many of those deaths came in brutal and spectacular fashion in bombing campaigns known as 'shock and awe.' However, the death toll compares to the hidden brutality of a four-year campaign of economic 'shock and awe'. Just as Iraq was invaded, the US has been invaded by a global banking cartel. Federal Reserve's economic policies — along with policies from the International Monetary Fund, World Bank and Bank of International Settlements — have caused rioting and uprisings over skyrocketing food prices and costs of living throughout the world. The fact of the matter, and very harsh and unfortunate reality of this crisis, is that the global economic central planners are deliberately carrying out genocidal economic policies.

When tens of trillions of dollars deliberately flow to the top economic one-tenth of one percent of the global population, while large percentages live in poverty, you have to conclude, in technical terms, that a Neo-Feudal-Fascist state is upon us.

These people, the global economic top one-tenth of one percent, are genocidal fascists carrying out a holocaust."

Some people studied the economic question: How can we get a lot of money without land, without high labor costs, without big production premises, without complex business structures, without the costs of production, and without supplying and allocating goods, and at the same time remaining incognito?

There is only one answer for these people: We must take away from the middle class and the upper class and the new rich all the wealth and we must take away from the production entities all the products and we must make them powerless and poor people. And we must get (without working) some cents from every single purchase made by the people around the globe, a kind of tax for the people on the hidden stage behind the curtains. The aim is set!

Now there are methods to achieve the aim:

- Forcing government to take on huge debt, buying public goods and leasing them back
- Offering to companies a lot of money for expansion to make more profit
- Offering people high mortgages (up to 120%) and loans with time-limited low interest
- Giving to all people credit and debit cards and heating up the 'easy consumption'
- Allowing the credit card holders to overcharge their limit (charged with heavy interest)
- Giving consumer loans, stimulating 'wants' through promoting a lifestyle by credit
- Offering millions of apartments and houses to the people for living or holidays

And then the next step follows:

- Creating political unrest, riots, proxy wars and murdering, the terrorism myth
- Triggering wars and selling weapons (with loans) to get total control over raw resources
- Implementing step by step the total control of all citizens (Internet, money, life)
- Playing out periodical financial crises and triggering with that financial earthquakes
- Speculating with food and resources, betting, bridge financing (for minutes or hours)
- Now the banks get the millions of homes, machines, land, wealth, and whatsoever more
- The middle and upper class looses wealth, homes, money, their businesses, and become poor
- Logically unemployment and poverty increase in many countries and intimidate entire folks
- And in 5-10 years the confiscated homes, machines, land, and wealth have increased in value
- The banks will dominate the entire real estate market with mortgages
- The private real estate market collapses, more bankruptcy brings more homes to the banks
- Interest is a way of making profit without having worked for it (as the work costs 2%)
- High public debt means giving the power to banks and investors that make billions in profit

- The potential 'enemies' of the people on the stage behind the curtains are eliminated
- Economic satisfaction, well-being, happiness as a tool to seduce converts into a nightmare
- The mad mega-agents are destroying nations, cultures, trust, peace, love, hope, confidence
- Now the super rich are richer and much more powerful without even having worked for it
- Dictatorship over people, CEOs, institutions, education, businesses, governments is re-born

4.2.5. Changes in Society

Changes in society are indispensable: Without a new Western life style and a new composition of the production market there will not be a sustainable solution for the huge amounts of unemployed people in most capitalistic countries; not to talk about developing countries.

We have in the European Union between 25-30m registered and unregistered unemployed people. There are sources that say the world needs 250-300m more jobs within the next 10 years. If we add the under-employed people and the one billion people suffering from extreme poverty, then we reach a demand of at least 2 billion jobs needed on this planet within 10 years, the increase of the world population (especially in Asia, Africa, Middle East, and Latin America) the next 20-30 years considered or not.

The dynamic of the global market with its 'invisible hand' will never be able to solve the immense problems. This 'invisible hand' is anyhow rubbish. The 'profit-maximizing lunacy' of the capitalistic economics will never solve this problem; it will make it even worse.
Those who still think that we – the capitalistic world – are in a 'free market' are ignorant, uniformed, naïve, and stupid. And if this problem of creating 1-2 billion of new jobs within the next 10-20 years will not be solved, then the entire humanity will experience an economic collapse of unimaginable dimension provoking even an Armageddon – not to talk about the included collateral human misery of 80% of the world population.

Small sustainable businesses can reduce unemployment:

➔ A small business must allow that a person or a family can live from the business.
➔ US & EU: A net income of minimum €1,500-2,500 (Dollars), means 30-

60% of the turnover, is aimed.

→ A business can grow and be expanded for 3-5 additional working places.
→ Human values and a new sustainable lifestyle is the core of businesses and marketing.

Hiring workers and wages:

There are three perspectives in interdependence that need to be considered:

1) The firms can't hire workers if they don't have work
2) Sustainability of work places is a factor of high importance
3) A wage must enable a person to make a modest basic life.

Exploring these three perspectives we need to consider as well the state of humanity, the development of humanity, of the world, and of the planet within the next 50 years. But here we can't develop these future perspectives. We explore this topic in Economics III. We assume that the readers already have a certain picture about the big problems of humanity today and tomorrow.

The crucial question is: How can the business world create hundreds of millions new jobs?

4.3. The Hidden Aims of Economics

4.3.1. Another Scientific View about Economics

The most important faults of economics lie in the neo-capitalistic economics:

- Most scientific terms have a wide connotation which is confusing and misleading.
- In general everywhere the understanding of humans is outrageously simplified.
- Human values, as essence of human life, and the characteristics of life is ignored.
- The manifold characteristics of consumers and producers are ignored.
- The varieties of entity structures of consumers and producers are ignored.
- The culture of consumers and producers, seen as a way of living, are ignored.

- The quality and efficiency of self-management in life and business are ignored.
- The natural limitedness of consumer's satisfaction is ignored; does not exist.
- That everything in life and business is permanently in development is ignored.
- The flexibility of the bundles of demand and supply is thoroughly ignored.
- The flexibility and levels of budgets of consumers for living a decent life is ignored.
- The environmental factors of costs for consumers and producers are ignored.
- The labor market on consumer and producer side is completely distorted.
- A worker is not a human, is simply a production factor and a cost factor for profit.
- Microeconomics is presented preponderantly from the view of corporations.
- The cost analysis is vague, undifferentiated and a chaos in terms and laws.
- The element 'marginal' is an expression of unlimited compulsion and greed.
- The term 'revenue' hides the manifoldness of making profit behind production.
- 'Maximizing profit' is the sole motive to do business ignoring any responsibility.
- The calculation of the parameter 'profit' is behind the curtains in the fog.
- Profit is never related to the workers' performance and excluded from its benefit.
- The variable costs are not specified and not put in the context of exploitation.
- The theory of 'opportunity cost' is an insane compulsion and monstrous greed.
- Cost calculations often focus on cents and seconds of workers' performance.
- The consumers' satisfaction theory is a Fata Morgana and a perverse distortion.
- The producers' satisfaction is only related to the highest possible profit for owners.
- The 'rational choice' theory is a neurotic and absurd construction beyond reality.
- The concept of 'equilibrium' is a mathematical model that never matches with reality.
- The importance of 'incentives' is highly exaggerated and may only work with dummies.

- The consumer's 'optimal choice' is a fantasy it never works in the real world.
- The law of 'demand and supply' does not work 'naturally' in a majority of the market.
- The term 'allocation' is abstract, diffuse and misleading in most contexts.
- The substitution theory is a phenomenon, but becomes irrelevant in the thousands of goods.
- The term 'efficiency' has the sole aim to exploit any opportunity and it leads to insanity.
- As everything is permanently in motion, the term 'elasticity' becomes very artificial.
- Income elasticity in real numbers is only of interest for the big corporations.
- The competitive market and the 'free market' are extremely limited by corporations.
- The real world of amoral operations of corporations is ignored or simplified.
- The crucial influence and power of the mega banks with centuries of history are ignored.
- Principles, models, concepts, laws and theories are vague and do not match with reality.
- The generalization of the theories, laws, models, graphs, and principles is a joke.
- The world of self-employed people, small and medium sized firms is mostly ignored.
- The characteristic economics of the manifold different service firms is thoroughly ignored.
- Everywhere and endlessly extended the economic statements refer to corporations.
- The very different kind of market dynamic (e.g. tourism, hospitality) is totally ignored.
- Externalities are ignored or simplified and devaluated in their consequences for the collective.
- The human cost factor of 'marketing' with billions of €/$ and its brainwashing is ignored.
- Everywhere we identified greed, compulsion, avarice, envy, restlessness, and disrespect.
- The radicalism of technological and mathematical models for doing business is unspoken.
- The destruction of small and medium size businesses through corporations is obvious.
- The outgoing cash flows from villages, towns, and cities to corporations is

ignored.

- The destructive function of debt, interest, and the concentration of money is ignored.
- The complicated constructions of most statements express neuroticism and psychosis.
- Neo-capitalistic practices accept the worst amoral doing in cooperation with political agents.
- Such understanding of economics leads immediately to sadistic falseness, strife, and wars.
- The humane 'picture' behind most theories and laws shows psychopathy and psychosis.
- The energetic drive of most theories, laws and economic statements is thoroughly anti-human.
- Most 'theories', multiplied by millions and extended by score and time, end in deicide.

We conclude with some normative statements:

→ The foundation and principles of economics is a scam, an ideology, not a science.
→ The development of such understanding of economics aims for a capitalistic global government.
→ The dynamic of neo-capitalistic economics destroys all societies, cultures and human values.
→ The power of economics has reached to destroy the mind and soul of people and governments.
→ The study books are full of regicide and in the end of deicide: an unimaginable madness.
→ The roots of such a mind are around 3,000 years old and its tree is growing since centuries.
→ The capitalistic 'science' is the program of dehumanization and elimination of human's dignity.
→ Everywhere we identify hate for life, hate for the Archetypes of the Soul, and hate for God.
→ The neo-capitalistic economy is evil, a lunacy, a blasphemy, and a terrible capital offense.
→ The real world of economics as presented in the study books will lead humanity towards doom.

With the neo-capitalistic economics humanity's future is at stake!

The result of the analysis about economic terms, principles, laws, theories, parameters, and suggestions is outrageous and frightening as can be seen from the following: The economic thinking reveals psychological dimensions that we consider to be the 'hell in human's mind and soul'. Everywhere is falseness, compulsion, cantankerousness, greed, envy, avarice, control, imperiousness, neuroticism, mania, insanity, lunacy, madness, psychosis, stubbornness, bullheaded minds, dehumanization, addiction drive, radical disrespect, exploitation, abuse, vanity, structural and institutional violence, conceptual radicalism, illimitableness, exploitation, meanness, deceit, lies, camouflage, arrogance, people imprisoned in lies, omnipotence, and individuals striving for dominance over the entire world.

Economics has destroyed all essential genuine human values like never seen before in the history. There is a horrifying scam especially as the corporations (banks included) operate in a way that is not presented in all these economic study books. The supreme economic agents are driven by a rage and hate that a normal human can't even imagine.

This is what capitalistic economics is about: The structures of global corporations allow for the domination of entire networks of corporations simply by occupying some of the top positions on the top level or via control of money flow. These people have much more power than most governments in the Western world and in developing countries. These people don't need to be in the governments; they give instructions (orders!) to governments, bribe and blackmail or simply finance political agents of any country. They are the Trojan horse that is nearly everywhere in the middle of governmental power and in most of the countries of their wishes. They have destroyed democracy (if it ever existed). They have destroyed the societies of many countries. They have destroyed the life of billions of people. They manipulate and brainwash billions of people to get them on a main stream of opinion. They have reached a level of control of privacy and freedom of speech and demonstration over most people of the capitalistic world that is worse than ever existed in the history of mankind. They have destroyed in union with Christian authorities (of most churches) the psychical-spiritual evolution.

The theory (ideology) of the capitalistic economics is the code program of the destruction of humanity and the planet. They destroy a project that needed billions of years to be realized. Why do they hate God, the source of everything in the universe, that much? These evil monsters have created an unimaginable sadness that covers the entire universe of which our earth is part.

→ Humanity lives since the 19th Century in an 'Age of Atrocity' like never seen before.
→ How can I forgive them? Can I? How can I? Do I have to forgive them?

Do you?

The most important question is: What has caused such a perverse and infernal economic thinking? Who was the first person (or group of persons) that developed such an economics that will lead humanity into the Abysm? Who are the architects and protagonists of this monstrous economics? What caused this cosmic pain and sadness in their soul forcing them to act in such ways?

Economics from another point of view that we get from the capitalistic economics study books is:

"June 6, 2012 – EARTH – Earth is rapidly headed toward a catastrophic breakdown if humans don't get their act together, according to an international group of scientists. Writing Wednesday (June 6) in the journal Nature, the researchers warn that the world is headed toward a tipping point marked by extinctions and unpredictable changes on a scale not seen since the glaciers retreated 12,000 years ago. "There is a very high possibility that by the end of the century, the Earth is going to be a very different place," study researcher Anthony Barnosky told LiveScience. Barnosky, a professor of integrative biology from the University of California, Berkeley, joined a group of 17 other scientists to warn that this new planet might not be a pleasant place to live. "You can envision these state changes as a fast period of adjustment where we get pushed through the eye of the needle," Barnosky said. "As we're going through the eye of the needle, that's when we see political strife, economic strife, war and famine."

Barnosky and his colleagues reviewed research on climate change, ecology and Earth's tipping points that break the camel's back, so to speak. At certain thresholds, putting more pressure on the environment leads to a point of no return, Barnosky said. Suddenly, the planet responds in unpredictable ways, triggering major global transitions. The most recent example of one of these transitions is the end of the last glacial period. Within not much more than 3,000 years, the Earth went from being 30 percent covered in ice to its present, nearly ice-free condition. Most extinctions and ecological changes (goodbye, woolly mammoths) occurred in just 1,600 years. Earth's biodiversity still has not recovered to what it was. Today, Barnosky said, humans are causing changes even faster than the natural ones that pushed back the glaciers — and the changes are bigger. Driven by a 35 percent increase in atmospheric carbon dioxide since the start of the Industrial Revolution, global temperatures are rising faster than they did back then, Barnosky said. Likewise, humans have completely transformed 43 percent of Earth's land surface for cities and agriculture, compared with the 30 percent land surface transition that occurred at the end of the last glacial period. Meanwhile, the human population has exploded, putting ever more pressure on existing resources. - MSNBC" [336]

→ It is time that the young generation and all people of good faith identify the monsters by name, address, institution, positions, activities, networks, tentacles, religion, and their ancestors in order to save humanity's psychical-spiritual evolution and the planet.

4.3.2. The Crucial Global Perspective

1. For 2-3 billion people there is not enough (healthy) food and clean drinking water, or the allocation doesn't work, or these people can't afford to buy the food due to lack of money (and work).

2. The global contamination is an immense threat to the entire humanity; on the one side it creates illnesses, and on the other side it damages and contaminates all kind of indispensable resources.

3. The global contamination, especially of the air, produces secondary effects through climate change, means: the entire food and water chains, including species, are already irreversibly damaged.

4. The big corporations over-exploiting nutrition resources such as seas and oceans, water reservoirs, forests (deforestation), and agricultural land are on a suicidal roadmap.

5. The concentration of money destroys the development of small and medium sized businesses, put billions into poverty, destroys the values of democracy, and establishes fascism.

6. The big corporations operating globally, also with their supra media power, destroy the mind of people, dehumanize and degenerate billions of people, and eliminate pioneering spirit, private initiatives, and genuine human values.

7. The United States (US-Army) and the European Union (NATO) is on the roadmap of re-armament and wars since 1989 creating one of the biggest threats for humanity.

---

[336] http://theextinctionprotocol.wordpress.com/2012/06/06/war-famine-strife-extinction-scientists-warn-planet-approaching-a-tipping-point-of-an-apocalyptic-nature/

8. Wars can be seen as a business – the most expensive business: There are the producers and sellers of weapons. There are those who have 'war' as a business aim and they trigger wars with a road map. The architects and project managers of a war do not have to be on the political stage (with governmental power). There is always a declared winner of a war. The winner of a war gets a lot of goods and reparation. The looser of a war has to give up nearly everything that is of economic (and political) interest. But for those who trigger wars it is unimportant who will be the winner. Who makes most profit from wars? 'Maximizing profit' and 'to get most of it' becomes here the revealed aim of capitalistic economics (and of its original authors).

9. The term 'economic war' is well known. It refers to fights between two or more mega competitors. But it also refers to a tool in order to destroy other countries' economy and with that their governmental power. Rearmament on a level of 100 billion dollars and on a level of a trillion dollars (per year) is the most powerful economic instrument to destroy the economy, the life standard of citizens, and the power of governments of other countries.

10. The financial crisis since 2008, caused by many corporations and institutions, brings into light amorality, scrupulousness, arrogance, and a criminal energy of destructive global dimension. In the bigger picture the question arises: What is the long-term superior aim of the financial crisis?

Presenting the planet Mars with 29 photos as a possible place to live in the future 'n-TV' writes on its website: "We know the reasons that in the long term significantly make life on earth more difficult or even impossible." [337] The media mentions: explosion of global population, scarcity of resources, and climate change. This is an outrageous perverse lie, typical for such media in many terrestrial criticalities. At least implicitly they say: these three factors are today of highest critical importance and urgency.

But these three reasons are absolutely not the original reasons. These three factors are human made and therefore humans are the reason that makes it more difficult or even impossible to live on earth in the future. And when we say 'humans', we mean these 100-300 hidden devilish monsters (maybe 500) with a 'mission' nearly 3,000 years old, the lured and seduced leaders in the past and today, the highly incompetent political leaders, the scam of religion, the archaic curriculum of public education, the madness of economics (including the monetary systems) that in the core all have many systemic

---

[337] http://www.n-tv.de/mediathek/bilderserien/wissen/Der-Mars-article6381991.html

faults, including psychopathy and psychosis; and finally a huge majority of humans that are stupid, lazy-minded, unwilling to learn and unable to love, archaic and infantile, ego-centered and narcissistic, arrogant and conceited, greedy and envious, neurotic and false, aggressive and cantankerous, suffocating the truth with attitudes of a child abuser, blind and naïve sheep or 'subhuman beings' following any dogmatic or ideological Fata Morgana that suits to them and to have at least a certain feeling of triumph over others.

The way people glorify their ideology and their leaders and the way they believe in God or pray to God is like pouring oil into the fire that destroys the planet and its ecosystems. Or in a moral statement: It's the evil in a majority of human's mind and soul that destroys the planet with its ecosystems. And it's also the evil in the mind and soul of these people that destroys the psychical-spiritual evolution of mankind – the planet and mankind, both a divine project.

Conclusions:

➜ All possible solutions require a complete transformation of these ten criticalities.
➜ There is no solution for 2 billion new jobs without an all-embracing global renewal.
➜ The scam of the economics is one of the worst engines of these dire developments.
➜ There is no solution if people can't get work with a wage that allows for a modest life.
➜ There is no solution if the marketing continues making people crazy with 50,000 goods.
➜ There is no solution if economics ignores human values and psychical-spiritual factors.
➜ Absolutely all big corporations must be split into manageable and controllable entities.
➜ Central political power must be delegated: 25% to provinces and 50% to local governments.
➜ Leaders, managers, CEOs, and board members must periodically undergo an integrity check.
➜ Politicians, especially members of governments, must periodically undergo an integrity check.
➜ A network of ethical institutions must be built up globally in every country and urban area.
➜ Global peace includes peace in the economic world and requires respecting all-sided balance.
➜ The all-sided balance must first be established in the mind and soul and

life of people.

> *If a servant of a king is envious of the king's wealth and power, he compulsively thinks about how he could get even more wealth and more power than the king has, without having or aspiring governmental power or a kingdom. The sole path for such an insane aim is the economics in theory and practice. Such servants exist since millenniums on the hidden stage behind the curtains. Here we have the monsters that commit deicide because they are angry at God.*

4.3.3. Studying Economics

Thesis: Students of economics must become the soldiers of the mad capitalistic economics.

Let's take some classical study books in economics; the ones we discuss in this book. In the average we calculate 750 pages per book, calculated only the pages of text. These books have a big size and each page is fully packed with texts and some with a lot of exercises. To read one page we calculate an average of one hour, including studying the graphs, and occasionally making notes. Doing at least 50% of the given exercises, a student needs additionally an estimated 150 hours.

We also include that the students must read some paragraphs or pages twice or three times to understand the texts. To elaborate one book and to do additional exercises given from the professor, a student spends an estimated 900 hours; additionally 300 hours of teaching (classes) with some little questioning (discussion) here and there. Alone this subject requires 1,200 hours for classes, reading, studying, and doing exercises from the book and from the teacher (home work); means 400 hours per year, or 200 hours per semester, or around 130 hours per trimester.

Studying the general Bachelor program of 'Business Administration' we calculate 30 weeks per year and 20 hours of teaching per week, included some short tests or final exams. Writing yearly 2-4 essays and the final thesis are not included. This Bachelor program during the 3-year-program includes estimated 12 subjects per year (6 subjects per semester or 4 subjects per trimester); means 36 subjects during these 3 years. 'Economics' is only one subject of these 36 subjects.

To draw a model study picture we estimate that a student works during the 3 years in total 90 weeks; additionally and here not included the essays and the final thesis or reading other books to extend specific knowledge. If a student works 40 hours per week (teaching and studying), he spends in total 3,600 hours for the entire program; 1,200 hours per year, 600 hours per semester or 400 hours per trimester. In this calculation each subject gets in the average 100 hours at disposal.

But for the subject 'economics' he must spend 1,200 hours 'to make the best of it'. And such an imbalance of performance distribution is not reasonable, even not possible.

As the students of economics have no time for critical thinking or for a pioneering thinking, they must simply copy all the statements, laws, theories, terms, definitions, graphs, and principles. Copying as a learning method leads to stubbornness, rigidity, compulsion, sheep behavior, and especially in the economics to neurotic thinking and acting.

A majority of experts, professors, and authors of economics started learning by copying 20-30-40 years ago and periodically with a further education (self-study), they are today mentally and as a personality a result of a distorted economics, the micro- and macroeconomics.

The economic world, the free market, shows us where such economic science leads humanity and the planet. The leaders in the economic world are essentially responsible for the destruction of people's soul and mind, for the collective dehumanization, and for the state of humanity and the planet.

The leaders in the economic world and the economic science together with the science of politics and agents in the political world they are not only predators, but also the supreme destroyers of humanity and the planet, of the evolution of mankind as a whole.

A lot of the classical study books about Western economics abuse, cheat and deceit, manipulate and brainwash the students in an outrageous way. That's like child abuse as the students have no chance to look through or to protect themselves from such evil doing.

The same problem we have with the Holy Bible and the 'Credo'. It's practically an identical structural and humane failure. At least, religions use spiritual words and create spiritual emotions. But certainly, in both cases: humans and humanity need a healthy and genuine, pioneering and balanced economics and genuine spirituality (or religion), based on the Archetypes of the Soul.

Students are well advised to open their eyes, to think critically, and to question everything they get on the study table to copy, including that from scientific authorities and institutions. Students must decide if they want to become a soldier or slave of economics and to lose their soul and to become neurotic and compulsive, or if they want to develop the potential of their soul and an economic science and world that is sustainable for the future of humanity and the planet.

→ You never know if an economic theory, principle, or law is for a 'Pizzeria' or a corporation.
→ Economic experts reveal the naked truth: "(Capitalistic) Economics (is) for Dummies"!

Something to learn for students and economic experts:

The capitalistic science of economics preaches the needs and wants and its satisfaction together with well-being as the highest aim of life. They never include human factors within a psychical-spiritual process aiming for complete fulfillment, nor do they include human values in general. There is absolutely no respect for the planet and the future generations or for the folks and their cultures.
It's logical and one can even calculate it with the right parameters that this understanding of economics and consumer society leads to the complete destruction of mind and soul of humans, of the world and the planet. That's why capitalistic economics is fundamentally in its system against humans and against the creation. Therefore such kind of economics is evil.

Good words from a University with highest reputation: "We want young people to use their minds as they never have before, thinking hard about realities and issues that strain their mental powers. They should be urged to be imaginative and inquiring." [338] We learnt from economics that any positive statement is helpful to hide reality.

The reality is different: "There are twelve (American Universities) that recur again and again on the list of those parents who demand the very best. We'll be calling them the Golden Dozen.

Harvard	Cornell
Yale	Penn
Princeton	Stanford
Dartmouth	Duke
Brown	Amherst
Columbia	Williams

---

[338] Hacker, p. 6

The Golden Dozen! For many parents, the stern fact is that there's a wide chasm between them and whichever school might come next.

Do these schools really represent the 'best educations in the nation'? And what does 'the best' mean anyway?" [339] We would say: 'sectarian chasm'. They all teach the neo-capitalistic economics with a hidden religious background!

Another fact is: "Teaching: good, great, and abysmal. When we come to Harvard, we have to understand it's not for the education we get, but for the reputation its degree gives us." [340] "The American colleges and universities (are a) bound by a caste system." [341] What is the price of such 'reputation' for the students, for a human life in general, and for humanity as a whole?

→ The formula for neo-capitalism: Economic scam + religious scam = doom.

4.3.4. Decadence of Colleges and Universities

Some authors put the failure of academic education (including or especially of economics) without ambiguity and pitiless on the table. Although the authors mostly speak about American colleges and universities, we can assume a similar or even equal development in Europe.

---

[339] Hacker, p. 64-65
[340] Hacker, p. 77-78
[341] Hacker, p. 15

The Nineteenth-Century Science

"Science and the development of a vibrant industrial economy have brought enormous advances in education to many millions around the world who have become literate and numerate for the first time in history. And yet, the myopic vision of science and industry has also failed our students and our future. The ways in which we educate students today are, in large part, a reflection of our worldview, which itself is an image of nineteenth-century science." [342]

→ The way social science sees the world is itself an image of nineteenth-century science.

→ The myopic vision of science and industry is a disastrous failure; there is nothing pioneering.

→ The academic failure is not only internal; it leads to a failure of the students' and in general of humans' future.

"Where many cultures over many centuries saw a hierarchy of being, we now see the sole remnant as an inert substance which, when compounded and set in motion, is thought to give rise to the epiphenomena of life and mind, values and purpose. Gone are life, consciousness, soul, and spirit. This view reflects itself in innumerable ways in the priorities and methods sanctioned throughout the academy." [343]

→ The social science's result (economics) is: gone are life, consciousness, soul, spirit, mind, values and purpose.

"(The) view of the mind and the world is partial as a consequence of seeing it only from (the) limited Western viewpoint." [344]

→ The very narrow view of social science (economics) of the Western world is blinkered and in its consequence catastrophic.

"The failure of traditional economics to account for what are called 'externalities' is a symptom of its tragic neglect of the interconnectedness we have been considering. For example, the additional health and environmental costs caused by the pollution associated with production are 'externalized', which is to say they are not borne by manufacturers but by the populace and

---

[342] Palmer, p. 59
[343] Palmer, p. 62-63
[344] Palmer, p. 65

the environment." [345]

→ Traditional economics is a failure. Externalities express a tragic neglect of the interconnectedness.

"The second recognized failure of neo-economic theory is the 'tragedy of the commons'. Our survival as a species depends fundamentally on such common resources as air that is suitable to breathe, water that can be drunk, fish in the sea, soil that will grow crops, and so on. But if fishermen, farmers, and other workers act rationally and purely in their self-interest, then the neo-classical economic calculation predicts the collapse of fish stocks, the disappearance of water, and so on. Without someone acting on behalf of everyone, without a selfless sense for the whole, the tragedy of the commons will take place." [346]

→ Another failure of neo-economic theories is the negligence of the commons, the common resources.
→ Acting (in economics and the market) rationally and purely in (…) the self-interest, then the neo-classical economic calculation leads to the collapse.
→ (Elite-) universities where consciousness, soul, spirit, mind, values and purpose are gone, lead humanity to the collapse and therefore are 'deadbeat'-universities. That's a tragedy.

The Network of Deicide

"The growing faith in universities reinforced, and was reinforced by, the growing influence of all large institutions. The mid-twentieth century was the era of the military-industrial complex and mass media. Large corporations, nonprofits, and government bureaucracies increasingly dictated the life of the 'organization man'. Universities had characteristics of all three." [347]

→ The military-industrial complex, the mass media, the large corporations, and the government bureaucracies dictate humans' life and this is a total failure for humanity's future.

"Universalistic principles form the all-but-invisible warp upon which the carpet of global civilization is woven. From individual examples (an apple falling on the ground), we expect that universal principles (gravity) can be

---

[345] Palmer, p. 83
[346] Palmer, p. 84
[347] Kamenetz, p. 11

derived and used to measure, predict, and control the outcome of events.

Hypotheses about the world can be deduced from observation and tested through repeatable experiments. ... these beliefs add up to nothing less than a 'rationalistic religion' that has supplanted the old mystical religions. The university's 'hidden curriculum', (...), has always been teaching its own importance." [348]

→ Social science (economics) is obsessed to find universal principles in order to predict the world.
→ Social science (economics) is aiming to measure, predict, and control humans' outcome.
→ Social science (economics) is nothing less than a 'rationalistic religion' that has supplanted the old mystical religions.

"The idea is that your value in the mind of a rational god is a standardized thing in this world.
The rationalistic god, (...), is a jealous and devouring god. It must be growing, advancing, enlarging, accumulating, till the end of time." [349]

→ Social science (economics) has created a rationalistic god, a jealous and devouring god.

"Today, the University of Phoenix, the largest example of a so-called market-driven institution..." [350]

→ Universities of highest reputation, such as for example University of Phoenix, worship a rationalistic god, a jealous and devouring god. That's the neo-capitalistic ideology.

The University's Party Life

"...what is going on at hundreds of campuses today is not higher education or even lower education. It's not really education at all, just one big, non-stop party." [351]

→ The student's advanced American dream: one big, non-stop party. It's

---

[348] Kamenetz, p. 21
[349] Kamenetz, p. 21
[350] Kamenetz, p. 5
[351] Brandon, p. xix

training for the casino-party to maximize profit on the top of the corporations.

"(Since the early 1990s) hundreds of college campuses have been deliberately transformed into heavens of adolescent hedonism, where student misbehavior has become the norm and college administrators allow it because they don't want their student customer to take their tuition money somewhere else ... Administrators have given students exactly what they said they wanted: more parties and less education." [352]

→ Heavens of hedonism is the ultimate satisfaction of all needs and wants, every day presented and heated up from the big American (and European) media brainwashing their TV-consumers.

"Party school policies also encourage students to stay in school longer than the four years that it is supposed to take to get a bachelor's degree. It now takes the average college student six years to complete a four-year program, adding a 50 percent surcharge to the advertised sticker price." [353]

→ Most American students show signs of degeneration and genetic damages due to the neo-capitalistic economics and its collateral damages (e.g. contamination).

"The vast majority of (...) students want to do as little work as possible. (There are) thousands of classes in party schools across the nation." [354]

→ That's what economics is about: least cost and maximum profit: the Bachelor diploma and later on a fat wage working in a corporation. A tragic illusion.

Teaching and Graduation

"Grades too low? Forget it. We'll use a 'grading curve' to transform your F magically into a B. Is it really worth tens of thousands of dollars to attend a college that is really nothing more than an adolescent resort?" [355]

→ American Colleges and Universities are really nothing more than an

---

[352] Brandon, p. 3
[353] Brandon, p. 6
[354] Brandon, p. 46
[355] Brandon, p. 4

adolescent resort.

"Professors are encouraged to make their classes student-friendly, and that means no outside reading assignments, no difficult concepts, no boring discussions, and no tests. Instead, they are encouraged to show movies, bring in guest speakers, and develop classroom presentations that are more 'entertaining'." [356]

→ That's exactly what the economic theories teach: Consumers want to get a benefit, a satisfaction, some sort of happiness or at least 'good mood', or a special incentive in order to buy the good.

"National statistics show that 60 percent of students require at least six years to graduate." [357]

→ It is the result of the implicit aim of neo-classical economics to destroy human's mind and soul in order to succeed with getting highest profit and their world governance.

University is a Business

"The inconvenient truth is that only the best colleges in America still consider 'education' to be their primary mission. Instead, since the early 1990s, colleges have been reinventing themselves using a business model, transforming themselves into Diplomas Inc., run by a new breed of college administrator more interested in retaining customers than in educating students. [358]

→ The body (institution, entity) can't be different from its main 'organ', the economic ideology that ignores all human values and externalities (collateral damages).

"Colleges with excess funds could give their administrators big pay raises, hire more administrators to lighten the load with many hands, and pay for non-stop construction projects designed to attract even more students. It was the winner-take-all strategy taught at business schools." [359]

→ The 'winner-take-all strategy' is also a fault of economics that has the

---

[356] Brandon, p. 5
[357] Brandon, p. 18
[358] Brandon, p. 3
[359] Brandon, p. 11

intrinsic coding to destroy humans, humanity, the planet, and in the end the aim of deicide.

"Nearly every major university in the country has a multi-million-dollar affinity relationship with a credit card company, wrote nearly $20 million to a single university … and, in most cases, the worse the card terms are for students and alumni, the more profitable they are for the schools." [360]

→ It's the same principle as in the market: the seller is the winner and the consumer is always in a certain way, psychologically, spiritually, and financially, the loser.

"Armed with the names and addresses of students provided by school administrators, credit card companies bombard students with marketing promotions, sometimes several per week in a relentless mailbox bomb." [361]

→ That's the typical corporation marketing: to win, one must bombard the consumers every day and from everywhere, all the time and with all sneaky and subtle psychological means.

Students' Performance Ability

"More commonly, the entire class is simply dumped down to elementary school levels from the start so that every student can pass the tests without studying or even reading the textbook." [362]

→ The young generation today has not experienced any significant development since childhood, the terrible twos; a majority of them is even stuck or regressed to the oral age.

"An increasing number of professors don't even bother assigning term papers anymore because the students simply refuse to complete them. They don't have the necessary skills and are not willing to take the time to do the research and the writing. Their language and thinking skills are too poor and they don't have enough familiarity with essays to write one. They don't know how to use source information and they have a hard time focusing on one thing for very long." [363]

---

[360] Brandon, p. 38
[361] Brandon, p. 38
[362] Brandon, p. 49
[363] Brandon, p. 54

→ They are all lured, seduced, and pampered by immature fathers and mothers. What else can we expect from mostly stupid parents with lowest level of personality quality?

"Now it is the students who set the standards and they can get really angry if they feel the standards are too high. Professors who have problems with the new rules can expect to be out of a job." [364]

→ The Authorities of Colleges and Universities want such students and professors must comply; they are generously paid in order to execute the hidden aims of the monsters.

"In countless written evaluations of faculty, students repeat the same complaints over and over. Classes are boring. Professors aren't entertaining enough, not funny enough. 'Bring a pillow', students sometimes write, or 'He needs some dancing girls or a monkey or something to make his class more interesting'." [365]

→ The only solution is: All these students need a long stay in a Chinese correctional facility.

"Teaching is often more about babysitting and joke telling than it is about education." Brandon, p. 59

→ This young generation is made stupid. It's an intrinsic aim of economics, the public education, and the religion to make people go soft in the head. Who is to be indicted for this?

"Today's classes, as a result, suffer from high absenteeism and a low level of student participation." [366]

→ Nowadays, wherever people (students) are, they are in a certain way 'absent' and do not really participate in their social interactions or in the nature. There is no motivation, no mind and no soul, and therefore no meaning of being and life. That's the spirit of America and Europe.

"Obsessed with their hair, their clothes, their cars, their boyfriends and

[364] Brandon, p. 56
[365] Brandon, p. 56
[366] Brandon, p. 60

girlfriends, and how many friends they have on Facebook, they have little that could be recognized as an intellectual life." [367]

→ Digging deeper in this obsession we find: narcissism, neuroticism, stupidity, stubbornness, rigidity, infantilism, falseness, defiance, a brainwashed and degenerated mind and lost soul.

"Most college students remain dangerously immature and unable to make the most basic choices about whether to attend classes do their homework, study for tests, use drugs, engage in unsafe sex, or drink themselves into unconsciousness." [368]

→ It is indeed dangerous as these patterns of behavior express their miserable state of the mind and soul, their lousy character, their inability to master life, their lack of responsibility, and a complete absence of human values. It can't surprise, as it is a copy of the economics and its representatives.

"They have no idea how to write a resume or a cover letter. They have no idea how to dress or what to say at a job interview. They have little understanding about how the cool photo of them with their heads in the toilet bowl throwing up that they posted on Facebook will look to recruiters." [369]

→ These students show us how their parents are and how they experienced teachers in the public school. It also shows us the evil market of insane entertainment (internet, other media).
→ As a child and adolescent they wanted something for their soul, but education, religion, governments, economics and the media gave them toxics for soul and mind.
→ They are the result of a completely rotten society where a majority of authorities are nothing more than liars, false people, cheaters, gamblers, deceivers, robbers, murderers, warmongers, cowards, perverts, sadists, psychopaths, scammers, a regicide and a deicide. In general, the authorities can't be better than those who elect them.
→ Where powerful authorities have stolen the highest Archetypes of the Soul to fool their folks and pretend to be 'in God', there is for the young

---

[367] Brandon, p. 74
[368] Brandon, p. 81
[369] Brandon, p. 146

generation no other solution than to play an infantile idiotic theatre.

Richard Arum provides a graph with the time use of students in the US: [370]

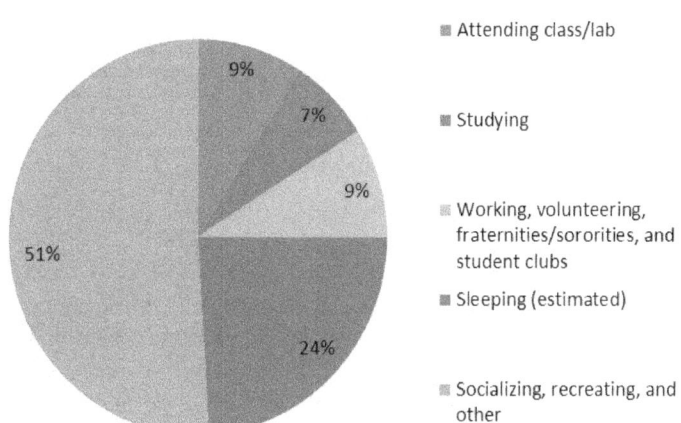

Figure 4.2. Student time use (percentages based on 168 hours - i.e., full seven - day week).

- Attending class/lab
- Studying
- Working, volunteering, fraternities/sororities, and student clubs
- Sleeping (estimated)
- Socializing, recreating, and other

9%
7%
9%
51%
24%

The Future of American Students

"More than 90 percent of employers rate written communication, critical thinking, and problem solving as 'very important' for the job success of new labor market entrants. At the same time, they note that only a small proportion of four-year college graduates excel in these skills: 16 percent excel in written communication and 28 percent in critical thinking/problem solving." [371]

→ The result for those students will be that they will never succeed in their life and professional career. They can never have a clear view about what's going on with their leaders' evil doing in economics, politics, religion, and education. That's very welcome by the authorities.

"The idea that there are thousands of corporate jobs waiting for brand-new college graduates as middle managers, researchers, and marketers is at least a decade out of date … They work in a cubicle at the minimum wage as a temporary employee with no benefits or are forced to accept jobs as pizza deliverers, mail carriers, clerks, and waiters … Most graduates of party

---

[370] Arum, p. 97
[371] Arum, p. 143

schools have absolutely no idea how to find a job. During their college year, they never really chose a career and only chose a major when the college told them they could not put it off any longer." [372]

→ The decadence in the United States and in the European Union is culminating. In the end this will hit all authorities and destroy the entire planet up to the elimination of humanity.

→ The more the young intelligence for tomorrow is infantilized, dehumanized, has lost the 'instinct' for genuine human values, the more the authorities in economics, politics and education can operate (unhindered) for their global master-plan.

Spirituality for Academic Life

"Professors agree with students concerning the high importance of values, meaning, and purpose in life, and they report that they personally cultivate them, but the role these should play in their teaching is unclear. Thus while student interest and expectations around spirituality are high, the academy is unsure of how to respond." [373]

→ High importance in academic teaching must also have human values, meaning, and purpose in life.

→ The academic teaching does not respond to the high interest and importance students give to human values.

"Spiritual or contemplative experience, on the other hand, is open to all who practice contemplation and is, therefore, open also to thoughtful study." [374]

→ Scientific activities (in economics) also must reflect human values with practicing contemplation.

"Truth has the power to liberate, but ignorance binds us to delusions and so to suffering." [375]

→ Social science (economics) is ignorant and binds (enslaves) students, professors, teachers, and in general humans to delusions and so to

---

[372] Brandon, p. 145
[373] Palmer, p. 118
[374] Palmer, p. 120
[375] Palmer, p. 121

suffering.

"So when I hear faculty dismiss the affective dimension of teaching and learning as 'touchy-feely stuff,' I have to conclude that they are projecting their personal discomfort with emotions rather than making a statement about the real world." [376]

➔ Scientists, experts, professors and teachers fear their own inner conflictive being and their own true face, and escape in rational statements about their field of social science.

The Academic Hope

"Never doubt that a small group of thoughtful, committed citizens can change the world. Indeed, it is the only thing that ever has." [377]

➔ A small group, or even 100,000 scientists committed to human values have no chance because the monsters govern everything. There is no hope in the science of capitalistic economics.

"We need to uncover and empower the heart of higher education in those faculty, administrators, students, alumni, and trustees who have a vision for reclaiming the unrealized potentials in the human and historical DNA that gave rise to academic life." [378]

➔ There are many brave pioneering scientists that have a vision for reclaiming the unrealized potentials in the human's mind and soul. But they don't have the golden key for renewal: the vivid superior Archetypes of the Soul. Absence of these Archetypes leads to decadence.
➔ The entire accreditation system in America and Europe does not allow uncovering and empowering the heart of higher education (e.g. in economics, business, education, psychology, and sociology). Logically, the archetypal evolution is paralyzed and this results in decadence.
➔ Visions and potentials in social sciences (economics) that do not match with the interests of corporations are not allowed at accredited universities. The so called 'pioneering spirit' is only reserved for technological visions and this is also a sign of an advanced decadence.

---

[376] Palmer, p. 42
[377] Palmer, p. 126
[378] Palmer, p. 21

4.3.5. The Economic Deicide Program

We have already uncovered with 'Economics I' that economics in its principles and terms is soulless. We have explored in other books that the governments and politics are soulless. We have uncovered in other books the soulless Western consumer society. We also have uncovered the soulless public education. And we have profoundly unveiled since 1987 the soulless Christianity. [379] Herewith, in 'Economics II', we have dug more in the economic theories and realities.

In general in the topics of this book we observe another nasty compulsion of the servant of the king, something like an accountant of the king or a postman for the king: Wherever this servant sees a movement of something on the side of the king, he wants to get a piece (margin) of it. Whatever the servant sees in the king's kingdom (realm), he has an idea how he could make more of it and then he could get a piece of it.

Mainly this servant is terribly avaricious, envious and compulsive. He always sees what others possess or get or move around. He never thinks what he could do himself to possess or get what he wants through his own potentials and performances. He would never give away for free any thin piece of whatsoever. He has lost himself and suffers from a psychosis. He never has an attitude of servicing and humility. He wants to be the king and he wants to possess everything that others possess or get or move around. He is insatiable forever. He infects everybody with his toxic virus, children, adolescents, students, and all consumers. That's the perfect regicide.

Economics is full of this sick attitude and also the governments with their tax obsession always want a piece of everything that makes a move or that people possess or get or use from the environment however. They would even ask for a tax for breathing or talking if they could. This is the crucial dynamic element of the systemic failure of economics and politics (Economics III).

We can multiply this servant by 7bn people: already babies suffer from this compulsion, envy, and addiction. They all want a piece of everything that makes a move or that people possess or get or use from the environment.

Or we can see it in that way: The servant gets everything under his control that's on earth and logically he has dethroned all the kings on earth (regicide). But as the 'last king' he will not be satisfied. He will want more: in the

---

[379] http://www.rcigi.com

culmination of his insanity he dethrones God.

Or see it that way: all servants want to dethrone each other and then, the last servant as the last king, will dethrone God. That's the outrageous atrocity we experience today!

This is what capitalistic economics and capitalistic politics is about! Let's call this a 'crucial topic' on the ladder of humanity's psychical-spiritual evolution – or a 'systemic failure' of theory and practice. But who knows, it could also be a systemic fault in the genes or in the brain. At least for sure it is a 'systemic fault' in the mind (and soul) of certain individuals.

100% sure is: Many religions have already dethroned the wise Kings, God and his Spirit. And also the hidden capitalistic elites on the stage behind the curtains have already dethroned the wise Kings, God and his Spirit – whatever 'God and his Spirit' is, or however 'God and his Spirit' could be described in terrestrial words and humane comprehension. Logically, capitalistic economics implies triggering wars.

What a sick world and lost humanity! Another way is possible!

There is hope: The spiritual potential, the intellectual potential, the cultural and creative potential, and the philosophical-psychological potential of the European folks is immense – probably on the highest level of the entire humanity; Americans have not got to offer much spiritual potential. There is so much potential around the world that, once explored and originated with the inner Spirit, this power could easily transform the entire world into a new state of peace, care, balance, justice, cultural creativity, understanding, cooperation, human rights, human values, and human dignity.

However, first the Europeans and other folks must undergo a profound inner catharsis. Then they must free themselves from the American occupation and other (economic) dependences. Then their governments must free themselves from lobbyism and the Jewish claws hysterically abusing the guilt from the past generations. Then they must disburden from their guilt from the First and Second World War. They must undergo a catharsis of their history back to the Middle Ages.

Finally they must find back to their authentic soul with their inner Spirit. Concerning the collective unconscious they all must find the real truth behind the First and Second World War, in general of history, because the real puppet masters, responsible for all big wars since more than 1,000 years, are still undiscovered up to today. It remains to be stated that there are other folks and cultures that could easily compete with the genuine inner potentials of the Europeans.

Everybody knows the proverb: "When two parties quarrel, a third party rejoices". The complementary part of this proverb is: Provoke (as the third party) as much as possible until two parties (or two states) quarrel; then heat up their rage and intrigue with all means (including all Machiavelli's strategies) as much as possible at any price even with own sacrifices until they go berserk and start a war. The third party supplies both sides with weapons, and then the third and the winner party can rejoice from the benefit during decenniums. This game also works if one party humiliates another party making his blood boiling until he gets berserk and a third party provides the humiliated party which got berserk with weapons and all necessary tools. In all cases the third part will win although it's never actively and never visibly in any way involved in the war game. Unfortunately the history of the 19th and the 20th century is completely falsified and distorted in the books about its real history.

It is indispensable for the collective catharsis to identify this third party operating since centuries on so many places: it's the servant from the king that has lost his kingdom due to his own fault and due to his own systemic failure in trying to get back his lost kingdom! Already Homer (B.C. 850 or 1200) knew about the insane unconscious mind; see: Odysseus; the God Zeus, the king and father of Gods and mankind.

There are since millenniums Archetypes (eternally infallible symbols) that express the power and destination of a King, an emperor, and a (highest) religious leader. These symbols and supreme Archetypes of the Soul are, here in short interpretation:

- Orb: God's Dominion over the World
- Crown: Royal Authority, Christ, the King of Kings
- Royal Scepter: Power, Dominion of a Monarch
- Scepter and Crown: Christ, Authority, King
- Pair of Balance: Justice, Jurisdiction, Spiritual Jurisdiction
- Owl: Pure Spirit, Wisdom
- Eagle (with open wings): Power above the World
- Circle-Cross-Mandala: Highest Fulfillment in God
- Sun: God, the Ultimate Source of Life
- King of the Holy Grail: Highest Transcendental Mission

In the history of mankind, the inner Spirit in the soul of some wise men, spiritual kings, has created (has made vivid) these Archetypes in their inner life (soul). There have been a few men since millenniums on varied places on this earth that have performed (made vivid) all the Archetypes of the Soul in their inner life, including all highest Archetypes of God and they all got the mission from God to bring forward the psychical-spiritual evolution and they were committed in God.

Religions have stolen the transcendental archetypal experiences these wise men, spiritual kings in their soul, had performed and received (experienced) in dreams. All Popes and Cardinals have stolen their archetypal experiences. Terrestrial Emperors and Kings have stolen their archetypal experiences. Supreme Rulers of folks, aristocrats and elites in the capitalistic economy have stolen their experienced inner archetypal processes, have copied the archetypal pictures (from dreams these wise men had), but never performed such inner transformations produced and guided by the inner Spirit. This is the systemic failure of economics, politics, religion, public education, and society in general.

All what these thieves do is to found their fake (stolen) legitimacy with gorgeous buildings, with historic paintings and other works of art of immense value, with 'holy' robes, with immense military and financial power, and with fake impressive ceremonies. And the stolen supreme Archetypes of the Soul they hang on their walls and buildings or have stuck them on their flags and emblems. They think that what they have stolen are the appropriate substitutes for the lost vivid supreme Archetypes of the Soul. They have all dethroned the spiritual kings, and God and his Spirit, expressed in these supreme Archetypes of the Soul. Finally, in the inner roots and final aims of these people, is nothing short of DEICIDE.

→ If everything continues as usual humanity will have to experience the worst 'lesson' of most dire dimension in its history within 35-40 years.
→ The planet and humanity is at highest risk to be eliminated in less than 100 years if billions of people do not take drastic measures in their personal life and if the governments and responsible economists do not take drastic measures for global catharsis, changes and renewal.

There is never a sustainable and balanced global solution of economics, of all the immense global problems, and of all the dire global poverty and misery until the terrestrial kings, the leaders, the religious authorities, the rulers, the super-powerful men, and the aristocrats accept the man that has brought again to the world and humanity for the first time since 2,000 years all the vivid and highest Holy Archetypes of the Soul.

4.3.6. The Vision

We say: Renewal of economics in theory and practice is indispensable and requires an all-embracing renewal of all (the six) systems of societies (as shown above with a diagram) and that includes all humans. The authors of 'Limits to Growth' write about it: [380]

"A sustainable world can never be fully realized until it is widely envisioned." The authors invite the readers to develop and enlarge their vision:

- Sustainability, efficiency, sufficiency, equity, beauty, and community as the highest social values.
- Material sufficiency and security for all. Therefore, by individual choice as well as communal norms, low birth rates and stable populations.
- Work that dignifies people instead of demeaning them. Some way of providing incentives for people to give their best to society and to be rewarded for doing so, while ensuring that everyone will be provided for sufficiently under any circumstances.
- Leaders interested in doing their jobs than in keeping their jobs, more interested in serving society than in winning elections.
- An economy that is a means, not an end, one that serves the welfare of the environment, rather than vice versa.
- Efficient, renewable energy systems.
- Efficient, closed-loop materials systems.
- Technical design that reduces emissions and waste to a minimum, and social agreement not to produce emissions or waste that technology and nature can't handle.
- Regenerative agriculture that builds soils, uses natural mechanisms to restore nutrients and control pests, and produces abundant, uncontaminated food.
- The preservation of ecosystems in their variety, with human cultures living in harmony with those ecosystems; therefore, high diversity of both nature and culture, and human appreciation for that diversity.
- Flexibility, innovation (social as well as technical), and intellectual challenge. A flourishing of science, a continuous enlargement of human knowledge.
- Greater understanding of whole systems as an essential part of each person's education.
- Decentralization of economic power, political influence, and scientific expertise.

---

[380] Meadows (et al.), p. 273-274

- Political structures that permit a balance between short-term and long-term considerations; some way of exerting political pressure now on behalf of our grandchildren.
- High-level skills on the part of citizens and governments in the arts of nonviolent conflict resolution.
- Media that reflect the world's diversity and at the same time unite cultures with relevant, accurate, timely, unbiased, and intelligent information, presented in its historic and whole-system context.
- Reasons for living and for thinking well of ourselves that do not involve the accumulation of material things.

The list expresses high ethical values, genuine human values, very relevant concerns about the planet and society, and in general a vision that is of highest importance to save humanity and the planet.

But a strange statement got our attention: "We are no more certain of the truth than anyone is." [381]

So no-one can be sure of the truth? The truth no one can have? It is uncertain? No one can have more of the truth than the authors of this book have? This is very arrogant and thoroughly ignorant – obviously totally wrong. It reflects the ideology of the neo-capitalism. It is not surprising as on the author's preface (ix) we can read that "The Volkswagen Foundation in Germany provided the funding for our work."

So obviously a critical look at the implication of the car industry in the destruction of the planet, the outrageous disaster of the nuclear waste, the immense re-armament of the US-Army and the NATO, the toxic contamination of the global natural food chains with pharmaceutics, the extreme stupidity and blindness of 6.5 billion and more people, the power of the mega-banks over governments, the wars since 1990 from the capitalistic coalition from the media and politicians with frightening falseness presented, the devilish scam of religion, the insane and hypocrite politics of Israel on stolen land and enslaved Arabs/Palestinians, triggering from there the global doom and forcing others to do the dirty war-job, the real rulers behind the stage of America and Europe, and much more did not get any light shed onto! How can we explain to them that the earth is not flat? The report is a total failure without any chance of significant success!

We also miss in the entire book a roadmap that shows at least the basic principles, rules, and systemic factors that characterize the way to go globally

---

[381] Meadows (et al.), p. 276

ahead aiming for such aims. We miss a clear advanced understanding of humans and of the archetypal evolutionary process in which humanity is embedded.

We miss a clear picture about the main agents in politics and economics and religion that are responsible for the dire developments of the planet. We miss that religions and most concepts of spirituality must re-start from the source of its inner origin (not from ancient 'holy' texts which are anyway a complete distortion of the truth). We miss the meaning of human's life that is rooted vivid inside in the soul (not in dogmatic statements). We miss a deeper critical approach to the economics (faults) and its implicit dynamic factors as shown in many economic terms, 'laws' and theories in this book (and in Economics I).

The declared vision of this Club of Rome is not the same language as all the analyses in this book. All approaches are technological. The language of the vision comes from social, humane, and spiritual fields. All people with spiritual attitudes would agree with the vision, but not with exclusively technological solutions. This 'vision' is simply a camouflage, a kind of a divine robe, hiding the real aims of this Club: a technocratic global order. The mixture of truth and facts with an ideological foundation of economic principles is extremely manipulative and dangerous.

In general, the actual and future criticalities mentioned in the book are of such a vague description that the entire message of the vision becomes 'castrated'. To simply say that there is a critical growth, an exponential growth, a critical acceleration, a rapid change, an overstressed state, and an 'overshoot' is only half of the real truth about the state of humanity, the world, and the planet. [382]

→ To see fully the truth about humanity one must be able to look into the eyes of the evil without being affected due to the high inner state of psychological-spiritual development.
→ The truth is referred to external realities, but also to internal realities. And inner realities seen also in the potential of its development lead us to the Archetypes of the Soul.
→ No one can stand for long in front of the cosmic devil if the he is not rooted in the truth and the Archetypes of the Soul. The Club of Rome ignores the Archetypes of the Soul.
→ Economics has intrinsically an immense social and humane dimension and importance. But all theories and laws exclude this world, alike the Club of

---

[382] Meadows (et al.), p. 17, 164, 174, 176, 234, 273-274

Rome. They sit in the same boat.

Fact is: The multi-dimensional systems together as a unity are in a human made momentum of growth with its hundreds of factors that are in mutual interdependences. And, for example, the effects of today's emissions and today's changes in the ecosystems we will experience in estimated 10 years. To mention is also the distorted and degenerated mind of a majority of humans. Or, as we also state: All relevant systems operate with internal faults and already with irreversible effects.

Herman Kahn, cited as a critical statement which is also a camouflage, said: "With current and near current technology, we can support 15 billion people in the world at twenty thousand dollars per capita for a millennium – and that seems to be a very conservative statement." [383] A practical answer would be: Humanity will be eliminated long before through nuclear wars and weapons of mass destruction, through toxic contamination and sewage with chemical and pharmaceutical elements from 5-9 billion people going to the oceans and from there back through the food chain to all humans.

The project 'The Limits of Growth' – with probably a 50 million dollar cost since 1972-2012 – and the critical words of H. Kahn (a trap!) – a typical capitalistic economic view; and a finger of the 'invisible hand' – will never solve the huge problems of humanity. The 'Limits of Growth' is a softener product that does not have a ghost of a chance. And people expressing attitudes like H. Kahn express extreme aggression and arrogance towards the archetypal human values.

Prof. Paul Ehrlich's answer is: "Cut world population and redistribute resources ... Nuclear disaster or plague likely unless population shrinks and natural resources are reassigned to poor ... If you want a battery chicken world where everyone has minimum space and food and everyone is kept just about alive you might be able to support in the long term about 4 or 5 billion people. But you already have 7 billion. So we have to humanely and as rapidly as possible move to population shrinkage." [384]

Both concepts express zero idea about the psychical-spiritual evolution, and zero awareness of the horrifying state of the mind and soul of billions of people. These factors can't be simply calculated, but they will be absolutely decisive in the future of mankind. The psychical energy of the suppressed, distorted, rotten and dehumanized mind and soul of billions of humans is

---

[383] Meadows (et al.), pre-page one
[384] http://www.businessinsider.com/paul-ehrlich-population-growth-2012-4#ixzz1tkPlk2xz

stronger than thousand nuclear bombs, once it collectively explodes. And this can happen within the coming two or three decades.

The process of deicide created from the supreme agents behind the curtains is already in motion since long. They have their road-map! Here we have that what is a thousand times more evil than what Hitler and his henchmen have done. It seems that nobody has a clear view about this devilish perspective: the opposite of an archetypal evolutionary vision for mankind.

The golden key of all solutions for humanity and the planet lies in the fundamental Archetypes of the Soul aiming for a balanced wholeness and also lies in the vivid supreme Archetypes of the Soul as the legitimation of highest spiritual power to lead humanity's evolution towards the eternal vivid source of all cosmic creation. This is about the sole inner path towards fulfillment of all longings in the soul and mind of people – in the end of humanity. This path requires the spiritual intelligence – the inner Spirit – completely lost in the systems of societies.

Therefore humanity is lost in a dark labyrinth without exit. In other words:

→ Sustainable external evolution (expressed in the vision of Meadows et al.) without the inner archetypal evolution of humanity is never possible to achieve.

Without a doubt, the economic concepts (microeconomics), the political concepts (macroeconomics), and all other systems of societies as well must take on a new frame and a new focus: humanity's archetypal evolution. Such a path first requires a complete catharsis before renewal.

→ Hope is real: The truthful 25-year roadmap for a new world and for humanity with the Archetypes of the Soul can be fully developed and implemented.

Either the leaders (the elites) of all relevant systems of societies and humanity as a whole want this archetypal evolution, or humanity will perish in their dark labyrinth without exit.

Either the students of social science, in general the young generation, want this archetypal evolution, or humanity will perish in their dark labyrinth without exit.

Either the students of economics and politics, tomorrow the leaders or agents of businesses and politics, want this archetypal evolution, or humanity will perish in their dark labyrinth without exit.

Never undervalue the invisible magic attractiveness of the evil! Never undervalue all the lies, deceit, cheat, fraud, falseness, orchestrations, and camouflage in economics, politics, religion, media, and public education. The global destruction is in increasing motion. The engine is the neo-capitalistic economics with hidden religious roots. You already have the deicide! You live in the 'Atrocity Age'! The frightening true face you can only fully see with your soul.

→ You can have the global archetypal evolution!
→ You can have a holistic social science with soul!
→ You can have an economic science with soul!

What do you want? You decide!

Literature – Economics I, II, III

Antonioni Peter, Flynn Sean Masaki: Economics for Dummies. Wiley 2011. Chichester, West Sussex, England.

Arum Richard, Roksa Josipa: Academically adrift. Limited Learning on College Campuses. University of Chicaco Press 2011. Chicago. London.

Brandon Craig: The Five-Year-Party. Benbella Books 2010. Dallas.

Chinn Menzie D., Frieden Jeffry A.: Lost decades. Debt Crisis and the long recovery. W.W. Norton & Company 2011. London.

Colander, D.C.: Microeconomics. 8th edition. McGraw-Hill 2010. New York.

Dasgupta Partha: Economics. Oxford University Press. 2007. New York.

Hacker Andrew, Dreifus Claudia: Higher Education. Times Books Henry Hold 2010. New York.

Haralambos Mike, Holborn Martin: Sociology. 7th edition. Collins 2008. London.

Kamenetz Anya: DIY U Edupunks, Edupreneurs, and the Coming transformation of Higher Education. Chelsea Green Publishing 2010. White River Junction VT.

Krugman Paul, Wells Robin, Graddy Kathryn: Essentials of Economics. Worth Publishers 2011. New York.

McConnell Campbell R., Brue Stanley L., Flynn Sean M.: Macroeconomics, Principles, Problems, and Policies. 19th edition 2012. McGraw-Hill. New York.

McDowell Moore, Thom Rodney, Frank Robert, Bernanke Ben: Principles of Economics. 2nd European Edition. McGraw-Hill Higher Education 2009. Berkshire.

Mankiw N. Gregory, Taylor Mark P.: Economics. 2nd edition. South-Western Cengage Learning. 2011. Hampshire. United Kingdom.

Meadows, Donella, Randers Jorgen, Meadows Dennis: Chelsea Green Publishing. 2004. Vermont.

Palmer Parker J., Zajonc Arthur: The Heart of higher Education. Jossey-Bass 2010. San Francisco.

Smith Adam: The Wealth of Nations. First copy 1776. Edition 2010. Simon and Brown. www.simonandbrown.com

Other Publications (English, German) from Dr. Edward Schellhammer: www.edwardschellhammer.com

www.ingramcontent.com/pod-product-compliance
Lightning Source LLC
Chambersburg PA
CBHW051439170526
45166CB00001B/42